MANAGEMENT INFORMATION SYSTEMS

[For Engineering, B.B.A., B.C.A., M.B.A., M.C.A., Information Technology, C.A./C.S., I.C.W.A. and other Postgraduate Students]

A.K. GUPTA

M.Sc. (Maths), Ph. D. (OR), M.B.A

Director

The Institution of Engineers (India)

8, Gokhale Road

Kolkata - 700020

S Chand And Company Limited

(ISO 9001 Certified Company)

S Chand And Company Limited

(ISO 9001 Certified Company)

Head Office: D-92, Sector–2, Noida – 201301, U.P. (India), Ph. 91-120-4682700

Registered Office: A-27, 2nd Floor, Mohan Co-operative Industrial Estate, New Delhi – 110 044, Phone: 011-49731800

www.**schandpublishing.com;** e-mail: **info@schandpublishing.com**

Marketing Offices:

Chennai : Ph: 23632120; chennai@schandpublishing.com

Guwahati : Ph: 2738811, 2735640; guwahati@schandpublishing.com

Hyderabad : Ph: 40186018; hyderabad@schandpublishing.com

Jalandhar : Ph: 4645630; jalandhar@schandpublishing.com

Kolkata : Ph: 23357458, 23353914; kolkata@schandpublishing.com

Lucknow : Ph: 4003633; lucknow@schandpublishing.com

Mumbai : Ph: 25000297; mumbai@schandpublishing.com

Patna : Ph: 4011400; patna@schandpublishing.com

First Edition 2000
Second Revised Edition 2003; Reprint 2007
Third Revised Edition 2008
Reprints 2010, 2012, 2013, 2014, 2016, 2018, 2019, 2020, 2021 (Twice), 2022, 2023, 2024, 2025

Reprint 2026

ISBN: 978-81-219-1993-7 **Product Code:** H3MIS50INFT10ENAC08O

PRINTED IN INDIA

By Shri Shyamlal Printing Press Private Limited, Plot 20/4, Site-IV, Industrial Area Sahibabad, Ghaziabad – 201 010 and Published by S Chand And Company Limited, A-27, 2nd Floor, Mohan Co-operative Industrial Estate, New Delhi – 110 044.

PREFACE TO THE THIRD REVISED EDITION

The rapid emergence of management information systems (MIS) in organisations during the past two decades has created an intense demand for well-trained, capable MIS managers to plan, organise, direct and control the powerful technology of computer-based information systems (CBIS). MIS managers are required to know the systems approach to management, coupled with the ability to participate in the design and utilisation of CBIS. They face increasingly rapid change in information technology, culture and environment in which they work. MIS management is therefore an intricate process, because it has become more interwoven into the complex fabric of modern organisations.

With the advent of many facets of information technology, it is necessary that all students and MIS personnel should develop a critical perspective and understanding about the potential and challenges of information systems and technologies so that they can understand, anticipate, push, and lead information technology strategy in the years to come. There is a general consensus among the faculty of technology and management in the university curriculum that information is a key currency in facilitating organisational change. Information systems and technologies effortlessly eliminate the barriers of time and space and has a far-reaching impact on the way we receive, process and share knowledge and information.

In this book, the aim is to provide students a thorough coverage of the principles, applications and design of MIS, which is suitable to the heterogeneous MIS courses taught in business schools for diploma in management; advanced diploma in management; BBA; MBA; graduate and postgraduate courses in information technology; different engineering courses; professional examinations, *viz.*, CA, CS, ICWA, Section B and M.Tech. examinations of the Institution of Engineers (India); and other management courses, who need to understand the principles of information systems design. Also, the book aims for managers and others in industry, commerce, public and private enterprises, and management consultants who wish to gain a working knowledge of MIS. The book accentuates the relevance and contribution of information systems not only to the growth and success of a business, but also to our personal lives.

Encouraged with the students' and teachers' constant critical comments and suggestions, *six* new chapters have been incorporated in the book, apart from thorough revision of the text, to make it more useful.

In a systematically and logically arranged 19 chapters, the book deals with managerial overview of information systems (Chapters 1-2); hardware, software and data management (Chapters 3-7); business applications of information systems (Chapters 8-11); managing the developments and maintenance of information systems (Chapter 12); strategic and managerial implications of information systems (Chapters 13-14); enterprise resource planning and supply chain management (Chapter15-16); applications of information technology in business and E-Enterprises (Chapters 17-18); and information security, ethics society (Chapter 19). Each chapter starts with an introduction and ends with review questions to test the knowledge and allow a person to apply the text in a creative manner. The chapters on Controls in Information Systems/Organizations; and Data Warehousing and Data Mining are appended at C and D, respectively. The framework for the text consists of many illustrations in the form of schematic diagrams or models. The diagrams facilitate to learn the text easily.

A book of this type obviously gained a lot of ideas from the books written by many authors on similar and allied subjects. I am able to recognise literary contributions in the bibliography by referencing outstanding authors contributed in this area. Finally, I am thankful to my family—Alka, Pragya and Udit—for putting up with rigorous effort and for their cheerful cooperation all through the period of revising the text.

Even though I have received a lot of help along the way, I am alone responsible for the manner in which the text is presented in its revised form. Therefore, any shortcomings in the book are my own. Valuable comments, suggestions, criticisms can make this book more valuable and useful to all of us. All feedback with a return address shall be answered.

—DR. A. K. GUPTA

CONTENTS

1

Management Information Systems : An Overview

1.1. INTRODUCTION

Today the need for an updated information has become inevitable to arrive at an effective decision in all walks of life. Whether it is industry, commerce, defence, banking, education, economics or politics, information is needed everywhere. A significant part of an executive's working and personal time is spent on recording, searching, absorbing and communicating information.

Information is 'live' as it is required to be updated all the time and is renewable. It is substitutable and transportable and can be made to travel. The all round exponential growth of information makes it necessary that information is collected, stored and retrieved in various fields so that it could be usefully exploited as and when needed. For example : (*a*) In setting up a new industry, information regarding the choice of technology (methods), skill (manpower), money and material becomes an important requirement for its growth and smooth functioning. In the absence of such information the proposed industry becomes sick over a period of time; (*b*) In a competitive market, before deciding about the price of an item, the producer needs information about the pricing policy of the competitors, specially of competitive products, sales techniques, etc. to effectively combat the effect of competition; and (*c*) In defence, considerable amount of money is spent in gathering information (intelligence) from all possible sources.

Information is considered as the sixth resource, the other five being men, machines, materials, money and methods. Figure 1.1 illustrates the flow of information in a production organisation along with other resources.

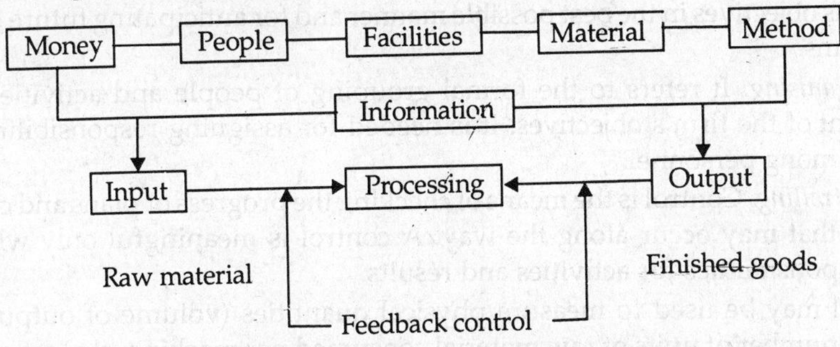

Fig. 1.1. Information as a Resource

1.2. MANAGEMENT INFORMATION SYSTEMS

The Management Information System (MIS) is an integrated man-machine system that provides information to support the planning and control functions of managers in an organisation. MIS can also be defined as the combination of human and computer-based resources that results in the collection, storage, retrieval, communication and use of data for efficient management of operations and for business planning.

MIS is something more than just a computer system. Before the evolution of computers, MIS techniques existed to supply users with information that would permit them to arrive at an effective decision. The computer has added new dimensions such as speed, accuracy and processing of massive data, that permit the consideration of more alternatives in a decision.

The scope and purpose of MIS is better understood if each part of the term MIS is explained in detail separately.

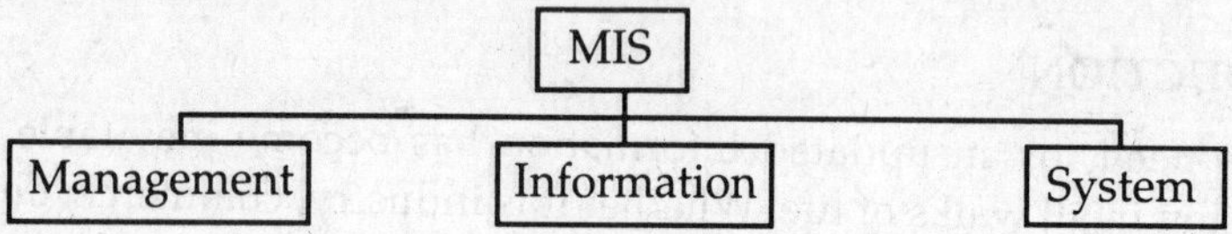

1.2.1. Management

Management has been viewed as a *function*, a *process*, a *profession*, and as an *elite* or a *class* of people. Management has also been described as an *art*; and as a *science*. And along with material, capital and labour, management is considered as a *resource*. It is possibly the most valuable resource because it provides the primary force for converting other resources into products and services.

This section is confined to the elaboration of only one point — management as a function. It refers to the kind of tasks and activities that are performed by managers. The specific nature of the activities are determined by such managerial functions as *planning, organising, directing, leadership* (initiating or coordinating) and *controlling*. In fact, management is a process of achieving an organisation's goals and objectives by judiciously making use of resources of men, materials, machines, money, methods, messages and moments (the last two in the context of information being a vital resource to the manager/decision-maker).

Various functions of management are briefly defined as follows :

(1) *Planning*. It is the process of deciding in advance the courses of action (or strategies) to be followed, and when and how to undertake these.

It is needed for committing and allocating the organisation's limited resources for achieving its objectives in the best possible manner and for anticipating future opportunities and problems.

(2) *Organising*. It refers to the formal grouping of people and activities to facilitate achievement of the firm's objectives. It is needed for assigning responsibilities, jobs, and hierarchy among personnel.

(3) *Controlling*. Control is the means of checking the progress of plans and correcting any deviations that may occur along the way. A control is meaningful only when there are defined responsibilities for activities and results.

Control may be used to measure physical quantities (volume of output, number of manhours, number of units of raw material consumed per machine, etc.), monetary results (value of sale, capital expenditure, return on investment, earnings per share), etc.

(4) *Directing*. It is the process of activating the plans, structure and group efforts in the desired direction. It is needed for implementation of plans by providing desired leadership, motivation and proper communication.

The management can also be grouped into three hierarchical levels — top, middle and junior. The functions of these categories can be studied by analysing TMJ (T-Top; M-Middle and J-Junior). Top (or strategic) management establishes the policies, plans and objectives of the organisation as well as a budget framework under which various departments will operate. Middle (or tactical) management has the responsibility of implementing the policies and overall plans of the top management. Junior (or operational) management has the responsibility of implementing day-to-day operations and decisions of the middle management to produce goods and services to meet the revenue, profit and other goals, which in turn will enable the organisation to achieve its overall plans and objectives.

The different levels of management are important for two reasons (Fig. 1.2) :

(*a*) Information needs tend to be different at different levels of management; and

(*b*) Amount of time required for any function varies considerably with each group.

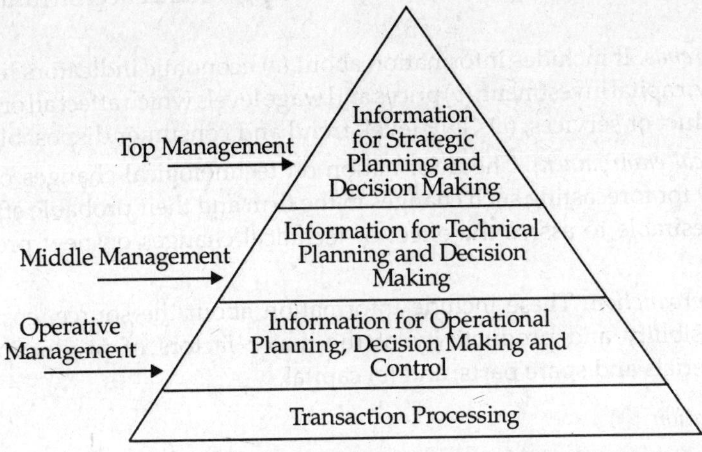

Fig. 1.2. Allocation of Manager's Time

The functions and job contents of various management levels are explained later.

1.2.2. Information

Information can be defined as the data which is organised and presented at a time and place so that the decision-maker may take necessary action. In other words, information is the result/product of processing data. The conversion process of data into decision is shown in Fig. 1.3.

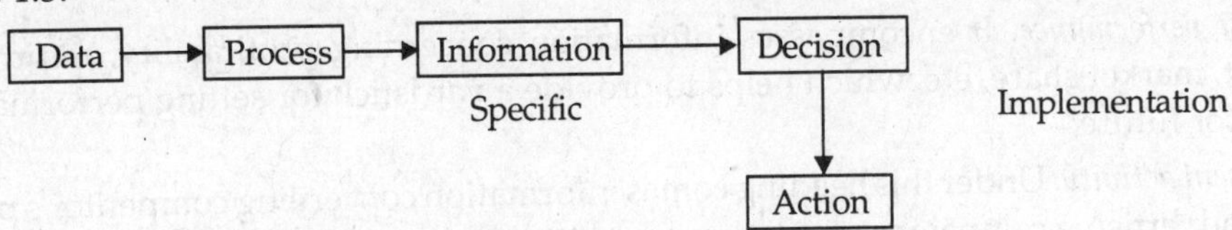

Fig. 1.3. Conversion of Data into Decision

From Fig. 1.3, it is clear that information consists of data that has been retrieved, processed or otherwise used, for informative or inferential purposes, arguments, or as a basis for forecasting. For example, some supporting documents, ledgers and so on, which comprise source material for profit and loss statements, may be used by the decision-maker for profit planning and control, or for other decision-making purposes. In fact, the relation of data with information is that of raw material to finished product. As mentioned earlier, information resources could supplement the existing list of 5 M's by introducing messages and moments in the context of information resource management. Information resources (in the sense of stored data of all types) are reusable.

Information contains an element of surprise, reduces uncertainty and triggers off action. It carries messages and when perceived by the recipients via any of the senses, it increases their state of knowledge or intelligence.

For planning, information requirements of decision-makers can be classified into three broad types as enumerated below :

Environmental Information

Environmental information requirement can be further classified and described as follows :

(1) *Government policies.* Information about Government policies or financial and tax affairs, political stability, etc. is required and may have a significant effect on future planning decisions.

(2) *Economic trends.* It includes information about (*a*) economic indicators like employment, productivity, capital investment; (*b*) prices and wage levels which affect all organisations regardless of product or services; (*c*) GNP level, trend and consumer disposable income.

(3) *Technological environment.* The information on technological changes or advancements is necessary for forecasting such changes in the firm and their probable effects on the same. It is also desirable to assess the effect of technical changes on new products and processes.

(4) *Factors of production.* These include information about the source, cost, location, availability, accessibility and productivity of the major factors of production such as (*a*) labour; (*b*) materials and spare parts; and (*c*) capital.

Competitive Information

Competitive information requirement can be classified and described as follows :

(1) *Industry demand.* This refers to the demand forecast of the industry for the product manufactured or about the area in which the firm is operating.

(2) *Firm demand.* This implies assessment of the firm's capabilities, activities and potentialities to meet demand relative to the capabilities and actions of the competing firms.

(3) *The competition.* This includes information about competing firms for forecasting own product demand and making decisions and plans to achieve the forecast. Such information falls into three categories :

(*a*) *Past performance.* It encompasses information concerning profitability, return on investment, market share, etc. which helps to provide a yardstick for setting performance objectives for future;

(*b*) *Present activity.* Under this heading comes information concerning competitor's price strategies, advertising campaigns, product mix, changes in distribution channels, etc. which help to evaluate one's own weaknesses or strengths; and

(*c*) *Future plans.* Information concerning new products, R & D efforts, availability of raw materials, etc. which help to decide future plans comes under this head.

Internal Information

It is the by-product of the normal operations of a business. Generally, it is historical or static in nature; it is after the fact data.

Internal information is aimed at identification of the firm's strengths and weaknesses. It includes the following :

(1) *Sales forecast.* Since all other internal plans of the firm are guided by the sales plan, it is considered as the dominant planning premise internal to the firm.

(2) *The financial plan.* Information on financial or budget plan is important because it represents a quantitative and time bound commitment about the allocation of total resources (workers, plant, materials, overheads, administrative expenses) of the firm. It provides information about a number of sub-plans of the firm and it acts as an important link between all activities of the firm.

(3) *Supply factors.* Information concerning availability and limitations of certain supply factors such as labour, capital, plant and equipment is important as these factors play a vital role in developing the financial and subsidiary plans for achieving firm's objectives.

(4) *Policies.* Long-term basic policies on product range, marketing, finance and about personnel do not permit flexibility in developing alternative courses of action in the short run.

1.2.3. System

Systems are diverse— economic system, computer system, decision-support system, communication system, transport system, educational system, solar system, etc. This means we live in an era of systems. But what exactly is meant by a system ?

A system is a group of elements or components joined together to fulfil certain functions. In a larger context, a system is an assemblage of procedures, processes, methods, routine techniques, etc. united in some form of regulated interaction to form an organised whole. The systems are either natural or man-made. An input-output relation and interdependence exists between the components (or sub-systems) of a man-made system.

A system is made up of sub-systems. A sub-system which may be composed of further sub-systems. However, a system itself is part of a supersystem. This could be termed as the environment in which the system operates. This relationship is shown in Fig. 1.4.

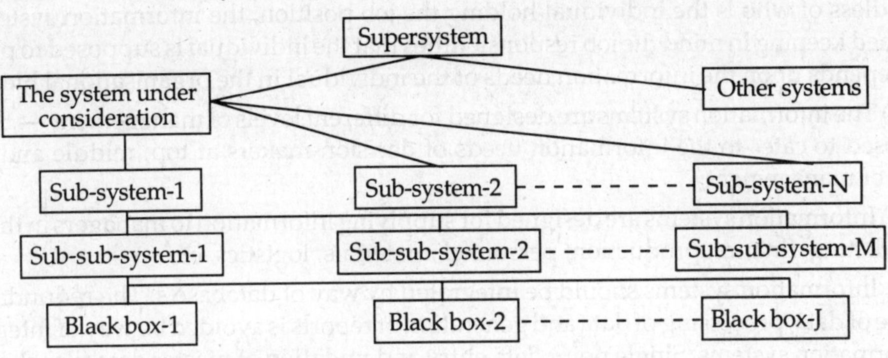

Fig. 1.4. System and its Components

The example given above is that of an industrial (or factory) system. It has various sub-systems such as production sub-system, marketing sub-system, personnel sub-system and financial sub-system. These sub-systems in turn are composed of further sub-systems. For example, a production sub-system could consist of sub-sub-system of production control, material control, quality control, etc. Again, the material sub-sub-system can be further broken down into 'black boxes' such as purchasing, stores, transportation, inspection, etc. This industrial system is a part (or sub-system) of the large economic system of the country which may be called as the super (or supra) system. Figure 1.4 and Table 1.1 describe various sub-systems and their links with the systems and the supersystem.

Table 1.1. Various Types of Systems

System	*Sub-systems*	*Usefulness*
Transport (Man-made)	Air transport, Rail transport, Road transport, Water transport	To provide movement of goods and passengers
Computer (Man-made)	Physical components like inputs, outputs, storage and connections	Processing of data for information
Business (Man-made)	Various departments like production, marketing, finance and personnel	Production of goods, services, earning of profit
Human body (Natural system)	Various systems like digestive, respiratory, circulatory, etc.	To keep human body alive and provide strength
Solar (Natural system)	All planets	To provide natural resources and basic necessities on earth

Now, combining management, information and system, it could be seen that management information systems are sets of related processes, activities, individuals or entities interacting together to provide processed data to the individual managers at various levels in different functional areas.

1.3. DEFINITIONS OF MIS

While defining the Management Information Systems, following characteristics should be kept in mind :

(*a*) Management information systems are primarily meant for providing information from the data after processing them. The information systems do not generate data. The data are generated, collected, recorded, stored, processed and retrieved after it has been generated by business operations in an organisation. The information systems follow the procedures designed for processing this data which has been generated within the organisation;

(*b*) Information systems are designed for the job positions rather than for individuals. Regardless of who is the individual holding the job position, the information systems are designed keeping in mind the job responsibilities that the individual is supposed to perform and depends upon the information needs of the individual in the organisational hierarchy;

(*c*) The information systems are designed for different levels of management — they are supposed to cater to the information needs of decision-makers at top, middle and junior levels of management;

(*d*) Information systems are designed for supplying information to managers in the areas of marketing, finance, production, personnel, materials, logistics, etc.;

(*e*) Information systems should be integrated by way of database's. The redundancy in storage of data, processing of data and generation of reports is avoided by way of integration of information systems. Single point data entry and updation of master data files should be ensured to minimize chances of discrepancies in the data integrity; and

(*f*) Information systems are facilitated with electronic equipment such as computers.

1.3.1. Definitions

The definition of the term 'Management Information System' varies from person to person. However, a few definitions are given here to make the concepts of MIS clear.

1. According to Schwartz, 'MIS is a system of people, equipment, procedures, documents and communication that collects, validates, operates on transformers, stores, retrieves, and present data for use in planning, budgeting, accounting, controlling and other management process'.

2. Coleman and Riley state that 'an MIS (*a*) applies to all management levels; (*b*) is linked to an organisational sub-system; (*c*) functions to measure performance, monitor progress, evaluate alternatives or provide knowledge for change or collective action, and (*d*) is flexible both internally and externally'.
3. Davis and Olson defined MIS as 'an integrated user-machine system designed for providing information to support operational control, management control and decision-making functions in an organisation. The information systems make use of resources such as hardware, software, men, procedures as well as supplies'.
4. Canith defined MIS as 'an approach that visualises the business organisation a single entity composed of various inter-related and inter-dependent sub-systems looking together to provide timely and accurate information for management decision-making, which leads to the optimisation of overall enterprise goals'.
5. Thomas R. Prince defined MIS as 'a computer based network containing one or more operating systems, provides relevant data to management for decision-making and also contains the necessary mechanism for implementing changes of responses made by management in the decision-making'.
6. Frederick B. Cornish defined MIS as 'structure to provide the information needed when needed and where needed. Further, the system represents the internal communication network of the business providing the necessary intelligence to plan, execute and control'.
7. According to Jerome Kanter, 'MIS is a system that aids management in making, carrying out, and controlling decisions'.

1.4. FRAMEWORK FOR MIS ORGANISATION AND MANAGEMENT TRIANGLE

For defining MIS organisation and its characteristics, it is necessary to understand the general framework which seeks to sharpen important distinctions in the types of information that support managerial decisions.

Robert Anthony in 1965 suggested that the area of management planning (deciding what to do) and control (assuring desired results) be divided into three categories as shown in Fig. 1.5.

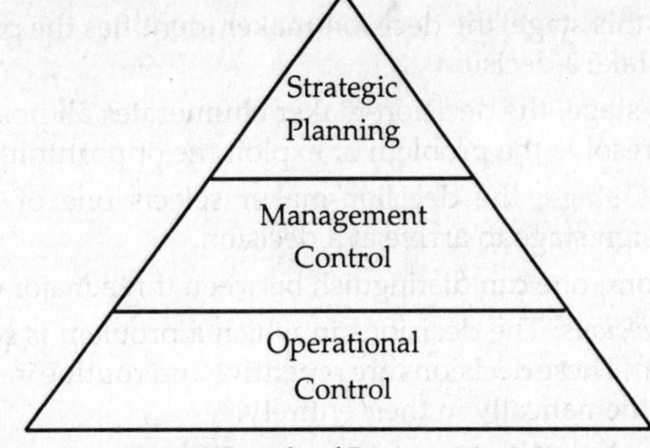

Fig. 1.5. Levels of Business Activity

(1) *Strategic planning.* It develops the strategy for (*a*) deciding objectives of the organisation and introducing changes in those objectives; (*b*) planning resources to be used to attain those objectives; and (*c*) formulating policies to govern procurement, use and disposition of those resources.

(2) *Management control.* It is needed by managers of various departments to (*i*) measure performance, (*ii*) decide on control actions, (*iii*) formulate new decision rules, and (*iv*) allocate resources.

(3) *Operational control.* It is the process of ensuring that operational activities are carried out to achieve optimum use of resources. It makes use of pre-established procedures and decision rules. Decisions and actions undertaken cover a short time span.

In essence, Anthony's framework is concerned with the objective of the decision-maker, *i.e.*, what the decision-maker is trying to do.

Table 1.2 illustrates with a specific example the planning and control activities in different functional areas of management.

Table 1.2. Planning and Control Activities in Different Functional Areas of Management

Function	*Strategic Planning*	*Management Control*	*Operational Control*
Finance	Raising funds by issuing new shares	Deciding maximum credit level for customers	Deciding the type of action to be taken against non-payment by a particular customer
Marketing	Deciding the possibilities to enter into the export market	Media planning for advertising	Planning sale contracts to be made by a salesman in the following week
Personnel	Changes in the organisation structure	Deciding promotions and vacancies to be filled up at the middle and lower levels in the organisation	Deciding on the workers' shift and their number
Production	Location of new plant	Deciding production planning and product mix for a specific period	Scheduling particular jobs on particular machines, shiftwise

While Anthony's framework is concerned with the objective of the decision-maker, Simon's framework examines the process of decision-making, *i.e.*, how the decision-maker arrives at a decision.

The process of decision-making, according to Simon, is divided into three stages :

(1) *Intelligence.* At this stage, the decision-maker identifies the problem or opportunity which enables him to take a decision.

(2) *Design.* At this stage, the decision-maker enumerates all possible courses of action that may help him to resolve the problem or exploit the opportunity.

(3) *Choice.* At this stage, the decision-maker selects one of the courses of action enumerated at the design stage to arrive at a decision.

With this framework, one can distinguish between three major classes of decisions :

(1) *Programmed decisions.* The decisions in which a problem is solved by a predefined procedure or algorithm. These decisions are repetitive and routine in nature and are capable of being modelled mathematically in their entirety.

The examples of such decisions are : (*i*) preparation of pay in accordance with the laid out regulations; and (*ii*) inventory ordering.

To arrive at the programmed decisions, a solution-manual to problems is prepared to help the users. Few characteristics of such decisions are : (*i*) These decisions can be delegated; (*ii*) The cost of solving a problem is low compared to non-programmed rules; and (*iii*) Such decisions can be made with the help of the computer system.

(2) *Non-programmed decisions.* These decisions are unstructured, occasional, of high consequence, complex and involve major commitments. There is no predefined program or set decision rule or algorithm available to solve these problems automatically.

The examples of such decisions are : (*i*) advertising budget; (*ii*) new product decisions; (*iii*) acquisition of capital projects.

Few characteristics of such decisions are : (*i*) These decisions are novel and difficult to structure in logical mathematical terms; (*ii*) These decisions cannot be delegated, and are based on management direction, thinking and deliberations, *e.g.*, purchase of scarce and capital items under fluctuating price conditions cannot be delegated; and (*iii*) Computers cannot be used directly for such decisions. However, they may be used to process large volumes of necessary data.

(3) *Semi-programmed decisions.* In these types of decision, at least one but not more than two of the above stages can be handled by a well-defined preset procedure. An example of such a decision is the intelligence phase, which is well-structured, having diverse kinds of variance analysis. Here a comparison with a budget is undertaken in a well-defined way to indicate the need for a decision. Subsequent stages of design and choice are, however, not handled by any set procedure.

1.4.1. Levels of Management

Each organisation is made up of several levels. These could be classified broadly into three categories : Top, Middle and Junior (TMJ) levels. In most cases, the top management performs strategic planning and the other two levels provide support in the form of processed information. The middle management level performs tactical planning and control, and needs information to discharge these managerial functions. The junior level is involved in day-to-day operational control and needs information for its working. Table 1.3 and Fig. 1.6 summarize the interaction and role of these three levels in an organisation.

Table 1.3. Organisational Structure

Task	*Location*	*Management Function*	*Level*
Strategic planning	Management	Management	Top
Management control	Office	Planning and control	Middle
Operational control	Factory and field	Execution	Supervisory

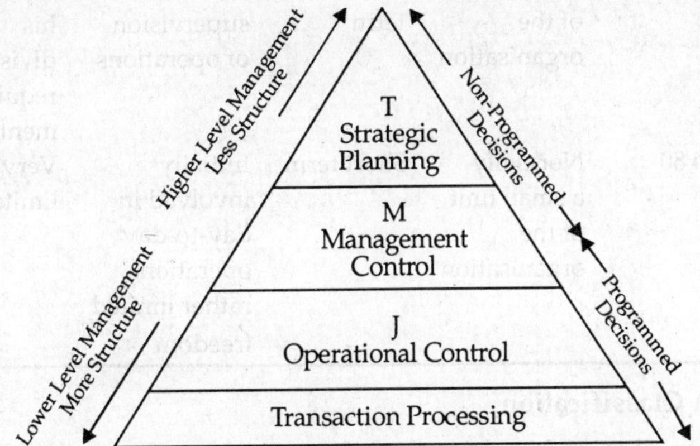

Fig. 1.6. Interaction of Management Levels

1.5. INFORMATION NEEDS AND ITS ECONOMICS

The availability of information to management at various levels has improved due to three reasons :

(1) *Development of telecommunications.* The information flow has been accelerated with

developments in communication technology like radio telephoney, microwave communication, laser communication and satellite communication.

(2) *Processing of data with computer.* The accessibility of information has been considerably improved as a computer can readily scan the available stored data to provide the required information.

(3) *Video technology.* Video technology permits the recording of activities on video cassettes and video discs. By combining the functions of a TV set and a computer it is possible to produce a video text which can be a storehouse for handy information.

Table 1.4 summarizes the information needs at various levels of management. All managers, whatever be their level in an organisation, are engaged in making decisions. It is only in the degree, influence and time-span that decisions made at various levels of management differ.

Table 1.4. Information Needs at Various Levels of Management

Level of Management	*Management Population in %*	*Extent of Organisation*	*Time Period*	*Nature of Decisions*	*Financial Powers*	*Nature of Information*
Top Level	5 (approx.)	Whole organisation	Long term	Selection of top personnel, policy approvals, emergency decisions	Extensive	Sporadic and one-shot
Middle Level						
(*a*) Staff	10 to 20	Whole organisation	Long term	Formulation of policies, framing of rules and procedures	Limited	Periodic information for special policies, procedures, etc.
(*b*) Line		A division of the organisation	Medium term	Actual supervision of operations	Limited to his divisional requirements	Operational (may be on daily basis)
Junior Level	70 to 80	Normally a small unit of the organisation	Short term	Initially involved in day-to-day operations, rather limited freedom	Very limited	Operational, instantaneous, on-line

1.5.1. Information Classification

The information obtained and used in the organisations can be classified into five categories :

(1) *Action vs. non-action information.* The information (or data) lying unnoticed is called non-action information, but the same information (or data) when processed and used in some context by the recipient is called action information.

(2) *Recurring vs. non-recurring information.* Information which is generated at regular intervals of time is called recurring (or repetitive) information. A particular type of

information which is arrived at through some special kind of study and which helps in management decision is called non-recurring (or non-repetitive) information.

(3) *Documentary vs. non-documentary information.* Information which is available in some document form, *i.e.*, either in some written form or on microfilms, magnetic tapes, floppy disks etc. is called documentary information. All other information is categorised as non-documentary (or oral).

(4) *Internal vs. external information.* The distinction is obvious. Managers at different hierarchies in the organisation require different combinations of internal and external information.

(5) *Historical information vs. future projections.* Here again the distinction is obvious because historical information would be futile unless it can be used for future projection.

1.5.2. Information Characteristics or Value

The value of information for a successful functioning of any organisation is now well recognised. The vital role of information as a link in the business system is shown in Fig. 1.7.

With business activities becoming more and more complex, the value of information is now vital, and hence greater managerial skill is required to perform the increasing range of business activities.

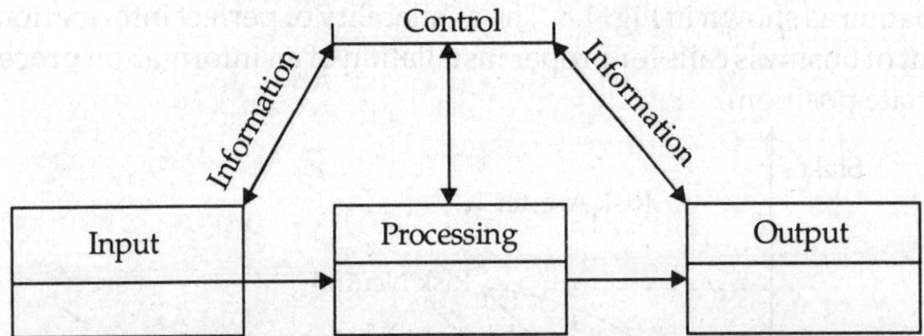

Fig. 1.7. Role of Information as a Link in the Business System

The information to be of 'value' must possess certain desirable quantitative and descriptive characteristics. The primary characteristics which an information must possess are : (*i*) Relevance; (*ii*) Availability; and (*iii*) Timeliness. Besides, certain desirable and necessary variable attributes of information are objectivity, sensitivity, comparability, consciousness and completeness. This information must be of quality. Since information is a critical organisational resource, low quality information has an adverse effect on organisational performance. The quality of information is determined by how it can motivate human action and contribute to effective decision-making. The measures of quality of an information are as follows :

(1) *Accuracy.* The degree of accuracy of an information depends upon the truthfulness with which data is collected either from primary or secondary sources. The information must be a true reflection of the situation; otherwise decision are bound to be incorrect and may lead to disastrous consequences.

(2) *Form.* The information value increases if the form in which it is to be supplied matches the requirements of the decision-maker. For example, if a decision-maker requires information on sales pattern in a graph form, then he appreciates receiving such information (or data) in a graphical form rather than in a tabular form

(3) *Relevance.* The available information needs to be updated all the time so that it could match its current utility. For example, in a service organisation, new data regarding

improvement in the service keeps coming in most of the time. Therefore, processing continues to take place so that updated information is available all the time.

(4) *Timeliness.* The information should be available when required. Delayed information has less value as a resource.

(5) *ABC nature of information.* Sometimes internally generated information can be categorised as follows based on its availability, cost and dependence :

Four basic principles of information management are :

Data + Relevance + Purpose = Information

Information + Insight = Understanding

Understanding + Communication = Intelligence

Intelligence + Action = Effectiveness

1.5.3. Business Risk due to Information Gap

Generally decisions are made in the absence of adequate information because efforts to get the required information are either tedious or too costly. Sometimes there is no knowledge of the availability of required information, and often it is not available in the form needed.

The risk of taking wrong decisions is minimized by maximizing the availability of the needed information as shown in Fig. 1.8. The availability of perfect information to minimize the risk element of business calls for proper installation of an information processing system at the appropriate position.

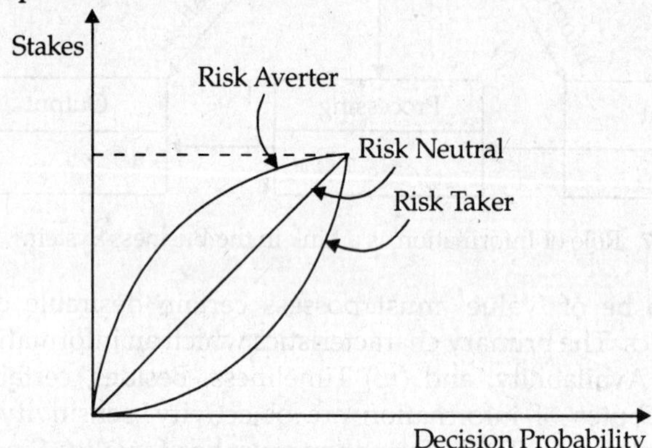

Fig. 1.8. Business Risk in Terms of Information Gap

A few observations can be made on Fig. 1.8 :

(*a*) With the increase in efforts of information collection (time and money), the probability of availability of information is increased;

(*b*) With the increase in availability of information about a particular business activity, the business risk is minimized; and

(*c*) In spite of all-out efforts for information collection, the importance of availability of information does not increase beyond a limit. Hence, it is necessary for a manager to know the limits of information availability in a given situation.

1.5.4. Information from Data

Data Life Cycle

Data has its own life cycle. The following aspects of the data life cycle are important in the development, design and operation of the information system.

(1) *Generation of data.* This may take place internally and/or externally by the occurrence of an event in a business organisation such as sales slips, personnel forms, purchase orders, etc.

(2) *Manipulation of data.* Manipulation of data involves addition, subtraction, multiplication, division, etc. based on certain formulae. This includes, for example, preparing pay slips for employees, bills of customers, determining optimal product-mix, economic order quantity, aggregate production planning, etc.

(3) *Storing/retrieving and reproduction of data.* The generated data is *stored* in a document in devices such as magnetic disks and tapes. The stored data is *retrieved* by searching for specific data elements from the device on which it is stored. The retrieved data may be *reproduced* or converted to a different form of storage by preparing documents, reports, etc. The data life cycle is shown in Fig. 1.9.

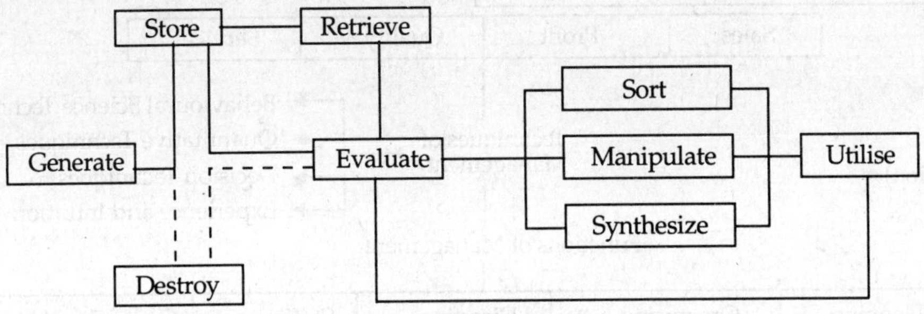

Fig. 1.9. Data Life Cycle

Data Processing Methods

Before the evolution of computers, data processing consisted of manual procedures whereby data operations were performed by hand with the aid of basic devices such as a pencil, paper, slide rule, etc. Then came the electro-mechanical method which is actually a symbiosis of man and machine. This was followed by the use of typewriters, cash registers, time clocks, etc.

The punched card equipment method came into use along with the 'unit record system', the principle being that data concerning a person, object, or event is normally punched (recorded) on a card. A number of cards placed logically and sequentially in a deck was termed a 'file'. There was considerable reduction in manual intervention. After the development of the electronic computer, a single machine became capable of performing most of the data operations without intermittent human intervention. Today, data processing is generally assumed to be *electronic data-processing* (EDP). Initially, computer systems were used in many organisations to perform essentially the *automatic data processing* (ADP). Recent technological developments, especially in the field of electronics, have reduced the cost and size of a computer. Thus, organisations of almost any size can benefit now by using computer data processing.

1.6. SYSTEMS APPROACH

In the past, decision-makers in a business organisation attempted piecemeal solutions, *i.e.*, thinking in isolation without relating the parts or other operational sub-systems (or units) in the organisation to each other and to the whole. For example, the marketing department used to perform without interaction with departments of design and production; production control was not coordinated with financial or personnel planning; and the classic or old management information system worked on individual reports rendered by the departments, and was guided by a chart of accounts without too much regard for organisational information needs. This kind of piecemeal approach for optimizing the effectiveness of business organisations is no longer adequate because business activities are increasingly becoming complex, and hence the consequences of wrong decisions are costly.

The systems approach to a business organisation implies a wholistic approach to the study of inter-relationships of sub-systems of an organisation, in view of the objectives set by the organisation. Thus, this requires an integrated approach which could reduce the conflict among different sub-systems and modify the objectives of these sub-systems in order to arrive at an optimum solution to the problems which may arise in the achievement of the main objectives or in the working of the whole system. A systems view of business is shown in Fig. 1.10.

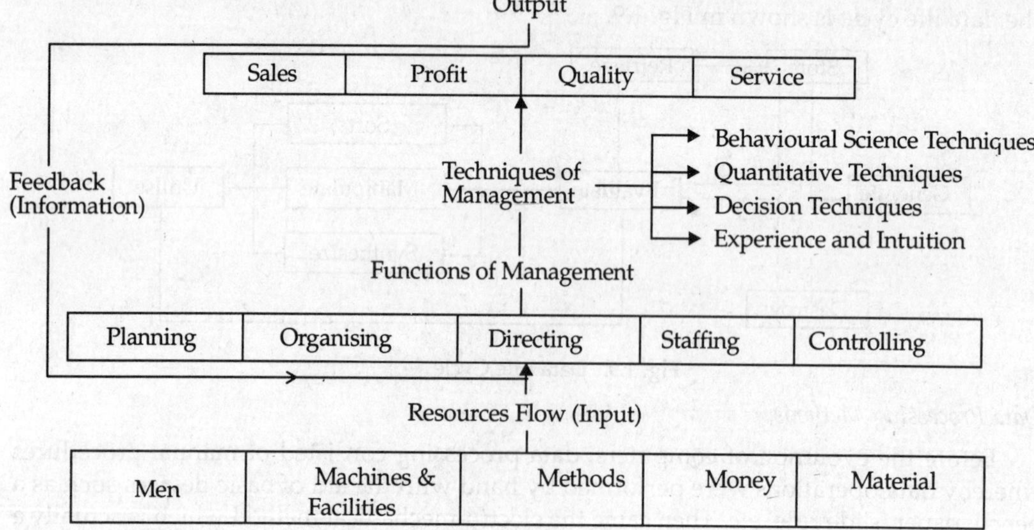

Fig. 1.10. Business Organisation — A system

1.6.1. Reasons for Systems Approach

The reasons for an increasing need for systems approach can be listed as follows :

(1) *Increased complexity of business.* Business activities are becoming complex due to (*a*) technological revolution; (*b*) research and development; and (*c*) an information explosion. Transportation, communication, agriculture and manufacturing units are some of the industries where advanced mechanisation and automation techniques have been adopted to improve output and productivity. The need for such changes is obvious but this requires an improved management. In order to cope with this revolution in technology, there is a need of going in for selective information for complex tasks and for decisions to be made in future.

There are two factors responsible for technological advances: first, the research and development; and second, the varying customer choice for product and services. The second factor has led to an increase in competition among manufacturing and service industries.

Further, the information explosion has been in progress for quite some time. It is said that people's knowledge is doubling in every 5 to 10 year period and that this rate of knowledge accumulation is accelerating. This exponential growth of information makes it necessary that information is properly collected, stored, processed, retrieved and displayed for the right decision as and when needed.

(2) *Increased complexity of management.* The decision-making ability of managers has improved due to the following reasons :

(*a*) Improved information feedback systems;

(*b*) A better understanding of decision-making processes;

(*c*) Quantitative techniques that permit an experimental or simulation approach to complex problems; and

(*d*) The increasing availability of computers.

1.6.2. Classification of Systems

The various types of systems are :

(1) *Conceptual and empirical systems.* The conceptual system is concerned with theoretical structures which may or may not have any counterpart in the real world. Examples of such systems are : economic theory, organisation theory, general system of relativity, etc.

Empirical systems are concrete operational systems made up of people, materials, machines, energy and other physical things. Other systems such as electrical, thermal, and chemical are also fall into this category. Since such systems may be derived from or based upon a conceptual input, therefore it represents the conversion of concepts into practice.

(2) *Natural and man-made systems.* The examples of natural systems are : human body, solar system, etc.

Examples of man-made systems are : Transportation system, communication system, education system, business organisation, etc.

(3) *Social system.* A system made up of people may be taken as a social system, such as business organisations, government agencies, political parties, social clubs, professional societies, etc.

(4) *Man-machine system.* Most empirical systems fall into the category of man-machine systems. One of the examples of this system is the aeroplane.

(5) *Open and closed systems.* An open system continually interacts with its environment. This type of system can adapt to changing internal and environmental conditions. Every social and business organisation is open because it reacts with its unpredictable environment.

A closed system is one that does not interact with its environment. This system does not change, or if it does, then a barrier exists between the system and the environment to prevent the system from being affected. However, any known system cannot continue its operation for a long period of time without interacting with its environment.

1.6.3. System Life Cycle

A management information system in business has the following four phases in its life cycle.

(1) *Study phase.* This phase is concerned with (*i*) identification of the problem; (*ii*) study of the present system and its effectiveness; (*iii*) identification and evaluation of various alternative courses of action; and (*iv*) selection of the most appropriate course of action as per the objective.

(2) *Design phase.* This phase is concerned with (*i*) identification of the functions to be performed; (*ii*) study of the input/output and life cycle design; and (*iii*) defining basic parameters of system design.

(3) *Development phase.* At this stage, the decision about the selection and use of hardware and software is taken.

(4) *Implementation phase.* The system so designed is given practical shape; and is adopted for use.

The adopted system is reviewed after a fixed interval of time to assess its weaknesses and usefulness. Such a review helps to modify the current system in view of changing environmental conditions.

1.7. MEANING AND OBJECTIVES OF MIS

Management information system (MIS) is an integrated man-machine system which collects, maintains, correlates and selectively displays information in the proper time frame consistently, to meet the specific needs of various levels of management, in order that decisions could be made and action taken for fulfilling the objectives of an organisation. In other words, it is a system which (*i*) provides information to support managerial functions (planning, control, organising, operating); (*ii*) collects information systematically and routinely in accordance with a well defined set of rules; and (*iii*) includes files, hardware, software and operations research models of processing, storing, retrieving and transmitting information to the users.

An effective MIS has the following objectives :

(1) *Facilitate* the decisions-making process by furnishing information in the proper time frame. This helps the decision-maker to select the best course of action.

(2) *Provide* requisite information at each level of management to carry out their functions.

(3) *Help* in highlighting the critical factors to the closely monitored for successful functioning of the organisation.

(4) *Support* decision-making in both structured and unstructured problem environments.

(5) *Provide* a system of people, computers, procedures, interactive query facilities, documents for collecting, storing, retrieving and transmitting information to the users.

1.7.1. Categories of MIS

The MIS can be sub-divided into following four categories :

(1) *Transaction processing system* (*TPS*). The system designed for processing day-to-day transactions in an organisation is called TPS. This system deals with collecting and processing a large volume of data which mainly helps junior level management in discharging their responsibilities (operational control).

(2) *Information providing system* (*IPS*). This system is meant for processing information, making a summary of information, and providing exception reports. The summary reports help in giving at a glance the information available, while exception reports indicate deviations (if any) and the reasons for shortfalls in performance.

(3) *Decision support system* (*DSS*). It is sometimes described as the next evolutionary step after MIS. It helps in improving the analytical capability of the decision-maker by creating an interactive model of the real-life situation.

(4) *Programmed decision-making system.* The word 'program' is derived from the jargon of the computer field, where it is defined as a plan for the automatic solution of a problem. Programs are simply a string of instructions to accomplish a job or a task. In this information age, the systems for programmed decisions are created so that decisions are made by the system rather than a person.

1.7.2. MIS and Organisation Structure

Organisation structure and information needs are inseparably linked like the human anatomy (as organisation structure) and the nervous system (as information system). The knowledge of organisation structure and proper record of delegation of authority within the organisation are prerequisites of MIS. This actually helps in defining authority and responsibility, demarcating decision-making areas, and measuring objectives of each sub-system (or unit). The outline of the design of an MIS for any organisation is shown in Fig. 1.11.

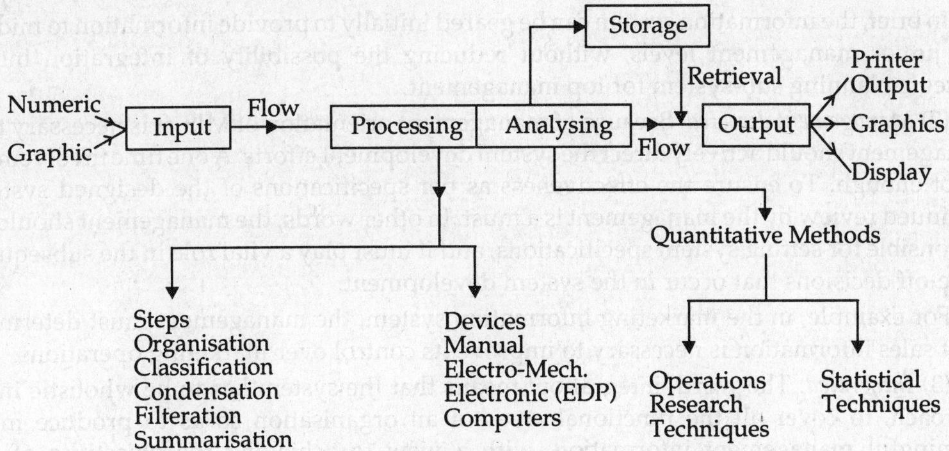

Fig. 1.11. Organisation of an MIS

1.7.3. Location of MIS in a Business Organisation

Different business organisations follow different procedures in locating an information centre in the organisation. Three forms of organisations of MIS/Data Processing (DP) set-up are generally known. These are as follows :

(1) *As part of financial department.* In this case, DP personnel headed by a DP Manager are placed under the charge of the financial controller or the chief accounts officer. This is so because historically financial applications were the first to be computerised and systematised.

(2) *DP organisation under a separate direction* (*MIS*). Sometimes other names such as director (management services) or director (data processing) are also used. In this form of organisation the DP Manager or the Director of MIS enjoys a status equal to the Financial Controller or the Chief Accounts Officer or any other chief of the functional divisions. This kind of organisation is adopted by companies, who recognise data processing and systems design as important functional areas.

(3) *DP organisation as a separate company.* This kind of organisation, followed largely by the consultancy units or subsidiaries of conglomerate of companies, is useful for the speedy and rapid growth of systems design and other related data processing activities both with respect to internal applications as well as external consultancy.

1.7.4. Characteristics of MIS

Some important features of MIS are summarized as follows :

(1) *Management orienited.* The system is designed from the top downwards. It does not mean that the system is designed to provide information directly to the top management. Other levels of management are also provided with relevant information. Here management orientation of MIS implies that the development of information system efforts should start from an appraisal of management needs and overall business objectives.

For example, in the marketing information system, the activities such as sales-order processing, shipment of goods to customers and billing for the goods are basically operational control activities. This information can also be tracked by a salesman to know the sales territory, size of order, geography and product line, provided the system is designed accordingly. However, if the system is designed keeping in mind the top management, then data on external competition, market and pricing can be created to know the market share of the company's product and to serve as a basis of a new product or market-place introduction.

In brief, the information system can be geared initially to provide information to middle and junior management levels, without reducing the possibility of integration into a strategic planning sub-system for top management.

(2) *Management directed.* Because of management orientation of MIS, it is necessary that management should actively direct the system development efforts. A one time involvement is not enough. To ensure the effectiveness as per specifications of the designed system, continued review by the management is a must. In other words, the management should be responsible for setting system specifications, and it must play a vital role in the subsequent trade-off decisions that occur in the system development.

For example, in the marketing information system, the management must determine what sales information is necessary to improve its control over marketing operations.

(3) *Integrated.* The word 'integration' means that the system has to be wholistic in its approach, to cover all the functional areas of an organisation so as to produce more meaningful management information, with a view to achieving the objectives of the organisation. It has to consider various sub-systems, their objectives, information needs, and recognise the interdependence that these sub-systems have amongst themselves, so that common areas of information are identified and processed without repetition and overlapping. In other words, an integrated system that blends information from several operational areas is a necessary element of an MIS.

For example, in the development of an effective production scheduling system, a proper balance amongst the following factors is desired : (*i*) set-up costs; (*ii*) manpower; (*iii*) overtime; (*iv*) production capacity; (*v*) inventory level; (*vi*) money available; and (*vii*) customer service. Ignorance regarding any of these factors would lead to a sub-optimal solution.

(4) *Common data flows.* Because of the integration concept of MIS, common-data-flows concept avoids repetition and overlapping in data collection and storage, combining similar functions, and simplifying operations wherever possible. However, it may be better to live with a little duplication to ensure system's acceptability and workability.

For example, in the marketing operations, orders received for goods become the basis of billing of goods ordered, setting up of the accounts receivable, initiating production activity, sales analysis and forecasting, etc.

(5) *Heavy planning element.* An MIS cannot be established overnight. It takes 3 to 5 years or even more to establish it properly in an organisation. Hence, long-term planning is required for MIS development to fulfil the future needs and objectives of the organisation. The designer of an MIS must ensure that it should not become obsolete before it actually gets into operation.

An example of such a feature of MIS may be seen in a transportation system where a highway is designed not to handle today's traffic requirements but to handle the traffic requirements five to ten years hence.

(6) *Sub-system concept.* Even though the system is viewed as a single entity, it must be broken down into meaningful sub-systems that can be implemented one at a time. The division of an MIS into various sub-systems opens a way for this phasing plan. In Fig. 1.12, various systems have been shown, which in turn can be broken into additional sub-systems to delimit boundaries to the problems.

(7) *Flexibility and ease of use.* While building an MIS system all types of possible means which may occur in future are added to make it flexible.

A feature that often goes with flexibility is the ease of use. The MIS should be able to incorporate all those features that make it readily accessible to a wide range of users with easy usability.

1.7.5. Classification of MIS

According to Mason, the MIS can be divided into four categories :

(1) *Data bank information system.* In this system, the link between the information system and the user is assumed to be weak. This type of system is more useful for unstructured decisions. The information system collects, classifies and stores data which may be useful to the user. The user makes request for data as per his need and determines the cause and effect in view of the actions, and makes judgement as to which outcome is suitable. The data does not help the user in making predictions or decisions, however, the nature and availability of data itself tend to suggest certain desirable alternatives to the user. The data bank information system is shown in Fig. 1.12.

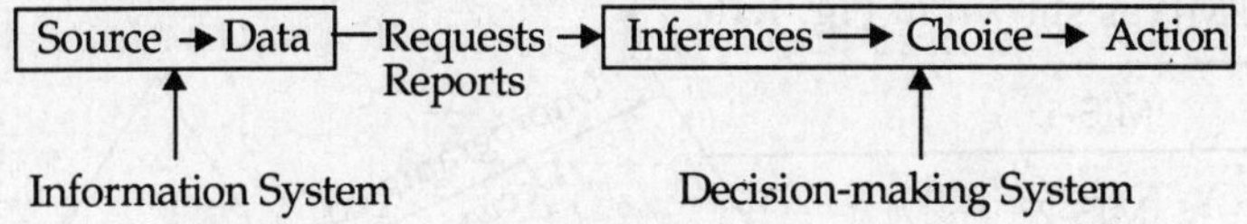

Fig. 1.12. Data Bank Information System

(2) *Predictive information system.* This class of system is an extension of the data bank information system. In this system, prediction and inference-making occurs when processing by the information system passes from basic data to conclusions about the source.

The decision-making system (or user) asks as to 'what if' certain actions are taken. In response to such enquiries, the information system responds in the vein of 'if' user goes for action 'then'. This is what he can expect, will occur. Here the outcome is not evaluated.

This class of MIS is helpful when decisions are semi-structured (relationship between input and output is either deterministic or probabilistic, but mathematical optimization is possible in the absence of unrealistic assumptions). Ultimately decisions are taken based on predictions that the user receives. The predictive information system is shown in Fig. 1.13.

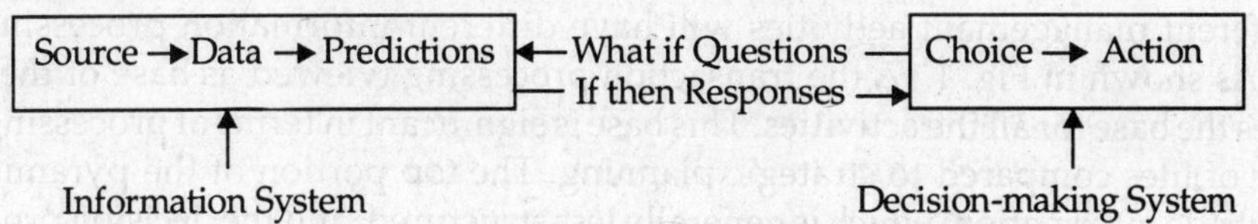

Fig. 1.13. Predictive Information System

(3) *Decision-making information system.* In this system, an organisation's value system and criteria for choice are incorporated. This level of MIS is useful for structured decisions (Fig. 1.14).

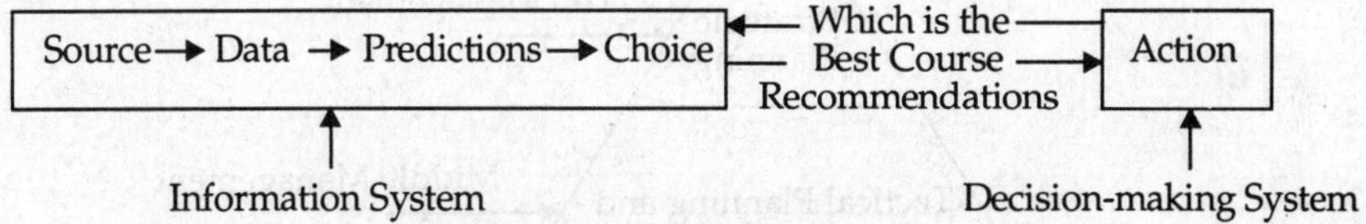

Fig. 1.14. Decision-making Information System

Optimization methods such as 'operations research' and 'cost effectiveness' are examples of this MIS system. The solution offered by such models with a specific objective function (for ranking outcome from each alternative course of action) and a set of constraints (for specifying functional relationship amongst various resources) recommend a single course of action for optimizing the policy. The decision-maker, however, may not act on the recommendation.

(4) *Decision-taking information system.* In this system (Fig. 1.15), the information system and the user are assumed to be one. For example, a purchase order is released automatically when an inventory level reaches or goes below the reorder point or sends reminders to vendors to supply goods when supply is overdue.

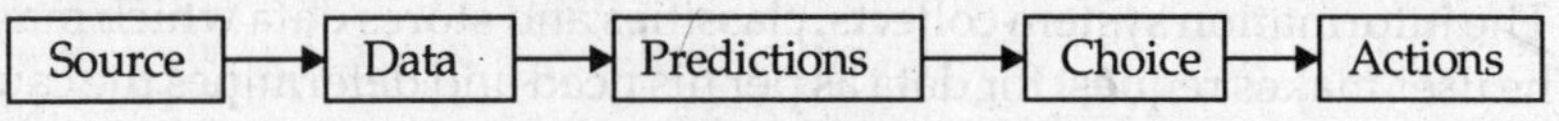

Fig. 1.15. Decision-taking Information System

1.7.6. MIS and Levels of Management

There exists an inverse relationship between Mason's categories of MIS and levels of management (TMJ) as shown in Fig. 1.16.

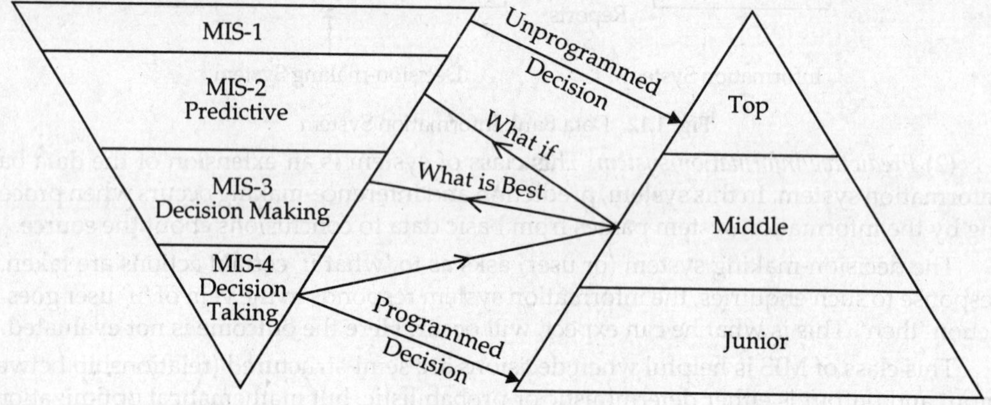

Fig. 1.16. Inverse Relationship

Levels of Management Activities

Different management activities will have different information processing requirements. As shown in Fig. 1.17, the transaction processing (viewed as base of the pyramid) provides the base for all the activities. This base is significant in terms of processing time and number of files compared to strategic planning. The top portion of the pyramid requires more outside information, which is generally less structured, and the decision process at this level will be more non-programmed. The lower portion of the pyramid tends to be more structured, precise, current and repetitive data.

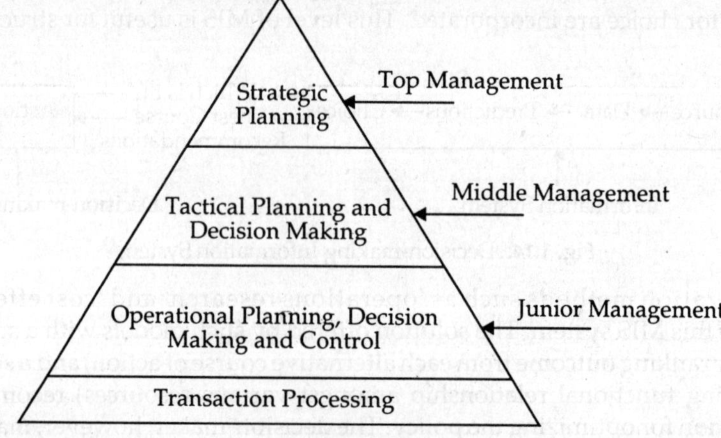

Fig. 1.17. Pyramid Structure of MIS

Table 1.5 shows the information requirement for different levels of management activity in the case of some selected information characteristics.

Table 1.5. Information Requirement for Different Levels of Management in the case of some Selected Information Characteristics

Information Characteristics	*Strategic Planning*	*Management Control*	*Operational Control*
Volume	Low	Intermediate	High
Source	Significant amount from external source	Mostly internal	Entirely internal
Scope	Very wide	Intermediate	Well-defined, narrow
Level of aggregation	Aggregate	Intermediate	Detailed
Time horizon	Future	Present	Historical
Currency	Quite old	Intermediate	Highly current
Accuracy	Low	Intermediate	High
Frequency of use	Infrequent	Intermediate	Very frequent

1.7.7. Design of an MIS

While designing an MIS, a general approach has to be followed so that a suitable system can be devised to cater to the needs of different organisations as per their functions and decision-making requirements. Irrespective of the organisation in question, the data gets generated at various levels of the management. These data when processed and analysed become information which, when properly communicated in time to the decision-maker, helps in making decisions and undertaking actions.

The following steps are generally taken in the design of an MIS (Fig. 1.18) :

(1) *Identifying information needs at all levels of management.* There are problems in every growing business organisation, but most of the time a clear definition of problems and a priority system for their solution is not known. Thus, as a first step in MIS design, the management should identify, in detail, the problems to be solved.

The mission statement for the business as a whole leads to objectives for the general business and these objectives help in framing various plans. Each of these business objectives and plans need some kind of feedback (or information). These information needs are actually the problems, to be solved by the MIS function.

The following steps are necessary to initiate the design process and are repeated until the information requirement and the problem to be solved are fully understood :

(*a*) Initiating the information need;

(*b*) Asking questions about the need;

(*c*) Suggesting interpretations of that need;

(*d*) Detailing the original statement; and

(*e*) Reviewing with the management the more detailed statement of the need.

(2) *Listing objectives of MIS and anticipated benefits.* The users must define system objectives in terms of information demands and not in terms of satisfaction of demands that are not related to an objective. For example, in several government departments, prior to the designing of an information system, the system objective was the automation of hundreds of reports without looking at the management of tasks related to functional or resource system represented by the report. These are training needs, employee relations, safety, recruitment, staffing. Such attention is possible only by automation of records or processing of existing data, otherwise the true objectives of the organisation represented by the system are overlooked.

The system objective should be defined in terms of what a decision-maker can do and how effectively he would be able to function after his information requirements have been complied with. The basic questions which are asked, while listing down the objectives of the MIS system design are : (*i*) What is the purpose of the system ? (*ii*) Why is it needed ? (*iii*) What is it expected to do ? (*iv*) Who are the users and what are their objectives ?

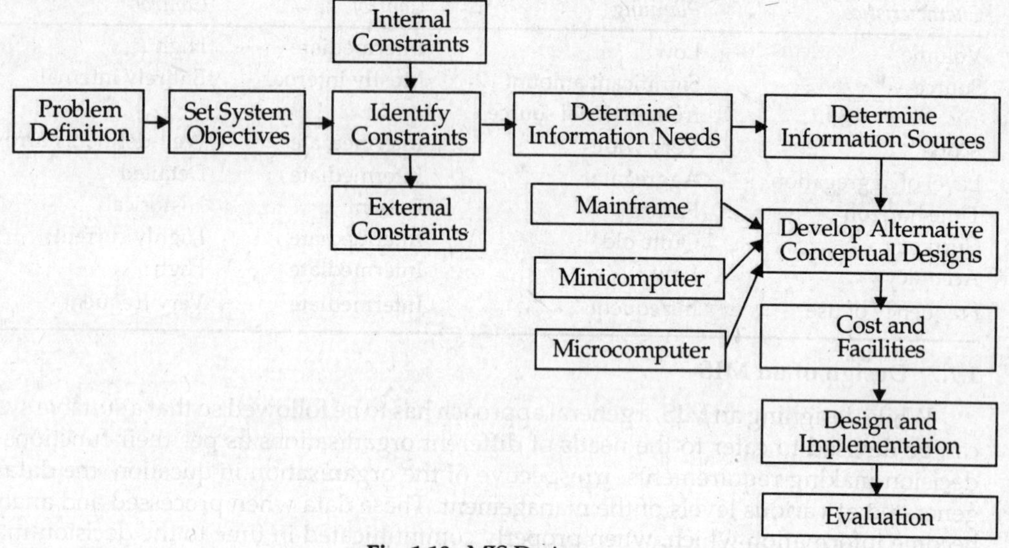

Fig. 1.18. MIS Design

Obviously, the objectives of the MIS system design have to match with the objectives of the organisation. However, a common fallacy in stating objectives of the MIS system is to emphasize these in vague terms : reduce costs, improve efficiency, keep accurate records, meet customer demands and meet the production schedule.

A few more examples of the fallacy and vagueness in stating objectives of the organisation and hence that of the MIS system design are given below : a university vice-chancellor may state his objective as to 'provide quality education'; whereas a minister may claim it to be to 'provide more jobs for the unemployed'. In both the cases, the objective so stated is not enough to provide a measure of performance of the system or to design an information system to help achieve the objective.

(3) *Identifying systems constraints* (*internal and external*). The systems constraints are also called problem boundaries or restrictions under which objectives may be achieved. These constraints (or limitations) in the design of the system are the creation of the manager-user or the designer himself, because of his limited freedom of action in designing a system, to achieve the objectives.

The internal constraints are viewed in terms of (*i*) top management support; (*ii*) organisational policy; (*iii*) personnel needs (manpower) and availability; (*iv*) cost and resource; and (*v*) acceptance (resistance in the acceptance of computerized MIS are : economic threat, threat to status, threat to ego, etc.).

The external constraints are mainly concerned with the customer. Ordered entry, billing and other systems that interface with the systems of the customer must be designed with the customer's need in mind. In addition to this, a variety of other external constraints exist, *i.e.*, Govt. (central or state) restrictions on the processing of data, unions, suppliers, etc.

(4) *Determining information needs and resources.* The system design must begin with determining the real information needs of the management : information that can increase

the perception of managers in critical areas such as problems, alternatives, opportunities and plans. In other words, if a decision-maker can define his objectives and spell out the items of information that are needed to attain the objectives, then he or she is at least half-way home in systems design.

A decision-maker needs information for a variety of reasons concerned with the management process. The type of information which is required at various times and for various purposes depends on two factors : (1) Personal managerial attitudes, *e.g.*, knowledge of information systems; managerial style; perception of information needs, etc. of the individual manager; and (*ii*) Organisational environment (nature of the company; level of management; structure of the organisation, etc.).

After estimating the need of information and clearly defining the objectives, the next step in MIS system design is to determine the sources of information. The sources of information may be categorized as follows : (*i*) *Internal sources.* It is in the form of written materials — file records, memoranda and letters, reports containing information about the existing system, etc.; (*ii*) *External sources.* It may be in the form of trade and Govt. publications; personal interviews of managers and personal interaction with decision-makers.

Information needs and sources of a few sub-systems may be stated as follows :

Sub-system		*Information*
Inventory	need	: Items falling below minimum inventory level
	source	: Stock level determination sub-system compares current balance against minimum inventory level
Production Control	need	: Cost variance over or under 5 per cent
	source	: Integration of costing with manufacturing applications — shop control, stores requisitioning, manpower availability, etc.
Purchasing	need	: Performance of individual vendors
	source	: Comparison of prices, quality, lead time with predetermined standards.

(5) *Developing alternative conceptual design and selecting one.* The conceptual design of MIS is considered as a skeleton of the MIS, which guides and restricts the form of the detailed design. The concept of design of an MIS consists of : patterns of information flow; channels of information; and role of decision-makers and competitors.

The alternative concepts of a system can be evaluated on the basis of the following :

(*a*) Compare anticipated performance of the conceptual design with respect to objectives of the system developed earlier;

(*b*) For quantified comparison amongst systems, prepare a preliminary cost-effectiveness data for the system;

(*c*) Examine the quality of databases and information to be made available. Study the number of operations, dispersions and duplication of files, and potential breakdown points; and

(*d*) Expand the conceptual designs in greater detail if none of these provide a preferred design.

(6) *Preparing the conceptual design report.* The conceptual design report is a proposal prepared for the expenditure of funds and possible changes in the organisational set-up. Since this report is submitted to management, it must contain the summary of problems that necessitate the system, the objectives, the general nature of the system, reasons why this concept was selected over others, and time and resources required to design and implement the system.

Along with this summary, a separate report about the performance specifications of the system may also be submitted. The performance specifications describe the functions, which must be performed by the system, and provide the yardstick for its assessment.

1.7.8. Implementation of MIS

Before installing a new MIS in any organisation, it is desirable to know whether there is already an old MIS in operation. If so, then the old system is allowed to operate parallely till the new system is fully in operation. This arrangement will be helpful in examining the relative advantages of the new system over the old one.

The implementation plan involves the following steps :

(1) Preparing organisational plans
(2) Planning of work flow
(3) Training of personnel
(4) Development of software
(5) Acquiring computer hardware
(6) Designing the format for data collection
(7) Construction of data files
(8) Operation of old and new systems in parallel
(9) Phasing out the old and inducting the new system
(10) Evaluation, maintenance and control of the new system.

The outline of implementation phase of an MIS is shown in Fig. 1.19.

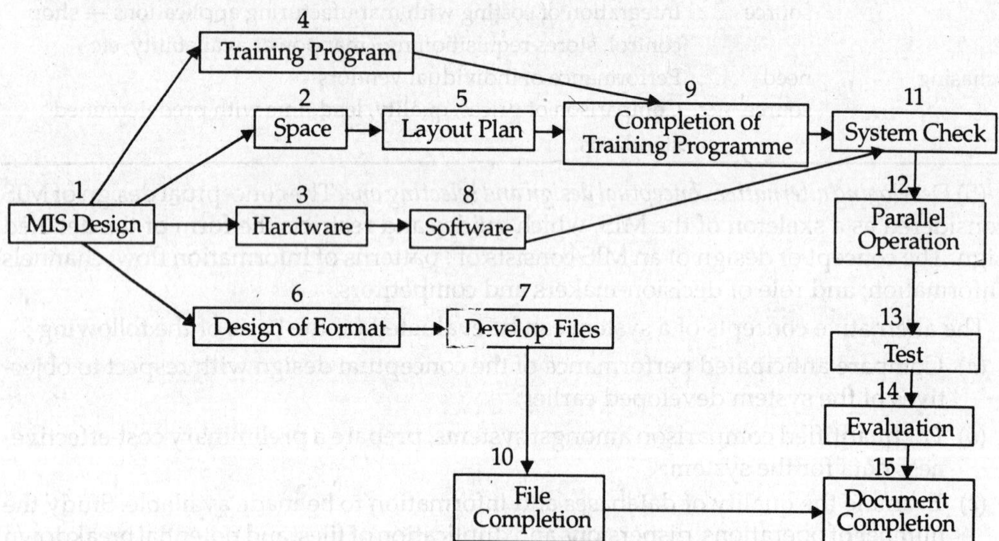

Fig. 1.19. Steps of Implementation of an MIS

1.8. DISADVANTAGES OF INFORMATION SYSTEMS

Many benefits can be derived from information systems and technologies by the organisations. However, at times, the same systems and technologies can have negative effects on people and organisations. Therefore, it is utmost essential that organisations take all possible precautions to ensure that information systems will not hinder their growth and progress. Following disadvantages are likely to be there from information systems :

1. *'Deskilling' of workers.* Introduction of new technologies, especially for automation, sometimes render obsolete the existing skills of some workers. Many industries such as the automobile, steel, insurance industries, banks, have gone through periods of massive layoffs because of intense automation efforts. Therefore, while computerisation can increase operational efficiency and improve profits, sometimes it is also the root cause of workforce reduction.

2. *Information overload.* Generation of excessive amounts of information can overwhelm managers who must digest it and use it to make decisions. At times, this improvement also has its downside.

3. *Employee mistrust.* Employees sometimes fear that computers will eventually replace them. They may view information systems with skepticism, unless they are assured that their jobs are not in danger.

4. *Increased competitive pressure.* There is increased pressure on small and medium-scale industries, failing which they are steadily being pushed out of the marketplace by larger companies.

5. *Disenchantment with IS.* Many organisations are unable to value the information systems and technologies to their organisations vis-a-vis the return on investment. In coming years, the MIS will experience close scrutiny of its abilities to deliver on its promises.

6. *Security breaches.* When organisations introduce new and sophisticated technologies, they must also find new ways to protect these assets from theft, pilferage, and security breaches. Therefore, computers and information systems actually increase the operating costs of an organisation.

1.9. APPROACHES OF MIS DEVELOPMENT

Generally, following seven approaches are used for developing MIS :

1. *Top down approach.* This approach develops a corporate plan as a guide for designing the information system. Here top management takes the lead in formulating objectives, policies and plans and communicates them down the line to middle and supervisory management for translating them into reality.

2. *Bottom up approach.* It consists of following *five* steps : (*a*) Individual functional applications are planned separately consisting of transaction processing, updating of files and simple reports; (*b*) Files of various functional applications are integrated by means of indexing and chaining into a database; (*c*) Various functions are added to operate on the database at management control level; (*d*) Integration of models into a model base having a wide variety of analysis, decision and planning models; and (*e*) Strategic planning data and planning models are added to the information system.

3. *Integrative approach.* This approach permits managers at all levels to influence the design of MIS. Here evaluation, modification and approval of top management continues till a final design is acceptable to all levels.

4. *Traditional approach.* Here activities are performed in sequence. Each activity is undertaken only when the previous activity is completed. Managers and users consider and review the work performed by MIS professionals during each stage of processing, in order to ensure accuracy and completeness.

5. *Prototyping approach.* In order to avoid any possible delay, prototyping approach is used. The goal is to develop a small or pilot version, called a prototype, which is built quickly and at lesser cost with the intention of modifying it when need arises.

6. *End user development approach.* With the increasing availability of low cost technology, end user development is popular in many organisations. Here the end user is responsible for system development.

7. *Systematic approach for development in small organisations.* Since fewer MIS professionals shall be working having with variety of responsibilities that they have little time to develop new systems for users. In a very small organisation, no MIS professional will exist. This does not mean that they cannot develop management information systems. They develop systems using the following steps :

1. Identify requirements.
2. Locate, evaluate and secure software development.
3. Locate, evaluate and secure hardwares.
4. Implement the systems.

1.10. CONSTRAINTS IN DEVELOPING AN MIS

Following are the constraints in developing an effective MIS :

1. No management system to build upon.
2. No clear definition of mission and purpose.
3. No objectives for the company.
4. Lack of management participation.
5. Misorganisation.
6. Over-reliance on the consultant/manufacturer.
7. Communication gap.
8. Performance of key people.

1.11. MIS AND USE OF COMPUTER

Following are the main advantages of using computer technology in MIS :

1. Expanding scope for using information system.
2. Enhancing speed of processing and retrieval of data.
3. Widening the scope of analysis.
4. Increasing complexity of system design and operation.
5. Integrating different information sub-systems.
6. Increasing the effectiveness of information system.
7. Extending more comprehensive information to business managers.

1.12. LIMITATIONS OF MIS

Following are the main limitations of MIS :

1. MIS cannot replace managerial judgement in decision-making. It is merely an effective tool for the managers in decision-making and problem-solving.
2. The quality of output of MIS is directly proportional to the quality of input and processes.
3. MIS cannot provide tailor-made information packages. It is required to analyse the available information before decision-making.
4. In a fast changing and complex environment, MIS may not have enough flexibility to update itself quickly.
5. MIS takes only quantitative factors into account.
6. MIS is less useful for making non-programmed decisions.
7. MIS is less effective in organisations where information is not being shared with others.
8. MIS is less effective due to frequent changes in top management, organisational structure and operational staff.

1.13 COMPUTER-BASED INFORMATION SYSTEMS

Managers make decisions to solve problems, and information is used in making the decisions. Information is presented in both oral and written forms by an information processor. The computer portion of the information processor contains each of the computer based application areas – Accounting Information System (AIS), Management Information System (MIS), Decision Support System (DSS), Office Automation (OA) and Expert System (ES). The term computer-based information system (CBIS) is used to describe the five subsystems that utilise the computer. All of the CBIS sub-systems provide information for problem-solving. These sub-systems have been thoroughly explained in subsequent chapters. Each CBIS subsystem can support quality management.

The firm sells its products and services to its customers. These are *external customers* that exist outside the firm. Information services interface with these external customers by means of the AIS. Much of the external customer's perception of the firm is based on the capabilities of the AIS to execute orders promptly and accurately. Hence, information system (IS) has a direct influence on the firm's product and service quality. IS also provides an indirect influence by providing information to users inside the firm. These are *internal customers*, and they exist on all organisational levels and in all functional areas. The information enables these internal customers to do their jobs better, resulting in better products and services. In addition, the standard financial reports produced by AIS, such as the income statement and cost analyses, serve as a scorecard of the quality effort, reporting cost of rework, scrap, customer returns, warranty claims, and so on. Figure 1.20 shows each of these subsystems which provide information to be used in quality management.

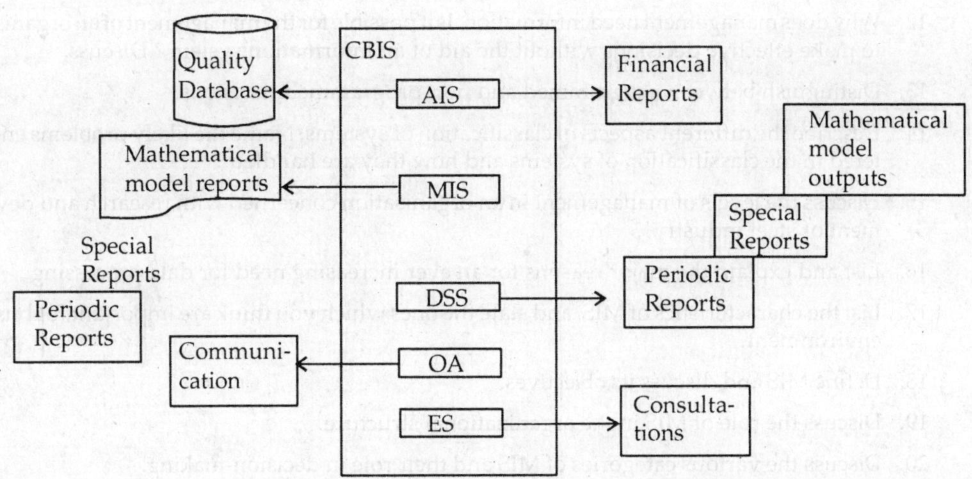

Fig. 1.20. CBIS sub-systems support - quality management

Review Questions

1. The fundamental idea behind the 'Systems Approach to Management' is the computer based information system. Comment.
2. 'Information' is an important resource. Discuss its special characteristics and show through a block diagram how information is processed.
3. What do you understand by programmed, semi-programmed and non-programmed decisions ? Illustrate with organisational examples that you have come across ?
4. How do you differentiate between planning and control activities in an organisation ?
5. Show how the systems approach would be useful in attacking the ecology problems of a large city. How can an industrial organisation cooperate with the government with regard to these problems ?
6. Show how the components of a management information system (management, information, system) are interrelated. Also, show how an MIS can facilitate the general functions of management (plan, organise, control).
7. Define the terms 'data' and 'information'. Discuss the difference between data and information. Give examples.
8. Take any situation in an organisation and illustrate how a data life cycle works in such a context.
9. List and explain the major reasons for an ever increasing need for data processing.
10. What impact would (*a*) the technological revolution, (*b*) research and development, (*c*) product changes, and (*d*) information explosion have on the need for information, by management of an engineering industry, and R&D organisation in electronics engineering ?
11. (*a*) Compare and contrast formal and informal information. Give three examples of each.

    (*b*) 'Formal information cannot do much to help top level decision-makers.' Discuss.
12. Why does management need information. Is it possible for the management of an organisation to make effective decisions without the aid of an information system ? Discuss.
13. Distinguish between programmed and non-programmed decisions.
14. Describe the different aspects of classification of systems. Name the likely problems encountered in the classification of systems and how they are handled ?
15. Discuss the levels of management in an organisation concerned with research and development of steel industry.
16. List and explain the major reasons for an ever increasing need for data processing.
17. List the characteristics of MIS, and state the ones which you think are important for business environment.
18. Define MIS and discuss its objectives.
19. Discuss the role of MIS in the organizational structure.
20. Discuss the various categories of MIS and their role in decision-making.
21. Write a short note on the importance of MIS and its different levels of management.
22. Mention the steps involved in designing an MIS for an organisation. What should be done to create 'acceptance' of the system in the organisation?
23. What are the chief factors to be considered in designing an MIS for a business organisation ? What considerations must influence the selection of a computer system for an MIS ?
24. What are the approaches for designing the strategies for implementing an MIS ?
25. List the steps for designing and implementing an MIS, and illustrate the same with a flow diagram.

26. Mention the disadvantages of information systems.
27. What are the approaches of MIS development in an organisation. Explain in detail *any two*.
28. List the constraints in developing an effective MIS.
29. Outline the limitations of MIS. Explain how these can be overcome for successful implementation.
30. What do you understand by computer-based information system? With a neat sketch, illustrate the subsystems providing information for quality management.

2

Information Systems for Decision Making

2.1. INTRODUCTION

The nature and scope of information required by managers at different levels in an organisation varies considerably. Organisations require different types of information systems to meet their needs. The field of information systems has come a long way in the last few decades. Innovative ideas from scientists, engineers and other users have contributed to the explosive growth of information systems and their applications. Information systems and computers function at the core of industries, such as automobiles, communications, education, entertainment, medicine, space and sports. Processing power of computers today can literally be held on the palm of one's hand. Data processing chips have become powerful yet inexpensive and have steadily found their way into our homes and offices. Software has become so versatile and user-friendly that even elementary school children can use it. Many organisations are in the process of tapping the versatility and power of computers by designing and developing systems tailored to meet their specific needs.

An increasing number of managerial personnel rely on computers and information systems to make decisions. As discussed in *Chapter 1*, managers at different levels in an organisation make different kinds of decisions (operational, tactical and strategic) so that the types of information necessary to support their decisions are also different. Accordingly, different types of information systems are designed to meet various information needs of managers, as shown in Fig. 2.1.

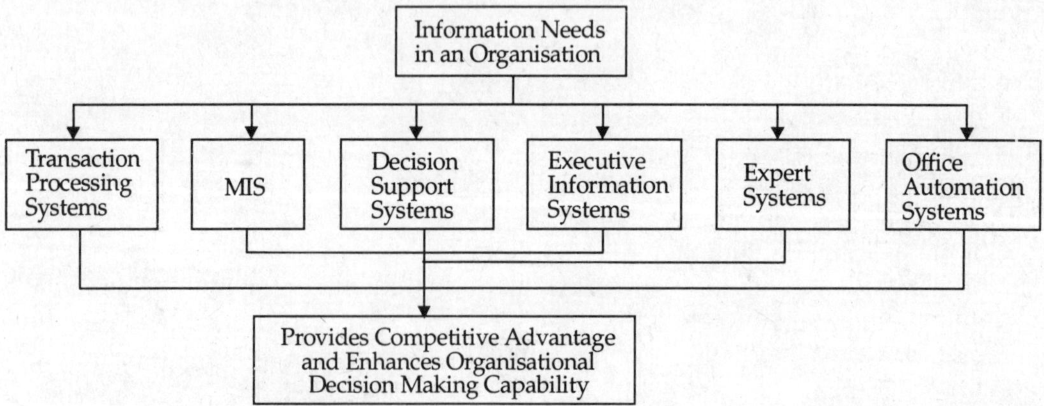

Fig. 2.1. Six Types of Information Systems for Enhancing Organizational Decision Making Capability

Four types of information systems exist :

1. Transaction processing systems (TPS).

2. Management information systems (MIS).
3. Intelligent support systems (ISS) consisting of decision support systems (DSS), executive information systems (EIS), and expert systems (ES).
4. Office automation systems (OAS).

No one system is superior to another. The types of information systems used by an organisation depend on its information needs. One organisation may rely on one system only, whereas another may use all four types of systems. However, different types of systems must be integrated to have free flow of information within and outside the organisation.

2.2. TRANSACTION PROCESSING SYSTEMS

The primary purpose of transaction processing systems is to record, process, validate, and store transactions that take place in various functional areas of a business for future retrieval and use. Transactions can be internal or external. When a department orders office supplies from the purchasing department, an internal transaction occurs; when a customer places an order for a product, an external transaction occurs. A TPS supports these tasks by imposing a set of rules and guidelines that specify how to record, process, and store a given transaction. There are many uses of TPS in our daily lives, *e.g.*, withdraw money at a bank, purchase at a stationery store, or register for courses at a university / college. Thus, almost all organisations, regardless of the industry in which they operate, have a manual or automated TPS. A TPS is the source of data for a firm to have other information systems, such as MIS and DSS. A TPS is also the main system like between the organisation and external entities, such as customers, suppliers, distributors, and others.

Transaction processing systems exist for various functional areas in an organisation, such as finance, accounting, manufacturing, production, human resources, marketing, engineering, quality control, and research and development. Many organisations so far viewed the TPS for each business function as a separate entity with little or no connection to other systems in the organisation. Today, organisations are trying to build cross-functional TPS to promote free exchange of information among different business units. This system, therefore, spans organisational boundaries and provides information to both internal and external entities.

2.2.1. Steps in Processing a Transaction

Data must be processed to become useful information. There are following six steps in processing a transaction :

1. Data entry
2. Data validation
3. Processing and revalidation
4. Storage
5. Output generation
6. Query support.

These steps are shown in Fig. 2.2 and also explained in detail.

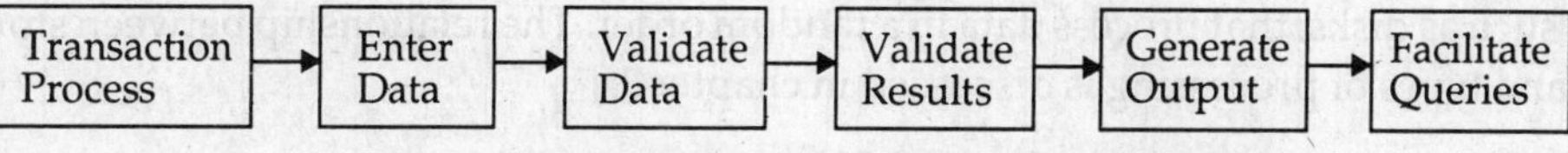

Fig. 2.2. Sequential Steps in Processing a Transaction

Data entry. Transaction data must first be entered into the system. A number of input devices exist for entering data, including the keyboard and the mouse. Other input devices are given in chapter 3. The documents generated at the source / point where the transaction occurs are called *source documents* and become input data for the system. For example, when a customer returns an item at a store, the sales receipt becomes the source document for the transaction 'return item for refund / replacement'. A cheque / cash deposit receipt for a bank transaction becomes the source document for updating a passbook.

Data validation. Data validation is essential in transaction processing. It ensures the accuracy and reliability of data by comparing actual data with predetermined standards or known results. There are *two* steps in validation : *error detection* and *error correction.* Error detection is performed by one set of control mechanisms, whereas error correction is performed by another.

Some commonly used error detection procedures are : checking the data for appropriate format, checking for aberrations, and checking for missing data, invalid data, and inconsistent data. *Missing data* refers to fields that are missing a mandated data value. For example, if the number of hours worked by a casual employee is missing on a payroll, it is called a missing error. Data, which are outside the normal range, are called the *invalid data.* For example, if the number of hours worked by a casual employee is 288 hours per month (36 days) instead of normal 30 days, then we have invalid data. The term *inconsistent data* means that the same data item assumes different values in different places without a valid reason. For example, if payroll records show that an employee worked 25 days, but the attendance register shows that the same employee worked 28 days, then we have inconsistent data. Although sophisticated validation techniques can detect many errors, some human errors are difficult to detect.

Error correction procedures are designed to ensure that all errors have been corrected and that no new errors have been introduced during the process. The technique used for correcting the error depends on the type of error and the nature of application. Some simple error correction measures include allowing only authorised people to correct errors, maintaining a log of revised data values and establishing a paper trail showing the nature and the source of each error and the techniques that were used to correct it. Sometimes a trail, showing who corrected each error and when and how each error was corrected, is called a *audit trail.*

Data processing and revalidation. After the validation of accuracy and reliability of the data, the data are processed in following two modes : Online transaction processing and batch processing.

Online transaction processing (OLTP). The term *online* means that the data input device is directly linked to the TPS and the data are processed as soon as it is entered into the system. The input device may be at a remote location and be linked to the system by networks or by telecommunication systems.

In this system, the information is always current since there is little or no time lag between data creation and data processing. Some examples of online transaction processing are ATM transactions, railway reservations and so on. Online processing is possible because of storage media, such as disks, that process data in a random order. The relationship between storage media and types of processing is discussed in chapter 3.

Batch processing. In batch processing, transactions are accumulated over time and processed periodically. Processing may be done on a daily, weekly, or monthly basis or any other time period appropriate to the given application. For example, an organisation may process its sale proceeds on daily basis at the end of each day, and its daily expenses on a monthly basis.

A *transaction file* contains information about a group of transactions that occurred in a given period of time. It is processed using techniques such as sorting, merging, and so on. After processing the transaction file, *master file* is updated. A master file is a permanent record of all transactions that have occurred in an organisation. Each time the master file is updated with information from the transaction file, an updated master file, including current transaction data, is generated.

Batch processing is still a popular method as it is often the most sensible and practical approach. Processing jobs in batches results in more efficient use of computer resources. Also, quality control is sometimes easier in batch processing, since errors detected at the end of a batch can be rectified before the next batch is processed. However, one of the disadvantages of batch processing is that there is a time lag between data creation and data processing, so that the information in the files may not be uptodate. Also, some errors in batch processing may be detected only after the batch has been processed, in which case the entire batch has to be processed again.

The use of the type of processing method depends on the user's needs. If a user needs periodic updates on system transactions, batch processing is appropriate; if a user needs up-to-the-minute information, online processing is required. Regardless of the type of processing used, once it is complete, the output should be validated for accuracy and reliability. Therefore, validation should be done both before the data is processed (to check input validity) and after the data is processed (to check output validity).

Data storage. Data storage is another important function because the value of usefulness of data diminish if data are not properly stored. For example, magnetic tape is often used to store data that is batch-processed. However, online transaction processing relies on other types of storage media, such as magnetic disks.

It is to be noted that storage and output may not always occur in the same order. One can output the results of the transaction to the decision maker and then store them, or store the result and then output them to the decision maker.

Output generation. The output can be communicated to the decision-maker, after the data are input, validated, processed, revalidated, and stored, in the following two ways :

1. Documents and reports
2. Forms — screens or panels.

Documents are a popular output method. Some examples of documents are invoices, paychecks, purchase invoices, sales receipts, and job orders.

In information system, a document is usually a record of one transaction, whereas a report is a summary of two or more transactions. Nevertheless, these terms are often used interchangeably.

Computer output can also appear on computer screens and panels. Such soft-copy presentations are known as *forms*.

Query support. Query (asking questions) facilities allow users to access data and information that may otherwise not be readily available.

The characteristics of TPS are summarised as follows :

1. A TPS records internal and external transactions for an organisation. It is a repository of data that is frequently accessed by other systems.
2. A TPS performs routine, repetitive tasks. It is mostly used by lower-level managers to make operational decisions.
3. Transactions can be recorded in batch mode or online.
4. Six steps are involved in processing a transaction. They are: data entry, data validation, data processing and revalidation, storage, output generation and query support.

2.3. MANAGEMENT INFORMATION SYSTEMS

Management information systems are designed for providing information to the key functionaries in an organisation. These systems make use of the already processed transaction data which is outputted from TPS and generate information reports after processing data. The examples of this kind of systems could be personnel information systems, marketing information systems, sales information systems, production and operations systems, etc. These systems are designed following the principles of organisational theory. The major group of users for this kind of systems are the middle level of management. The output of an MIS takes the form of *summary reports* and *exception reports.* A summary report accumulates data from several transactions and presents the results in condensed form. For example, a bank manager may get a summary report listing the total amount of deposits and withdrawals made the previous day. An exception report outlines any deviations from expected output. Its main purpose is to draw the attention of middle managers to any significant differences between *actual* performance and *expected* performance. For example, a sales manager may study an exception report that lists all sales personnel who sold less than Rs. 10,000 or more than Rs. 50,000 in the preceding month. Reports of both kinds should be succinct, accurate, timely, reliable, verifiable, and readily usable. Both types of reports are used in tactical decision making over a longer period of time, such as a year or more.

Figure 2.3 shows the relationship between TPS and MIS.

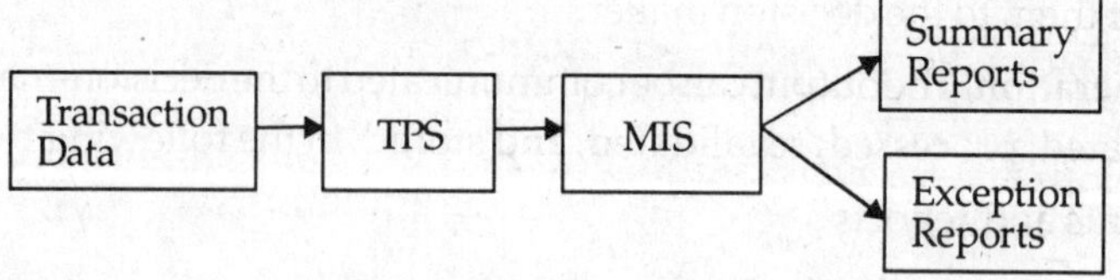

Fig. 2.3. Interaction between TPS and MIS for Information Needs of an Organisation

2.3.1. Decision Making in MIS

Decision making is an essential part of management. Some have even suggested that management is synonymous with decision making. Therefore, management and decision making are complex activities that involve many dimensions of human behaviour. Early classical models of management stressed the functions of managers, namely, planning, organising, staffing, coordinating, reporting, budgeting. Depending on the level at which managerial decision makers are, they perform a different mix of managerial functions. There are primarily three levels of management and decision making termed as strategic, technical/

tactical and operational decision making. These three levels of decision making relate to one another closely (Fig. 2.4). In essence, management decision making quality depends on the vital output of information so as to support the functions that a manager performs, the levels at which the decision maker is, and on the type of decisions.

The process of deciding is intimately related to the whole process of knowing (or 'cognition'). Knowing 'what the problem is' will assist in deciding 'what to do about it', that is finding the best solution. This is basic for each individual and also for a professional manager. However, the process by which one arrives at a decision is quite complex; in fact no one process can be applied to all decisions. Over the decades, decision making methods have evolved from primitive to supersophisticated, ranging from the instinctive/intuitive approach, to traditional precedent based approach, to the commonsense approach, to the scientific method. A decision involves many intuitive and deep-seated cognitive mechanisms that cannot be observed fully or directly influenced. What can be influenced are the behaviour patterns, the analytical procedures and the sequence of logic that are followed in making a decision . Ideals, objectives and goals form the background against which decisions are made.

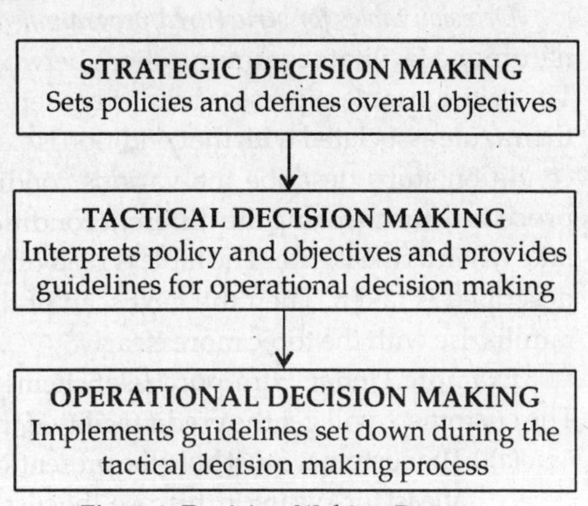

Fig. 2.4 Decision Making Process

Types of Decisions

There are many types of decisions, some that are completely specified, some partly specified and many unspecified. Primarily two types of decision making are discussed here : (*a*) Structured decisions; and (*b*) Unstructured decisions.

Structured decisions

Structured decisions are those that can be programmed. These decisions can be taken objectively. They are essentially repetitive, routine and involve a definite procedure for handling them. Herbert A. Simon termed 'structured decisions' as 'programmed decisions'. Programmed decisions are in fact those that are made in accordance with some policy, rule or procedure so that they do not have to be handled *de novo* each time they occur. It is for these reasons that such managerial problems are relegated to the supervisory level. Decisions implemented by the supervisors might feel elated, but when compared to managers at higher levels, the supervisory level decisions are straight-forward and simple because of their structured nature. These decisions are in fact routine decisions as they require little deliberation from the top man's viewpoint. Most programmed decisions are solvable by the 'force of habit', *i.e.*, by 'experience' gained in an organisation. It usually takes time and money for newer recruits to acquire this experience.

The 'force of habit' in fact leads to certain traditions, conventions and practices which might become a platform towards formal statement of rules, procedures, policies, etc. A *rule* is a specific policy statement about the conduct of certain affairs. It is frequently used when confronting a well structured problem. Rules are usually rigid which might specifically tell about 'dos and donts'. They are generally framed in a manner to take care of almost all situations. A *procedure* is a series of steps, sequencing in nature, and interrelated to address a well structured problem. It is a kind of direction in using a series of steps in either diagnosing a problem or solving it. The procedure has the additional advantage of forcing a certain amount of detailed planning, because it cannot be adequately designed, reviewed, or implemented without careful thought. *Policy* is a general guideline which sets up parameters for the judgement within which to operate and is general and judgemental in nature.

Decision tables for structured/programmed decisions. Decision tables are quite graphical in nature and facilitate communications between user, analyst, supervisors and affected parties. The decision table expresses primarily a series of conditions; when the conditions are fulfilled, then a rule associated with the condition is executed. A 'header' is used to identify the table and condition stubs describe the various conditions. As already explained earlier, a rule is a procedure for checking the different conditions, and the action statement tells what action to take when a rule is true. The table is read until the conditions for a rule are met and the action described is taken. Then the next scan of the table begins. A live example is illustrated to familiarise with the topic more clearly.

Example. Under 'Hire-purchase Scheme' there is a credit facility scheme for the customers. The customers will get the credit facility if they satisfy any of the following conditions :

(*a*) The customer must hold the present job for more than 6 years and reside in the same area atleast for 4 years. In this case, the customer will be entitled to get the credit up to Rs. 5000.

(*b*) The customer's monthly pay must be more than Rs. 3000 and hold the present job for more than 6 years. In this case, the credit will be given up to Rs. 6000.

(*c*) The monthly pay must be more than Rs. 3000 and reside in the same area at least for 4 years. In this case, credit will be given up to Rs. 6000.

(*d*) The customer's monthly pay exceeds Rs. 3000, holds the present job for more than 6 years and also resides in the same area at least for 4 years. In this case, credit will be given up to Rs. 8000.

(*e*) The credit facility is rejected for all other customers.

Prepare a decision table for this hire-purchase scheme.

Solution. The decision table for the programmed decision situation of hire-purchase is given as follows :

Condition Stub/	**Decision Rules**						
Allowing Credit Facility	**R1**	**R2**	**R3**	**R4**	**R5**	**R6**	**R7**
C1. Customers hold the present job for more than 6 years	Y	Y	Y	Y	N	N	N
C2. Resides in the same area at least for 4 years	Y	Y	N	N	Y	Y	N
C3. Monthly pay of the customer exceeds Rs. 3000	Y	N	Y	N	Y	N	—
Action Stub							
A1. Give credit up to Rs. 5000		X					
A2. Give credit up to Rs. 6000			X		X		
A3. Give credit up to Rs. 8000	X						
A4. Reject credit				X		X	X

Key : Y — Yes; N — No; X — Action to be taken.

Unstructured decisions

Unstructured decisions are those in which the decision maker must provide judgement, evaluation and insights into the problem definition. These decisions must be taken subjectively. There is no defined method of solving the problem. Unstructured decisions are more repetitive in nature, usually 'one-shot' occurrences for which standard responses are usually not available. Hence, they require a creative process of problem-solving which is specially tailored to meet the requirement of the situation on hand. In fact managers at higher levels in an organisation are usually faced with more such unstructured decision making situations. Some have aptly described the situations as somewhat 'strategic' in nature as compared to the 'tactical' orientation of the structured decisions at the lower levels of management. Strategic decisions are non-repetitive, vital and important and aim at determining or changing the ends or means of the enterprise.

Since each manager, in the case of such unstructured, non-programmed decisions, may bring his own personal beliefs, attitudes and value judgements to bear on the decision process, it is possible for two managers to reach distinctly different solutions to the same problem, each claiming that he is acting rationally. In fact the ability to make good non-programmed decisions helps to distinguish effective managers from ineffective managers. Unstructured decisions are not simple. They are usually quite complex in nature. One can't shy away from them for someone has to ultimately make these decisions even though there are inherent dangers when confronting ill-structured problems. Non-programmed decisions are essentially new and unique. They have to be often solved *de novo*. There is no tried and true method of handling them.

Hence, decisions can be classified in the following two classes :

Class I : Unstructured, Non-programmable, Strategic, Major, Routine, Repetitive, Complex, Long-run.

Class II : Structured, Programmed, Tactical, Minor, Non-routine, Non-repetitive, Simple, Short-run.

Departmental, inter-departmental and enterprise decisions

The department level decision is strategic in nature whereas inter-departmental level is tactical in nature. For example, sanctioning leave to an employee is a departmental decision; minor changes in the design of the product is an inter-departmental decision; and entering a new line of business is an enterprise decision.

Organisational and personal decisions

The transfer of an executive is an organisational decision whereas the decision of an executive to leave the organisation is a personal decision.

Individual and group decisions

Decisions may be taken by an individual or by a group. It is difficult to say which is a better method of taking decisions. Each method has its strength and weaknesses.

Individual decisions. According to Simon, 'It is impossible for the behaviour of a single isolated individual to reach any high degree of rationality. The number of alternatives he must explore is so great, the information he would need to evaluate them is so vast, that even an approximation to objective rationality is hard to conceive. The individual decision maker is an individual human being — the one factor most vital and most difficult to understand because of various factors such as age, perception, intelligence, experience in a given area, confidence in decision-making, time available, resource position, upbringing, family background, and so on that could come into play. The most mysterious factor is still the decision making by an individual human being. How and why an individual acts in a certain way at a certain time is still quite a mystery. The individual decision maker could have quite an amount of prejudice and bias that is inherent on account of perceptual processes which act as great filters. One only accepts what one wants to accept and hence only such information filters down to his senses, and second, the perception is highly subjective. The information gets distorted to coincide with pre-established beliefs, attitudes and values.

These are additionally 'cognitive' constraints. Psychologically one is always uncomfortable with decision making. One is never sure if his choice of the alternative was correct and optimum, until the impact of implication of the decision has been felt. This makes him feel very insecure and could be one of the many causes of 'stress' in individuals leading to hypertension and other health complications.

No doubt it is important to have adequate and accurate information about the situation for good quality decision making. However, it must be recognised that "an individual has constraints of nature such as physical, psychological, sociological, etc. These limit the amount of information the individual can handle".

Group decisions. These are usually taken for major issues in order to secure wider cooperation, acceptability and coordination. Usually in a group like situation, the chances of subjective errors are reduced and more options are thrown open. If the group is larger, such decisions suffer from unnecessary delays, deadlocks and petty party politics.

Some *advantages* of group decisions are :

1. Increased acceptance by those affected and hence implementation is easier.
2. Easier coordination.
3. Easier communication.
4. More information processed on account of availability of a larger number of specialists in the group.
5. Participative group process builds up a training ground for subordinates and others which allows for smooth handover when individuals leave the scene (no vacuum is created).

Some *disadvantages* of group decisions are :

1. Group decisions take longer time.
2. Groups can be indecisive.
3. Groups can compromise.
4. Groups can be dominated.
5. Group members may exhibit "focus effect", *viz.*, the group may just focus on one or a few suggested alternatives and spend all the time in evaluating these and may never come up with other ideas, thus limiting the choices.

2.4. INTELLIGENT SUPPORT SYSTEMS

Systems which facilitate decisions requiring the use of knowledge, intuition, experience and expertise, are called intelligent support systems (ISS). Decision support systems (DSS), executive information systems (EIS) and artificial intelligence (AI) and expert systems (ES) fall into this category. These systems are explained in brief and their role in organisational decision making.

2.4.1. Decision Support Systems

Decision support systems are interactive, well-integrated systems that provide managers with data, tools and models to facilitate semi-structured decisions or tactical decisions. It automates the routine and repetitive elements in a problem while simultaneously supporting the use of intuition and judgement. DSS are ideally suited for problems like location selection, identifying new products to be marketed, scheduling personnel, and analysing the effect that price increases for resources have on profits.

Where to apply DSS: DSS are man/machine systems and are suitable for semi-structured problems. The problem must be important to the manager and the decision required must be an important one. In addition, if an interactive computer-based system is to be used, then some of the following criteria must be met :

(*a*) There should be a large data base;

(*b*) Large amount of computation or data manipulation;

(*c*) Complex interrelationships;

(*d*) Analysis by stages;

(*e*) Judgement required; and

(*f*) Communication.

It follows from the above criteria that DSS are inappropriate for unstructured problems and unnecessary for completely structured problems because they can be dealt with wholly by the computer. In outline, DSS require a database, the software to handle the database and decision support programs including, *e.g.*, modelling, spread sheet and analysis packages, expert systems, etc.

A DSS also allows managers to perform *goal-seeking*, which specifies the action a manager should take in order to accomplish a certain goal. Another important feature of DSS is that an individual or a goup of individuals can use them. DSS that support group decision making are called **Group Decision Support Systems (GDSS).** In most organisations, decisions of any significance are made collectively by a group, not by a single person. GDSS are a set of interactive, well integrated systems that facilitate and support group decision making.

2.4.2. Executive Information Systems

Executive information systems (EIS) are forms of data retrieval systems that provide selected and summarised information for senior executives, engaged in long-range planning, crisis management, and other strategic decisions. It is a user-friendly interactive system. It has excellent menus and graphic capabilities. A typical way that an EIS works is by exception reporting and *drilling down* to investigate the causes. For example, a director of an organisation may be alerted that a particular department is well over budget. (An exception to budget or target is known as a *'hot-spot'* and would be highlighted by the EIS.) The manager would then drill down the data by pursuing lower and lower levels of detail.

The main difference between a DSS and an EIS is that the goal of an EIS is not so much to generate alternatives for a given problem as it is to integrate data from different sources and present it in a useful format to the decision maker.

The characteristics of DSS and EIS are :

1. DSS and EIS are intelligent support systems designed to provide middle and top managers with information necessary to make decisions that require intuition and judgement.

2. Both the systems are intuitive, interactive, user-friendly systems that augment the decision making capabilities of a manager. They are menu-driven and often have excellent colour and graphic capabilities.
3. DSS and EIS use internal and external data to solve problems. Managers at this level tend to rely more on external data than on internal data.
4. An EIS provides managers with information integrated from a variety of sources. A DSS uses various decision making models to provide managers with alternative solutions to a given problem.
5. Both systems are equipped with decision making tools such as 'what if' analysis and goal seeking. In addition to these tools, an EIS is equipped with drill-down capabilities.
6. A DSS can support both individual decision making and group decision making. DSS that support group decision making are referred to as group decision support systems.

A detailed discussion of EIS is given in chapter 8.

2.4.3. Artificial Intelligence and Expert Systems

Artificial intelligence (AI) is a branch of computer science whose goal is to design and develop machines that emulate human intelligence. It attempts to endow machines with capabilities and characteristics that would indicate intelligence in a human being.

Expert systems (ES), also known as knowledge-based systems, is a software designed to capture the knowledge and problem-solving skills of a human expert. It has three main components : a knowledge base, an inference engine, and a user interface.

Expert systems are good at solving semi-structured and unstructured problems and can solve problems that require theoretical knowledge and practical experience. They help organisations acquire and retain knowledge that is of significance to the competitiveness and the success of an organisation.

The first component of the expert systems, the knowledge base, serves as a storehouse of knowledge and experience gained from experts in a given field, including facts and principles to a field of study. Once the expert's knowledge is acquired, it is translated into a language that the computer can use. This process is called *knowledge-representation.* For example, a car mechanic may be the source of knowledge for an expert system designed to solve car problems.

The inference engine, second component of an expert system, uses rules of behaviour and interrelationships between different pieces of knowledge to solve the given problem. It selects the appropriate knowledge, applies it to the problem, and resolves any conflicts that may arise in the process.

The user interface consists of tools like menus, graphics and explanation facilities that help users to interact with the system. In particular, explanation module provides explanations as to how a problem was solved and how the knowledge was used to solve the problem.

Main characteristics of expert systems are :

1. An expert system is a program designed to capture the knowledge and problem-solving skills of a human expert. Expert systems is a branch of artificial intelligence.
2. Expert systems handle problems that require knowledge, intuition, and judgement.
3. Expert systems, unlike DSS and EIS, can replace decision makers.

4. It has three main components : the knowledge-base, which stores the knowledge, the inference engine, which stores the reasoning principles used by the expert, and the user interface, which allows the user to interact with the system.
5. Expert systems are not designed for any one level of management, their primary function is to disseminate expertise throughout the organisation.

Three types of information support systems discussed above have several differences. For example, a DSS is intended for middle managers who solve semi-structured problems. EIS is intended for top managers who solve unstructured problems. Expert systems are not for managers at any specific level; they are simply designed to assist in the solution of complex semistructured and unstructured problems.

The primary aim of both DSS and EIS is to facilitate and enhance the quality of decision making. The expert systems aim to gather and apply organisational knowledge for problem solving. A DSS uses both data and models to solve problems and present alternatives, while an EIS integrates data and present it in a useful format to decision makers. While DSS and EIS do not replace managers, expert systems have, in some cases, displaced knowledge workers.

2.5. OFFICE AUTOMATION SYSTEMS

Office automation systems (OAS) refers to the use of mechanical, electrical, and electronic devices to enhance communication in the workplace and increase the efficiency and productivity of knowledge workers and clerical workers. Office automation systems include :

1. **Word processing.** It is the use of an electronic device that automatically performs many of the tasks necessary to create written documents such as letters, memos, and reports that are directed to the manager.
2. **Electronic mail.** Electronic mail, popularly known as **E-mail,** is the use of a networked computer that allows users to send, store, and receive messages using the computer's terminals and storage devices. It sends mail electronically from one computer to others.
3. **Voice mail.** Voice mail is just like electronic mail and performs storing, accessing, retrieving, and distributing messages using the telephone.
4. **Electronic calendaring.** It is the use of a networked computer to store and retrieve a manager's appointment calendar.
5. **Audio conferencing.** Audio conferencing is the use of voice communications equipment to establish an audio link between geographically dispersed persons for conducting a conference. The *conference call*, which allows more than two people to participate in a telephone conversation, was the first form of audio conferencing and is still in use.
6. **Video conferencing.** Video conferencing is the use of television equipment to link geographically dispersed conference participants to engage in face-to-face communication. The equipment provides for audio as well as video linkage. Like audio conferencing, video conferencing does not require a computer.
7. **Computer conferencing.** Computer conferencing is the use of a networked computer to all members of a *problem-solving team* to exchange information concerning the *problem* that is being solved.
8. **Teleconferencing.** Teleconferencing includes all three forms of electronically-aided conferencing — audio, video and computer.
9. **Facsimile transmission.** Facsimile transmission, popularly known as fax, is the transfer of written or pictorial information by the use of special equipment that can read a document image at one end of a communication channel and make a copy at the other end.

10. **Desktop publishing.** Desktop publishing is the use of a computer to prepare printed output, using software with sophisticated publishing capabilities.
11. **Videotex.** Videotex is the use of a computer for displaying a stored narrative and graphic material on a CRT screen.
12. **Imaging.** Imaging is the use of optical character recognition to convert paper or microfilm records to a digital format for storage in a secondary storage device for easy retrieval and processing.
13. **Multimedia systems.** Multimedia systems are well integrated systems that store, retrieve, and process different types of data such as text, graphics, images, full motion video, audio, and animation. It helps users to create, process, share, and display information in a broad variety of formats.

Characteristics of four broad categories of information systems, *viz.*, TPS, MIS, ISS (DSS, EIS, ES) and OAS are summarized in Table 2.1.

Table 2.1. Characteristics of Information Systems

Types of System	*Input*	*Processing*	*Output*	*Users*	*Applications*
TPS	• Transaction-related data	• Uses procedures and rules • Repetitive tasks • Control-oriented	• Summaries of transactions	• Lower-level managers	• Sales transactions • Credit and payments • Insurance claims
MIS	• Output from TPS • Other internal data	• Measures and monitors operational performance	• Summary and exception reports	• Middle level managers	• Monthly production reports • Safety violation reports
ISS(DSS, EIS, ES)	• Internal and external data and models • Knowledge and experience	• Interactive, ad-hoc reporting • Generates alternatives	• Alternatives • Analysis reports	• Top managers • ES: knowledge workers	• Investment portfolios • Enterprise: wide performance • Plant expansion
OAS	• Data and information	• Formatting • Summarizing • Displaying	• Documents • Graphics • Multimedia	• Knowledge and clerical workers	• Fax • Multimedia • Video conferencing

Although many organisations have information systems, only a few seem to be able to make full use of these systems. Two factors are critical to the success of information systems. First, it is important to plan and develop integrated systems so that all employees in the organisation get a consistent view of information. Second, organisations should promote the idea of information stewardship rather than information ownership. This will improve the flow of information while ensuring that each individual is responsible for the quality and timeliness of the information.

Review Questions

1. Why does an organisation need different types of information systems to meet its information needs ? Does an organisation need *all* types of systems discussed or does it depend on the information needs of the organisation ? Discuss.

2. List *four* types of information systems and explain each one of them in brief.
3. What is a transaction processing system and how does it support operational decision making ? Why is a TPS often considered the data lifeline of an organisation ?
4. When you deposit your salary-cheque in a bank, a transaction takes place. Describe the *six steps* in processing a transaction and show how they apply to your bank deposit.
5. Outline the characteristics of TPS.
6. Why are management information systems designed ? Show the relationship between TPS and MIS by a neat diagram.
7. A middle manager receives a monthly report on the number of hours worked by the employees in his department/unit. A top manager receives a report on accidents that occurred on the factory floor because of safety violations. Which of these two is a summary report and which is an exception report ? Discuss.
8. Explain decision making in MIS. What are *two* types of decisions ? Explain each one of them with suitable examples.
9. What are individual and group decisions ? Enumerate their advantages and disadvantages.
10. It is said that *information system* will avail you nothing unless it is supported by a *management system.* Explain.
11. Identify *three* reasons why an organisation may need ISS. Explain *any two* differences among TPS, MIS and ISS.
12. Describe DSS. What are their major *three* components. How are they used ? How are they similar to MIS ? How are they different ?
13. Suppose a company uses a DSS to decide where it should build a new plant. What kind of internal and external information would be necessary to make this decision ?
14. How a DSS allow managers to perform goal-seeking ?
15. Which concept is older, artificial intelligence or DSS ? Discuss.
16. What is an ES and what are its three main components ? Who are some of the primary users of an ES ?
17. How is EIS used ? Outline the characteristics of DSS and EIS.
18. Identify *any two* types of problems that can be solved using a DSS, an EIS and an ES.
19. What is an expert system ? Mentioning the main components of expert systems, outline its main characteristics.
20. Is it necessary for the EIS to include computer-produced information ? Discuss.
21. Identify *at least six* office automation systems and explain each of them in brief. Identify *any two* goals of OAS.
22. What is a multimedia system ? How can a multimedia system enhance communication in the workplace ? Give an example of a business presentation in which multimedia can be used.
23. Explain characteristics of TPS, MIS, ISS and OAS in terms of input, processing, output, users, and applications.
24. What are *two* steps that an organisation can take to realise the full potential of its information systems.
25. Identify any organisation in your knowledge that has laid off employees and downsized its managerial staff. Find out if information systems and technologies are among the causes of the layoff.

- Controls in Information Systems/Organisations (Appended at C)
- Data Warehousing and Data Mining (Appended at D)

3

Computer Hardware for Information Systems

3.1. INTRODUCTION

Every organisation, regardless of its size or purpose, is concerned with processing of facts or data for its smooth and efficient functioning. With the ever-increasing amount of data to be processed in shortest possible time, organisations felt the need for faster, cheaper and more efficient methods of processing data. To fill this gap, various types of automated devices were developed and foremost among them was the introduction of the electronic computer in the later half of the twentieth century. Nowadays, the computers have come up in such a big way that their presence is felt in our personal and professional lives in one form or another.

A computer is an automatic machine made up of electronic and electro-mechanical devices that processes data under program control to generate meaningful information with speed and accuracy. It can perform long and complex calculations, and analyse complex scientific or mathematical data. On the other hand, even the most sophisticated computers cannot have power to *think.* Intelligence and creativity are still exclusive and endearing qualities of the human mind. Thus, memory, search and processing are difficult tasks for the human mind, but simple tasks for the computer.

In this chapter, a broad overview of computer hardware, which includes the physical computer and its peripheral components, is given. Input, output and storage devices, along with other types of computers, are identified and explained.

3.2. BASICS OF DATA REPRESENTATION

Data are usually represented in a computer by using the numbers, alphabets — A to Z, symbols, graphs and images. This form of representation is used to formulate problem and fed to the computer. The processed output is required in the same form. This form of representation is called *external data representation.* However, the computer can understand data by strings of binary digits, or *bits.* A bit is the smallest unit of data in a computer. It is represented by a 1 (to indicate the presence of an electronic signal) or a 0 (to indicate the absence of an electronic signal). A unique combination of eight bits, referred to as a *byte,* represents each character in a computer. The letter R, the number 5, and the symbol ? are each represented in a computer by eight bits.

Two most important characteristics of hardware in a computer are *speed* (the rate at which the computer can process data and instructions) and *size* (the amount of memory required to store the data and instructions). Computer processing time is measured in millionths of a second; the number of instructions processed per second is expressed in MIPS (millions of instructions per second). The units of time and size used to describe a computer are as follows :

Unit	Size of Memory
Byte	8 bits
Kilobyte (KB)	1,000 (10^3) bytes*
Megabyte (MB)	1,000,000 (10^6) bytes
Gigabyte (GB)	1,000,000,000 (10^9) bytes
Terrabyte	1,000,000,000,000 (10^{12}) bytes

*Actual value is 1024 bytes.

3.3. TYPES OF COMPUTERS

Computers are of three main types — Analog, Digital and Hybrid. The analog computers work on the principle of measurement, whereas digital computers work on the principle of counting. Hybrid computer combines the features of both analog and digital computers. Normally, when we speak of a computer, it is understood as a digital computer. Nowadays, these are the most widely used machines. Digital computers can further be classified into different types based on memory size and processing speed. Following types of computers are discussed here : supercomputers, mainframes, midrange machines, workstations, microcomputers, laptops, hand-held computers, and pen-based computers. Fig. 3.1 illustrates different types of computers — organisation-wide, work-group, and personal information systems. Supercomputers and mainframe are organisation-wide systems; midrange computers and workstations are work-group systems; and remaining types of computers are personal information system. Organisation-wide systems provide an overall view of an organisation; work-group systems allow groups of decision makers to process and exchange information; and personal information systems are designed to meet the individual needs. Essentially, a computer performs three functions : (*a*) It accepts data (input); (*b*) It processes data by performing desired arithmetic and logical operations (processing); and (*c*) It generates data in the desired form (output).

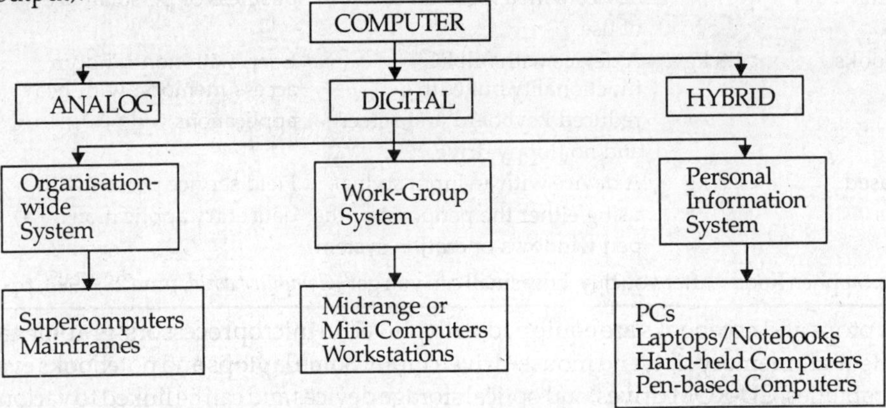

Fig. 3.1. Types of Computers

3.3.1. Personal Computers/Microcomputers

Microcomputers, also generally known as personal computers (PCs), are regarded as one of the greatest inventions in history. The memory size and processing capabilities of PCs are smaller than those of mainframes and minicomputers, but in many cases outperformed the larger units because of advances in hardware technology. Many organisations in India are replacing their mainframes, installed a few years ago, with PCs for sophisticated applications.

There are *four* basic units of a PC : System unit; the video display unit (VDU); a keyboard; and a mouse. The system unit is the rectangular metal box that houses the processor, where data are input, processed, stored and retrieved. This unit also contains primary memory, disk drives, a power supply, and outlets for connecting input and output devices. The VDU provides users with images of data, instructions, and output. The keyboard and the mouse are the most popular input devices for PCs.

When the components of a PC are customised to meet the particular information needs of the user, the process is called *configuration.* A system having built-in fax capability or a system having a communication device, *e.g.*, a modem, is the example of configuration.

Today, *plug-and-play* is emerging as the central theme in computing. It is a standard that allows different brands of hardware and software components to be 'plugged-in' and 'play' on the same computer system. It allows users to run different kinds of software on different types of desktop machines manufactured by different vendors.

Laptops and notebooks provide mobile computing technology. These are battery-operated portables and can be used any time and anywhere. Laptop computers are small enough to fit on the lap of a user; notebook computers are even smaller. Some popular portable computing devices and applications are shown in Table 3.1.

Table 3.1. Portable Computing Devices and their Applications

	Weight	*Description*	*User*
Pocket devices	< 454 g	Pocket-size machine for organisational applications	A mobile user who does not need communication capabilities
Hand-held computers	< 454 g	8086-based machines that contain an inexpensive docking station	Field service person with data entry applications
Personal digital assistants	< 1.4 kg	A powerful hand-held communication-intensive device with a focus on ease of use	Mobile users who desire two-way communications for business or personal use
Notebooks	< 1.8 kg	A device with full PC functionality but with a reduced keyboard and screen and no floppy drive.	User, with non-random access memory, with heavy applications
Pen-based devices	< 2.5 kg	A device with an input stylus, using either the penpoint or the pen windows operation system.	Field service person with data entry applications.

Source. Stephen Rood. 'After you buy, how small can you get', *Computerworld*, June 28, 1993, pp. 112-13.

Laptops and notebooks are equipped with powerful microprocessors, graphic capabilities, adequate memory size, and mouse-driven input. Some laptops and notebooks even have fax capabilities, CD-ROM drives, and optical storage devices and can be linked to various input and output devices.

The portability of laptops and notebooks has increased the productivity of marketing personnel. Today, marketing executive has a notebook computer that is linked to the corporate database, thereby information can be retrieved almost readily. This enhances the quality of decisions.

Hand-held computers are smaller than notebooks. They are primarily used to collect field data. A hand-held computer holds more than 1200 records. It is mainly useful for police officers, archaeologists, and other field personnel.

Pen-based computers are portable computers consisting an electronic writing pad and a light-sensitive electronic pen, thus free from the constraints of a keyboard. When the user writes on the pad, the writing is converted into digital input and stored in a file in the computer. Since most people are comfortable using a pen, pen-based computing is becoming increasingly popular. Although the first pen computers were promoted as being able to interpret the handwritten data, that capability has thus far been very limited. Some users attach keyboards and screens to their pen computers, thereby providing them with conventional input and output capabilities.

3.3.2. Minicomputers and Workstations

The recent trend has been not to use larger computers but to smaller ones. In the 1970s, this trend got its start with *minicomputers* or *minis*. This is a small, powerful multiuser system with excellent memory capabilities and processing speed. It is more powerful than a PC. A good example of a minicomputer is the IBM AS/400.

Workstations are faster and more sophisticated than PCs and are equipped with a number of productivity tools that increase their efficiency. Advances in microprocessors and sophisticated software have significantly increased the capabilities of these machines. Some popular workstations are : IBM RS/6000s, Hewlett-Packard's Series 700, and SPARC stations from Sun Microsystems. These workstations are being used by engineers, designers, architects.

3.3.3. Supercomputers/Mainframes

Supercomputers are the fastest, more powerful and largest computers available. They are used in a wide variety of applications. Supercomputers have large memories and high processing speeds; they can process up to a billion instructions per second. They are used mainly for large-scale scientific calculations. There are two common characteristics in supercomputers : (*a*) ability to recover automatically from failures (fault-tolerance); and (*b*) having multiple processors (or CPUs) that process multiple instructions at a time, also known as **parallel processing.** Parallel processing is ideally suitable for some business applications like resource optimization, image processing, graphics, and financial portfolio analysis. The popular brand is the Cray supercomputer. In India, Centre for Development of Advanced Computing (C-DAC), Pune had undertaken to develop a massively parallel processing high performance state-of-the art computing system (PARAM) for applications in defence, space, meteorology, science and engineering. It will have a peak power of 100 GFLOP scalable to 1 TETRAFLOP.

The main disadvantage of supercomputers is their high cost; the software that runs on them is also very expensive.

Mainframe. A mainframe is a large, general purpose computer with extensive memory and high processing speed. Mainframes are organisation-wide systems and ideally suited for transaction processing, payroll, airline reservations, railway reservations, weather forecasting, and other applications that require large computations and massive processing. Unlike PCs, mainframes serve many users at the same time. The main disadvantage of the mainframe computer is that it is expensive to purchase, operate and maintain. It requires customised software and highly trained computer personnel to run and operate them. Nonetheless, mainframe computers have been in use since the late 1950s and continue to be used for a wide variety of applications.

3.4. BASIC COMPONENTS OF COMPUTER SYSTEMS

The computer system consists of *five* basic units :

1. Input unit
2. Central processing unit (CPU) consisting of arithmetic logic unit (ALU), control unit and memory unit.
3. Secondary storage
4. Output unit
5. Communication devices

Figures. 3.2 and 3.3 illustrate first four necessary components and their interrelationship. Last component, communication devices, is optional.

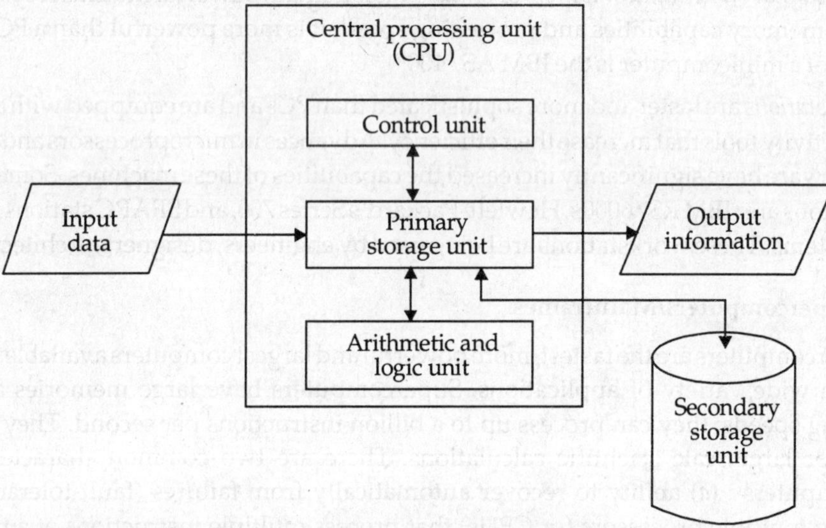

Fig. 3.2. Ways of Entering Input Data into the Computers

3.4.1. Input Unit

There are four basic ways of entering data into a computer. One can operate a keyboard device, a pointing device, the data can be read optically or magnetically, and one can speak to the computer. Fig. 3.4 illustrates these devices.

Keyboard device. The most popular unit is the keyboard of a terminal or microcomputer. It allows the user to input data by pressing the appropriate keys. Most computer keyboards are equipped with a number of extra keys, *e.g.*, *numeric keyboard* to facilitate entry of numeric data, *cursor control keys* to move the cursor, *function keys* to accomplish particular tasks for the user, depending on the software. The *cursor* is a small symbol that the keyboard operator uses to point to areas on the screen where operations are to be performed. The keyboard is linked to the CPU, which is also linked to video display terminal (VDT), or computer screen, for displaying the input given to the keyboard.

Pointing devices. (*a*) *Mouse* is a hand-held 'point-and-click' device, approximately the size of a deck of cards, that fits into the palm of the hand. Attached to the computer by a thin cable, it has a small ball on its underside, and the user can press the left and / or the right button on the mouse to execute various commands. Moving it around on a flat surface causes the ball to rotate. The rotation is interpreted by the computer, and the cursor is moved on the screen

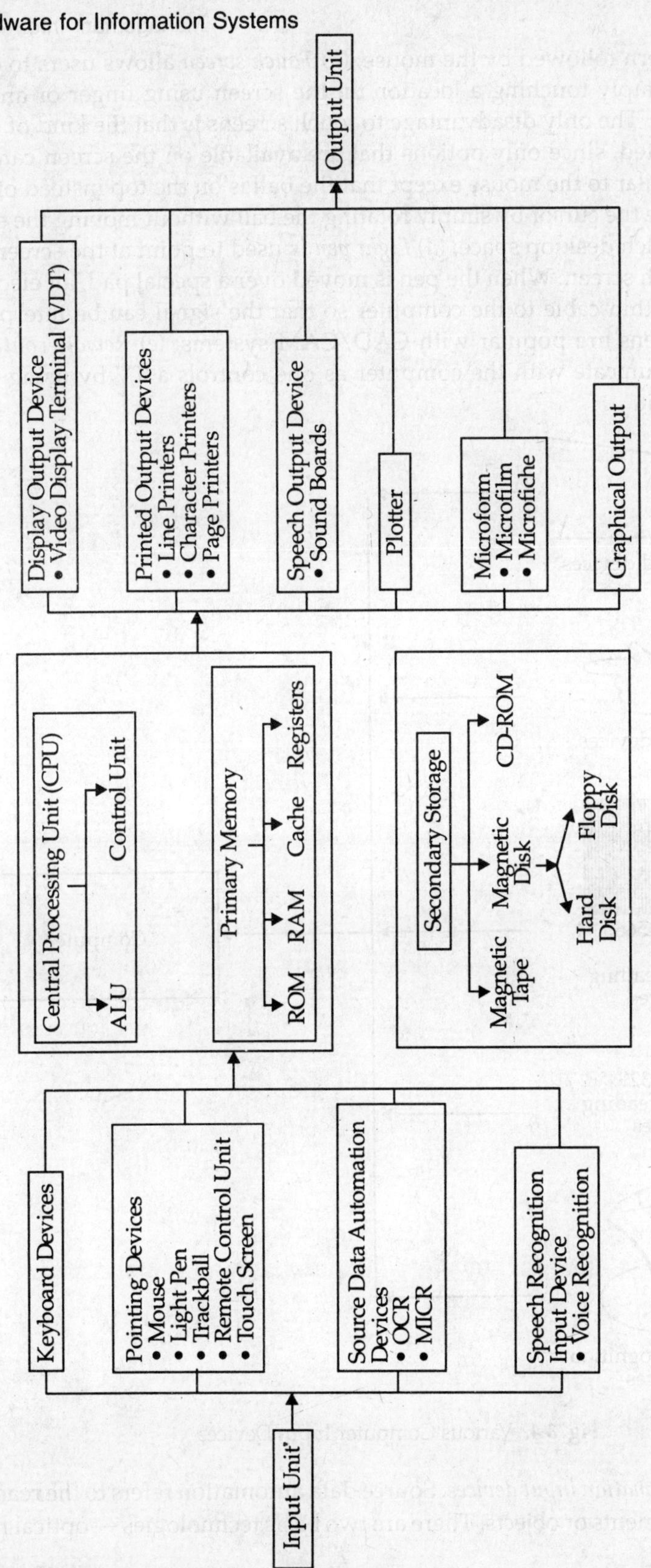

Fig. 3.3. Basic Components of a Computer System

to match the pattern followed by the mouse; (*b*) *Touch screen* allows users to enter data or instructions by simply touching a location on the screen using finger or any other non-transparent object. The only disadvantage to touch screens is that the kind of data that can be entered is limited, since only options that are available on the screen can be selected; (*c*) *Trackball* is similar to the mouse except that the ball is on the top instead of the buttom. The user can move the cursor by simply rotating the ball without moving the entire device. It does require much desktop space; (*d*) *Light pen* is used to point at the screen in a similar manner as in touch screen. When the pen is moved over a special pad, an electronic signal is sent through a thin cable to the computer so that the signal can be interpreted by the program. Light pens are popular with CAD/CAM systems; (*e*) *Remote control unit.* It is possible to communicate with the computer as one controls a TV by using a hand-held remote control unit.

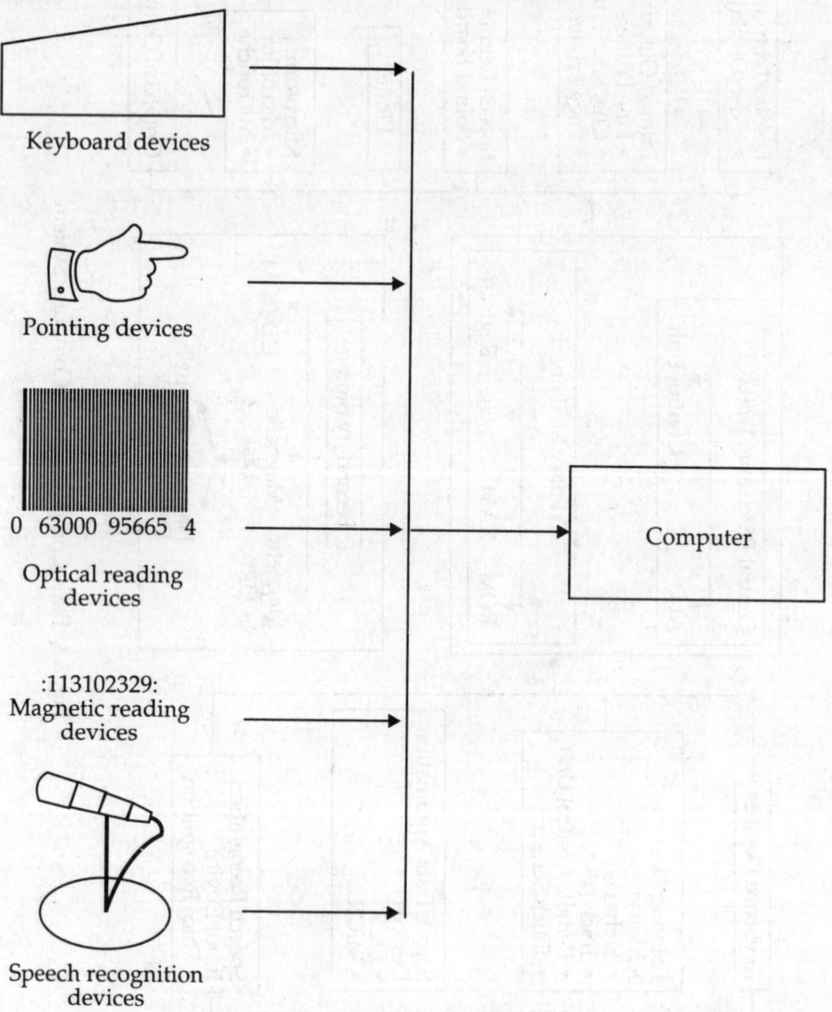

Fig. 3.4. Various Computer Input Devices

Source data automation input devices. Source data automation refers to the reading of data directly from documents or objects. There are two basic technologies — optical reading and magnetic reading.

Optical character recognition (OCR) device reads data by shining a bright light on it and then capturing the reflected image on a matrix of photoelectric cells. There are several classes of optical reading units. These are : (*a*) *Optical mark readers* detect only the presence or absence of marks on paper. The examples are test scoring machines that grade true-false and multiple-choice exams; (*b*) *Bar code readers* are capable of deciphering the meaning of data that is recorded in the form of bar codes. The pattern of the bars represents information about the product that can be used for managing inventory and sales. Bar code scanners are nowadays extensively used in libraries, publishing houses, departmental stores, etc.; (*c*) *Optical character readers* are capable of reading numeric, alphabetic, and special character data from paper; (*d*) *Handprint readers* are capable of reading characters that are written on documents by hand.

Magnetic ink character recognition (MICR) was introduced in late 1950s primarily for the bank industry to increase the speed, efficiency, and accuracy of cheque processing. MICR input devices automatically read characters printed along the lower edge of cheques.

Speech/voice recognition input devices. In a voice recognition device, it recognises and executes a set of instructions based on voice commands. In this system, the human speech is first converted into a digital pattern and is then compared to a set of pre-recorded patterns. If a match is found, the command is executed.

3.4.2. Central Processing Unit

The central processing unit consists of the arithmetic logic unit (ALU), control unit, and the primary storage.

The arithmetic logic unit performs actual processing of data including addition, subtraction, and logical operations. The CPU directs all mathematical and logical calculations to the ALU.

The *control unit* accesses the data and instructions stored in the computer and transfer them to the ALU. (An instruction tells the computer how to perform a given task.)

Primary storage is made up of memory cells, which are used temporarily to store data and instructions. It consists of several electronic components called *semiconductors*, or chips; each chip holds several thousand transistors / circuits; each transistor represents the binary state of a bit (on / off, zero / one). A chip with a small number of circuits is called an integrated circuit (IC). As the number of circuits on the chip increases, it is referred to as a large-scale integration (LSI), very large-scale integration (VLSI), or ultra large-scale integration (ULSI).

There are four types of primary memory :

1. **Random access memory (RAM)** (*Volatile memory*). Memory in which data and instructions are stored temporarily. RAM loses its contents when the power is turned off or fails.

2. **Read only memory (ROM)** (*Non-volatile memory*). Memory in which some basic instructions are permanently stored. Programs and instructions that are frequently used, but not frequently changed, are 'burned in', meaning etched into ROM, by the hardware vendor.

There are two variations of ROM — **PROM** and **EPROM.** In programmable read only memory (PROM), there are customised data and instructions, which are non-erasable, etched on a chip using special equipment. In erasable programmable read only memory (EPROM), the instructions etched on the chip can be erased and rewritten, using ultraviolet rays.

3. **Cache memory (pronounced as cash)** (*Volatile memory*). Since cache memory is physically located closer to the CPU than RAM, the computer can retrieve information from cache memory more quickly. Cache memory is more expensive than other types.

4. **Registers** (*Volatile memory*). This is a type of special storage that holds data values, programming instructions, and memory addresses. Registers are located in the ALU and the control unit; they are designed to increase the efficiency of the CPU. Types of registers include *accumulators, address registers, instruction registers,* and *general purpose registers,* which hold various types of data.

Secondary storage. It is a non-volatile memory that resides outside the CPU on devices such as magnetic disks and tapes. Data is stored on secondary storage devices, retrieved, and put into primary memory, where it is processed, and then is transferred back to secondary storage. There are two types of secondary storage : (*a*) *Sequential storage* — Data can be accessed and retrieved only in the order in which it was stored in the system; and (*b*) *Direct access storage* — Data can be retrieved in any order and is essential for online systems where information must be processed as it arrives.

3.4.3. Secondary Storage Devices

Magnetic disks are a popular storage medium for both large and small computers, provide direct access to data. These disks are essential for online systems where data has to be stored and retrieved almost instantaneously. They are of *two* forms : *Floppy disks* and *hard disks.* Floppy disks are 5.25 inch or 3.5 inch storage diskettes made of polyester film with a magnetic coating, used mostly on microcomputers. They are reliable and portable, and have fairly large memory capacities (between 720 KB and 2.88 MB). The floppy disks of 3.5 inch size are currently used most widely. They are of 1.44 MB memory. However, floppy disks of 1.3 inch size, with larger memory capabilities, are on the way to replace 3.5 inch diskettes.

Hard disk consist of several 'hard' disks or rigid platters (each hard disk usually has about 11 disks), a read/write head mechanism, and an electronic drive interface. These disks access data more quickly and efficiently than floppy disks and are reliable. They have fairly large storage capacities (between 20 MB and 7.5 GB).

Decisions about storage device must be made carefully as they can influence the productivity of an organisation.

Magnetic tape is mostly used for storing historical data or for keeping backups of important files. It is a sequential storage device, and is well suited to batch production. It is a low-cost, portable, and fairly reliable storage device that holds large volumes of data and information.

CD-ROM (Compact disc—read only memory). It is a special kind of optical disk that has excellent storage capacities (between 440 MB and 1 GB) and stores different kinds of data, such as text, pictures, audio, video, animation, and graphics. Telephone directories and dictionaries are well suited to the CD-ROM medium. CD-ROMs have helped many companies to increase productivity and reduce operating costs. There are *five* main features in a CD-ROM drive : (*a*) Access time; (*b*) Sustained throughput price; (*c*) Sound card; (*d*) Interfaces; and (*e*) Buffer.

Storage is a critical function for any organisation because data loss can cause heavy financial losses for an organisation. Hence, a good understanding of data storage and its organisation implications is essential for information systems managers.

3.4.4. Output Unit

The end product of all computer processing is some form of output. Fig. 3.5 illustrates the basic options — displayed, printed, and spoken — as well as specialised options such as plotters and computer output microform.

Displayed output devices. (*a*) *Video display terminal.* Most display terminals use a cathode ray tube (CRT) to shoot a stream of electrons on to the computer screen. This allows us to see text and images on the screen. Display screens vary in their size, resolution, and colour capability. However, a growing number of portable microcomputers use a flat panel. The *flat panel technology* consists of a liquid crystal display or plasma display that requires only a relatively thin package, such as the hinged cover of the portables.

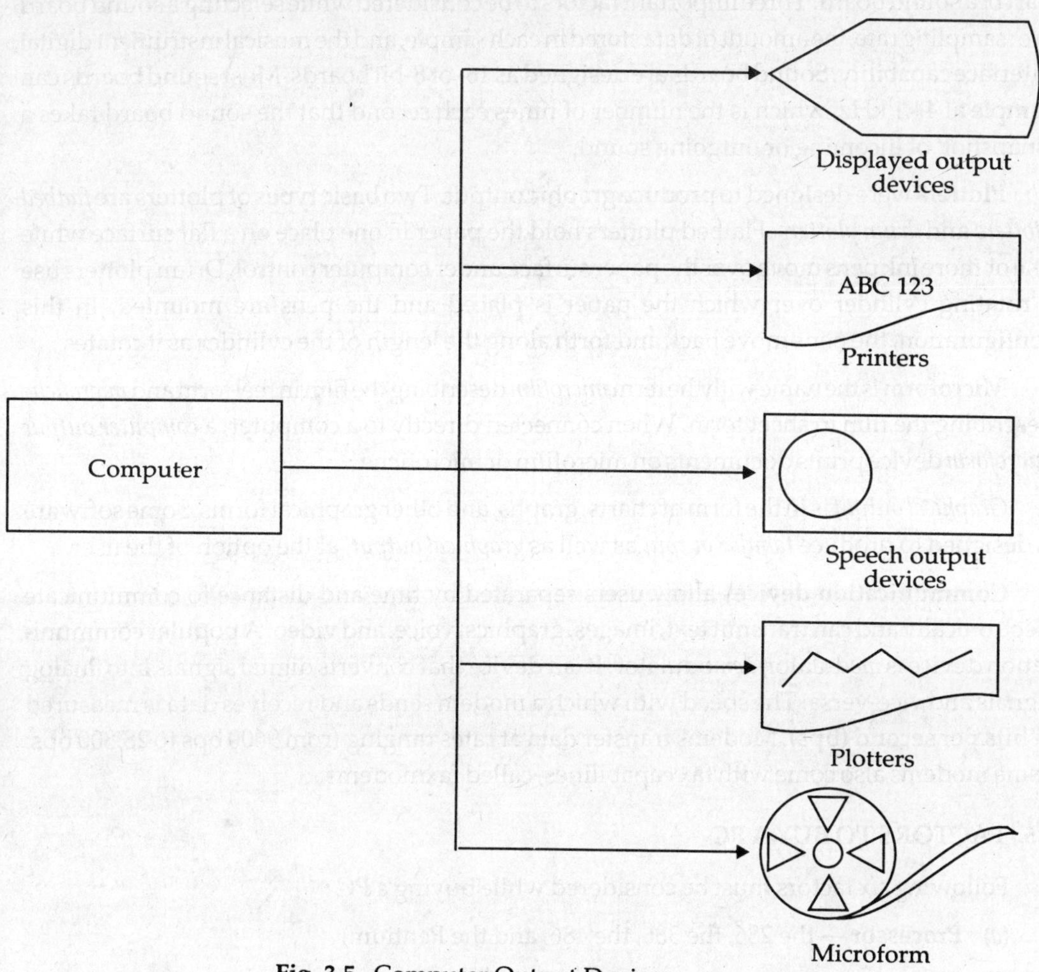

Fig. 3.5. Computer Output Devices

Printed output devices. Output devices, called printers, produce hard copy output. There are *three* basic types — line, character and page: (*a*) **Line printers.** Line printers print a line at a time. They are still used in mainframe configurations and operate at speeds ranging from 300 lines to 3000 lines per minute; (*b*) **Character printers.** Character printers print one character at a time. The most popular impact character printer is the *dot matrix printer*, which prints the characters in the form of a matrix of ink dots. *Non-impact printers* do not involve the striking of an object against an ink ribbon. Popular non-impact character printers include the **ink jet printer** which sprays droplets of ink on to the paper to form the character shapes, and the **laser printer** which causes ink to adhere to the paper through an electrostatic process. Although non-impact printers offer greater printing speeds than impact printers, impact printer can print multiple copies in a single process, whereas non-impact printers cannot; (*c*) **Page printers**

print a page at a time. Ranging from desktop printers, that can produce from four to ten pages per minute, to large systems that produce as many as 500 pages per minute, they are all non-impact printers that operate in a similar manner as a copying machine.

Speech output devices. Spoken computer output has been in use for some time. Sound, generated by a sound board, is useful to many business applications. Speakers are an important part of a sound board. Three important factors to be considered while selecting a sound board are : sampling rate, the amount of data stored in each sample, and the musical instrument digital interface capability. Sound boards are designed as 16- or 8-bit boards. Most sound boards can sample at 44.1 kHz, which is the number of times each second that the sound board takes a 'snapshot' of incoming or outgoing sound.

Plotters were designed to produce graphic output. Two basic types of plotters are *flatbed plotters* and *drum plotters.* Flatbed plotters hold the paper in one place on a flat surface while one or more ink pens move over the paper surface under computer control. Drum plotters use a rotating cylinder over which the paper is placed and the pens are mounted. In this configuration, the pens move back and forth along the length of the cylinder as it rotates.

Microform is the name with the term *microfilm* describing the film in reel form and *microfiche* describing the film in sheet form. When connected directly to a computer, a *computer output microform* device prints documents on microfilm or microfiche.

Graphical output is in the form of charts, graphs, and other graphical forms. Some software is designed to produce *tabular output* as well as *graphical output,* at the option of the user.

Communication devices allow users separated by time and distance to communicate electronically and can transmit text, images, graphics, voice, and video. A popular communication device is *mo*dulator-*dem*odulator. It is a device that converts digital signals into analog signals and vice-versa. The speed with which a modem sends and receives data is measured in **bits per second (bps).** Modems transfer data at rates ranging from 9600 bps to 28,800 bps. Some modems also come with fax capabilities, called faxmodems.

3.5. FACTORS TO BUY A PC

Following *six* factors must be considered while buying a PC :

(*a*) **Processor** — the 286, the 386, the 486, and the Pentium;

(*b*) **Clock speed** — varies between 25 MHz and 100 MHz;

(*c*) **RAM** — speed ratings in the range of 60, 70 and 80 nanoseconds;

(*d*) **Expansion slots and buses** — adding features and capabilities to one's own computer and the type of electrical connection used in an expansion slot.

(*e*) **Monitor** — size, resolution (sharpness), tricolour, interlaced or non-interlaced, radiation levels, and video boards.

(*f*) **Upgrade** — Combining some parts of an existing PC with some new components, with the result cost may be lower than that of a new system.

Review Questions

1. How data are represented in a computer ? What are the *two* important hardware considerations in representing data in a computer system ?
2. What are the size of memory of byte, kilobyte and megabyte ?
3. Name the four main categories of computers in terms of their size. Which category was the first that evolved ? Which was the last ? In which category/categories would you find a small business computer ?
4. What are the three main components of the CPU ?
5. Identify the time and space units of a computer. What does MIPS stand for ?
6. Identify the five basic components of a computer system and briefly describe their functions.
7. Since RAM is volatile, how do you prevent loss of its contents when the power is shut off ?
8. Would an organisation likely keep its database in cache memory ? Explain why or why not.
9. Identify any two differences between primary storage and secondary storage. Identify atleast two reasons why we need secondary storage.
10. Briefly explain each of the four types of primary storage.
11. What is the major distinction between a mouse and a trackball ?
12. What is the difference between RAM and ROM ? What are the two types of ROM ?
13. What is a similarity between touch screen and light pen technologies ? What is a difference ?
14. What are the differences between volatile and non-volatile memory ? Give at least two examples of each.
15. What is the main difference between OCR and MICR in terms of how the data is read.
16. There are two types of secondary storage : sequential storage and direct-access storage. Briefly describe each type.
17. Name three output devices that can produce graphics.
18. Describe a CD-ROM ? What are some applications of CD-ROM technology ?
19. Name the input and output devices that play direct roles in problem solving.
20. Name and describe any two input or output devices.
21. Describe parallel processing. What is the difference between a parallel-processing machine and a PC ?
22. What is the difference between a workstation and a PC ?
23. Computers are classified based on mainly memory size and processing speed. Identify the different types of computers discussed in this chapter, from the most powerful to the least powerful.
24. What are some technical considerations that a user should keep in mind while buying a PC ?
25. Outline the factors that should be taken into account when selecting a computer monitor.
26. Which are the two approaches for managing the growth of PCs in an organisation ? Which approach would you advocate and why ?
27. What type of computer(s) do you think is best for educational institutions, given the critical nature of educational administration tasks ?

4

Computer Software for Information Systems

4.1. INTRODUCTION

In order to build an information system, both hardware and software are essential. Various kinds of software are identified in this chapter, and explained their critical role played in an organisation to meet its information needs. The software developed in an organisation can monitor sales volume, generates reports, monitors employee attendance, processes marketing information, and tracks inventory, and so on.

Systems being used in organisations are driven by programs. A *program* is a set of stepwise instructions given to a computer to accomplish various tasks. Programmers write software using special languages, called programming languages. The process of writing programs is referred to as programming.

Today, hardware accounts for less than 15% of system costs, customised software accounts for about 85%. This is because of increase in the complexity and sophistication of software. Since computers are being used in a wide variety of fields for a number of complex tasks such as automating the factory floor, conducting scientific research, etc., writing software is one of the complex and creative activities of human mind. Moreover, it is a fact that users function in a dynamic environment in which their information needs are continuously changing. Therefore, it is necessary that software be frequently updated.

4.2. PROGRAMMING LANGUAGES

A programming language is a special type of computer language, with its own syntax and grammar, that is used to write software. Two types of programming languages exist : *Procedural* and *non-procedural* languages. A language, which explains stepwise sequential explanation to accomplish a given task, is called as *procedural language.* A *non-procedural language* focuses on *what* needs to be done, without specifying exactly *how* it should be done. Earlier programming languages were completely procedural, whereas several powerful and user-friendly non-procedural languages are available today, *e.g.*, Focus.

First Generation Languages — Machine Language. The early computers were programmed in **machine language**, or **first generation language** — a series of zeros and ones that the CPU can interpret and execute. Machine language is important because it is the only language that the computer understands. Since machine language was difficult to use, computer scientists developed programming languages which more closely resembled human communication.

The program is written in the programmer's language and is translated into machine language before it is run. The program written by the programmer is known as the **source**

program, and the machine language is called the **object program**. The system software that translates the source program into the object program is called the **translator**. Figure 4.1 illustrates the translation process and how the object program is used to process the user's data.

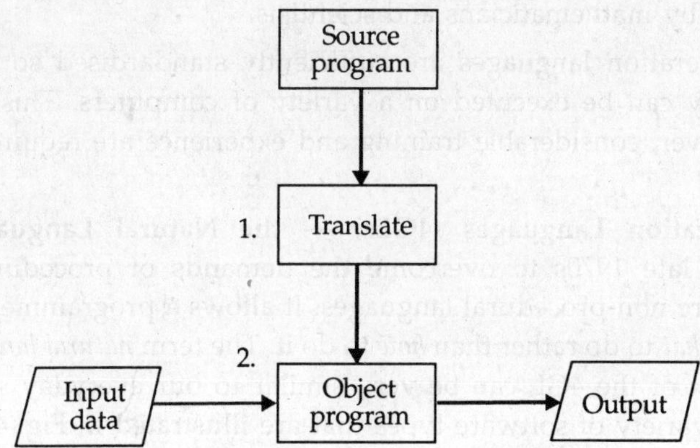

Fig. 4.1 Program Translation Process

Second Generation Languages — the Assemblers. The first translators were called **assemblers.** They permitted the programmer to code programs in **assembly language**, or **second generation language**. An assembly language uses *mnemonic names* (such as DIV for divide) for the operations that are to be performed, and *symbolic names* (such as PAYRATE) for the data that is processed. Also, there is generally a one-to-one relationship between source instructions written by the programmer and the object instructions that are generated. It means that if the object program requires 500 instructions, the programmer has to code almost that much.

Although assembly language was a big improvement over machine language from the programmer's point of view, it had several drawbacks. The assembly language programs tended to be lenghty and were difficult for programmers to read. Another disadvantage was that the assembly languages were different for every model of CPU. Thus, if a firm wanted to replace its computer with a newer model, all of the programs had to be rewritten. This requirement led to the development of a new generation of translators.

Third Generation Languages (3 GLs) — the Compilers and Interpreters. Unlike assembly languages, a **third generation language** can produce multiple object program instructions from a single source program instruction. It means that programmers have to produce fewer lines of code. In addition, the syntax of third generation languages is more like the user's language. Popular third generation languages are COBOL, FORTRAN, PL/I, and BASIC.

COBOL, FORTRAN, and PL/I are compiler languages. A **compiler** produces a complete object program in one process; then the object program is executed. An **interpreter**, on the other hand, translates a source language instruction and executes it before going on to the next instruction. There is no complete object program as such. BASIC programs are most often translated by an interpreter.

The terms procedure-oriented and problem-oriented are also associated with third generation languages. In a procedure-oriented language one must code the instructions in exactly the same sequence as they will be executed by the computer. A problem-oriented language is designed to address the needs of a specific application or set of problems. COBOL, for example, was designed to solve business problems, and FORTRAN was aimed at problems faced by mathematicians and scientists.

The third generation languages are sufficiently standardised so that, with minor modifications, they can be executed on a variety of computers. This feature is called **portability**. However, considerable training and experience are required to program in 3 GLs.

Fourth Generation Languages (4GLs) — the Natural Languages. 4GLs were developed in the late 1970s to overcome the demands of procedural programming languages. 4GLs are non-procedural languages. It allows a programmer/user to instruct the computer on *what* to do rather than *how* to do it. The term *natural language* is also used because the syntax of the 4GL can be very similar to our everyday speech. The 4GLs include the wide variety of software types that are illustrated in Fig. 4.2. The types are positioned in the graph based on their decision-support power and user-friendliness. Here *power* means their capability to provide support for each step of the problem-solving process, and *user-friendliness* means the ease with which the language can be learned and used.

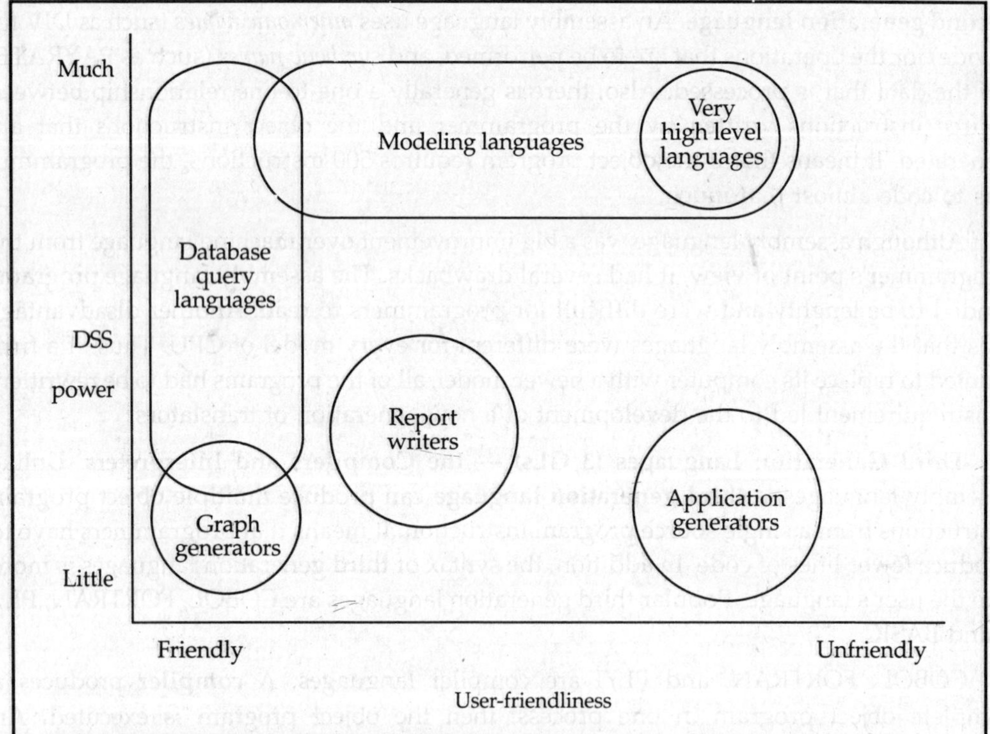

Fig. 4.2 Fourth Generation Languages having Decision-support Power and User-friendliness

- **Database Query Languages.** It is shown here how a manager can use a *database query language* that provides a special report from database contents without the need to code a program. The 4GL used inthe example is FOCUS. Assume that a manager wants a report of the sales for each of the company's products by sales region. If you have ever coded a program to prepare such a report, you can appreciate how much the 4GL has simplified the process.

- **Modeling Languages.** A *modeling language* is especially designed to make the building of mathematical models easier than when a problem-oriented language is used. One of the first modeling languages was GPSS (General Purpose Simulation System), developed by IBM in the early 1960s. The more popular ones that followed include DYNAMO, SLAM, SIMSCRIPT, GASP, MODEL, and IFPS.
- **Very High Level Languages.** The term *very high level language* is often used to describe a programming language, such as APL, that offers succinctness and power (but not necessarily user-friendliness) over and above that of conventional languages.
- **Graph Generators.** A *graph generator,* also called a *graphics package,* is used to display or print data in a variety of graphical forms.
- **Report Writers.** A *report writer* is specifically designed to prepare reports. The first example was RPG (Report Program Generator). COBOL has a report writer feature, as do most of the database management systems.
- **Application Generators.** An *application generator* produces an application program, such as inventory or payroll, without programming. Examples are MANTIS and MARK V.

Most managers are expected to use the 4GL types classified as friendly in Fig. 4.2. An important point to recognise, however, is that there are 4GLs in the upper portion of the figure that offer substantial power. These are the 4GLs that are likely to be used by information specialists, because they are characterised by: (*a*) interactive coding; (*b*) a limited amount of user training; (*c*) an emphasis on end results; (*d*) large increases in programmer productivity; and (*e*) increased CPU memory requirements.

Some popular third- and fourth-generation programming languages are briefly explained here:

BASIC: BASIC is an acronym for Beginners' All-Purpose Symbolic Instruction Code, a program developed at Dartmouth College in 1964 by John Kemeny and Thomas Kurtz. It is usually the first computer language that novice programmers learn. BASIC is a procedure-oriented, general-purpose language that is widely used for commercial and scientific applications. It is flexible and easy to learn, but is not portable.

FORTRAN: FORTRAN is an acronym for FORmula TRANslation. The program was developed by IBM in the mid-1950s. LIke BASIC, FORTRAN is a general-purpose, procedure-oriented language. It is widely used for scientific and engineering applications and number crunching. A large number of languages developed after FORTRAN have been influenced by its structure. However, it lacks flexibility in input/output operations.

COBOL: COBOL is an acronym for Common Business-Oriented Language. The program was developed at the Pentagon in 1959, the product of a joint effort by the federal government and the computer industry. COBOL is the dominant language of the business world and many industries use thousands of lines of code written in COBOL. It is easy to learn and has an English-like structure. It is excellent for processing large data files and performing repetitive tasks.

PASCAL: PASCAL was developed by Niklaus Wirth of the Federal Institute of Technology in Zurich, Switzerland, in 1968. It is named for the seventeenth-century French mathematician Blaise Pascal. PASCAL is widely used for business and scientific applications. The language is easy to learn and allows a programmer to structure programming problems. PASCAL is a popular language in computer science courses, because it lays the foundation for a structured programming framework.

C Language: C is a general-purpose language. It is called C because it was an improvement over another language called B that was developed at AT&T Bell Labs in the eary 1970s. C was developed by Brian Kerninghan and Dennis Ritchie. It is closely associated with the UNIX system since the C language was developed on UNIX. Although UNIX was initially written in assembly language, Dennis Ritchie later rewrote UNIX in C language. In a short time C has become an extremely popular language and is now widely used in system development applications and for commercial uses. C is a concise language that provides a high level of modularity.

4.2.1. Object-Oriented Programming

Object-oriented programming, also abbreviated as OOP, is also a programming language to enhance the productivity of programmers and reduces software development time. In OOP, systems are modeled using chunks of programming and data, called *objects.* Each object includes proramming code that specifies how it should behave, how it should manipulate data, respond to messages from other objects, and send messages of its own.

A significant benefit of OOP is *code reusability, i.e.,* the same piece of code can be used for different applications. Today, code reusability has not only become desirable but also essential in many software development environments. It is estimated that half of the code required for most applications already exists and that an estimated 40% to 60% of all new code can come from software libraries of reusable components. Also, OOP reduces the amount of testing required. OOP software is easier to update because some aspects of an object have often to be modified. Objects can inherit attributes from a parent object, so that only the differences have to be modeled. Further, full advantages of OOP can be accrued only if an organisation is willing to start from scratch, rather than making gradual transitions from existing code. However, many organisations are reluctant to adopt this practice.

4.2.2. Visual Programming

Visual programming facilitates users to visualise their code and its impact on the system. The program allows a user to download competitor's advertised prices from an external database. It then compares the competitor's prices with those of the user's organisation and graphically displays comparisons of the prices.

Microsoft company has developed Visual BASIC, designed to allow users to integrate Microsoft Windows applications. This feature can reduce the development time for many applications. Visual BASIC serves as a common macro language for Access, Power Point, Word and Excel.

4.3. CLASSIFICATION OF SOFTWARE

Two types of computer software are available : **system software** and **application software.** Computer-related tasks are performed by system software such as managing input and output devices. People-related tasks, such as marketing, are performed by application software.

4.3.1. System Software

There are three basic types of system software:

(a) System control software;

(b) System support software; and

(c) System development software.

System control software. System control software helps to monitor, control, coordinate, and manage the resources and functions of a computer system. System control software can be classified into two categories : (*i*) Operating system and its functions; and (*ii*) Operating system environments.

Operating system and its functions. The operating system manages the computer's processes, functioning as an interface between the user, the software that processes the firm's data, and the hardware. Major functions of an operating system include: (*a*) helping a CPU to manage or control internal computer operations; (*b*) facilitating communications between an user and a CPU; (*c*) enabling a CPU to communicate with other peripheral devices; and (*d*) automating certain program functions to increase the operating efficiency of the computer system as a whole. Other six basic functions, that an operating system can perform, are:

- Schedule jobs
- Manage hardware and software resources
- Maintain system security
- Enable multiple user resource sharing
- Handle interrupts
- Maintain usage records.

Some of the important operating functions of an operating system are listed in Table 4.1.

Table 4.1. Some Important Functions of an Operating System

Function	*Description*
Load programs	Moves programs to be executed into primary memory and indicate when program execution is complete.
Manage I/O operations	Enables and manages the use of multiple I/O devices. Ensures the efficient utilisation of I/O devices.
Manage files	Allows application programs to read and write files. Performs other file-related operations such as copying, deleting, moving, and so on.
Manage memory	Allocates memory so that users can create, execute, and retrieve different applications. Ensures that memory is fully and efficiently utilised.
Detect errors	Brings system and execution errors to the attention of the user so that timely action can be taken.
Allocate resources	Manages all computer resources, including the CPU, primary memory, secondary storage, and I/O devices and other peripherals.
Monitor resource use	Tracks use of computer resources for cost accounting and statistical purposes. Mostly done for enterprise-wide systems.
Resolve conflicts	Acts as an arbitrator among competing programs, taking into account factors such as the criticality of the application or the priority of the program.

All computers have operating systems, but the systems vary in the number of basic functions and how these functions are performed.

Operating system environment. There are two types of operating system environments: (*a*) **Multiprogramming** is a computing environment in which multiple users can run multiple programs on a single-CPU computer at the same time. The CPU switches between programs; however, at any given time is executing only one program; and (*b*) **Multiprocessing** system has a number of processors that process data and instructions, unlike systems that have only one CPU. It is ideally suited for complex and computationally intensive operations that require extensive processing.

Examples of operating systems are: MS-DOS; UNIX; Windows; Windows NT, and OS/2. Some of these operating systems, such as MS-DOS, are exclusively for PCs, whereas other operating systems, such as UNIX, are available for both large and small computers.

Some popular operating systems and their characteristics are given in Table 4.2.

Table 4.2. Important Operating Systems and their Characteristics

Operating System	*Characteristics*
DOS	A single-user system. Commands are somewhat cryptic and not very user-friendly.
Windows	Uses icons to execute programs. Uses point-and-click method to execute commands. Applications appear in windows on the monitor. A highly integrated environment, in which different applications have the same "look and feel".
Windows NT	Has multitasking and multiprocessing capabilities. Processes data in 32-bit chunks. Ideal for large business applications that run in a network environment.
UNIX	Powerful, interactive, multiprogramming, multitasking, multiuser, operating system. Highly portable.
OS/2	This 32-bit operating system supports multitasking, making it faster than DOS. It can run programs written for OS/2 or for other operating systems such as DOS and Windows.

System support software. Programs which support the smooth execution of various programs and operations of a computer are called system support software. System support software includes *utility programs. programming services software, database management systems, security software,* and *system documentation.*

Utility programs are among the most popular types of system support software. They perform tasks such as formatting disks, locating free space on a disk, retrieving lost or damaged files, sorting and merging data, converting files from one format to another, backing up important files, and providing online help.

Programming services software includes (*a*) language translators; (*b*) system loaders; (*c*) link editors; (*d*) system librarians. Language translators include *assemblers, compilers* and *interpreters.* Language translators that translate assembly language into machine language are called *assemblers;* language translators that translate an *entire* program written in 3GL or 4GL into machine language before program execution are called *compilers;* language translators that translate a statement and execute it before translating the next statement are called *interpreters. System loader* typically 'fetches' a computer program from a disk and loads it into primary memory in preparation for execution. *Link editors* enable a computer system to access modules, subroutines, overlays, and other segments of an application program that are stored on disk. A *librarian* program is required to catalog all other programs and to maintain a directory where these programs are stored.

A *database management system* is a set of computer programs that enable a user to define, create, access, manipulate, and output the information in records stored on a database. A detailed discussion on database management system is given in chapter 6.

Security software protects a computer system and its files from unauthorized access. Examples of security software include : (*a*) password programs; (*b*) file-protect programs; and (*c*) encryption software.

System documentation includes manuals, flowcharts, reference guides, and other operating instructions.

System development software helps design and build better systems, *e.g.*, a collection of programs that assist developers in developing an information system, also called as computer-aided software engineering (CASE). Shells are also system development software; a *shell* is a set of tools and techniques that allows developers to build a prototype of a system. Shells can be used to build expert systems, decision support systems, and executive information systems.

4.3.2. Application Software

Application software assists in managing the organisation's physical and conceptual resources. Application softwares are nowadays being used to meet information needs. There are two types of application software:

1. General-purpose software
2. Dedicated software.

General-purpose software is designed for general applications such as payroll, inventory management, accounting. Dedicated software is designed for specific applications such as space shuttle. Tables 4.3 and 4.4 list general-purpose software and commercial application software, respectively.

Dedicated software includes specialised or customised applications designed for specific purposes. For example, logistic software helps firms handle the flow of goods and services from one location to another in order to cut costs, minimize inventory, and reduce the time it takes for goods, services, or information to reach their destinations.

Table 4.3. Types of General-purpose Application Software

Type of Application Software	*Description*
Word processing	Computerisation of the creation and management of documents. Allows easy correction and manipulation of text.
Desktop publishing	Produces documents such as memos and pamphlets. Has many of the features of word processing along with more sophisticated text and graphics capabilities.
Spreadsheets	Electronic calculators used for extensive number crunching, such as financial analysis, budget preparation, and other numerical analysis. Also used for "what-if" analyses.
Computer graphics	Provides for the creation and management of sophisticated graphics, charts, and figures. Often comes with extensive colour capabilities and clip art.
Accounting software	Automates accounting functions, such as general ledger, accounts payable, and accounts receivable. Often can be interfaced with other financial systems, such as payroll, budgeting, and so on.
Imaging	Scans text and graphics from paper documents and converts them into digital images.

Table 4.4. Application Software Packages and their Operating Systems

Type of Application	*Software Package*	*Vendor*	*Operating System*
Word Processors	Word	Microsoft	DOS, Windows
	WordPerfect	WordPerfect	DOS, OS/2, Windows
	Ami Pro	Lotus	DOS, Windows
Spreadsheets	Lotus 1-2-3	Lotus	DOS, OS/2
	Excel	Microsoft	Windows
Graphics	Power Point	Microsoft	OS/2, Windows
	Freelance Graphics	Lotus	OS/2, Windows
	Photo Shop	Adobe	Windows
Desktop Publishing	Publisher	Microsoft	DOS, Windows
	Printshop	Broderbund	DOS, Windows
Accounting	Peachtree Accounting	Peachtree	DOS, Windows
	In the Black	Microrims	Windows
	DacEasy Accounting	DacEasy	Windows
	MYOB Accounting	Teleware	Windows
	Simply Money	Kiplinger	Windows
Integrated Packages*	Microsoft Works	Microsoft	DOS, Windows
	Claris Works	Claris	Windows

*Packages that combine a number of capabilities, such as word processing, spreadsheets, and graphics.

4.4. ROLE OF SOFTWARE IN PROBLEM SOLVING

Software can play either a direct or an indirect role in problem solving. System software always plays an indirect role. On the other hand, application software can play either a direct or an indirect role. Most general business and industry-specific packages are designed to play an indirect role by creating and maintaining the database that provides the basis for the information-oriented subsystems. However, some industry-specific packages go beyond data processing, providing components that directly contribute to problem-solving.

Some organisational and personal productivity software only indirectly affects problem-solving, by simplifying the creation and transmission of data. However, other productivity software such as electronic spreadsheet, project management, forecasting, and statistical analysis packages provides direct support.

4.5. CRITERIA FOR INVESTMENT IN HARDWARE AND SOFTWARE

Investment in information systems and technologies include the acquisition of hardware, software, networks, and other computer-related systems and technologies. *Criteria for investment* means the standards that an organisation uses to make computer-related investment decisions. Table 4.5 lists some criteria that organisations use to make information system and information technology investment decisions and the extent of use of each criterion.

Table 4.5. Criteria for Investment Used in Organisations for Purchasing Hardware

Criteria	*Percentage of Companies Using Criteria*
Financial Criteria	
Discounted Cash Flow (DCF)	
1. Net Present Value	49
2. Internal Rate of Return	54
3. Profitability Index Method	8
Other Financial	
4. Average/Accounting Rate of Return	16
5. Payback Method	61
6. Budgetary Constraints	68
Management Criteria	
7. Support of Explicit Business Objectives	88
8. Support of Implicit Business Objectives	69
9. Response to Competitive Systems	61
10. Support for Management Decision Making	88
11. Probability of Achieving Benefits	46
12. Legal/Government Requirements	71
Development Criteria	
13. Technical/System Requirement	79
14. Introduce/Learn New Technology	60
15. Probability of Project Completion	31

Source : *MIS Quarterly*, September 1992, p. 341.

However, using financial criteria alone for investment decisions has certain inherent limitations. For example, in a reputed publishing firm of New Delhi, every information system project is decided on the basis of its return on investment. On the other hand, in a publishing and printing firm at Bangalore, without doing any ROI analysis, top management had a feeling that the project was essential for the future of the firm, *i.e.*, qualitative factors outweighed financial considerations.

Review Questions

1. Define a 'program' and explain the need of hardware and software to build an information system.
2. Explain the four generations of programming languages. Identify some improvements between the generations. Give an example of a language from each generation.
3. What are procedural and non-procedural languages ?
4. Explain some popular third- and fourth-generation programming languages.
5. Define the following: Graph generators, Report writers, Very high level languages, and Application generators.
6. Explain in brief OOP and visual programming, and their significant characteristics.
7. What are the three types of system software ? Explain each of them in detail.
8. What is a basic difference between an assembler and a compiler, and also between a compiler and an interpreter ?
9. Is BASIC a procedure-oriented language ? Why or why not ?
10. Define an operating function and explain its primary functions. Name some operating systems that can be used on PC-based systems.
11. Explain multiprogramming and multiprocessing. Outline the difference between the two.
12. What are important operating systems and their characteristics ?
13. What are the two basic ways of acquiring application software ? Give an example of each.
14. What is programming services software ? Discuss in brief.
15. Outline different types of general-purpose application software and explain each of them in brief.
16. Which type of software plays only an indirect role in problem-solving ?

5

Data Communications System

5.1. INTRODUCTION

Data communications is the movement of coded data and information from one point to another by means of electrical or electromagnetic devices, fibre-optic cables, or microwave signals. A basic data communications schematic is shown in Fig. 5.1. This is

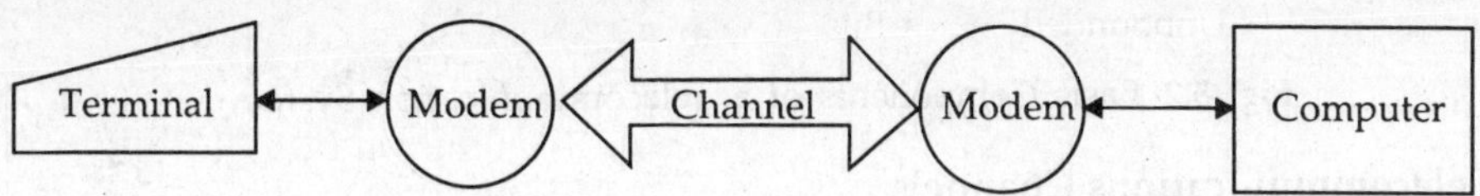

Fig. 5.1 Basic Data Communications Schematic

the simplest form of computer communication. A single terminal is linked to a computer. The terminal can be the sender and the computer can be the receiver, or vice-versa. As with communication between humans, computer messages must travel along a channel. The most common channel being used for data communications is the telephone circuit as is used for voice communication. For a telephone circuit to be used for data communication, a special device must be included at each end. The device is called a modem, which stands for **modulator-demodulator.** The modems convert the electronic signals of the computing equipment to the electronic signals of the telephone circuit, and vice-versa.

There are many variations in data communications network arrangements, but the basic types are the local area network (LAN) and wide area network (WAN). Today, both LANs and WANs are being used for client/server computing. The wide variety of data communications hardware has prompted equipment manufacturers to establish standard network architecture, pioneered by IBM. However, the quest for international standards has culminated in the Open Systems Interconnection (OSI) model. Data communications is so important to firms that a sound network management program based on planning and control is essential. Data communications helps managers by removing the geographic barriers to computer use, and helps the firms by enabling a strategy of either centralised or decentralised decision making.

5.2. TELECOMMUNICATIONS SYSTEM

Telecommunication system has five basic components. These components and their connections are shown in Fig. 5.2.

Since input and output devices are already described in Chapter 3, other components of a telecommunication system are discussed in this chapter.

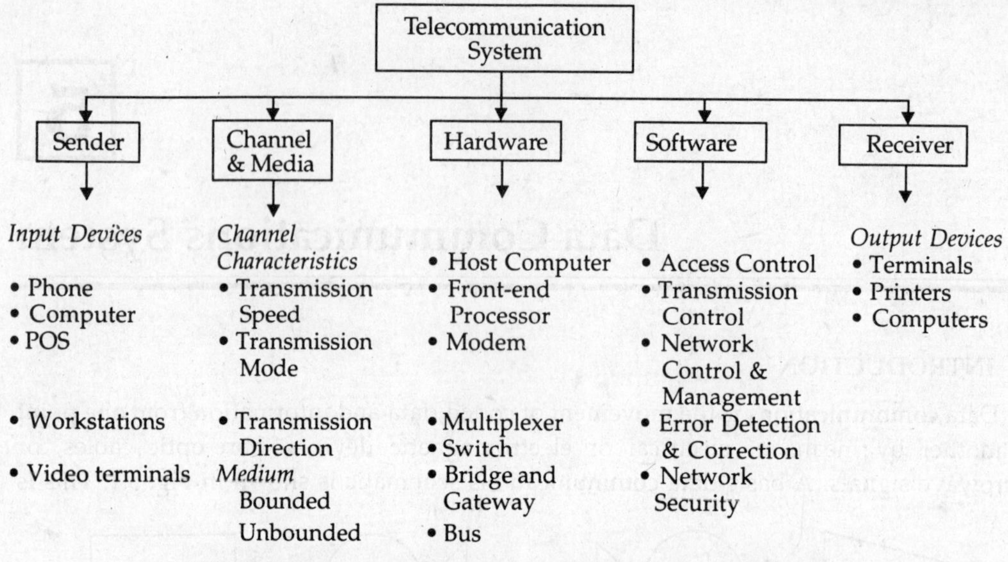

Fig. 5.2 Basic Components of a Telecommunication System

5.2.1. Telecommunications Channels

A data communications channel is a path through a medium that data can take to accomplish a communications task. In effect, channels are 'data highways' carrying signals from sending stations to receiving stations along predefined routes. Telecommunications channels are characterised according to transmission rate, transmission mode and transmission direction.

Transmission rate is the capacity of a telecommunication channel depending on the bandwidth. The bandwidth is the difference between the highest and the lowest frequency carried over the channel. The greater the bandwidth, the greater the amount of information that can be simultaneously transmitted over the channel. Bandwidth is of three types: voice-band (300 bits per second (bps) to 9600 bps); medium-band (9600 bps to 256,000 bps) and broadband (256,000 bps to a very large number, say, in billions).

In *transmission mode,* data are transmitted over the network. There are two modes of data transmission over a network: synchronous and asynchronous. Synchronous transmission transmits a group of characters at a time, whereas asynchronous transmission transmits one character at a time.

Transmission direction is the direction in which data is transmitted. There are three directions in which data can be transmitted: *simplex, half duplex,* and *full duplex. Simplex* is a term for a data communication device that can either send or receive data, but cannot do both. For example, television broadcasting and news wires. *Half duplex* is a data exchange device in which two parties alternately send data. When one party completes a transmission, control of the channel switches to the other party, allowing it to transmit data. *Full duplex* is a data exchange device in which both parties can send and receive information at the same time. An example of full duplex is the telephone.

Data communication carriers. Telephone and telecommunication firms that provide telecommunication services to move data and information from one location to another. There are two types of carriers: *common carriers* and *special-purpose carriers.* A *common carrier* is a private organisation that provides communication services to businesses and to the general public, and is regulated by central agencies, for a fee, called a *tariff.* For example, Mobilink. *Special-purpose carrier* is an organisation that add features to the basic communication services provided by a common carrier. They lease communication services provided by common carriers and add amenities such as E-mail, video-conferencing, backup services and network management. They charge their clients a basic monthly/annual fee; additional charges are levied based on volume and type of use. The example is Videsh Sanchar Nigam Ltd.

5.2.2. Telecommunications Media

There are two different types of media over witch data is transmitted: **Bounded media** and **unbounded media.** In a *bounded medium,* the signals are confined to the medium. Most common bounded medium are : (*a*) Twisted-pair wire; (*b*) Coaxial cable; and (*c*) Fibre-optic cables. *Twisted pair* is a pair of insulated, copper wires twisted into a angle, wrapped set. It is the most common type of circuit in standard phone lines, and is commonly used for data communications as well as voice-grade communications. A *coaxial cable* consists of a single wire covered with insulation and contained within an outer cylindrical shell. Coaxial cabling is commonly used both in local area networks, undersea data communications, and in the cable television industry. *Fibre-optic cables* consist of hair-thin strands of glass, or plastic, through which pulses of light are passed. The pulses are coded to represent the data.

In an *unbounded medium,* or wires, signals are not restricted to the medium. Wireless media propagate signals through the atmosphere, the ocean, and outer space. There are four types of wireless communication: (*a*) Microwaves; (*b*) High-frequency radio telephones; (*c*) Cellular phones; and (*d*) Communication satellites. **Microwaves** are high-frequency radio waves that can transmit data signals up to 40 miles. Microwave signals are commonly transmitted and received by antennas placed on tall buildings or mountain tops. **High-frequency radio telephones** use radio to transmit information over long distances. High-frequency signals radiate from an antenna using two paths: a *ground wave,* follows the earth's surface, can communicate over distance of up to 400 miles; and a *sky wave,* bounces between the earth and the ionosphere, can reach points up to 4000 miles away, with a path reliability of over 90%. **Cellular phones** are wireless personal telephones. A cellular system partitions geographical areas into cells; each cell has a base station with a radio transmitter, a receiver, an antenna, and a computer. Cellular phone technology uses a low-power transmitter attached to each cell (a small area), thus increasing the number of frequencies considerably available to mobile phone customers. Incoming calls are transmitted to a user's telephone with radio waves, using a unique set of radio frequencies for each cell, while a central computer and other communication devices send, receive, track, and manage calls and handoffs from one cell to another. **Communication satellites** are launched into geosynchronous orbits at an altitude of approximately 36,000 km above the equator. The satellite period is 24 hours, so it revolves at the same rate as the earth under it. Satellites are powered by solar panels. They carry a variety of signals such as television broadcasting, telephone transmissions, and high-speed data. Surface stations all over the world use *dish antennas* to transmit data to communication satellites, which amplify the signals and transmit them to other surface stations. Satellites cannot be used for real-time data processing because there is some delay between the transmission and the arrival of data.

5.3. DATA COMMUNICATIONS HARDWARE

As one moves from the user end of the network, other hardware components are found, including host computer, front-end processor, modem, multiplexer, frequency division multiplexing, time division multiplexing, data collection terminals, switch, bridge and gateway. Each of these components are briefly explained and illustrated in Fig. 5.3.

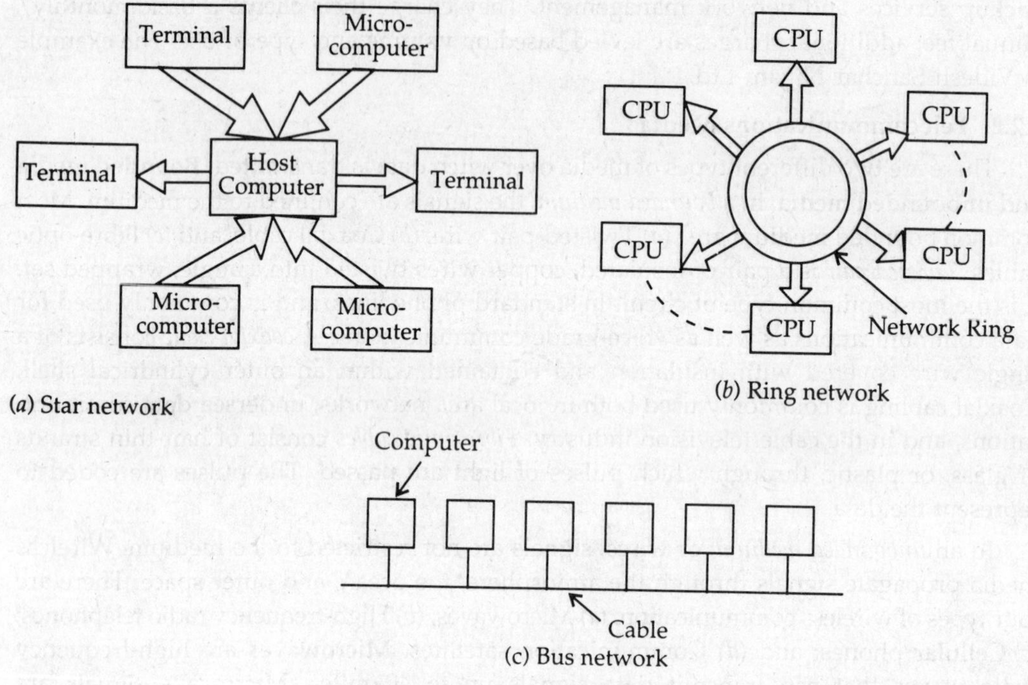

Fig. 5.8 Topology of Computer Network

Host computer. The host performs the data processing for the network. The incoming messages are handled in the same manner as data received from any other type of input unit. After the processing, messages can be transmitted back to the front-end processor for routing.

Front-end processor. The front-end processor is a minicomputer that acts as a buffer between the client device and the host computer. It increases the operating efficiency of

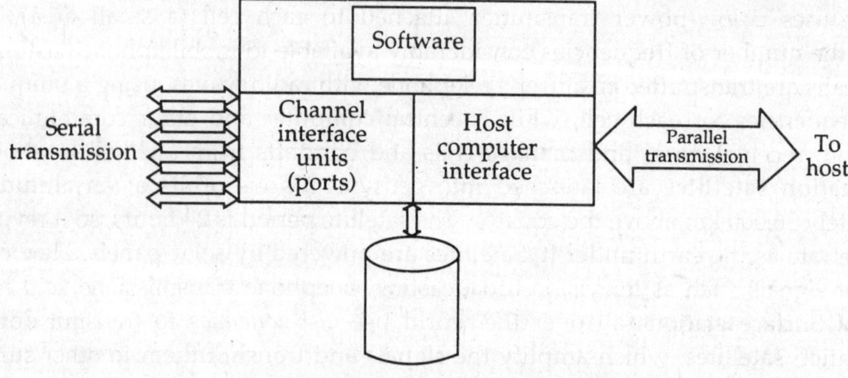

Fig. 5.4 Front-end Processor

the network by taking care of routine tasks such as coordinating peripherals and ensuring error-free transmission. The working of the front-end processor is shown in Fig. 5.4.

Modem. Digital signals are converted into analog signals (and vice-versa) by a modem, and can be carried over telephone lines. At the receiving end, the analog signals are converted into digital signals, in the form of binary digits such as 1s and 0s, that a computer can interpret.

Multiplexer. A multiplexer is a device that permits the simultaneous sending and receiving of multiple messages over a single channel. A multiplexer collects signals from several terminals, interwaves the signals and transmits them over a single channel.

Frequency division multiplexing. In frequency division multiplexing, a channel with a large bandwidth is divided into subchannels and each subchannel carries individual analog signals, which are then bound together. At the receiving end, the bound signals are separated into individual signals.

Time division multiplexing. It can only be used for digital data. It requires time synchronisation for the slots, which can be provided by a reference station.

Switch. An electronic device which determines the data transmission path by making connections. Switches can control the transmission path across national or local networks.

Bridge and gateway. A device that links two or more compatible networks. Bridge allows information to be sent between users on different networks. Gateways enable PCs on LANs to access a mainframe computer.

Bus. It has connections to all hosts and can simulate broadcasting by sending a message to all of them, one at a time.

5.4. DATA COMMUNICATIONS SOFTWARE

Software enables all of the data communication hardware units to work as one system. Most of the software is located in the host and in the front-end processor, but some can be located in the cluster control units and the terminals. It is necessary that communications software must interface the user's applications programs with the access method that has been selected to control the network, keeping in view that the telecommunications access methods themselves are control programs of a sort. In addition, this software must operate under the control of the operating system used in the host computer or in the user's data communication network. In essence, data communications software must provide the means of controlling the specific data communications environment defined by the user. The following are normally included in the basic functions of the control software:

- Activation and deactivation of the links and stations
- Establishment of logical connections over physical links
- Processing of network commands
- Detection and correction of line errors
- Recording of network status.

Various types of computer software are explained:

Access control software. This software establishes access between different devices, terminals, and computers in the network and checks the transmission mode (synchronous/asynchronous), transmission speed (low/medium/high), and transmission direction (simplex, half duplex, or duplex). It also includes automatic dialing and redialing of telephone numbers and the enforcement of access restrictions. Access control is of two types : centralised and decentralised. In centralised control, a host computer controls access between different devices on the network. In case central unit is down, whole network gets upset. In decentralised or distributed control, any device on the network can communicate directly with any other.

Terminal control software. This software controls the transmission of data over the network.

Terminal emulation software. This software enables a microcomputer to behave like a specific terminal when it interacts with a mainframe.

Network control software. This software coordinates, controls and manages the complete operations of the network. It establishes priorities for data waiting to be transmitted, checks for any transmission error, route messages, and maintain statistics on system use.

Error correction and detection software. It ensures that errors, caused by any other problem, are detected and corrected.

Security software. This software prevents unauthorised access to data and monitors the use of the network.

5.5. COMMUNICATION NETWORKS

There are five types of communication networks:

1. Private Branch Exchanges (PBXs)
2. Integrated Services Digital Networks (ISDNs)
3. Local Area Networks (LANs)
4. Wide Area Networks (WANs)
5. Value Added Networks (VANs).

A brief explanation about these networks are given below.

5.5.1. Private Branch Exchanges (PBXs)

A PBX is an electronic switching device located in the organisation that automatically switches between the organisation's telephone lines and that of the city's Central Telephones department and, therefore, acts like a small telephone exchange. Business houses use PBXs because (*a*) PBXs handle inter-office calls internally and thus lower the amount of 'outside' telephone traffic; and (*b*) PBXs save money by enabling business houses to lease fewer outside lines. Networks that carry only voice and data from PBXs are referred to as PBX-based networks; those that integrate voice, data, and images are referred to as integrated services digital networks (ISDNs). Nowadays, PBXs have become an integral part of the 'smart office' with their ability to coordinate, control, and communicate data among various devices on the network. The major advantage of a PBX is that it requires only a telephone jack to become operational, unlike telecommunication devices that require extensive wiring of existing facilities. The disadvantages of a PBX are: (*a*) It can cover only a small geographical area, unless it is connected to other PBXs or to value-added networks; and (*b*) PBXs cannot handle large volumes of data since PBXs use only telephone lines. PBX systems have now replaced some intraorganisation demand for public telephone services, public-access data banks, and public information services which are growing rapidly.

5.5.2. Integrated Services Digital Networks (ISDNs)

The ISDN is a digital communication network that uses the public telephone network and allows users to transmit data, voice, text, and video communications in digital form over telephone lines. Since it is a digital network, it eliminates the need for a modem to convert analog signals into digital signals and vice-versa; it does not require any rewiring since ISDN uses the coaxial or fibre-optic cables; it promotes uniformity and standardisation through a set of standard interfaces. Because of these reasons, ISDN is regarded as the heart of a global information revolution.

ISDN works basically on *five* principles :

(*a*) Openness;

(*b*) Modularity;

(*c*) Communication-based intelligence;

(*d*) Network management and control; and

(*e*) Integrated products and services.

Openness means that all ISDN products will be standardised. This brings order and uniformity to the complex task of developing a network.

Modularity enables the organisation to upgrade or replace any part in a network without replacing the entire network.

Communication-based intelligence provides users with a way to configure their network connections to meet their requirements.

Network management and control is one of the complex and challenging tasks that information system managers face.

Integrated products and services allows the use of a wide variety of products and services on the network, such as voice networking, data networking, teleconferencing, etc. Recent computerised railway reservation network throughout the country is one of the examples of ISDN.

The basic building block of ISDN is a 64-kbps (thousand bits per second) channel, referred to as a *B-channel.* Each B-channel is used to transmit user information. Another channel, called the *D-channel*, carries signalling and control information used to initiate, redirect, or terminate calls.

5.5.3. Local Area Networks (LANs)

The network that currently creating the most interest is the LAN. Figure 5.5 shows a LAN consisting of four workstations located in users' offices. A *workstation* is a micro configuration that is tailored to a user's needs. Each workstation can be used in a stand-alone manner, but each can also access storage or output devices, called *peripherals,* that are located elsewhere in the network. Peripherals are under the control of another micro-computer called a *network server* or *file server.* The network server in the figure controls three peripheral devices — a letter quality printer, a plotter, and a hard disk drive. In this particular LAN, the workstations are connected to the server by means of a **bus.** A bus is a single circuit of limited length.

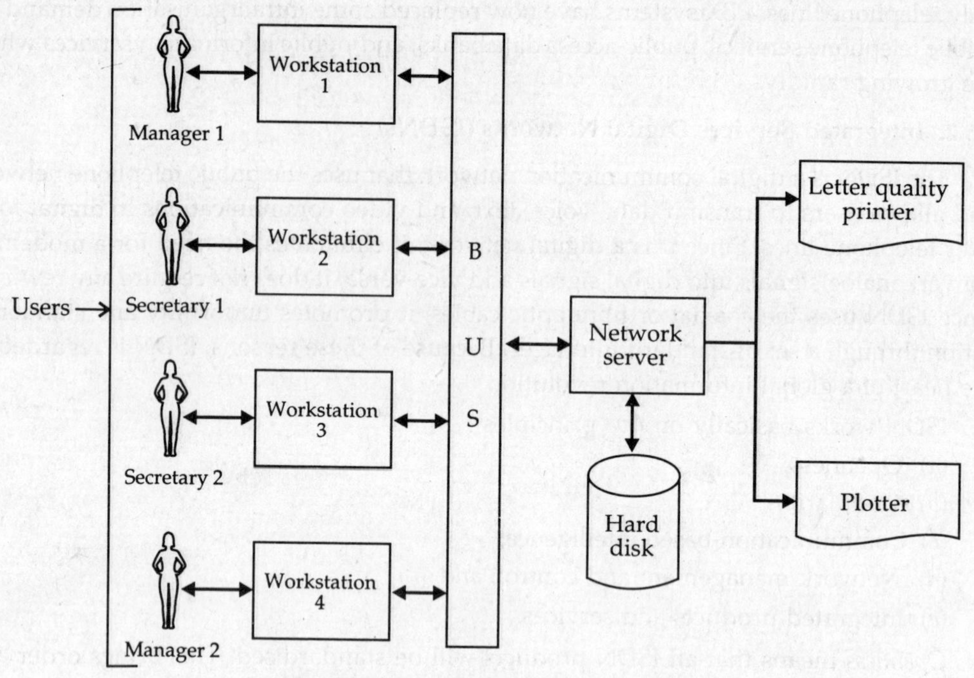

Fig. 5.5 An Example of Local Area Network

A local area network is constructed of high-capacity lines, such as a coaxial cable. If the cable is long, electronic devices are attached to keep signals strong and clear as they move along the line. A device to be attached to the network cable has an interface (connection) containing a microprocessor that manages the logic of the attachment and transmission. If LAN is small, the attachment logic may be handled by a computer that controls the entire network. Devices on the LAN have a **peer-to-peer relationship**, in which all of them have equal status and privileges where a central computer controls all the other devices on the network. There are a number of proprietary designs for building a LAN : Ethernet, Token ring and Appletalk, although in recent years wireless LANs are becoming popular.

Ethernet is a popular system that connects computers using coaxial cables. A typical Ethernet network has a maximum speed of 100 megabits per second (Mbps). It was developed jointly by DEC, Intel, and Xerox.

Token ring network was developed by IBM and has a maximum speed of 16 Mbps. It uses a special-type of twisted-pair cable.

Appletalk has a maximum speed of 230 kbps, and is most commonly used on twisted-pair. It is built into all Macintosh computers.

Local area networks designed only for data communications are termed as *baseband* networks. A *broadband* network is a larger capacity cable that can be divided into separate channels, each channel acting as a separate line. The extra capacity means the broadband network can carry data communications, television, telephone, etc., on the same cable. It is more expensive than a baseband network and is cost-justified only where there is a consistently high volume of communications.

The basic differences between a LAN and a PBX are : (*a*) LAN carries only data whereas PBX carries both voice and data; and (*b*) PBX uses the existing wiring of the telephone system whereas LAN is not the part of a telephone system and as such requires wiring.

5.5.4. Wide Area Networks (WANs)

A wide area network covers a large geographic area with various communications facilities such as long distance telephone service, satellite transmission, and undersea cables for data and voice communications. The WAN typically involves host computers and many different types of communications hardware and software. Examples of WANs are banking networks, airline reservation systems and railway reservation systems. Figure 5.6 illustrates a wide area network that a large organisation might use to connect regional computers. Here manufacturing units, marketing centres, and regional offices are all connected to headquarters of the organisation, and therefore to each other, for communication purposes.

There are many methods to set up a WAN. Typically, they are *direct distance dialling (DDD), wide-area telephone service (WATS) lines, leased lines,* and *satellites.*

One of the easiest ways to set up a WAN is *direct distance dialling.* It uses the services of the telephones department and a long distance carrier, such as AT&T and VSNL, to transmit voice and data. Although DDD is simple and easy to use, long distance data communications can become expensive and are error-prone. Also, DDD is restricted to sites that are linked by a telephone network.

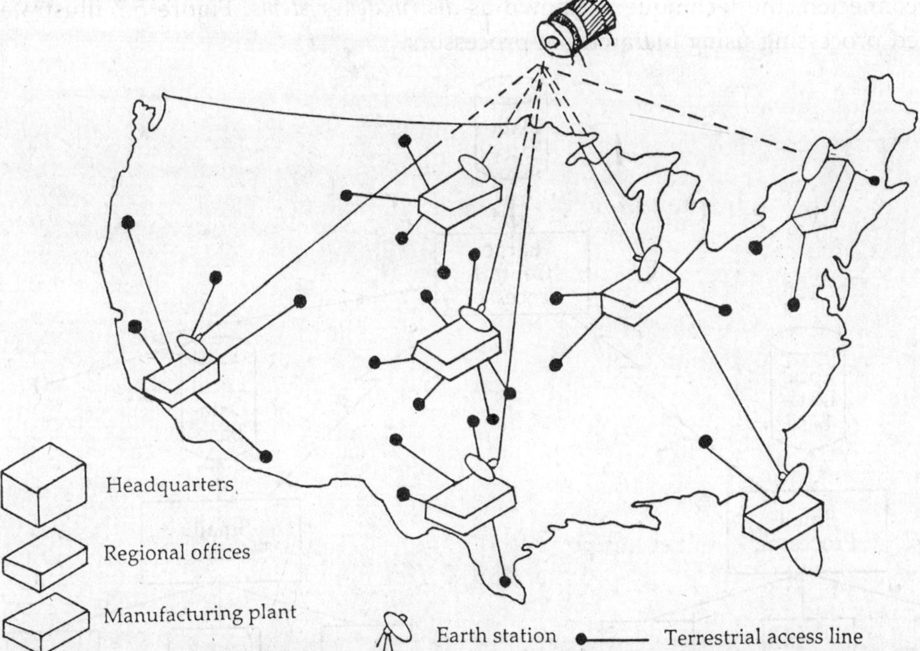

Fig. 5.6 A Wide Area Network for a Large Organisation and Connections with its Various Regional Offices, Marketing Centres and Manufacturing Units

In case of *wide area telephone service,* an organisation is required to pay a flat monthly fee whether it uses the network or not. It is similar to DDD.

In case of *leased lines*, telephone lines are leased to an organisation for its exclusive use. It is a dedicated line between two locations. Although it is more expensive, but it tends to be less error-prone than a public telephone line.

Use of *satellites* for setting a WAN is a good choice for organisations that have many remote locations and moderate data transmission needs. It is a relatively inexpensive way to transmit data.

The main advantage of WANs over LANs is that they can link sites that are remotely located. Inspite of many significant benefits, *e.g.*, remote data entry, remote job entry, centralising information, time sharing, using specialised databases, facilitating communications, they also pose some challenges. First, managing WANs is a difficult task. Second, when things go wrong, it is difficult to identify the source of the problem because many elements come together in many different ways to make the network operational.

5.5.5. Value Added Networks (VANs)

The public data networks that add value to the basic communication services provided by common carriers by offering specialised services are termed as *value-added networks*. The specialised services include access to commercial databases and software, correction of transmission errors, providing compatibility between incompatible computers and terminals, E-mail, and video conferencing. A subscriber to a VAN service pays a monthly fee depending on its level of use.

5.6. DISTRIBUTED SYSTEMS

When small computers became popular, organisations changed their strategy and began *distributing* the minis and micros throughout the organisation. When these systems are interconnected, the technique is known as *distributed systems*. Figure 5.7 illustrates distributed processing using hierarchy of processors.

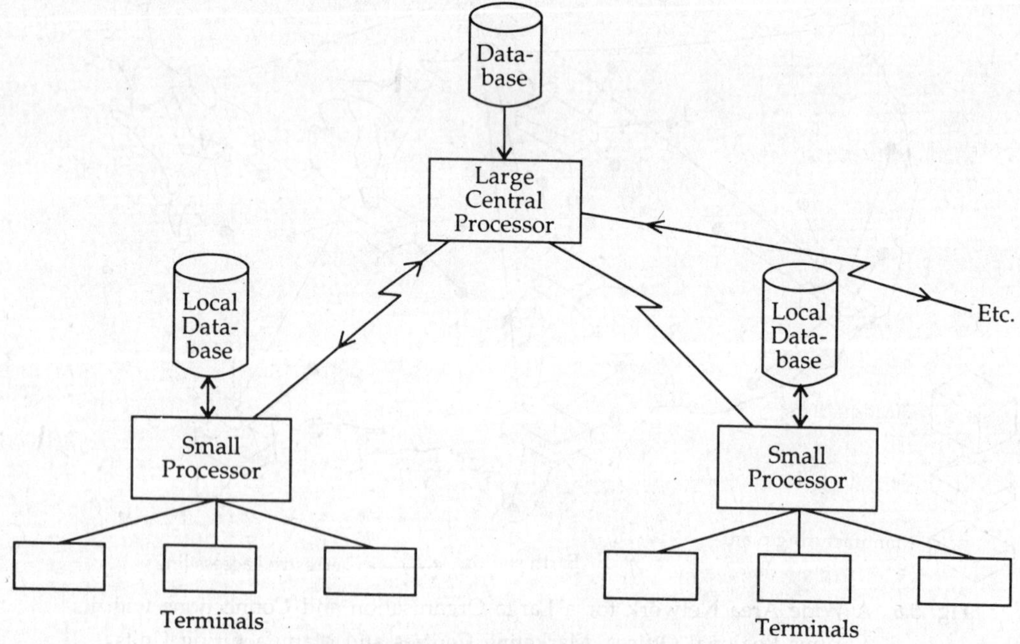

Fig. 5.7 Distributed Data Processing

There are a number of variations of distributed systems depending on the distribution of hardware and data:

- Separate computer system in each location
  - — each system has its own data
  - — systems share data
  - — systems share data managed by a designated computer
- Central computer with
  - — input/output devices in other locations connected to central computer
  - — data preparation and data entry equipment at other locations.

When physically separated computers are interconnected through communications facilities, the configuration is called *distributed computing* as shown in Fig. 5.6.

Alternatively, there may be a ring structure of minicomputers of equal power and no large central processor. Each minicomputer does local processing and accesses data from the other locations as required. The way a distributed processing system is configured usually depends on the needs of the application.

There are several advantages of distributed computing over a centralised computer. Since the bulk of computing is performed at the local site, communication costs can be considerably reduced. Also, if one processor does not function, its processing can be shifted to other processors, and there is minimal disturbance to the entire system. On the other hand, if a central computer 'goes down', all processing stops. In case of the hierarchical configuration, users may benefit from local control over a relatively inexpensive system and still have access to more powerful computers as needed.

5.7. TOPOLOGY OF COMPUTER NETWORKS

A computer network can be configured in many different ways, depending primarily on the applications and geographic locations to be supported. The placement of the nodes

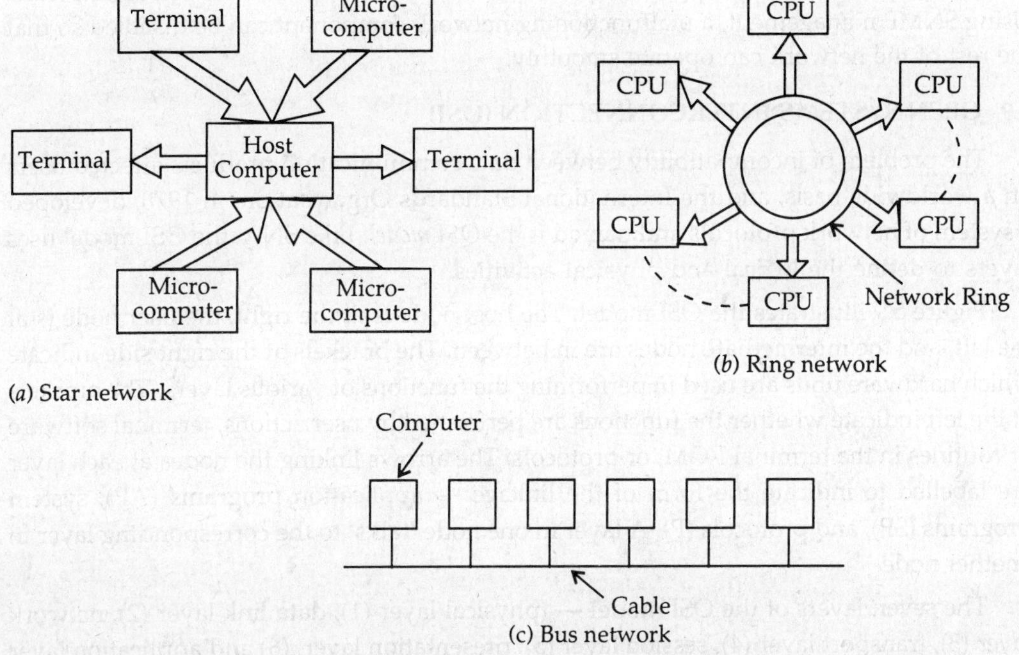

Fig. 5.8 Topology of Computer Network

and the number of alternate communication paths between them determine the configuration. There are three common network topologies: star topology, ring topology and bus topology. In a *star network*, all messages are received by the central computer and switched to the proper location; this process is called **message switching.** In the *ring network*, messages are passed from one node to another in a given direction. In a *bus network*, network may be structured to have multiple access paths between any two nodes. The control and management of a bus network is usually more complicated than a star or ring network. Figure 5.8 shows the three configurations.

5.8. PROTOCOLS AND NETWORK ARCHITECTURE

When two devices are communicating, there must be agreement as to the meaning of control information being sent with the data and agreement as to how the control information and data shall be packaged. Thus, protocols are the rules and formats that ensure efficient and error-free electronic communication.

A protocol has three major components: a set of characters having same meaning to the sender and to the receiver; a set of rules for timing and sequencing messages; and a set of methods for detecting and correcting errors. Some popular protocols are: TCP/IP (Transmission Contorl Protocol/Internet Protocol), Systems Network Architecture (SNA), System Application Architecture (SAA), XMODEM, YMODEM, and Kermit.

A *network architecture* is a set of standards, or protocols, for telecommunication hardware and software. It is intended to maximize modularity, user-friendliness, reliability, and ease of network maintenance. Also, it must establish standards for all its elements: the hardware, the software, and the user interface.

The simple network management protocol (SNMP) is a popular network architecture. Using SNMP management, a malfunctioning network component can be disabled so that the rest of the network can operate smoothly.

5.9. OPEN SYSTEMS INTERCONNECTION (OSI)

The problem of incompatibility between data communication products affected users on a worldwide basis, and the International Standards Organisation, in 1978, developed a system of network protocols and named it the *OSI model.* Like SNA, the OSI model uses layers to define the logical and physical activities.

Figure 5.9 illustrates the OSI model. The host node is at the right, the user node is at the left, and the intermediate nodes are in between. The brackets at the right side indicate which hardware units are used in performing the functions of various layers. The brackets at the left indicate whether the functions are performed by user actions, terminal software or routines in the terminal ROM, or protocols. The arrows linking the nodes at each layer are labelled to indicate the form of the linkage — application programs (AP), system programs (SP), and protocols (P). A layer in one node 'talks' to the corresponding layer in another node.

The seven layers of the OSI model — (physical layer (1), data link layer (2), network layer (3), transport layer (4), session layer (5), presentation layer, (6) and application layer (7) — are identified and the functions of each layer are given.

1. *Physical layer.* Transmits the data from one node to another.

2. *Data link layer.* Formats the data into a record called a **frame** and performs error detection.

3. *Network layer.* Causes the physical layer to transfer the frames from node to node.

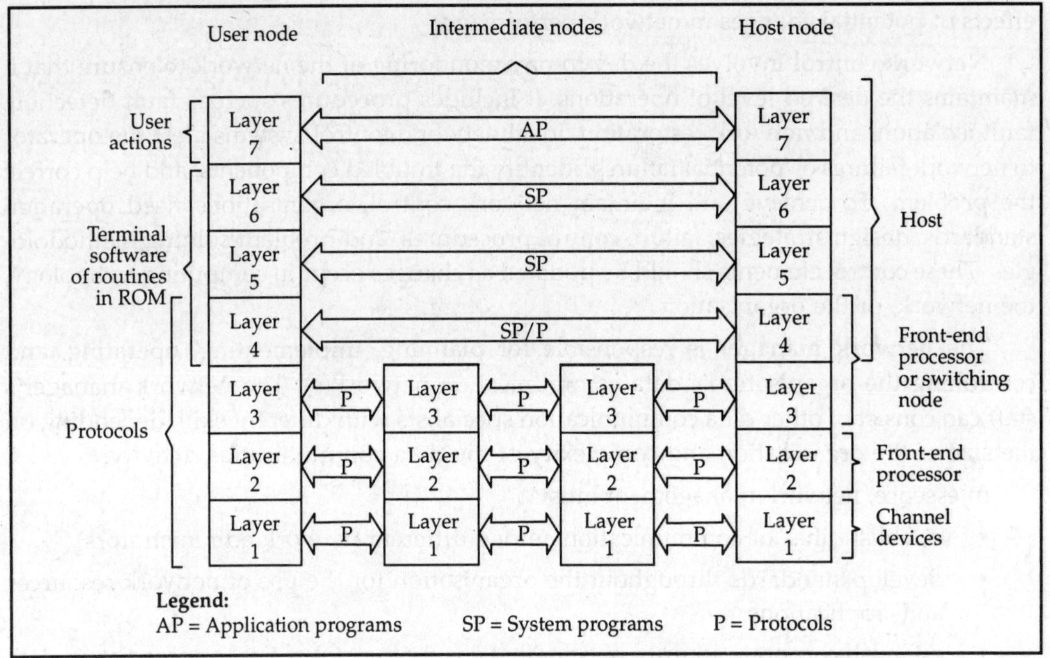

Fig. 5.9 Topology of Computer Network

4. *Transport layer.* Enables the user and host nodes to communicate with each other. It also synchronises fast- and slow-speed equipment as well as overburdened and idle units.

5. *Session layer.* Initiates, maintains, and terminates each session. A **session** consists of all the frames that compose a particular activity, plus signals that identify the beginning and end. A session is like a telephone call that begins with 'hello' and ends with 'good-bye'. Standard log-on and user identification routines are used to initiate data communication sessions.

6. *Presentation layer.* Formats the data for presentation to the user or the host.

7. *Application layer.* Controls user input from the terminal and executes the user's application program in the host.

It is observed that the bottom three layers appear in all nodes, but the upper four layers appear in only the host and user nodes. Layer 1 is the only layer that physically exists. The other layers use the physical layer for transmission of their signals.

5.10. NETWORK MANAGEMENT

Networks are the nervous system of the organisation's operations, and failures can cost crores of rupees every minute if the network is out of service. Network management is aimed at reducing the opportunity for network failures, primarily through planning and control.

Network planning consists of all of the activity aimed at anticipating the organisation's network needs. It includes *three* main components — capacity planning, staff planning, and performance monitoring. **Capacity planning** analyses and plans for traffic volumes that the network can handle. **Staff planning** helps determine the number of persons necessary to manage a network and their required level of expertise. **Performance monitoring** includes analysing response times for a given level of traffic to anticipate the effects of potential changes in network performance.

Network control involves the day-to-day monitoring of the network to ensure that it maintains the desired level of operations. It includes procedures such as fault detection, fault isolation, and network restoration. Ideal network control systems alert the operator to network failures or potential failures, identify the troubled components, and help correct the problem. To achieve and maintain network control, organisations need operation standards, design strategies, failure control procedures, and problem-solving methodologies. These control elements should be updated as changes occur in computing technology, the network, or the organisation.

The **network manager** is responsible for planning, implementing, operating, and controlling the organisation's data communication network(s). The network manager's staff can consist of other data communication specialists with different skill, depending on the size of the organisation and complexity of the data communication activity.

In essence, network management must:

- establish lines of communication among different network administrators.
- develop standards throughout the organisation for the use of network resources and applications.
- establish corporate security policies that ensure that: (*a*) critical or proprietary data are well protected; (*b*) network configuration is carefully documented, (*c*) distributed to all network managers, and (*d*) updated frequently.
- establish backup procedures for all corporate data and strictly enforce backup policies.
- eliminate or at least reduce redundancies in firm's databases.

Global networks. Global networks is difficult to manage not simply because of their size and technical complexity, but also because of a number of uncontrollable factors, such as poor infrastructure, monopolistic rules and regulations, and a different set of business ethics, come into play. A local presence in the countries where they operate is fundamental to their success; further, the best way to acquire and coordinate accurate and timely information from business units in different countries is through global networks. Inspite of many challenges, some organisations are building global networks. They are coming up with creative solutions, such as forming alliances with telecommunication carriers in different countries or building private networks. Everyone is fully aware that, as the world becomes a smaller place and electronic commerce becomes a common phenomenon, global networks will be a necessity.

Internet. The internet is a network of networks that serves as a storehouse of information on diverse topics and is often cited as an excellent model of the information superhighway. It allows millions of people all over the world to exchange and share ideas and information, and send messages to one another, around the clock. Some important tools on the Net are information retrieval tools (ftp and Gopher), communication tools (E-mail, Telnet, and Usenet), multimedia tools (World Wide Web), and information search tools [Wide Area Information Server (WAIS), Archie, and Veronica]. Many organisations set up a 'home page' on the Net which allows potential or existing customers to electronically view the products, services and other related news.

Electronic Data Interchange (EDI). EDI is a direct computer-to-computer exchange of data over a telecommunications network, thus eliminating the need for retyping data. Although EDI has been around for a long time, in recent years, many organisations are using EDI as a way to reduce processing errors and cut operating costs. Costs associated with EDI are software, hardware, VAN charges, software interface, program maintenance, and process reengineering. EDI is a powerful technology because it can create meaningful partnerships and replace sluggish bureaucracies with responsive organisations.

Review Questions

1. What do you understand by data communications ? Support your explanation with illustrative diagram.
2. What are the five components of the basic communication model ? List out sub-components of each component.
3. What device performs the coding and decoding function in a data communication network ? Is it always required ?
4. What is a channel and what are its three characteristics ? Briefly describe each characteristic.
5. What determines the transmission speed of a channel ?
6. What are the three types of transmission direction ? Give an example of each.
7. Explain the difference between common carriers and special-purpose carriers ? In what circumstance an organisation chooses a special-purpose carrier over a common carrier ?
8. What is the difference between bounded and unbounded media ? Outline the three types of bounded media and the four types of unbounded media.
9. Explain each of the four types of unbounded media.
10. Describe the working of a cellular phone system. Why are cellular phones gaining popularity.
11. What is a host computer ? What role does the front-end processor play in a data communication network ? Justify your answer with appropriate illustration.
12. Identify the hardware components of a telecommunication network with a neat diagram. Explain about each component in brief.
13. In what ways data communications software helps ? Outline the points that are normally included in the basic functions of the control software.
14. Explain various types of softwares being used in data communications.
15. Distinguish the five different types of networks. Explain the working of a PBX and mention one or two merits and demerits of this type of network.
16. What does ISDN stand for ? What are the two types of channels included in an ISDN ? Which are transmits data ? What does the other one do ?
17. Outline one five basic operating principles of ISDN. Briefly explain each of them.
18. Explain the working system of a LAN with an illustrative diagram. What is meant by a peer-to-peer relationship ?
19. Explain briefly Ethernet, Token Ring, and Apple Talk.
20. What do LAN, WAN, and VAN stand for ? What are some differences between a LAN and a PBX ? Identify any two advantages of LANs.

21. What are baseband and broadband ? What is the difference between the two ?
22. What are the different methods for setting up a WAN ? Mention some difficulties being faced by a network manager while setting up a WAN.
23. Outline the specialised services provided by VAN to the basic communication services.
24. Classify and explain the three types of network topology, with neat diagram of each topology.
25. Explain distributed data processing system with an appropriate sketch. What are the merits and demerits of the distributed system.
26. Define network architecture. Mention three characteristics of a protocol and the need for these protocols. Name any one protocol.
27. What does OSI stand for ? Illustrate and explain how many layers of the OSI model connect all nodes. How many layers transmit data ?
28. What are seven layers of the OSI ? Explain each of them in brief.
29. What are the three main components of network planning ? Explain each of them.
30. What are the essential requirements expected from network management.
31. Explain briefly about global networks, internet and EDI.
32. How does data communications provide flexibility in carrying out the firm's decision-making philosophy ?

6

Database Management Technology

6.1. INTRODUCTION

A *database* is a centrally controlled, integrated collection of logically organised data to manage an organisation. It excludes transient data such as input documents, reports and results obtained during processing. A database models the data resource of an organisation using the relationship between different data items. The model is independent of any application program.

Database contains data, not information. By itself, the database is meaningless. With some assertions about the meaning of the data and some rules for processing the data, one is able to produce information from the database. Management can act upon information. Thus, through proper design and use of the database, it can be an essential tool for producing information for making management decisions.

Since databases are large and the queries asked are varied, it is impossible to process such queries correctly and ensure a reasonably fast response time. To meet the specific requirement of fast and accurate access to large databases, use of computers is at the core of modern database technology. When access is to be extended to several users simultaneously, database technology meets such demanding requirements efficiently.

6.2. DATA *vs.* INFORMATION

Although the terms *data* and *information* are sometimes used interchangeably, they have distinct implications in the study of information systems. Data consists of numbers, letters, symbols, raw facts, events and transactions which have been recorded but not yet processed into a form which is suitable for making decisions. It is known that when data are processed, they become information only when they are presented to the decision maker in a meaningful manner. Note that only when the input (data) is accurate, timely and reliable, the output (information) will be useful and reliable. The GIGO principle (Garbage-In-Garbage-Out) was formulated as a warning about data because bad data cannot provide useful information, irrespective of the manner it is processed. There are many disadvantages to poor data quality. Many organisations are spending 30% to 40% of information systems time on data correction and revision, which is an enormous waste of resources. Therefore, it is essential to continuously monitor the quality of data, establish a continuous process of data improvement, and educate users about the impact of low-quality data.

Any data to be useful in decision making must meet three main criteria:

(*a*) It must be accessible to the people who need it;

(*b*) It must be well organised, cross-referenced, and efficiently managed; and

(*c*) It must be easy to create, update and maintain.

The basic qualities of good information are that it should be : complete, relevant, timely, accurate, understandable, significant, communicated to the right person, and communicated via an appropriate channel.

6.3. DATA HIERARCHY

Data and information are stored in computer files for processing, retrieval, and dissemination. If data files are not carefully organised and managed, decision makers will not be able to find the data when they need it. While many organisations are good at collecting data, only few organisations are good at *managing* their data and making it accessible to decision makers in a timely and useful manner.

The data in a computer system are organised in a hierarchy, known as the *data hierarchy chain.* The hierarchy, in ascending order, includes bits, bytes, fields, records, files, and databases. Hence, a database is made up of records, records consist of fields, fields contain bytes, and bytes are made up of bits. An example, showing the relationship among these elements, is shown in Fig. 6.1.

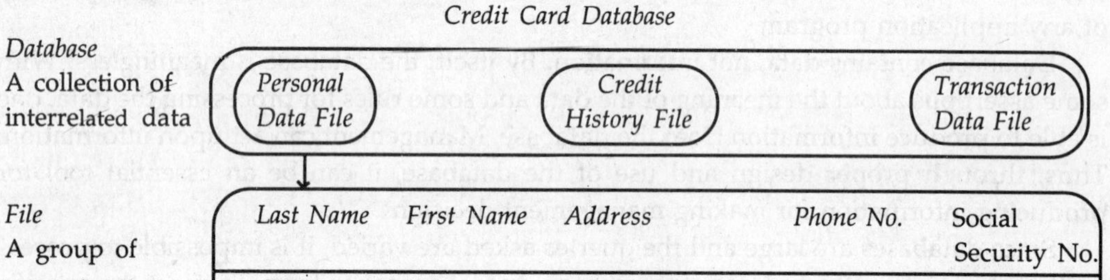

Credit Card Database

Database
A collection of interrelated data

Personal Data File | *Credit History File* | *Transaction Data File*

File
A group of interrelated records

Last Name	*First Name*	*Address*	*Phone No.*	Social Security No.
GUPTA	Udit	188A/238 Lake Gardens Calcutta-700045	033-4177861	19-00003466

Record

Gupta	Udit	188A/238 Lake Gardens Calcutta-700045	033-4177861	19-00003466

Field
Gupta (Last Name)
Udit (First Name)
188A/238 Lake Gardens, Calcutta-700045 (Address)
033-4177861 (Phone Number)
19-00003466 (Social Security Number)

Byte
| U | d | i | t |

Bit
0 (or 1)

Fig. 6.1 A Database Hierarchy for a Credit Card Company

A *bit* is a value that represents the presence/absence of an electronic signal and is represented as a 1 or 0 — an on-off switch. Eight bits make up a *byte* and a byte is required to represent a character (numeric, alphabetic, and so on) in a computer. For example, six bytes are required to represent the name Pragya in a computer. Since each character is represented using 8 bits, the name Pragya requires 48 bits. A meaningful group of characters/bytes is referred to as a *field*. For example, Pragya's last name, first name, and phone number are three fields. A group of interrelated fields is called a *record*. Thus, Pragya's last name, first name, phone number, identity number, and home address can make up a record because they constitute relevant data about Pragya. Record can alternately be viewed as a description of an entity (*e.g.*, Pragya). An entity can be a person, a place, a thing. The characteristics of the entity are called *attributes.* Pragya can be described by using attributes such as her phone number, identity number, gender, and so on; the value of each attribute can be found by referring to the relevant field. Each record must contain at least one field that uniquely identifies the entity.

A *file* is a collection of records of the same type grouped together. An integrated repository of logically related data that facilitates easy access and processing of data is called a *database.* The personnel data file, the employee benefits file, and the employee salary file are a group of interrelated files that provide information about employees, and hence can be brought together as a database. On the other hand, employees benefit file, suppliers' addresses file and an organisation's inventory file would not make a good database as these files are not interrelated.

6.4. METHODS FOR ORGANISING DATA IN FILES

A number of methods are available to organise data in files. The choice of the method is based on the factors such as storage media, access methods, processing techniques, etc. Here three file organisation methods are discussed. These are: sequential file organisation, direct file organisation, and indexed sequential file organisation.

6.4.1. Sequential File Organisation

In sequential file organisation, records are written and stored on a secondary storage device (such as a magnetic tape or magnetic disk) in the same sequence in which they were collected. The records are arranged in order using a unique key (such as identity number) and are physically adjacent to one another. Although sequentially organised files can be stored in different types of storage media, magnetic tape is the most popular storage medium for this type of data organisation. Figure 6.2 shows a sequential file organisation. If one desires to retrieve record 199 out of 200, records 1 through 198 must be read first.

Fig. 6.2 Sequential File Organisation

It is necessary that data sequencing and ordering must be done before the file is created, because the ordering of data cannot be changed when the file is processed. When records are modified, the entire file must be rearranged. This may be a time-consuming task.

Sequential file organisation is well suited to batch processing applications, such as payroll. This method uses very little storage space and is useful for applications in which records have to be retrieved in the same order every time the file is processed.

6.4.2. Direct File Organisation

Direct file organisation allows data to be retrieved quickly in a random manner, irrespective the manner in which the data were originally stored. A unique key is used to organise files (such as identity number), which is converted directly to a memory address, using a mathematical formula, called a *hashing algorithm.*

For this type of file organisation, the magnetic disk is ideally suited and many applications today use some form of direct file organisation. They are particularly well suited to quickly retrieve a single record. Figure 6.3 shows the direct file organisation. In this method, the computer goes directly to Record 199 and the hashing algorithm identifies the secondary storage address.

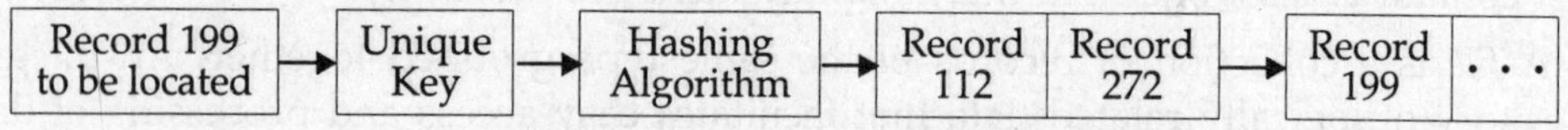

Fig. 6.3 Direct File Organisation

6.4.3. Indexed-sequential File Organisation

In this method, data are stored in a sequence (as in sequential method), but an index is created additionally which shows the memory address of each data. A file index shows the memory address or physical location of each data, making it easier and quicker to access data. Figure 6.4 shows indexed-sequential file organisation. Here the computer goes directly to Record 199. It refers to an index to locate the memory address for Record 199 and retrieves it from that address.

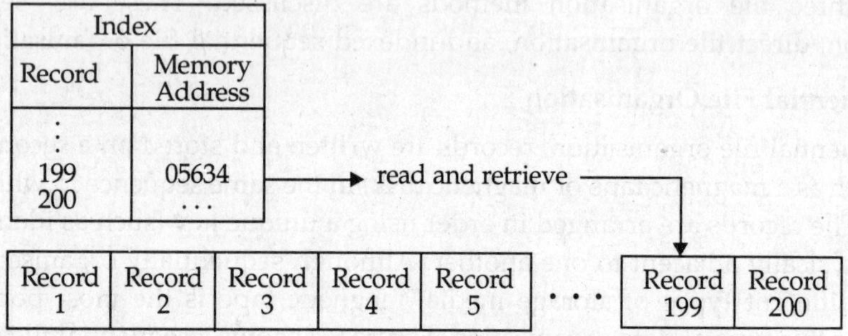

Fig. 6.4 Indexed-sequential File Organisation

Table 6.1 shows the organisation of files in three different ways before the evolution of databases.

Table 6.1. Summary of Methods for File Organisation

Type of File	*File Organisation*
Sequential	Data are stored sequentially based on a unique key. They are accessed in the order in which they are stored.
Direct	The memory address of the data is identified using the hashing algorithm and this accelerates the process of retrieving data.
Indexed-sequential	Data are stored based on a unique key and can be accessed directly. The location of the data is identified using an index.

6.5. LIMITATIONS OF FILE-BASED SYSTEMS

Conventionally data were stored and processed using file processing systems. Nowadays, databases are preferred because of many drawbacks in file processing system. Each file is independent of (or unrelated to) other files, and data in different files can be integrated only be writing individual program for each application. Also, the data and the application that uses the data are so arranged that any change to the data requires changing all the programs that uses the data. This is because each file is 'hard-coded' with specific information such as data type, data length, and so on. Many times it is even difficult to identify all the programs using that data. Therefore, this is often done on a trial-and-error basis.

Following are the main disadvantages when this approach is used:

1. Data redundancy
2. Data integrity
3. Data availability
4. Management control.

In *data redundancy,* data may be duplicated, and the same data resides in several files. This results in wasted storage, difficulty in updating and maintaining files, and inconsistency of data values, leading to poor decisions. *Data integrity* problem arises due to updating of one file while another file containing the same record may not be updated. *Data availability* problem comes due to non-uniformity in file design. *Management control* problem arises when organisations grow in size and the volume and complexities of their data increase. In such cases, files become more difficult to maintain and less reliable.

Databases and systems to manage databases overcomes most of the limitations of file processing systems as databases are independent of the application programs that access and process the files.

Figure 6.5 shows a file processing system. Each functional area in the organisation creates, processes and disseminates its own files. Files such as inventory and payroll generate separate files and do not communicate with each other.

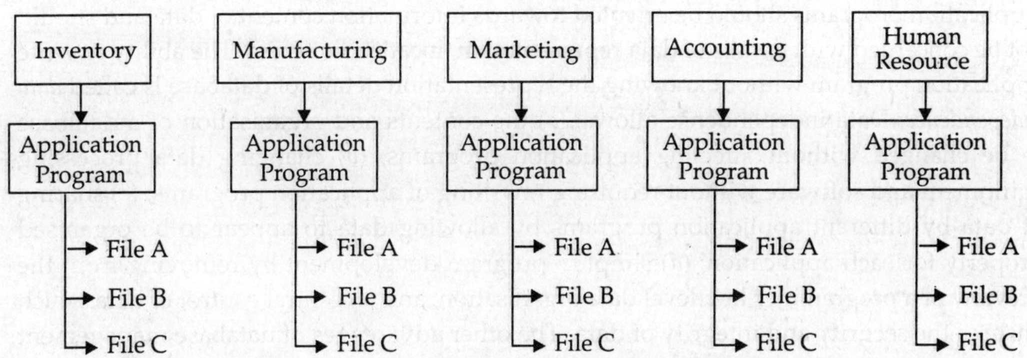

Fig. 6.5 File Processing System

6.6. DATABASE AND DATABASE MANAGEMENT SYSTEMS

A *database* is an integrated repository of logically related data, organised in such a way as to facilitate easy accessing and processing of data. It excludes transient data such as input documents, reports and intermediate results obtained during processing. A database models the data resource of an organisation using the relationships between different data items. The model is independent of any application program. Database systems require the use of direct access storage devices.

Database management systems (DBMS) are support programs that work in conjunction with the operating system to create, process, store, retrieve, control and manage data. Table 6.2 shows the primary functions of a DBMS. The DBMS acts as an interface between the application program (say, payroll) and the data in the database (say, employee records).

Hence, if a user wants to retrieve the employment number of an employee, the DBMS locates the data and displays it for the user.

Table 6.2. Five Primary Functions of a DBMS

Function	*Application*
1. Define, create and organise a database	1. Establish the logical relationships among different data elements in a database and define schemas and sub-schemas using the data definition language.
2. Input data	2. Enter data into the database through an input device, such as a data screen, a touch screen, or a voice-activated system.
3. Process data	3. Process and manipulate data using the data manipulation language.
4. Maintain data integrity and security	4. Limit database access to authorised users.
5. Query database	5. Provide decision makers with information they need to make dependable decisions. Query the database using structured query language.

6.6.1. Advantages of Databases over Traditional Files

One of the main advantages of a DBMS is *data independence*, which means that a user can have access of data based simply on its contents and its associations with other data. Application programs should be oriented towards information content of data and should not be concerned with details of data representation, location or access. The ability to write application program without knowing the representation details of database is called *data independence.* Data independence allows: (*a*) the contents and organisation of a database to be changed without affecting application programs; (*b*) changing data processing equipment and software without requiring rewriting of application programs; (*c*) sharing of data by different application programs by allowing data to appear to be organised properly for each application; (*d*) simplify program development by removing from the preview of a programmer low-level data organisation; and (*e*) central control of data which ensures the security and integrity of data. The other advantages of database management are:

(*a*) Control redundancy;

(*b*) Relating data items;

(*c*) Data integrity;

(*d*) Data security;

(*e*) Database performance; and

(*f*) Management controls.

6.6.2. Disadvantages of Databases

The primary disadvantage of a database is that it requires considerable outlay of resources. Mainframe hardware is expensive and although today there are a number of PC-based databases, multiple copies of the software, combined with training, can become an expensive proposition.

6.6.3. Data Management

The data management activities include:

(*a*) **Data collection:** The necessary data is collected and recorded on a form called a *source document* that serves as input to the system. For example, data describing a sale is entered on a sales order form.

(*b*) **Integrity and verification:** The data is examined to assure its consistency and accuracy based on prescribed constraints and rules.

(*c*) **Storage:** The data is stored on some medium such as magnetic tape or magnetic disk.

(*d*) **Maintenance:** New data is added, existing data is changed, and data no longer needed is deleted for keeping the data resource current.

(*e*) **Security:** The data is safeguarded to prevent destruction, damage, or misuse.

(*f*) **Organisation:** The data is arranged in such a way as to meet the information needs to users.

(*g*) **Retrieval:** The data is made available to users.

Prior to the computer era, all of these activities were performed by clerical employees, supported by the primitive punched-card and keydriven machines. Today, people are still required for much data collection and verification, but the computer has taken most of the data management responsibility.

6.6.4. Differences between Databases and Traditional Files

It is to be seen here why the location of data has to be specified in a file processing environment, whereas a database automatically retrieves the data. The main reason for this difference is that in a DBMS, the logical and physical views of the data are separate, whereas in a file processing environment, the logical and physical views of the data are firmly interwoven.

The *logical view* of data presents the logical relationship between different data elements in a database; the *physical view* shows how the data are physically stored in a storage medium. The managerial personnel are concerned only with the logical relationship between data. For example, a payroll administrator is simply interested to view the relationships among gross pay, taxes, other deductions, and net pay, and is not interested in the memory locations of the data.

A data base *schema* is a logical description of each piece of data and its relationship with other data elements. It does not identify the actual value of data. For examplé, the database schema might include such employee files as retirement, health insurance, or employment test results.

A *subschema* is a subset of the fields and records in a schema. Subschemas provide a user-oriented view of the database. When the user defines the schemas and subschemas, they are automatically generated by the DBMS. Schemas and subschemas increase the efficiency of databases and make them more user-friendly than traditional files. Table 6.3 outlines the differences between flat files and relational databases.

Table 6.3. Differences between Files and Relational Databases

Files	*Relational Databases*
1. Store data in a one-dimensional files.	1. Store data in two-dimensional tables.
2. Store, organise, and retrieve information from one file at a time.	2. Store, organise and retrieve information from tables in which information is linked by a common column or field.
3. Leave the management of data relationships to the applications that access the data.	3. Establish relationships between files and views within the database itself.
4. Require a programmer to write code for data management functions.	4. Consist a database engine that performs different functions.
5. Are typically created and maintained by application programs.	5. Are typically created and maintained by database administrators.
6. Are often associated with older programs on mainframe and mid-range systems.	6. Are popular on UNIX processors and powerful servers within a client/server architectural framework.

6.6.5. Components of a DBMS

A DBMS has three main components. These are the data dictionary system (DDS), data definition language (DDL), and the data manipulation language.

Data dictionary system. The data dictionary is an encyclopaedia of information concerning each data element. It describes the data and its characteristics, such as location, size, and type of data; it identifies the origin, the use, the ownership, and the methods of accessing and securing data. The data dictionary can exist either on paper or as a computer file. When it exists as a file, special software is necessary to create and maintain it, and make it available for use. Such software is called a *data dictionary system* (DDS). DDSs can be acquired as separate software packages or as modules within systems such as DBMSs and computer-aided software engineering tools. Database experts emphasize that it is important to standardise both *data items* and *process terms* in the data dictionary. A good data dictionary would ensure consistent definitions of data across different databases, and if there were a change to the data, it would also identify all the databases affected by the change.

Data definition language. Data definition language (DDL) is used to create and describe the data and define the *schema* in a DBMS. It serves as an interface for application programs that use the data. Once the data dictionary has been created, its definitions must be entered into the DBMS. For example, if a payroll program needs the employment number of an employee, the DDL defines the logical relationship between the employment number and the other data in the database and acts as an interface between the payroll program and the files that contain the employment numbers. Figure 6.6 shows how the DDL uses the data dictionary to produce the schema.

Data manipulation language. A language that processes and manipulates the data in the database is called *data manipulation language* (DML). It also allows the user to query the database and receive summary reports and/or customised reports. DML enables the user to (*a*) access, (*b*) update, (*c*) replace, (*d*) delete and (*e*) protect database records from unauthorised access.

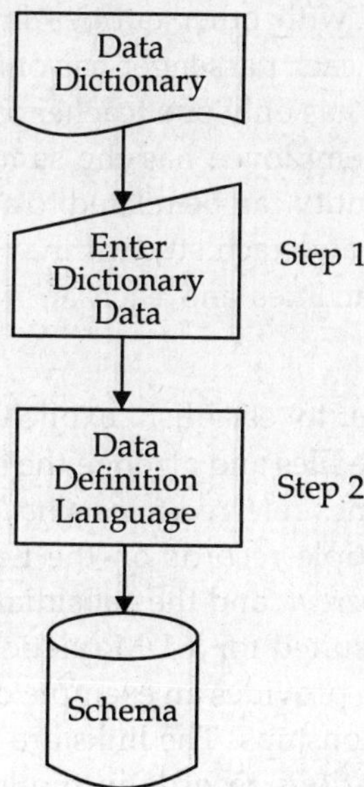

Fig. 6.6 Defining the Database Contents

Unlike other types of high-level programming languages, DDLs and DMLs usually perform specific data functions as part of the software of the database management system. The DML is usually integrated with other programming languages, many of which are 4GLs, to implement sophisticated database functions.

Structured Query Language (SQL). It is a non-procedural language exclusively deals with data: data integrity, data manipulation, data access, data retrieval, data query, and data security. It was developed by the American National Standards Institute. It allows users to elicit responses from their databases to specific queries, both on mainframes and on PCs. Here users can transform their experience from one database system to another without going into much learning.

There are four basic operations in SQL: Select, Update, Insert, and Delete. The Select statement enables users to query the database for specific information; Update, Insert and Delete allow users to update the data, insert new data, and delete existing data, respectively. Two types of questions can be asked by users in SQL: static questions and dynamic questions. Static questions are routine and standardised and once defined, can be used repeatedly for generating weekly, monthly, and quarterly reports. Software packages generating static questions are sometimes referred to as *report writers*. Dynamic questions are ad hoc and specific to the decision maker. Most query tools, today, allow users to ask dynamic questions.

6.6.6. Database Models

A database model is the method of organising data and represents the logical relationships among data elements in the database. Popular database models are **hierarchical models, network models** and **relational models.**

Before explaining the different types of models, it is prerequisite to look at three types of relationships: (*a*) **1-1 (one-to-one)** —This relationship indicates a unique relation between two entities. Examples are: a student and his/her grade; a child and its biological mother; and a person and his employment number; (*b*) **1-M (one-to-many)** — Here an entity can have multiple relationships with other entities in the database. Examples are : an airbus has many passengers, but each passenger has only one flight number; a teacher has many students, but each student has only one teacher for that course; and an organisation has many employees, but each employee has the same organisation title; and (*c*) **M-M (many-to-many)** — Here every entity can be related to a number of entities. Examples are : each teacher has many students and each student may have many teachers; each airport has many airlines that use its facilities and each airline has access to many airports.

Hierarchical Data Model

Hierarchical structure helps to establish explicit or logical relationships among various data elements of multiple files and arrange the elements in a hierarchy. Each 'box' in the model is a record, sometimes referred to as a *node*. In such a model, each record on one level can be related to multiple records on the next-lower level. A record that has subsidiary records is called the *parent*, and the subsidiary records are called *children*. Data elements in this model are well suited for a 1-M relationship with other data elements in the database. Figure 6.7 at the top provides an example of the hierarchical model. Here link fields establish the explicit relationships. The links are represented by the thin lines that connect data elements of the various records in the lower portion. Once a salesperson record is retrieved, the link in that record can lead to another record that is logically related to that salesperson. A link field in the second record leads to a third record, and so on, creating a chain reaction through an entire set of files.

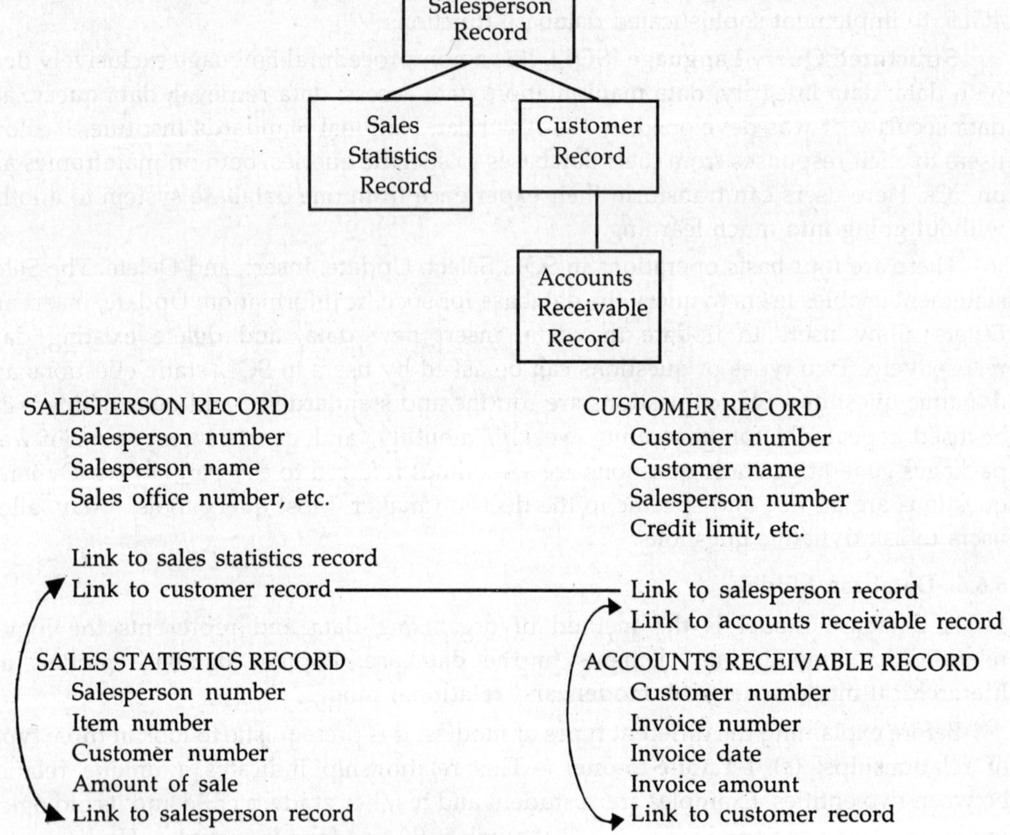

Fig. 6.7 An Example of a Hierarchical Model

The computer retrieve records from the hierarchy through *pointers*, which are pieces of data that identifies the link between different records. The data nodes in a hierarchical database are linked to one another through a series of pointers, one of which is attached to the end of each record in the database.

Advantages and disadvantages. This model is ideally suited for problems in which the data elements have a natural hierarchical structure. Although this model represented a giant step towards eliminating physical constraints, the use of logical relationships has its disadvantages. It is necessary to identify the groups of files that must be logically integrated *before* the database is created. Hence, a hierarchical data model may not always be flexible enough to accommodate the dynamic needs of an organisation.

Network Model

In a network model, each record in a database can have multiple parents, that is, the relationships among data elements can be many-to-many (M-M). Figure 6.8 shows a network model for an inventory system. In network model, databases can be translated from hierarchical form to network form and *vice-versa.* Data elements in a network model are also linked through pointers. The main difference between the network model and the hierarchical model is that in a network model a child can have a number of parents, whereas in a hierarchical model a child can have only one parent.

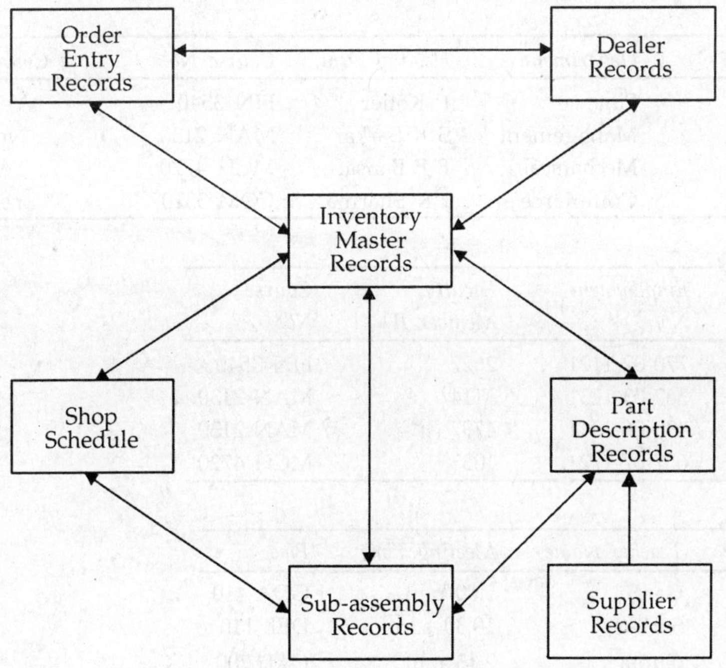

Fig. 6.8 Network Model for an Inventory System

Advantages and disadvantages. The network model promotes flexibility and data accessibility, since data elements at a lower level can be accessed without accessing the data elements above them. This model is efficient, easy to understand, and can be applied to many real-world problems that require routine transactions. Disadvantages of a network model are: (*a*) It is complex to design and develop; (*b*) It has to be fine-tuned frequently so that relationships among different pieces of data are true representations of the real world; (*c*) It requires that the relationships among all data elements be defined before development starts, and changes often demand a major programming efforts; and (*d*) For large databases, operation and maintenance of the network model are time-consuming and expensive.

An example of a network DBMS is Integrated Database Management Systems.

Relational Model

In relational model, data is represented using two-dimensional tables, called *relations* or *flat files*, which are made up of columns and rows. Each column represents a field, also referred to as an attribute; each row represents a record, also referred to as a *tuple*. Relational databases are a popular way of organising data for business needs because of their flexibility. The main advantage of this model over others is that it can relate data in a table to data in any other table as long as the two tables (or files) *share at least one common attribute.* Most commercial databases for microcomputers use relational databases.

Relational databases use three fundamental operations: Select, Project and Join. The Select operation is a horizontal cut so that only selected rows (records) are included in the query results. The Project operation creates a subset of columns (or a new table) designed to meet the information needs of the user. The Join operation joins, or links, two or more tables, if the information requested by the user is not found in one table.

Some popular relational databases are Access (Microsoft), dbase IV, and DB 2 (IBM).

Figure 6.9 shows a relational database with three tables: Institute, Faculty, and Course. In the figure, each column (*e.g.*, Course No.) is a field and each row (*e.g.*, MAN 2130) is a record, or tuple.

Institute Table

Institute	*Department*	*Head of Dept.*	*Course No.*	*Core Course*
Business	Finance	P Kotler	FIN 3540	Yes
Business	Management	S K Sarkar	MAN 2130	No
Engineering	Mechanical	B B Bansal	MCH 4720	Yes
Commercial	Commerce	J K Sharma	COM 3310	Yes

Faculty Table

Name of Faculty	*Employment No.*	*Faculty Member ID*	*Course No.*
Gupta	770-02-1121	2627	FIN 3540
Garg	362-03-1231	3114	MAN 2130
Banerjee	435-06-1341	4797	MAN 2130
Sarkar	657-07-1721	1033	MCH 4720

Course Table

Course No.	*Teacher Name*	*Meeting Time*	*Place*
MAN 2130	Garg	5.00 p.m.	GOA 410
MCH 4720	Sarkar	10.30 a.m.	DEL 110
FIN 3540	Gupta	2.15 p.m.	CAL 700

Fig. 6.9 An Example of a Relational Model

Advantages and disadvantages. Two major advantages of a relational model are: (*a*) It enables a computer system to accommodate a variety of file inquiries in an efficient manner; and (*b*) Additional indexes can be constructed at a later point of time as new data processing requirements dictate. Three major disadvantages of relational model are: (*a*) The index portion of the file must be created and maintained along with the file records themselves. This means two separate files are created, only one of which stores user information; (*b*) In some cases, the index file portion of the file may be larger than the file itself. This wastes storage space; and (*c*) The file index must be searched sequentially before the actual file records are obtained. This wastes time. Table 6.4 summarizes the advantages and disadvantages of three data models.

Table 6.4. Advantages and Disadvantages of Three Data Models

Data Model	*Advantages*	*Disadvantages*
Hierarchical	• Some problems lend themselves to this model • Easy to understand • Continues to be widely used	• Difficult to access values at lower levels • Changes to the model require extensive programming
Network	• Easy access to data • Flexible	• Complex to design and develop • Large models consume a great deal of computer memory
Relational	• Widely used • Easy to understand • Provides excellent support for ad hoc queries • Users need not consider issues such as storage structure and access strategy.	• Relatively slow to execute for large databases • Data redundancy

Large databases are difficult to deal with by all three data models discussed. Most databases are considered large when they reach tens to gigabytes in size.

6.7 OBJECT-ORIENTED DATABASE STRUCTURE

Object-oriented database model is one of the important technologies of a new generation of multimedia web-based applications. An *object* consists of data values describing the attributes of an entity, and the operations that can be performed upon the data. This *encapsulation* capability allows the object-oriented model to better handle more complex types of data (graphics, pictures, voice, text) than other database structure. An example of object, from the customer and bank viewpoints, is shown below :

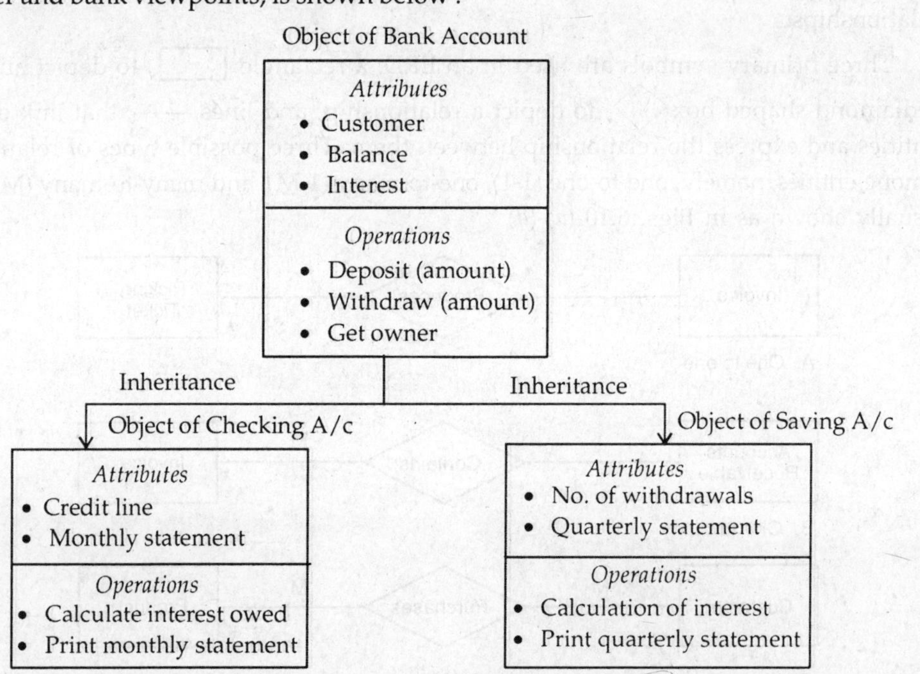

The object-oriented model also supports that new objects can be automatically created by replicating some or all of the characteristics of one or more *parent* objects. In the above example, checking and savings account objects can both inherit common attributes and operations of the bank account object. Such types of capabilities have made *object-oriented database management systems* (OODBMS) popular in computer-aided design and a number of other applications. Another similar example of object technology is to allow designers to develop product design, store them as objects in an object-oriented database, and replicate and modify them to create new product designs. Apart from this, multimedia Web-based applications for the Internet and corporate intranets and extranets have become a major application area for object technology.

6.8. ENTITY RELATIONSHIP DIAGRAM

An entity-relationship diagram (ERD) is a graphical tool that identifies and represents the entities in an enterprise or system and the logical relationships among those entities. It is useful to capture the data elements in a system. ERD uses three features to describe data: *Entity, Relationships* and *Attributes.* An **entity** can be (*a*) an environmental element, (*b*) a resource, or (*c*) a transaction, which is of such importance to the enterprise that it is documented with data. Examples of entity types are teachers, students, administrators, courses and classrooms in a college. A **relationship** is the way entities interact with one another. Since entities are linked to each other through relationships, a graphical tool that depicts the entities and their interrelationships plays a useful role in gaining a better understanding of the 'big picture'. An **attribute** is an item of data that describes an entity. The attributes are actually data elements, and each is given a single value, called the *attribute value.* Attributes that serve to identify the entity are called *identifiers.* An example is customer number. Other attributes describe the entity, and they are called *descriptors.* Examples are customer name and territory.

An ERD represents static data and is used for many modelling tasks, such as modelling an enterprise, its entities, and the relationships among them. It also plays an important role in the design and development of information systems. The ERD is a useful tool in the logical design of a database, because it graphically portrays the entities and their relationships.

Three primary symbols are used in an ERD: a rectangle ▭, to depict an entity; a diamond-shaped box ◇, to depict a relationship; and lines, ——, that link different entities and express the relationship between them. Three possible types of relationships among entities, namely, one-to-one (1-1), one-to-many (1-M), and many-to-many (M-M), are usually shown as in Figs. 6.10 (*a*)-(*d*).

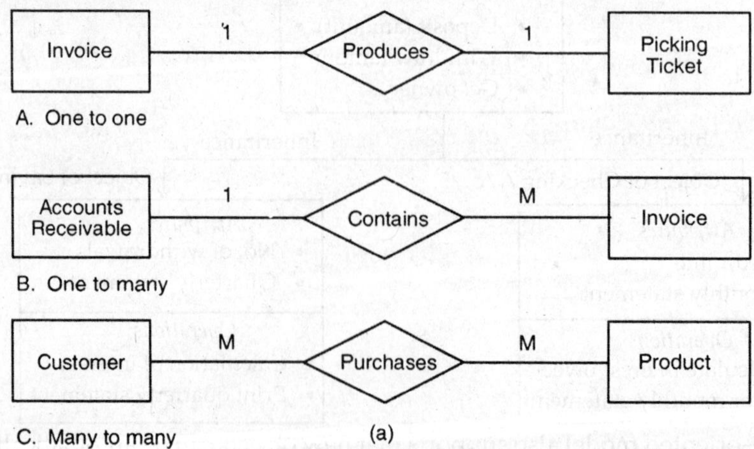

(a)

Supplier Number
Supplier
1
Fills
M
Purchase Order Number
Purchase Order
M
Contains
M
Raw Material
Item Number
M
Represents
1
Supplier Number
Accounts Payable

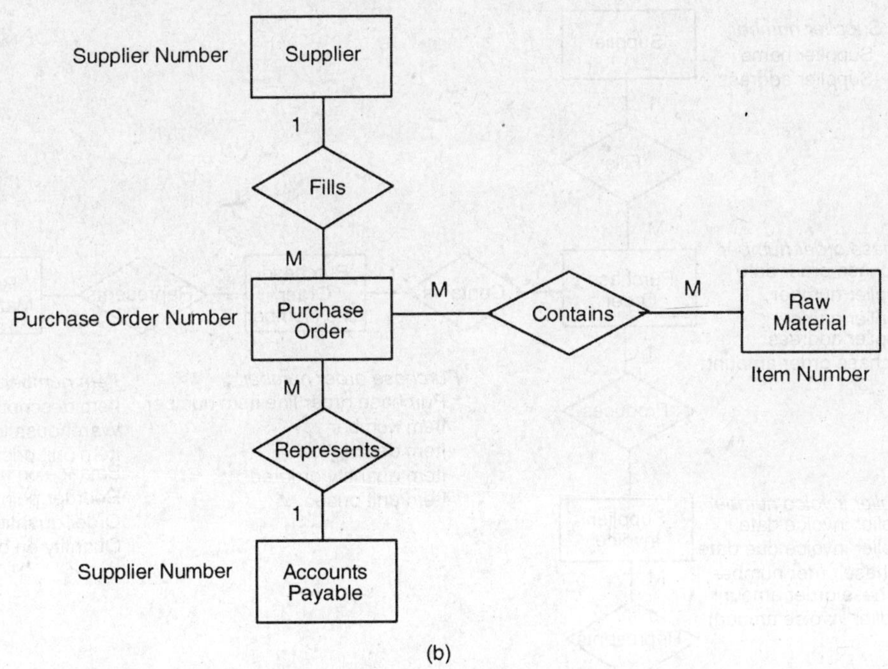

(b)

Supplier number
Supplier name
Supplier address
Supplier
1
Fills
M
Purchase order number
Purchase order rate
Supplier number
Supplier name
Supplier address
Item number (occurs n times)
Item description (occurs n times)
Item quantity ordered (occurs n times)
Item unit price (occurs n times)
Item extended price (occurs n times)
Purchase order amount
Purchase Order
M
Contains
M
Raw Material
Item number
Item description
Warehouse location
Item unit price
Balance on hand
Reorder point
Order quantity
Quantity on order
1
Represents
1
Supplier number
Supplier name
Supplier address
Total amount payable
Accounts Payable

(c)

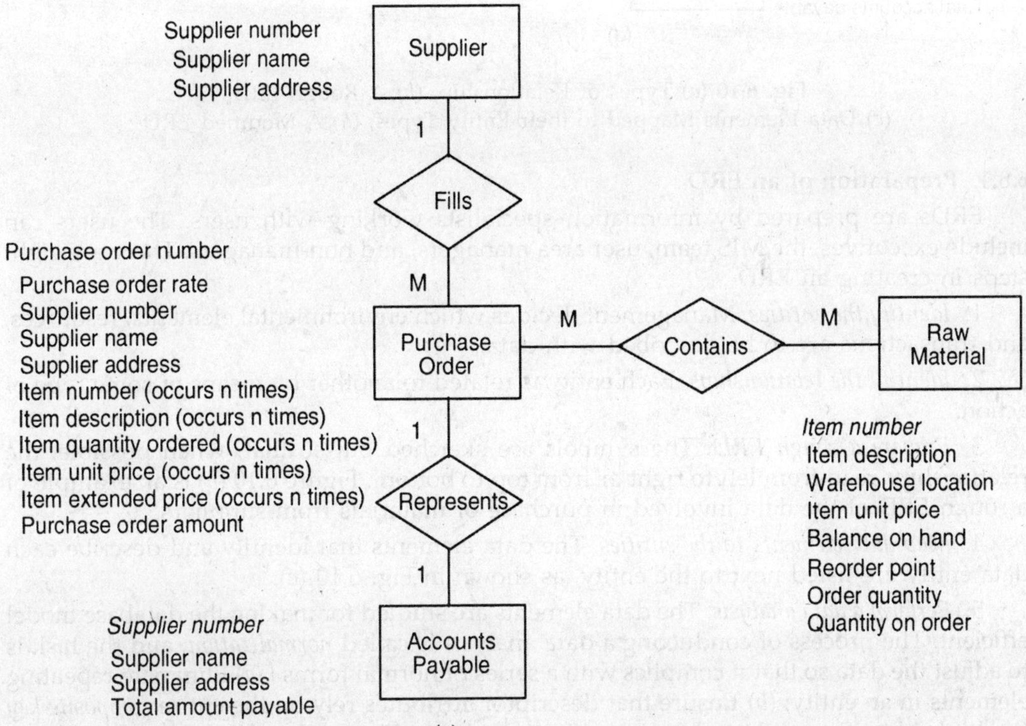

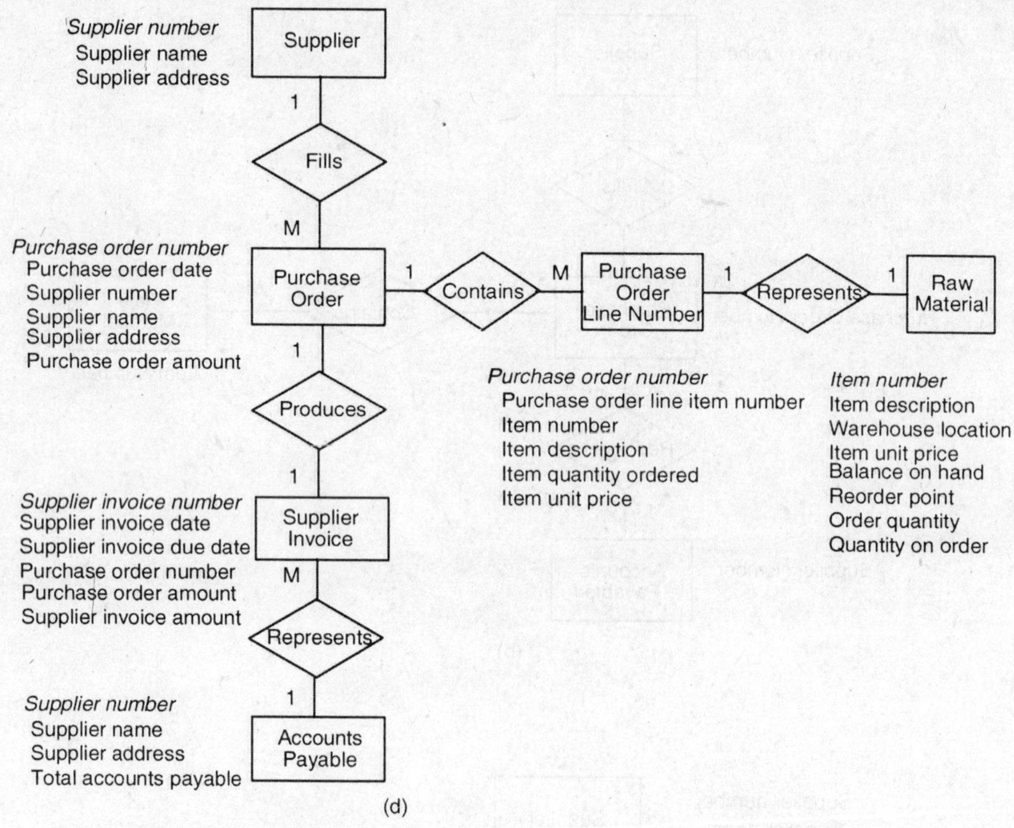

Fig. 6.10 (*a*) Types of Relationship, (*b*) A Rough ERD, (*c*) Data Elements Mapped to their Entity Types, (*d*) A Modified ERD

6.8.1. Preparation of an ERD

ERDs are prepared by information specialists working with users. The users can include executives, the MIS team, user area managers, and non-managers. There are eight steps in creating an ERD :

1. *Identify the entities.* Management decides which environmental elements, resources, and transactions are to be described with data.

2. *Identify the relationships.* Each entity is related to another by means of some type of action.

3. *Prepare a rough ERD.* The symbols are sketched out so that, when possible, the relationships read from left to right or from top to bottom. Figure 6.10 (*b*) is an example of a rough ERD of the data involved in purchase of materials from suppliers.

4. *Map data elements to the entities.* The data elements that identify and describe each data entity are listed next to the entity, as shown in Fig. 6.10 (*c*).

5. *Perform a data analysis.* The data elements are studied for making the database model efficient. The process of conducting a data analysis is called *normalization*, and the task is to adjust the data so that it complies with a series of normal forms : (*a*) Eliminate repeating elements in an entity; (*b*) Ensure that descriptor attributes rely on the entire *composite key* (multiple identifier attributes) for identification; and (*c*) Ensure that the values of attributes do not rely on the values of other attributes in the same entity.

6. *Prepare a modified ERD*. The results of the data analysis are incorporated into a new ERD.

7. *Review the ERD with users and revise*. The information specialist reviews the diagram with executives, managers, and non-managers in the user area and revise it when necessary.

Since ERD was introduced in the mid 1970s, it has now become a useful tool for conceptualising the contents of a database. The best ERD approach is to use it at the enterprise or business level. However, such an approach demands a commitment from top management to engage in strategic planning for information resources and participate in data modelling.

6.9 FOURTH GENERATION LANGUAGES (4GLs)

These are high level user-friendly fourth generation languages. These are designed for end users who write programs to query or extract information from a database. These 4GLs typically include SQL as their core product. Since SQL lacks formatting features, 4GLs provide formatting to produce quality reports. Many of the 4GLs also provide a means of quick application for user input and some other form screens for user output. By filling, full or in part, the input screen, the required outputs can be generated even by an occasional end user, who may be a novice to computers and databases.

Facilities exist to edit/format the user data (case conversion, numeric/character alignment), database validation (alpha, numeric, range check), database look-up and feedback.

6.10. RECENT DEVELOPMENT IN DATABASES

6.10.1. Distributed Databases

A distributed database is a database distributed over single- or multi-vendor computer hardware located in different geographic areas. Examples are: Network of bank transactions/credit; a network of libraries; and a network of corporate offices across the country. Distributed databases have become popular in recent years because of two main reasons. First, earlier many organisations created individual databases for different applications, such as, payroll, personnel data, employee benefits and so on. Unfortunately, many of these databases could not communicate with one another because they were created on different systems. Distributed databases provide a way to overcome this problem. Second, the business units of an enterprise may be geographically dispersed and the information needs and demands of each location may be very different. Distributed databases help to store the data where it is most needed or used, and help to customise the data to meet the needs of individual business units.

6.10.2. Client-Server Architecture

With client-server architecture, a network user can initiate several client processes in many windows among many servers; they could be heterogeneous hardware and a software running on machines that are geographically dispersed. Yet the user feels that he is being served by all the servers.

6.10.3. Object-oriented Databases

Object-oriented programming (OOP) methodology uses information hiding principles to ensure that data are processed only by the correct programs and in a correct manner. Also, using a concept known as *polymorphism*, the OOP methodology permits multiple views of data in a significantly better fashion than the view mechanism of relational systems.

6.10.4. Multimedia Databases

Databases to handle complex data objects, like scanned images (maps, line drawings, pictures, photographs, etc.), audio and video images, are known as multimedia databases. A new generation of databases are being built to accommodate multimedia. OOP is a promising technique to handle multimedia databases.

6.11. PRINCIPLES OF DATABASE MANAGEMENT

Database management technology has revolutionised the way organisations store, process, and disseminate data by providing instantaneous access to large volumes of information. In order to have full utilisation of databases, following principles have been identified:

1. Database technology must be aligned with business strategy.
2. It should be easy to access and process data residing in different databases.
3. Data resources are critical to an organisation and must be fully utilised and protected.
4. Control and security are important issues in databases, particularly distributed databases.
5. Database tools must be carefully selected. For this, following points should be taken into consideration : (*a*) Understand the resources required; (*b*) Understand database utilities; (*c*) Understand SQL optimisation; and (*d*) Understand connectivity issues, *e.g.*, speed, installation and configuration, database administration, querying capabilities, event alerts, simple reports, complex reports, and documentation and technical support.

6.12. THE DATABASE ADMINISTRATOR

An information specialist who has responsibility for the database is called a database administrator (DBA). The duties of the DBA fall into four major areas: Database planning, implementation, operation, and security. Typical responsibilities of a DBA are:

1. Helps an organisation decide which department will be responsible for the maintenance and update of each data field in a database.
2. Assures access to database information to each department that needs it.
3. Secures databases or portions of databases from unauthorised use.
4. Protects databases from physical harm by supervising the creation of backup copies and establishing fallback procedures.
5. Coordinates the work of individuals making file modifications, policy changes, and improvements to databases.

Ideally, DBA is a mature individual with years of computer experience, a wide diversity of technical abilities, and superior managerial skills.

Review Questions

1. Why are databases created ? What problems encountered leaving everything as separate data files ?
2. Explain the difference between data and information. How are data useful in decision making.
3. Outline the elements of a data hierarchy in ascending order. Suppose the Registrar's office of an engineering college has three student files in a database : personal data of the students, financial data (such as scholarships and financial aid), and classes in which each student has registered in the last three semesters, including the current semester. Develop a data hierarchy (files, records, fields, bytes, bits).
4. Define the terms : database, file, record, field, byte and bit, illustrating with example of each.
5. Describe three methods to organise data in a file-oriented environment. Which method is the most efficient and why ?

6. Why are sequential files usually inadequate for use as databases ? Why are direct-access files more suitable ?
7. What are some limitations of file and how can they be overcome using databases ?
8. What is the single-most important advantage of databases over conventional file processing systems ? Illustrate with the help of an example.
9. What is a DBMS and what are its primary functions ?
10. Prepare a comparative chart of the strengths and weaknesses of two competing DBMS products in the market, *e.g.*, Oracle and Sybase.
11. What is a database schema and subschema ? How are they used to define database information ?
12. What is the difference between a logical file and a physical file ? Why are these distinctions important to business information systems ? How are they related to the concept of a database ?
13. Outline in brief data management activities.
14. What are the differences in files and relational databases ?
15. Define a schema, a subschema, and a DDL. What are the relationships among the three ?
16. (*a*) What is a data dictionary ? What would be contained in one ? How is it used ?

    (*b*) Why is the data dictionary a vital tool for the Information System Manager ?
17. What are data definition languages (DDLs) and data manipulation languages (DMLs) ? How are they related to DBMS ?
18. Explain in detail advantages and disadvantages of database management systems.
19. Name at least *five* functions of DBMS.
20. Define SQL and explain its role in decision making.
21. What are the four basic operations in SQL. Refer to schema STUDENT, which is present in a database called UNIVERSITY. The Registrar would like to retrieve the name of every female student whose GPA is greater than 3.0 and who is currently registered in at least three classes. Identify the SQL operators necessary to retrieve this information.
22. What is a data model ? What are the three popular data models and what is the nature of relationship (1-1, 1-M, M-M) of the data elements in these models ?
23. Compare and contrast the advantages and disadvantages of hierarchical, network, and relational models.
24. What is a network model ? What type(s) of data might best be stored in a network model ? How these files use pointer addresses to create database relationships ?
25. Explain the structure of relational model. Why is it considered flexible ?
26. Is SQL, DDL and a DML or DML only or merely a DDL ? Explain.
27. What is an entity relationship diagram ? What is the main purpose of an ERD ?
28. (*a*) Draw a rough ERD of the data entities and relationships that are involved when a customer orders products from a firm. The customer places a sales order. Each order contains one or more inventory items and represents an addition to the accounts receivable. When drawing the diagram, keep in mind that a firm is supplier's customer, and use Fig. 6.10 (*b*) as an example.

    (*b*) Map data elements to your rough ERD. Use Fig. 6.10 (*c*) as your basis.

    (*c*) Modify your rough ERD by performing a data analysis. Use Fig 6.10 (*d*) as a basis.
29. What is distributed databases ? Identify *any four* types of distributed databases.
30. Identify *any three* principles of database management.
31. What are complex databases ? What is meant by object databases ? Elucidate.
32. Who is a database administrator ? Identify several functions that such a person might perform.

7

Client-server Computing

7.1. INTRODUCTION

Client-server computing is an approach to network use and is based on the concept that some function are performed best on a local basis and some are performed on a central basis. Therefore, client-server computing is a blend of the time-sharing approach, which features central use, and the distributed processing approach, which emphasizes local use. Client-server computing can involve WANs, but the configuration typically consists of one or more interconnected LANs.

In a typical client-server computing network, application processing is shared between clients and one or more servers. A **client** is a user who accesses the network by means of a desktop computer. A **server** can be a computer of any size — a mainframe, a mini, a workstation, or even a micro — that provides a control function for the network.

Client-server computing is a much more complex hardware and software configuration than either time-sharing or distributed processing. When implemented in its most sophisticated form, any system in the network can access and use any other available systems. Thus, unused computing capacity in a desktop can be utilised by other desktops in the network, or work can be downloaded to the desktop from a server. The key to client-server computing is the network server software that provides control points for critical functions such as hardware sharing, data sharing, database management, storing and forwarding, network management, batch processing, and the interconnection of multiple networks.

The current interest in client-server computing is a result of technological, economic, and organisational forces working together. The technological forces consist of advances in microcomputers and data transmission technologies, database management systems tailored to network use, and graphical user interfaces. Economic forces are applied by an international marketplace that demands maximum efficiency in the use of information resources. Organisational forces include those generated by end-user computing.

In the client-server environment, the information specialists focus on the firm's main applications that run on the servers, and the end-users develop applications to run on their desktops. For client-server computing to be used to full advantage, applications must be developed specifically to run in such an environment. A client-server system is shown in Fig. 7.1.

Increasing competitiveness in the global marketplace has compelled many organisations to re-engineer and streamline their business processes. Re-engineering requires firms to analyse what they do and ask themselves the question 'Why do we do what we do ?' In many instances, firms implement a certain process or processes simply because 'that's how it has always been done', creating waste and underutilisation of existing resources. Client-server systems play an important role in minimizing waste, although in some cases, firms downsize not so much to cut costs as to increase profits.

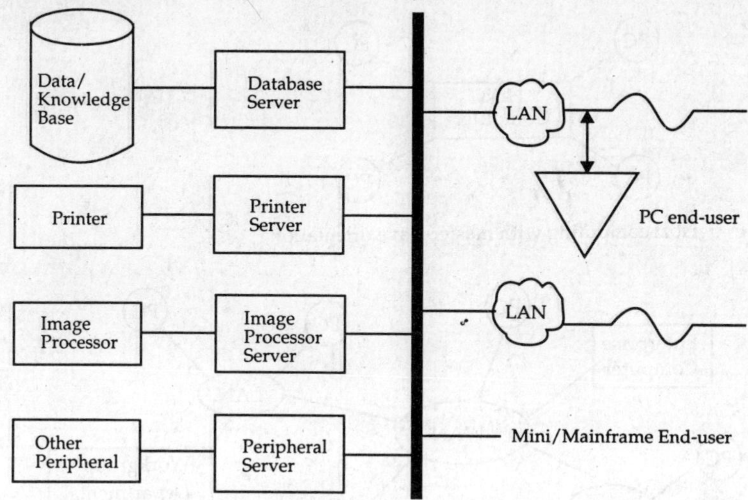

Fig. 7.1 Schema for a Client-server System

By making a wide variety of information readily accessible to users, client-server systems have helped many organisations improve productivity, enhance customer service, and minimize the time necessary to bring products to market. Before the emergence of client-server technology, information was often isolated and compartmentalised, leading to data redundancies and information bottlenecks. Client-server technology can provide significant benefits to organisations that make a long-term commitment to it and use it to build new infrastructures.

It is in this context, the client-server paradigm was born, and is the focus of this chapter. The resources of a client-server system are examined.

- Hardware (processor and user interface)
- Software
- Communications facilities
- Human resources
- The organisational environment necessary for the client-server to be successful.

Also, concern of corporate management with 'downsizing' and 'rightsizing', advantages and disadvantages of the client-server paradigm are examined in this chapter.

7.2. DEFINITION OF CLIENT-SERVER COMPUTING

The client-server technology is defined, as per Newton's *Telecom Dictionary,* as follows:

" A form of shared, or distributed, computing in which tasks and computing power are split between servers and clients. Servers store and process data common to users across the enterprise; these data can then be accessed by client systems for individual processing requirements."

7.3. COMPONENTS AND FUNCTIONS OF A CLIENT-SERVER SYSTEM

An overview of the client-server approach is shown in Fig. 7.2. It is compared with the earlier configuration with a host acting as 'master' and the connected PCs (or minis) acting as 'slaves'.

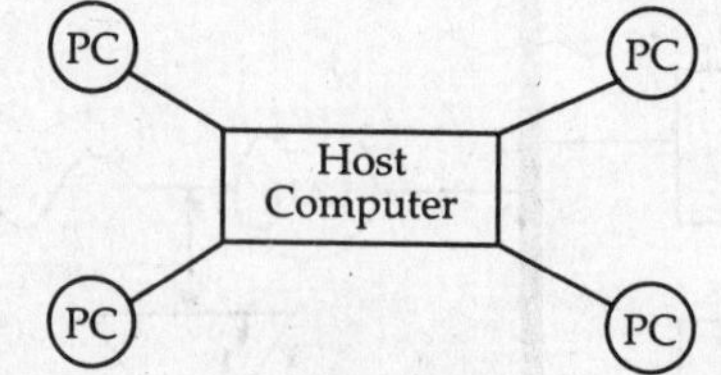

Host computing with master-slave orientation

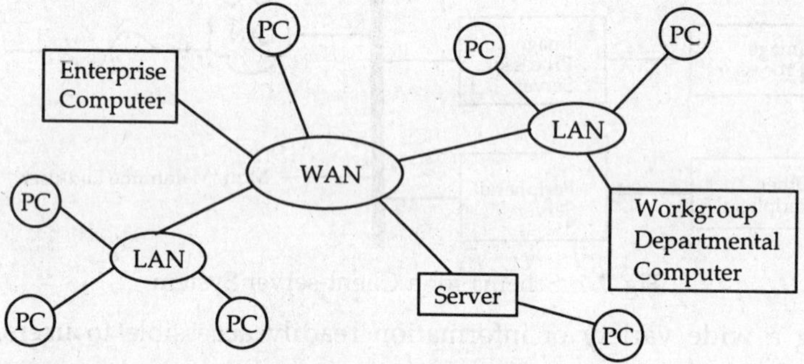

Distributed networking with client-server orientation

Fig. 7.2 Host Computing vs. the Client-server System

Figure 7.3 identifies different types of front-end and back-end software.

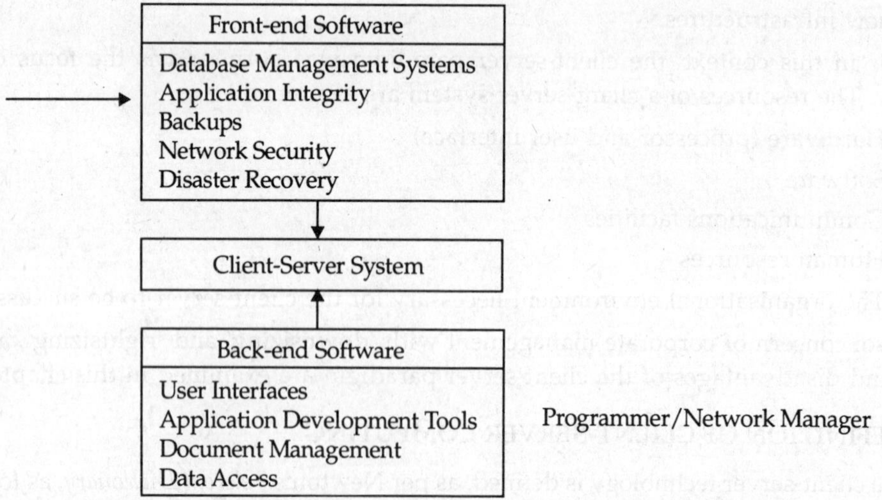

Fig. 7.3 Different Types of Frond-end and Back-end Software

As illustrated in Fig. 7.3, the client-server architecture, in addition to server and client software, includes front-end (client) software and back-end (server) software. The front-end software provides the user interface (what the user sends and receives), communication with at least one server, and data manipulation. The back-end software primarily controls data acquisition and integrity, supports transaction management, and recovers lost transactions, in cases of system failure. Other components of client software are tools for developing user interfaces, applications, communications software to communicate with the server; document management systems (systems managing different forms of written information, such as memos, manuals, documents, invoices, etc.), and relational database management systems (RDBMS).

In a client-server system (*a*) the server influences the way the client responds to a user request, (*b*) a number of clients can access the server at the same time, and (*c*) client processes and server processes are independent of each other. This independence has one of the greatest advantages of the client-server environment, because clients can be added to or deleted from the network, without affecting the server or other clients.

7.4. DEVELOPMENT OF CLIENT-SERVER SYSTEM

Following five steps are required before development of a client-server system:

1. Identify and define the type of application (problem definition).
2. Assess network requirements.
3. Select the architecture (hardware, software, and network capabilities).
4. Develop the logical and physical design of the system.
5. Test, implement, and maintain the system.

The development of client-server applications is then based on the following six components:

- Communication services
- Distribution services
- Application services
- Organisation-specific applications
- Industry-specific applications
- System management and security.

7.5. CLIENT-SERVER SECURITY

The security of client-server environments is a critical issue for network managers. Access privileges and application security are two issues that must be carefully addressed in order to ensure that client-server environments are well secured. Network managers should know at all times who is on the network and what each user is doing. As such, network security is a balancing act between control and access and there are no easy answers. Another issue in client-server environments is preserving the integrity of system applications.

7.6. CLIENT-SERVER COSTS COMPUTATION

Client-server technology is applicable to only those organisations that have a long-term commitment to it and are willing to make a large financial investment in it. Estimating the cost of client-server computing is one of the most challenging tasks confronting Information System Managers. Some of the factors that must be taken into account when computing client-server costs are hardware, software, peripherals, accessories, training for end-users, managers, and network administrators, contract negotiations, outside consultants, and various unexpected costs.

7.7. ADVANTAGES OF CLIENT-SERVER SYSTEM

The advantages of a client-server system is context-sensitive and depends on one's vantage point. If a person is a corporate manager, he will have advantages of downsizing and the reduction of costs in his organisation. If a person is an end-user, he will be getting control of the system even though it may mean that he cannot blame computer personnel for things going wrong and instead have to take certain responsibilities for the system (at the client-end).

If a person is one of the computer personnel, especially at the management level, then he will be somewhat happy at his reduced responsibilities for the system but he is concerned about the integrity and security of the system, especially that of the data/ knowledge base. On the whole, considering the system from the enterprise point of view, there are more advantages overriding the disadvantages.

Following are the advantages of a client-server system:

- Reduction of responsibilities and cost overhead at centre.
- Better local cost control of operations and development (original and modifications).
- Faster response time to requests for processing.
- Greater access to corporate data and knowledge otherwise maintained in a highly protected and centralised data structure. The client-server system strips data off transactional systems and stores it in the server to be shared for analysis and even local manipulation.
- Enables distribution of processing from centralised to desktop computing.
- Offers cooperative processing between individuals and group departments across organisational boundaries, geographies and time zones.
- Rewriting systems for the client-server system is often an opportunity to purge obsolete software from the application portfolio and to consolidate, integrate and make the system more efficient.
- Offers more friendly interfaces for end-users — especially knowledge workers and customers.

  Greater involvement of end-users in IT implementations.

  The open architecture and open systems offer flexibility in choosing different configurations of hardware, networks, and DBMS from multiple vendors.
- There is greater possibility for expansion by adding hardware (even laptop computers) to networks without replacing existing hardware. The plug-and-play possibility applies (at least in theory) when parts of a system can be replaced without impact on the rest of the system.

7.8. DISADVANTAGES/OBSTACLES OF A CLIENT-SERVER SYSTEM

There are some disadvantages of client-server system. Some problems exist, which are associated with downsizing and the need for greater coordination and cooperation among the end-users of the system. There is the problem of resistance, which must be expected of all new technological changes. Also, problems of conversion, especially the need to train personnel in the use of the new system prevail.

Training may be considered as a technological obstacle. End-users have to be trained not only on using the client and knowing the functions of the server, but end-users need to be educated about networking and trained in navigating across the LAN and perhaps even the internet. Other technological obstacles are the lack of tools of development and products of the client-server system; the lack of methodologies for the development of client-server systems; the lack of experience in the planning and implementation of a client-server system; and the lack of available standards relating to the equipment and operations of such systems. These, and other, disadvantages of a client-server system are as follows:

- Organizational
  - — Lack of personnel skill in the client-server system and in networking
  - — Resistance to change and new technology
  - — Risks of downsizing
  - — Costs of conversion
  - — Need for greater coordination and control of more end-users.
- Technological
  - — Need of LAN/WAN infrastructure
  - — Lack of skills and equipment resources
  - — Lack of methodology/experience in planning for a client-server system
  - — Lack of client-server products and tools of development
  - — Lack of client-server applications
  - — Lack of national and international standards for the client-server paradigm.

Review Questions

1. Client-server technology is viewed as vital to the growth of a business. Discuss.
2. Enumerate some factors that led to the evolution of client-server technology.
3. What do you mean by a 'server' and a 'client' ? Explain the meaning of client-server technology.
4. Explain the reason for similarity of client-server system and distributed databases.
5. Explain about front-end software and back-end software. Are these essential for a client-server system to function ?
6. Why preplanning is prerequisite before investing in client-server applications ?
7. List out some advantages of client-server systems.
8. What are the disadvantages of client-server systems ? List some hidden costs associated with this technology.
9. What are the different components of a client-server system ? Explain in brief about each component, with illustration.
10. Explain the factors on which development of client-server system is based.
11. Enumerate the factors involved in computing client-server costs.
12. What measures should be taken to ensure the security of the client-server system ?

8

Decision Support System

8.1. INTRODUCTION

Decision support system (DSS) in an outcome of management information system, providing support for management at operational control, management control, and strategic planning. Management activity of each of these classes includes planning, control and decision making. Support functions for these three functions are focused in this chapter. The design of systems supporting decision making is first explained. Another class of support systems, named executive information systems, is also discussed. Development of DSS using different approaches is followed.

A feature of the DSS that is currently receiving much publicity is computer graphics. Graphs are good only in certain situations. However, in those situations some graphs are more effective than others.

The most recent embellishment of the DSS concept is the group decision support system (GDSS). The GDSS endeavours to improve communications among group members by providing stimulating environments.

8.2. DEFINITIONS

The term decision support system refers to a class of systems which support the process of making decisions. The emphasis is on 'support' rather than on automation of decisions. DSS allows the decision maker to retrieve data and test alternative solutions during the process of problem-solving.

Keen and Scott Morton (1978) defined DSS as:

(*a*) The impact is on decisions in which there is sufficient structure for computer and analytic aids to be of value but where manager's judgement is essential;

(*b*) The payoff is in extending the range and capability of manager's decision processes to help them improve their effectiveness; and

(*c*) The relevance for managers is the creation of a supportive tool, under their own control, which does not attempt to automate the decision process, predefine objectives, or impose solutions.

However, this definition has certain limitations.

In 1984, Freyenfeld (1984) proposed the following empirical definition of DSS based on discussions with some 30 supplier, user and academic organisations:

" A Decision Support System is an interactive data processing and display system which is used to assist in a concurrent decision making process, and which also conforms to the following characteristics:

(*a*) It is sufficiently user-friendly to be used by the decision maker(s) in person;

(*b*) It displays its information in a format and terminology which is familiar to the user(s); and

(*c*) It is selective in its provision of information and avoids its user(s) in information overload."

Another definition of a decision support system is: "A set of well-integrated, user-friendly, computer-based tools that combine data with various decision-making models — quantitative and qualitative — to solve semi-structured and unstructured problems."

8.3. EVOLUTION OF DSS

The notion of decision support as a formal concept was coined by G. Anthony Gorry and Michael S. Scott Morton. They felt a need for a framework to channel computer applications toward management decision making and developed a grid, known as the **Gorry and Scott Morton grid** (Fig. 8.1). The grid is based on Simon's concept of programmed and non-programmed decisions and Robert N. Anthony's management levels. The decision types are described in terms of problem structure, ranging from structured to semi-structured to unstructured. A fully *structured problem* is one in which the first three of Simon's phases — intelligence, design and choice — are structured. The decisions are routine and straightforward. By following a set of pre-established steps, a solution to the problem can be found. Such a problem does not require intuition or judgement. Therefore, the system returns the same solution every time. An *unstructured problem* is one in which none of the three phases is structured. The decisions are unique and non-repetitive. Because they require intuition, experience and judgement, there may be no one 'best' solution and solutions may differ from one decision maker to the other. A *semi-structured problem* is one in which one or two of the phases are structured. The decisions in this category fall somewhere between structured decisions, which are routine and repetitive, and unstructured decisions, which are unique and non-repetitive.

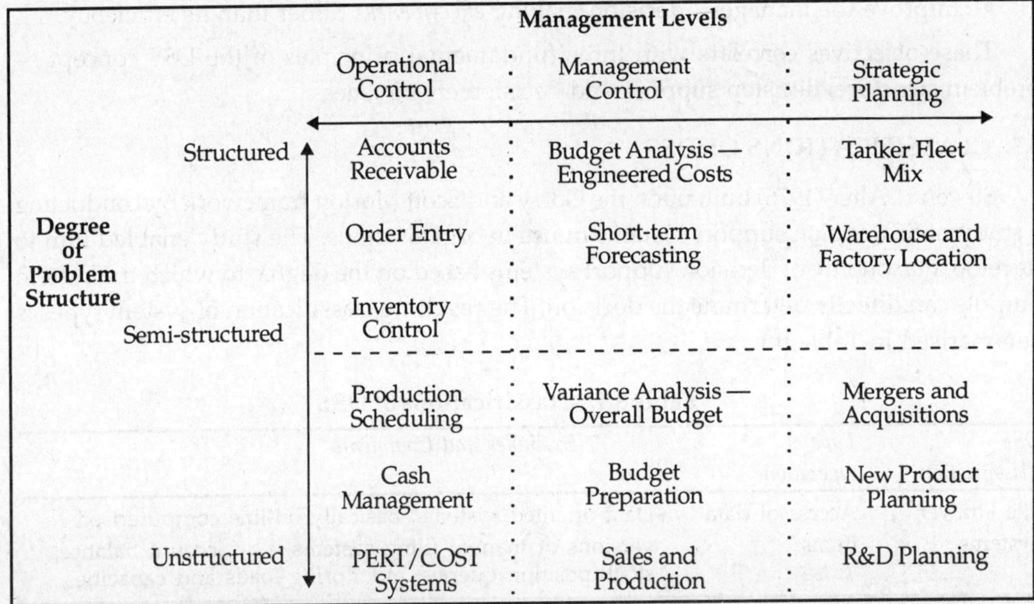

[**Source:** G. Anthony Gorry and Michael S. Scott Morton. 'A Framework for Management Information Systems', *Sloan Management Review.* 13 (Fall 1971), 55-70.]

Fig. 8.1 Gorry and Scott Morton Grid

Gorry and Scott Morton entered types of business problems into their grid. For example, accounts receivable is solved by managers on the operational-control level making structured decisions. R&D planning is accomplished by strategic planning managers making unstructured decisions.

The horizontal dotted line through the middle of the grid is significant. It separates the problem that had been successfully solved with computer assistance from those problems that had not been subjected to computer processing. The upper area was named *structured decision systems* and the lower area was named decision support systems.

DSS are especially useful for semi-structured problems where problem-solving is improved by interaction between the manager and the computer system. The emphasis is on small, simple models which can easily be understood and used by the decision maker. Examples of semi-structured decisions are : planning a mix of investments for a portfolio, looking at the financial implications of various ways of financing a short-term cash flow deficit, consideration of alternative production and pricing policies, assessing the impact of potential future changes in exogenous variables such as interest rates, analysis of the credit-worthiness of corporate clients, and assessing the likely impacts of departmental reorganisation.

8.4. OBJECTIVES OF DSS

Peter G.W. Keen and Michael S. Scott Morton (1978) defined three objectives that a DSS should achieve. These are :

- Assist managers in making decisions to solve *semi-structured* problems.
- *Support* the manager's judgement rather than try to replace it.
- Improve the manager's decision-making *effectiveness* rather than its efficiency.

These objectives correlate with three fundamental principles of the DSS concept — problem structure, decision support, and decision effectiveness.

8.5. CLASSIFICATIONS OF DSS

Steven L. Alter (1976) built upon the Gorry and Scott Morton framework by conducting a study of 56 decision support systems in use in organisations. The study enabled him to develop a taxonomy of decision support systems based on the degree to which the system outputs can directly determine the decision. The resulting classification of system types is summarised in Table 8.1.

Table 8.1. Classifications of DSS

DSS Classification	*Type of Operation*	*Examples and Comments*
File Drawer Systems	Access of data items	Data oriented systems. Basically on-line computerised versions of manual filing systems, *e.g.*, account balance, stock position queries, monitoring loads and capacities.
Data Analysis Systems	Ad hoc analysis of data files	Data oriented systems. Used to analyse files containing current or historical data, *e.g.*, analysing files for overdue account, bad payers.

Analysis Information Systems	Ad hoc analysis using databases and small models	Data oriented systems. Extension of data analysis systems to include internal and external databases with limited modelling, *e.g.*, a marketing support DSS could include internal sales data, customer data and market research data.
Accounting Models	Estimating future results using accounting rules	Model oriented systems. Typically these generate estimates of cash, income, costs, etc. based on accounting relationships and rules, *e.g.*, cash and expenditure budgeting, balance sheet projections.
Representational Models	Estimating results, consequences where risk exists	Model oriented systems. These generate results using probability based simulation models, *e.g.*, risk analysis for new project, traffic simulation with variable flows.
Optimisation Models	Calculating optimal results where constraints exist	Model oriented systems. These are used for structured decisions where constraints exist and there is a clear objective, *e.g.*, machine loading, material usage, production planning.
Suggestion Models	Producing suggested results where decision rules are known	Model oriented systems. These compute suggested decisions for semi-structured problems. Expert systems are one of the tools, *e.g.*, credit authorisations, insurance rate calculations.

8.6. CHARACTERISTICS OF DECISION SUPPORT SYSTEM

The main characteristics of DSS are:

- The computer must *support* the manager but not replace his/her judgement. It should, therefore, neither try to provide the 'answers' nor impose a predefined sequence of analysis.
- The main payoff of computer support is for *semi-structured* problems, where parts of the analysis can be systematised for the computer, but where the decision maker's insight and judgement are needed to control the process.
- Effective problem solving is *interactive* and is enhanced by a dialogue between the user and the system. The user explores the problem situation using the analytic and information-providing capabilities of the system as well as human experience and insights.

8.7. COMPONENTS OF A DSS

There are three main software components of a DSS. These are: a *database management system* (DBMS), a *model management system*, and *support tools*.

8.7.1. Database Management Systems

To solve a problem, the necessary data may come from internal or external databases. In an organisation, internal data are generated by systems such as TPS and MIS; external data come from a variety of sources such as newspapers, on-line data services, databases (financial, marketing, manufacturing, human resource, and others). Some examples of external data are government regulations, tax codes, census figures, competitors, market shares, economic indicators, interest rates, and inflation. The data in the DSS database are managed by the DBMS, which covers compilation of data, manipu- lation of data, data generation, data updating, data maintenance, and dissemination of data.

8.7.2. Model Management Systems

Model management system stores and accesses models that managers use to make decisions. Such models are used for designing a manufacturing facility, analysing the financial health of an organisation, forecasting demand for a product or service, and determining the quality of a particular batch of products. Although most models are quantitative, decision makers use qualitative models also to make decisions.

The *model builder*, a component of many model bases, provides a structured framework for developing models by helping decision makers identify the variables and the interrelationships among the variables in the model. A model builder creates, identifies, processes, stores, updates, and maintains different decision makiing models and ensures that these models are consistently applied when decisions are made. The model builder also contains a model dictionary for consistency in the definitions and uses of models.

Some models that decision makers use to make decisions are: statistical models, production models, marketing models, human resource models, financial and accounting models, and strategic models. These models are extensively used in different functional areas of a business.

8.7.3. Support Tools

Support tools — online help, pull-down menus, user interfaces, graphical analysis, error-correction mechanisms — facilitate users' interactions with the system. Interfaces are an important support tool especially in the case of a DSS. The better the interface, the greater the chances that users will accept the system. Although managers recognise the power and potential of DSS, the main problem to its adoption is a lack of people with training in computer technologies. In such an environment, good interfaces can make or break the system.

8.8. FUNCTIONS OF A DSS

There are *five* functions of a DSS facilitating managerial decision making. They are :

- Model building
- 'What-if' analysis
- Goal seeking
- Risk analysis
- Graphical analysis.

Model building allows decision makers to identify the most appropriate model for solving the problem at hand. It takes into account input variables, interrelationships among the variables, problem assumptions and constraints. For example, a marketing manager of Videocon is charged with the responsibility of developing a sales forecasting model for colour TV sets. A model builder uses a structured framework to identify variables like demand, cost and profit, analyse the relationships among these variables, identify the assumptions, if any (*e.g.*, assume the prices of raw materials will increase by 5% over the forecasting period), and identify the constraints, *viz.*, the production capacity of the plant. All this informations are then integrated by a system into a decision making model, which can be updated and modified whenever required.

'What-if' analysis is the process of assessing the impact of changes to model variables, the values of the variables, or the interrelationships among variables. This helps managers to be proactive, rather than reactive, in their decision making. This analysis is critical for semi-structured and unstructured problems because the data necessary to make such decisions are often either not available or imcomplete. Hence, managers normally use their intuition and judgement in predicting the long-term implications of their decisions. Managers can prepare themselves to face a dynamic business environment by developing a group of scenarios (best-case scenario, worst-case scenario and realistic scenario). Spreadsheet packages, such as Excel and Lotus 1-2-3, have 'what-if' applications.

Goal seeking is the process of determining the input values required to achieve a certain goal. For example, house buyers determine the monthly payment they can afford (say, Rs. 7000) and calculate the number of such payments required to pay the desired house.

Risk analysis is a function of DSS that allows managers to assess the risks associated with various alternatives. Decisions can be classified as low-risk, medium-risk, and high-risk. A DSS is particularly useful in medium-risk and high-risk environments.

Graphical analysis helps managers to quickly digest large volumes of data and visualise the impacts of various courses of action. First, the Lotus system enabled users to easily display and print information in a graphic form. S L Jarvenpaa and G W Dickson (1988) studied the relative advantages and disadvantages of tabular and graphic output. They recommended the use of graphs when:

- Seeking a quick summary of data
- Detecting trends over time
- Comparing points and patterns at different variables
- Forecasting activities
- Seeking relatively simple impressions from a vast amount of information.

The researchers suggest that a tabular presentation be used when it is necessary to read individual data values.

Jarvenpaa and Dickson also offer the following tips when choosing between the various types of graphs:

- Line or bar charts are preferred for summarising data.
- Grouped line or bar charts are good for showing trends over time.
- Grouped bar charts are better than pie charts for presenting parts of a whole.
- Grouped line or bar charts are good for comparing patterns of variables.
- Use horizontal rather than vertical bars when comparing variables.
- Use single-line or bar charts to compare individual data points between variables.
- Put data values on the top of the bars in a bar chart for easier reading.

Spreadsheets have sophisticated graphical analysis capabilities. For example, Microsoft Excel gives the user a wide choice of graphs and charts in many colours and patterns.

8.9. DEVELOPMENT OF DECISION SUPPORT SYSTEMS

The development of a decision support system is determined by the types of information and the facilities needed for taking the decision. Decision support systems are developed using programming languages or produced by packages specially incorporating decision support development tools.

Conventional high-level languages, such as C^{++} and BASIC, can be used to develop DSSs. They are extremely flexible. However, DSSs using these languages involve a lengthy analysis and design phase. Fourth-generation or very high-level languages are more appropriate. They are particularly useful as they are generally database-oriented. This is important for those systems that rely on data retrieval and analysis for decision support. An example of a prominent fourth-generation language is SQL, which can be used on many relational database systems such as ORACLE. The selection of a language depends on factors such as:

- Availability of language and support for it.
- Experience of developers with various languages.
- Amount of manipulation *vs.* presentation of data.
- Need to document and maintain the program.
- Frequency of use and number of users.

The advantages of using programming languages are that:

- Applications development is speedy.
- Many are end-user orientated.
- They are more likely to be declarative rather than procedural.

In general, there are three methods for developing a DSS:

1. DSS generator
2. DSS shells
3. Customer made software.

8.9.1. DSS Generator

A DSS generator is comprised of programs such as data management tools, electronic spreadsheets, report generators (user-friendly programs that allow decision makers to produce customised reports), statistical packages, graphical packages, query languages, and model-building tools, that help in the development of a DSS. Some known DSS generators are FOCUS, Excel, and Lotus 1-2-3.

8.9.2. DSS Shells

A DSS shell is a program used to build a customised DSS. Shells eliminate the need for developing the DBMS, model management system, and user interfaces, because skeletal versions of these modules are already available in the shell. A user can simply connect the shell with the appropriate external and internal databases and input the appropriate models in order to have a fully functional DSS.

System development can proceed at a rapid pace because of availability of basic versions of the DBMS, the model management system, and the set of interfaces in the shell. Shells have become user-friendly, allowing even users with little or no programming background to develop fairly sophisticated systems. The main disadvantage of a shell is that it may have to be customised to meet the needs of the decision maker or the user may have to adopt the problem to the tool.

A DSS, called Advia, assists entrepreneurs in developing a plan, analysing the marketing and financial aspects of their businesses, and implementing it. This DSS has two components — Manage and Decide. **Advia Manage** is a financial model that allows managers to forecast income statements, project operating cash flow, automatically create forecasted balance-sheets, and analyse key financial data and ratios. **Advia Decide** is designed to analyse market issues such as the status of our organisation in the market, aims of our organisation in the next five years, and how do we get there ? Advia Decide has two components : Situation Analysis and Vision. Some questions asked by the system from the user are structured whereas other questions are open-ended, allowing the user to provide input in a variety of ways. Depending on the size of the company and the amount of information available, a single session with Advia can last 5 to 6 hours. The output of this DSS is a first draft of a business plan, along with some interesting and useful insights about the company's market possibility and strategy.

The second module, Advia Manage, is designed to assist users through complex financial decision making processes and has two components: Forecast and Tracking. Many CEOs of small firms struggle to assess the performance of their firms. Advia provides an objective framework to help each of them evaluate his/her firm and its performance.

8.9.3. Custom-made Software

Custom-made software is designed and developed by an organisation, who is committed to DSS technology but cannot find a suitable generator or shell. The software is developed using a procedural language, such as C, or a 4GL, such as FOCUS. Organisations may also choose to combine shells and customised software.

The primary disadvantage of this approach is that the system may be expensive and time-consuming to develop, and organisations may run into unexpected bottlenecks and cost overruns.

8.10. GROUP DECISION SUPPORT SYSTEMS

The decision support systems considered so far have been concerned with computerised support for an individual taking a decision characterised as semi-structured or unstructured. Many decisions taken within an organisation are not by a single individual but as a result of group deliberations. **Group Decision Support Systems (GDSS)** are computer-based information systems that facilitate the free flow and exchange of ideas and information among group members while maintaining their anonymity. Other terms have also been coined to describe the application of information technology to group settings. These terms include **group support system (GSS), computer-supported cooperative work (CSCW), computerised collaborative work support,** and **electronic meeting system (EMS).** The software used in these settings has been given the name **groupware.**

Groups typically consist of less than 20 people, who arrive at decisions through communication. The communication serves to share information and implement the decision-taking process. The decision may be taken by vote but is more often by negotiation, consensus, or preference ranking.

Three types of computer-based support are available :

1. **Decision networks:** This type allows participants to communicate through networks with each other or with a central database. Applications software may use commonly shared models to provide support. The commonest implementation is using a local area network and microcomputers. The technology filters out many of the typical group dynamics of a participative meeting.

2. **Decision room:** Participants are located in one place — the decision room. The purpose of this is to enhance participant interaction and decision making by computerised support within a fixed period of time using a facilitator. Specific computer-based tools are provided (Fig. 8.2).

3. **Tele/computer conferencing:** If groups are composed of members or subgroups that are geographically dispersed, tele/computer conferencing provides for interactive connection between two or more decision rooms. This interaction will involve transmission of computerised and audiovisual information. Whereas decision networks can be viewed as the use of local area networks, for decision making involving groups the decision room is an entirely new development.

The decision room is used by an organisation to create an environment in which groups may enhance their decisions. The decision-making process is guided by a *facilitator*. The facilitator is usually not from within the organisation but a trained professional in group dynamics brought in for the decision-making sessions. There will also usually be a computer controller whose responsibility is to maintain computer communications and software support within the room.

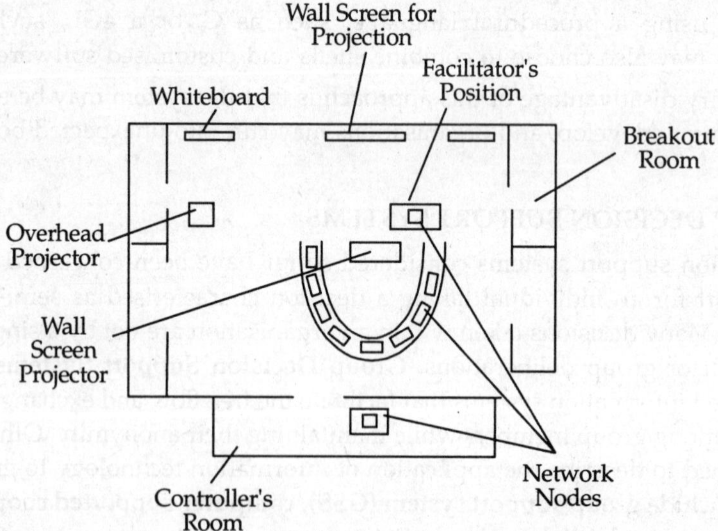

Fig. 8.2 A Typical Layout of a Decision Room

The decision room (an example of which can be seen in Fig. 8.2) consists of a table with networked workstations for the participants and workstations for the facilitator and controller. The screen of any node of the network can be projected onto the wall screen. The facilitator can also ensure that, if required, any participant's screen can replace some or all of the other nodes for demonstration or interactive purposes. Breakout rooms, used for smaller discussions, are also equipped with similar networked machines. A combination of overhead projector, flipchart, photocopier and other presentation devices are provided as well.

The software may take many forms but will always consist of tools that aid group decision making, are easy to use and are interactive. Examples of software (as well as spreadsheet and statistical/graphical packages) are:

- **Brainstorming:** Brainstorming software may be used at any stage of the proceedings but is particularly valuable at early stages when members of the group need to think and converse freely on issues. A problem or statement can be entered for comment. This will appear on all screens. Each individual may then produce comments, which are anonymously consolidated and displayed. The tool increases creativity and lateral thinking.

- **Voting:** It is frequently important to obtain a swift view on the acceptability of proposals from a group perspective before proceeding. Voting software enables this to happen. It is not merely restricted to yes/no but will also enable different formats for expressing preferences including multiple choice and 1-5 scales.

- **Policy formation:** Software can aid policy formation by allowing decision makers to identify connections and relations between issues and communicate this to all present for comment.

The software will be used as part of a methodology followed by the facilitator in arriving at decisions. Much work is still to be done in the area of development of tools to support decision rooms.

Decision rooms are expensive to equip and all but the largest organisations would find it difficult to justify the expenditure — particularly so as the use of the decision room is not regarded as an everyday occurrence. It is becoming more common for establish-ments, especially academic institutions, to hire out these facilities to organisations when needed.

It is difficult to analyse the effectiveness of these group decision support systems although it appears that they are most likely to be beneficial (and to be regarded as beneficial by participants) for larger group size (size eight and above). Participants are aware of the need to impose some structure on groups of this size and welcome the direction given by the decision room and the facilitator.

The primary advantage of GDSS is that it fosters an environment that is conducive to decision making. A second advantage of GDSS is that whereas in traditional meetings, extroverts or politically powerful people can dominate the shy and the introverted, GDSS allows all members of the group to participate. Another advantage of a GDSS is that it greatly enhances the efficiency of group meetings, since the system generates and processes ideas in parallel and there is no cross talk among group members. Further, the system has good 'organisational memory'. It captures all ideas instantaneously, which reduces the need for documentation and the risk of loosing or misinterpreting ideas.

8.11. EXECUTIVE INFORMATION SYSTEMS

An Executive Information System (EIS) is a set of computer-based tools with features such as colour graphics, touch screens, voice-activated commands, and natural-language interfaces, that help managers to quickly retrieve, analyse, navigate, summarise, and disseminate large volumes of data. An EIS is frequently connected with on-line information services so that top managers can quickly access external data as well. The primary aim of an EIS is, therefore, the delivery and display of information, rather than the analysis or diagnosis of problems and possible solutions. This is one of the major differences between an EIS and a DSS.

The executive information system (Fig. 8.3) sits atop the functional systems, and makes information available to the executives. The information originates both within the firm and within its environment. It is generally accepted that environmental information is especially important at the top level.

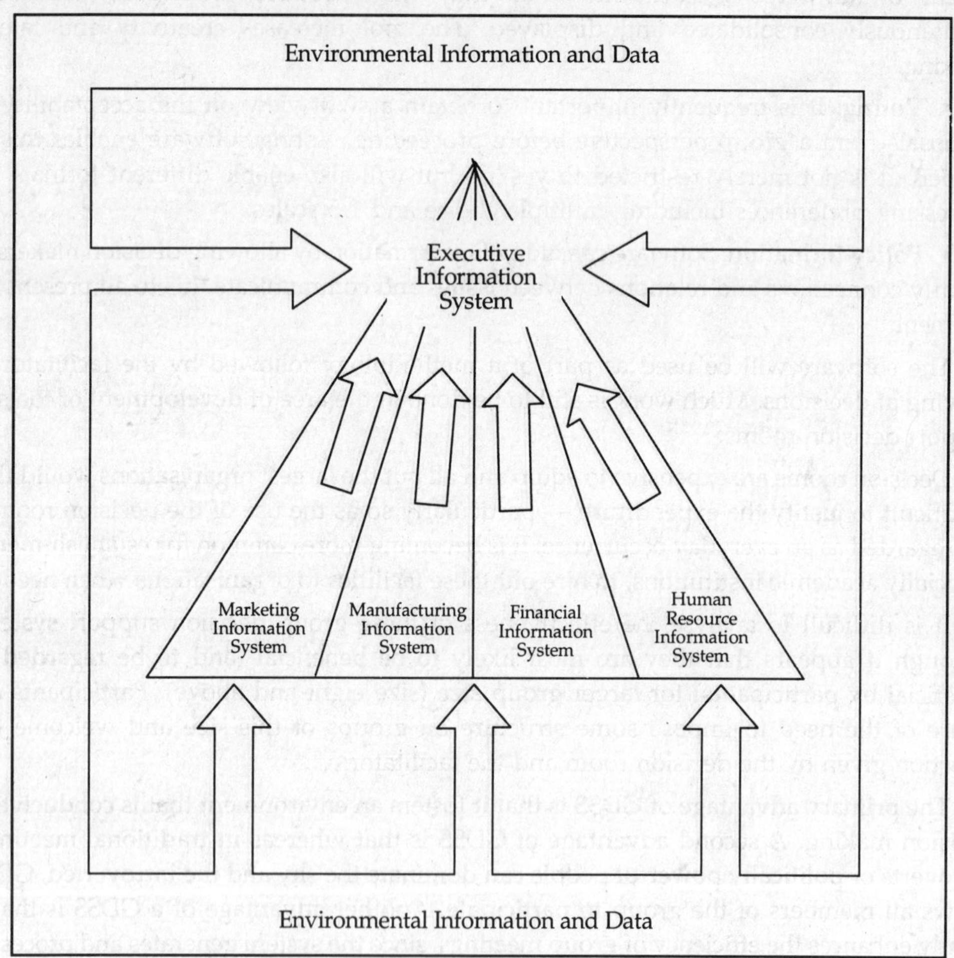

Fig. 8.3 An Executive Information System in an Organisation

J P Kotter (1982) believes that executives cope with the challenges of their jobs by following a three-step strategy :

- *Agenda* — the objectives that the firm is to achieve.
- *Networks* — co-operative relationships among those people who are to accomplish the agendas.
- *Environment* — establish the right environment of norms and values so that the network members can work to achieve the agendas.

It was felt that executives should strive to improve the non-computer components as well. These components are:

1. Take an inventory of incoming information transactions.
2. Stimulate high value sources.
3. Take advantage of opportunities.
4. Tailor the system to the individual.
5. Take advantage of technology.

The configuration of a computer-based EIS is shown in Fig. 8.4.

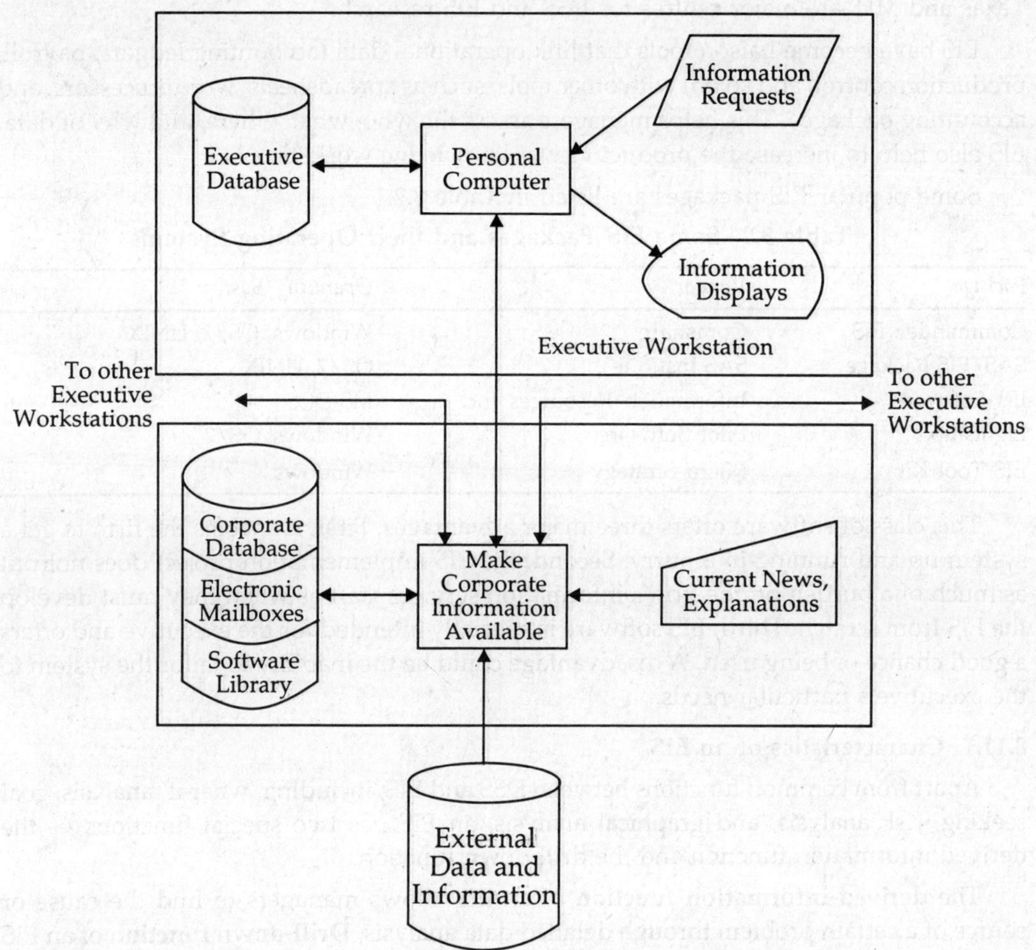

Fig. 8.4 A Computer-based EIS Model

Interest in EIS took off like a rocket during the late 1980s. The interest reflected a combination of greater computer awareness on the part of the executives and the availability of improved hardware and software.

Peter Drucker, the **management guru**, in a recent article in *Harvard Business Review*, identifies the different kinds of information top managers need to make good decisions. The primary goal of an enterprise is to create wealth, not merely control costs. This requires *four* sets of diagnostic tools that provide decision makers with the right information to make sound decisions:

- Foundation information (cash flow, liquidity and so on)
- Productivity information (economic value-added analysis)
- Competence information (competence and its competitors)
- Resource-related information (capital, manpower, environment and so on).

The market for DSS and EIS is expected to be more than double because of their versatility. EIS is considered such an important technology that some universities in the U.S. spent a considerable portion of their research fund to EIS research. The University of Texas and MIT are major centres for DSS and EIS research.

EIS have become liaison tools that link operational data (accounting ledgers, payroll, production control, and so on) with other tools, such as spreadsheets, wordprocessors, and accounting packages. This helps managers assess the who, what, where, and why of data. EIS also help to increase the productivity of knowledge workers.

Some popular EIS packages are listed in Table 8.2.

Table 8.2. Some EIS Packages and their Operating Systems

Package	*Vendor*	*Operating System*
Commander EIS	Comshare	Windows, OS/2, UNIX
SAS/EIS Package	SAS Institute	OS/2, UNIX
IRI Software	Information Resources Inc.	MS-DOS
Lightship	Pilot Software	Windows, OS/2
EIS Tool Kit	Micro Strategy	Windows

This class of software offers three major advantages. First, it enables the firm to get a system up and running in a hurry. Second, the EIS implementation project does not put as much of a burden on the firm's information services staff as when they must develop the EIS from scratch. Third, EIS software is specially intended for the executive and offers a good chance of being used. A disadvantage could be the inability to tailor the system to the executive's particular needs.

8.11.1. Characteristics of an EIS

Apart from common functions between DSS and EIS, including 'what-if' analysis, goal seeking, risk analysis, and graphical analysis, an EIS has two special functions — the derived information function and the drill-down function.

The **derived-information function** of an EIS allows managers to find the cause or source of a certain problem through detailed data analysis. **Drill-down function** of an EIS precisely locate and retrieve necessary information at any desired level of detail.

Another recent feature found in DSS and EIS that increases the usefulness of drill-down and *derived-information* is a software agent. Comshare is one of the leading producers of agents for DSS. Many spreadsheets have some simple EIS-like capabilities. Microsoft Excel also has many EIS features.

8.12. SUCCESS CRITERIA FOR DSS/EIS

Rockart and Delong (1988) identified *eight* critical success factors for achieving a successful DSS/EIS. These are :

1. Commitment from top management.
2. Availability of accurate and reliable data.
3. Careful problem selection.
4. Integration of DSS and EIS with existing technologies.
5. Meaningful analysis of costs *vs.* benefits.
6. A clear link to business objectives.
7. Management of organisational resistance.
8. Management of the spread and evolution of the system.

These critical success factors essentially boil down to good planning. If the firm has embraced information resources management (discussed in Chapter 14) and does a good job of strategic planning for information resources (Chapter 13), the achievement of a good EIS and other organisational informational systems as well is a realistic goal.

8.13. RELATIONSHIP BETWEEN MIS AND DSS

There are several views who disagree with making any distinction between MIS and DSS. Some of the views on the relationships between the two are summarised in Fig. 8.5. There do not appear to be any significant differences about what constitutes the combined area of MIS and DSS.

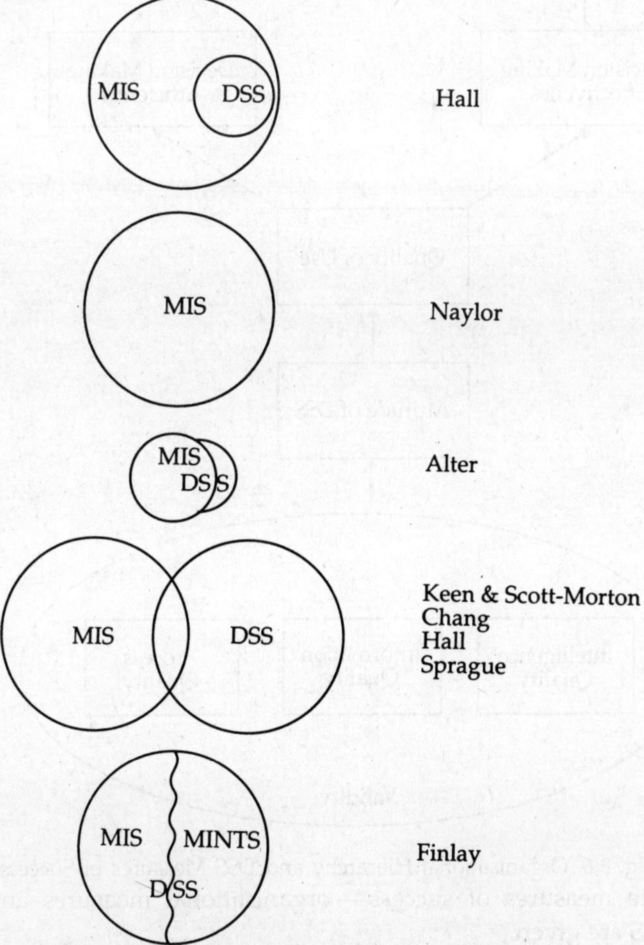

Fig. 8.5 Relationships between MIS and DSS

8.14. DSS MEASURES OF SUCCESS IN ORGANISATIONS

In practice, it is likely that the effects of a DSS on the organisational goals will be difficult to identify. Thus, the search for indirect measures of DSS success that can more likely be operationalised. A broad indication of the form of these indirect measures is shown in the lower portion of Fig. 8.6, where intra-DSS measures are listed. The hierarchy of organisational measures is shown in the upper portion of Fig. 8.6. Where possible, success of a DSS would be sought in terms of how well it helped the organisation meet goals on these dimensions. These measures are supra-DSS measures.

A hierarchy of organisational and DSS measures of success are shown in Fig. 8.6.

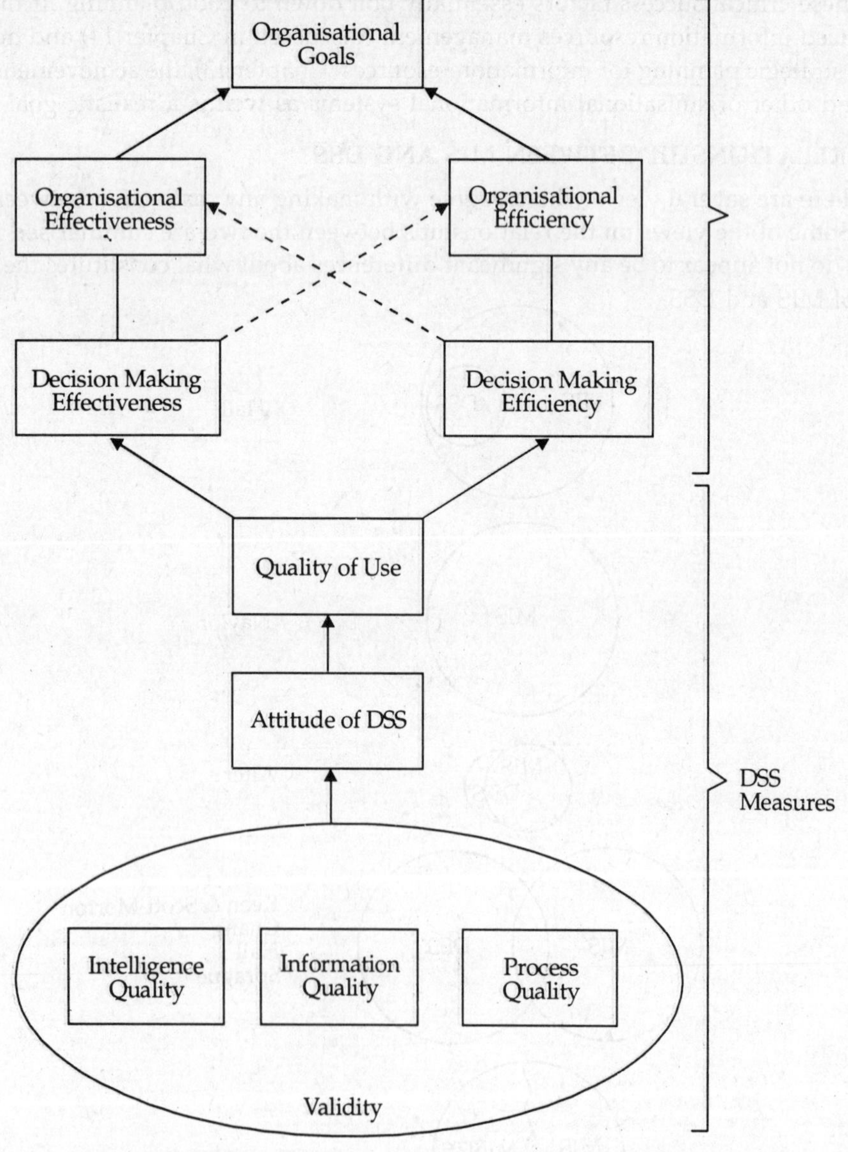

Fig. 8.6 Organisational Hierarchy and DSS Measures of Success

Appropriate measures of success — organisational measures and intra-DSS measures — for DSS are given.

Organisational Measures

Organisational Effectiveness

Faster and better adaption/response to 'the new'

Improved cash generation

Greater growth

More and better innovation

Increased market share

Enhanced profitability

Satisfactory return on investment

Technical excellence

Organisational Efficiency

Enhanced communication between stakeholders

Greater and more appropriate control

Cost savings

Enhanced productivity

Greater team work

Time savings

Decision Making Effectiveness

The ability to carry out ad hoc analysis

Increased depth of the analysis undertaken

More alternatives examined

The procedural and substantive rationality of the process

Decision Making Efficiency

The better use of available data

A reduction in the time taken for decision making

Improvements in the predictive accuracy of the decision making process

Greater focusing of the process on key issues.

Intra-DSS Measures

Attitudes to DSS

Enhanced employee welfare

Improved tangible and intangible relationships

Satisfaction with the procedures for getting reports

Satisfaction with the procedures for getting systems enhancements and maintenance

Quality of Use of DSS

The application of the DSS to a major problem area

Repeat use

Utilisation ratio

Widespread use.

Information Quality

Accuracy/reliability of the information

Communications thoroughness

Format and contents of reports
Information scope
Timeliness of this information
Value of information

Intelligence Quality

Better understanding of the organisation and its environment
Generation of ideas
New insights and learning

Process Quality

An enhanced commitment to action
Improved negotiation quality
Fuller consensus formation
A belief that more intelligent decisions are being taken
Increased confidence in the decision
More participants
More and more equal participation
Enhanced openness of the process
Less emotive meetings
Decreased domination by one or a few individuals
A fuller and deeper ownership of the outcomes
Enhanced meeting interest
Willingness to work with the group again

Validity

Construct validity
Content validity
Theoretical validity.

8.15. APPLICATIONS OF A DSS

Applications of a DSS can be classified into following *three* categories:

1. **Independent problems.** The independent probelms are 'standalone problems' whose solutions are independent of other problems. The goal is to find the best solution to the given problem. In the business world, independent problems are rare.

2. **Interrelated problems.** In interrelated problems, solutions are interrelated, by each other, to find the most effective solution to the group of interrelated problems. These type of problems usually require team effort. Suppose Thums Up's goal is to increase sales of its soft drink by 10% this summer. This requires the coordination of a set of interrelated tasks, such as developing an effective advertising campaign, motivation of the sales force, developing pricing strategies, and offering incentives to distributors. To accomplish these tasks, talents of a group of experts are required.

3. **Organisational problems.** In organisational problems, all departments within an organisation are included. Such problems require team effort. Total quality management is a good example of an organisational effort, because for it to be effective, it requires a joint effort from all departments/units in the organisation.

A DSS is ideal for interrelated and inter-organisation problems. For example, in a manufacturing environment, a DSS can help a production manager answer complex and data-intensive questions such as the number of machines to be operated, the amount of materials required to fill a new order, production scheduling, and labour scheduling.

Another application of DSS is forecasting, demand management, and supplier evaluation. A DSS can consolidate data from different sources to forecast demand, determine the appropriate quantity and mix the resources necessary to meet the demand, and balance supply and demand for a wide variety of products. It can also present managers with comprehensive data about different company projects, programs, and products so that they can make sound decisions. Other applications of DSS include corporate planning, developing effective advertising strategies and pricing policies, determining an optimal product mix, and handling investment portfolios. DSS are used all over the world by public, private and government agencies to solve complex and data-intensive problems. In India, DSS is being especially used to develop regional health care plans.

8.16. TPS, MIS, DSS AND EIS

A transaction processing system (TPS) is designed to capture data related to various transactions within the organisation and is well suited to highly structured and routine tasks that support operational decision making. The output of the TPS becomes the input to the MIS. While TPS and MIS primarily support operational decision making, DSS and EIS support tactical and strategic decision making. Today, DSS and EIS are used at all levels in the organisation. The overall goal, however, is to integrate the different systems to meet the overall needs of the business.

The differences among TPS, MIS, DSS and EIS are given in Table 8.3.

Table 8.3. Differences and Similarities among TPS, MIS, DSS and EIS

	TPS	*MIS*	*DSS*	*EIS*
Targeted Audience	Operational Management	Operational Management	Middle Management	Top Management
Primary Purpose	Capture Transaction Data	Generate Summary and Exception Reports	FacilitateGenerate Decision Making	Clear, Concise, Enterprise-wide Information
Nature of Tasks	Highly Structured	Highly Structured	Semi- or Unstructured	Semi- or Unstructured
Type of Data	Internal	Internal	Internal and External	Internal and External

8.17. FUTURE DEVELOPMENTS IN DSS

Although the technology of DSS is now reasonably well established, there remains a substantial mismatch between the information and intelligence made available, which is necessary for managerial decision making. There is also a mismatch between the means by which information is made available and intelligence is produced. This is especially true at strategic levels, where the need is to be able to handle qualitative, ill-structured and messy information. Most recent DSS are only able to handle quantitative, certain and well defined data.

Three general areas can be identified where the future thrusts of DSS lie. These are improvements in current DSS (generally single-user DSS); the inclusion of Expert System methodologies into DSS; and developments in GDSS. In all cases, there should be strong moves into the softer, more qualitative areas.

Review Questions

1. Define a DSS. What are the other definitions of DSS ?
2. How did Gorry and Scott Morton initially view the DSS ?
3. Explain structured, semi-structured and unstructured problems and the decisions arrived at in each category. Outline the differences among them.
4. Can a computer make decisions ? Discuss.
5. 'DSS are especially useful for semi-structured problems'. Comment on this statement. Give examples.
6. Does Alter's *make decisions* type of DSS replace the manager ? Explain.
7. Explain *three* objectives of DSS.
8. Explain Alter's classification of DSS with type of operation and examples in each class.
9. What is the difference between a set of structured decision rules and a decision support system.
10. Give examples of type of problems for which each of the seven classes of decision support systems would be appropriate. For each, specify who would operate the system.
11. Identify and explain *any three* characteristics of a decision support system.
12. What are the three main components of a DSS. Explain each type of component.
13. Outline the functions of a model builder.
14. Name and describe the *five* functions of a DSS.
15. If you are designing a weekly report for a departmental head, showing the hours that each employee worked each day, would you use a graph or a tabular display ? Support your answer.
16. When are graphs required to be used ?
17. Outline the key points for choosing between the various types of graphs.
18. How is development of DSS determined ?
19. What are the factors involved in the selection of a language for DSSs ?
20. What are the *three* advantages of using programming languages for DSSs ?
21. What are the *three* methods for developing a DSS. Explain each of them in detail with examples.
22. What is a GDSS and how does it facilitate group decision making ?
23. What are the *three* types of computer-based support available in a GDSS ?
24. What is an EIS and how does it support unstructured decision making ?
25. What is the role of facilitator in a GDSS.
26. Explain the drill-down function through an example.
27. How does Kotter's use of the term 'environment' differ from how we have been using it ?
28. Is it necessary for the EIS to include computer-produced information ?
29. What are the critical success factors for EIS technology ? Why is selecting the right problem a critical step ?
30. Outline the success criteria for DSS/EIS.
31. Establish a relation between DSS and EIS with the help of a suitable diagram.
32. Outline the measures of success of DSS in organisations, with appropriate illustration.
33. What are the differences among TPS, MIS, DSS and EIS ?
34. Describe *any three* applications of DSS.
35. What are your suggestions for future developments in DSS ?

9

Artificial Intelligence

9.1. INTRODUCTION

Every organisation, irrespective of the business in which it operates, depends on the knowledge and skills of its employees. Knowledge workers make up a critical resource. The output of knowledge is reflected in many ways. For example: a new idea for a product or an elegant solution to a nagging problem or a new approach to a procedure. Therefore, knowledge must be preserved, protected, enhanced, consolidated, and coordinated. It must be *preserved* so that it is not lost when an employee leaves the organisation; it should be *protected* from competitors if an organisation is to succeed in the long run. The organisation must make all efforts to *enhance* its knowledge in order to sustain in the marketplace. Knowledge *consolidation* is the integration of knowledge from a variety of experts. Knowledge from different sources must be *coordinated*, particularly for companies having world-wide network, this task becomes more and more challenging.

The technologies that assist in the handling of knowledge are broadly referred to as artificial intelligence (AI). A broad overview of artificial intelligence and a more detailed view of its two branches — expert systems and neural networks — are given in this chapter.

9.2. DEFINITIONS

Artificial intelligence (AI) is concerned with using computers to perform tasks that would be called 'intelligent' if people did them. The objectives are two-fold: to improve understanding of human cognition and to improve the potential of the computer as a tool for problem-solving.

According to Holsapple and Whinston (1987), 'artificial intelligence is the activity of providing such machines as computers with the ability to display behaviour that would be regarded as intelligent if it were observed in humans.'

Another definition of artificial intelligence is: 'A field of study that designs and develops machines capable of performing tasks that would require intelligence if performed by a human being (Rich, 1987).'

A more formal definition of artificial intelligence, from Barr and Feigenbaum (1981), is : 'A branch of computer science concerned with designing intelligent computer systems, that is, systems that exhibit the characteristics associated with intelligence in human behaviour — understanding, language, learning, reasoning, solving problems, and so on.'

9.3. HISTORY OF AI

The term AI was coined by John McCarthy as the theme of a conference held at Dartmouth College. In the same year, the first AI computer program, called Logic Theorist, was announced. This program encouraged researchers to develop another program, called the General Problem Solver (GPS), that was intended for use in solving problems of all kinds.

For the past 15-20 years, there has been an increasing interest in using the computer for artificial intelligence. The idea is to develop a machine that can reason, learn, understand, recall and explain its behaviour, and actions can be viewed as an intelligent machine. However, even today, three to four decades after AI was conceived, the creation of truly intelligent machines is still not quite a reality.

9.4. AREAS OF AI

The areas that influence AI and the branches of AI are expert systems, robotics, natural language, learning, computer vision, perceptive systems, AI hardware, and neural networks. These areas are illustrated in Fig. 9.1, which indicates certain amount of overlap among the areas. The overlap illustrates the way that one area can benefit the others. A brief explanation of various branches of AI is given.

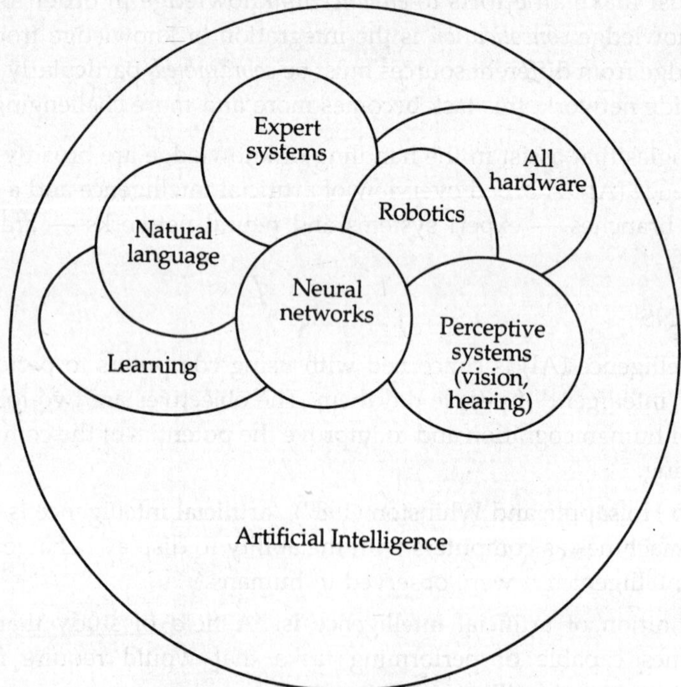

Fig. 9.1 Areas of Artificial Intelligence

- **Expert systems** are computer programs that attempts to represent the knowledge of human experts, in the form of heuristics, in a specialised area. An expert system stores the knowledge of an expert in a specific area of study, such as production engineering and genetic engineering. The system applies various reasoning methods to the information stored in it, in order to solve complex problems that require both knowledge and intuition. Sometimes, the problem-solving capabilities of such systems are as good as, or even better than, those of human experts.

- **Perceptive systems** use visual images and auditory signals to instruct computers or rather devices, such as robots.
- **Computer vision** is to endow computers with the ability to recognise and identify objects and the context to which they belong. Vision capabilities enhance the ability of computers to emulate human intelligence.
- **Natural language processing** enables users to communicate with the computer in foreign languages.
- **Learning** encompasses all of the activity that enables the computer or other device to acquire knowledge in addition to what has been entered into the memory by its manufacturer or by programmers.
- **AI hardware** includes the physical device that aid in AI application.
- **Robotics** consists of computer-controlled devices that mimic the motor activities of humans.
- **Neural networks** are highly simplified models of the human nervous system that exhibit abilities such as learning, generalisation, and abstraction. These abilities enable the models to learn human-like behaviour.

Each of these areas has the potential for use in solving business problems, but so far the main benefits have come in the form of expert systems.

9.5. EXPERT SYSTEMS

An expert system is a computer application that guides the performance of ill-structured tasks which usually require experience and expertise. Using an expert system, a non-expert can achieve performance comparable to an expert in that particular domain. Expert systems can be considered an instance of a decision support system. The unique and distinguished feature of an expert system is the *knowledge base,* the data and decision rules which represent the expertise.

The concept of expert systems is based on the assumption that an expert's knowledge can be captured in computer storage and then applied by others when the need arises.

There are a number of significant problems with expert systems. They are costly to develop. Some large experimental systems require 10 to 25 work-years of effort and millions of rupees. Eliciting knowledge from an 'expert' to incorporate in an expert system is costly and difficult. One reason is that experts establish heuristics to reduce the problem space (within their own knowledge domain) and aid their search for a solution. Often, to merely ask experts how they reason is not adequate; to ask them to 'think aloud' as they respond to a problem situation may be useful but results are not certain of completeness. Another problem with the development of expert systems is the need for a simple but flexible user interface with a non-expert user. The development of expert systems represent a very active area of ongoing research. Some examples of expert systems in experimental or practical use illustrate the variety of applications.

Task domain	**Expert system**
Oil exploration	DIPMETER ADVISOR
Computer configuration	R 1
Mineral exploration	PROSPECTOR
Medical consultancy	MYCIN

For example, the doctor seeks additional expertise from a specialist for diagnosis and prescription for an ailment with which the doctor is not familiar. The accountant, in recommending a business plan for a client, will seek specialist advice from a tax consultant. Before embarking on a major contract with another company, a business executive will require expert advice on that company's financial health. All of these cases involve consultation with an expert prior to decision taking.

Not all expert systems are used for decision support. Other uses include training personnel, archiving important knowledge within an organisation.

Expert systems can be developed in a conventional programming language such as Pascal, BASIC, C^{++}, Lisp.

9.6. COMPONENTS OF AN EXPERT SYSTEM

The components of an expert system, as illustrated in Fig. 9.2, consists of *four* main parts — user interface, knowledge base, inference engine, and development engine.

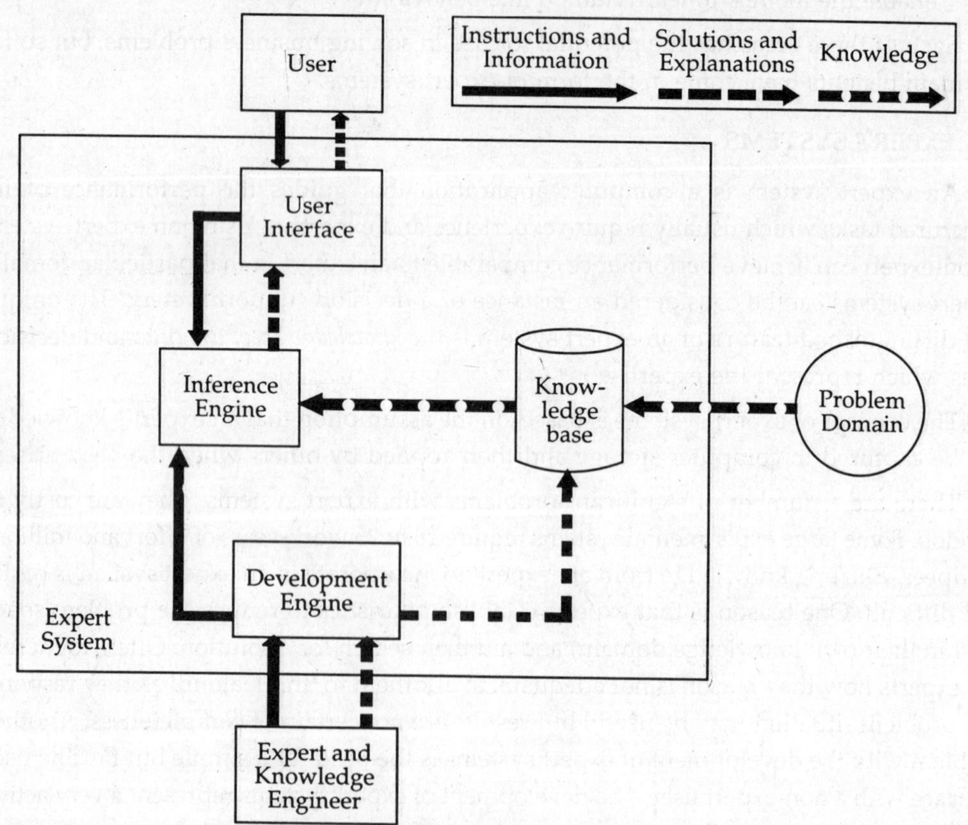

Fig. 9.2 Components of an Expert System

9.6.1. The User Interface

The user interface enables a person to enter *instructions* and *information* into the expert system and to receive information from it. The instructions specify the parameters that guide the expert system through its reasoning process. The information is in the form of values assigned to certain variables.

Expert system inputs. A person can use *four* methods for input: menus, commands, natural language, and customised interfaces. **Menus** are like those of Lotus; **Commands** are like the dot commands used with dBASE III Plus; **natural language** is like that used with a 4GL query language; and **customised interfaces** reflect particular aspects of the problem being solved.

Expert system outputs. Expert systems are designed to recommend solutions. These solutions are supplemented by explanations. There are two types of explanations: **Explanation of questions** —The person may desire explanations while the expert system performs its reasoning; **Explanation of the problem solution** — After the expert system provides a problem solution, the person can ask for an explanation of how it was reached. The expert system will display each of the reasoning steps leading to the solution.

The user interface is user-friendly, although the inner workings of the expert system can be complex. A person accustomed to interact with a computer should have no difficulty using an expert system.

9.6.2. The Knowledge Base

The knowledge base contains facts that describe the problem area, and knowledge representation techniques that describe how the facts fit together in a logical manner. The term **problem domain** is used to describe the problem area. The popular knowledge representation techniques are *rules* and *networks of rules*. The *rules* in the knowledge base are usually coded in the form, IF X THEN Y, where X is a condition, Y is an action to be taken if the condition is true.

The knowledge is often represented in the form of interconnected rules. An example of a rule from a system designed to aid a bank manager on whether to grant a loan to a client might be : If the client is a houseowner, then establish :

1. the amount of the mortgage.
2. whether there have been any payment defaults.

Many similar rules can be incorporated in such a system. The aim of the system would be to provide a recommendation, based on the bank's standard lending policy, on whether to lend to the client, the amount of the loan, and any other conditions attached to it. It is decision support rather than decision replacing because it is just one of the factors that the bank manager would take into account. There may be other circumstances, not covered by the system, that the bank manager finds relevant. Using discretion, the manager could 'overrule' the advice of the expert system.

The rules of a rule set are not physically linked, but their logical relationships can be established.

9.6.3. The Inference Engine

The inference engine of an expert system takes the rules that define how the expert processes his factual knowledge and interprets them as appropriate. Unlike a simple conventional computer program, the steps are not sequentially determined by the programmer, but follow from the data input and the results obtained at earlier stages in the use of the system.

The inference engine works in either *forward chaining* or *backward chaining*, mode or both. Backward chaining proceeds faster than forward chaining because it does not have to consider all of the rules and does not make multiple passes through the rule set. Backward chaining is especially appropriate when:

- There are multiple goal variables.
- There are many rules.
- All or most of the rules do not have to be examined in the process of reaching a solution.

Similarly, forward chaining is preferred if the goal is to draw some conclusions based on a given set of facts.

Some inference engines are designed to perform both forward and backward chaining. In that case, the user specifies which one to use.

9.6.4. The Development Engine

The development engine is used to create the expert system. This process essentially involves building the rule set. There are two basic approaches: **programming languages** and **expert system shells.**

Programming languages. An expert system can be created using any programming language; however, two are especially suited to the symbolic representation of the knowledge base : Lisp and Prolog.

Expert system shells. An expert system shell is a readymade processor that can be tailored to a specific problem domain through the addition of the appropriate knowledge base. In most cases, the shell can produce an expert system quicker and easier than by programming. Today, applying expert systems to business problems involves the use of shells. The first commercial shell was KEE, for Knowledge Engineering Environment. It was designed for use on a computer designed especially for the Lisp language — a **Lisp machine.** However, the introduction of faster devices such as RISC (for reduced instruction set computing) has caused most development to move away from Lisp machines and onto the new platforms. Development work is also beginning to branch out to multiprocessing machines that combine multiple CPUs.

Role of the systems analyst. The term *knowledge engineer* has been used to describe the person who works with the expert in designing an expert system. For developing conventional computer applications, the systems analyst must (*a*) understand how experts apply their own knowledge in solving problem, and (*b*) be able to extract a description of that knowledge from the expert. The process of extracting the knowledge has been termed *knowledge acquisition.*

Svstem development process. The system development process for developing an expert system consists of the following steps:

1. Study the problem domain
2. Define the problem
3. Specify the rule set
4. Test the prototype system

5. Construct the interface
6. Conduct user tests
7. Use the system
8. Maintain the system.

9.7. ADVANTAGES AND DISADVANTAGES OF EXPERT SYSTEMS

As with all computer applications, expert systems offer some real advantages, but there are also disadvantages. The advantages can accrue to both managers and the organisation.

9.7.1. Advantages of Expert Systems to Managers

Following are the advantages of expert systems to managers:

- Make better decisions by considering more alternatives.
- Apply a higher level of logic in evaluating the alternatives.
- More time to evaluate decision results.
- Achieve a consistency in the decisions taken.

9.7.2. Advantages of Expert Systems to the Organisations

An organisation that implements an expert system can expect:

- Better performance for the organisation.
- Maintain control over the organisation's knowledge.

9.7.3. Disadvantages of Expert Systems

The disadvantages of expert systems are:

- They cannot handle inconsistent knowledge.
- They cannot apply the judgement and intuition recognised as important ingredients of problem-solving.
- They cannot apply to unstructured/partially structured problems.

9.8. BUSINESS APPLICATIONS OF EXPERT SYSTEMS

Business applications of knowledge-based systems are many. Some of them are given.

Manufacturing

- Maintaining facilities
- Analysing quality and providing corrective measures
- Determining whether a process is running correctly
- Scheduling job-shop tasks
- Selecting transportation routes
- Assisting with product design and facility layouts.

Marketing

- Establishing sales quotas
- Responding to customer inquiries
- Assisting with marketing timing decisions
- Determining discount policies.

Accounting and Finance

- Providing tax advice and assistance

- Helping with credit-authorisation decisions
- Selecting forecasting models
- Providing investment advice.

Personnel

- Assessing applicant qualifications
- Giving employees assistance in filling out forms.

General Business

- Assisting with project proposals
- Recommending acquisition strategies
- Educating trainees
- Evaluating performance.

9.9. CRITERIA FOR ADOPTING EXPERT SYSTEM

The following factors should be taken into account if an expert system is required to be developed for a potential application area:

- **Availability** — One or more experts are capable of communicating how they go about solving the problems to which the expert system will be applied.
- **Complexity** — Solutions of the problems for which the expert system will be used is a complex task that requires logical inference processing, which would not be easily handled by conventional information processing.
- **Domain** — The domain, or subject area, of the problem is relatively small and limited to a well-defined area.
- **Expertise** — Solutions to the problem require the efforts of experts. This means only a few people possess the knowledge, techniques, and intuition needed.
- **Structure** — The solution process must be able to cope with ill-structured, uncertain, missing, and conflicting data, and a dynamic problem-solving situation.

9.10. NEURAL NETWORKS

Neural networks is another growing branch of artificial intelligence. A neural network is a program that models the pattern-recognition capabilities of the human brain, thereby endowing machines with the ability to identify and classify faces, voices, pictures, and written characters. Neural networks are programs that model the inter-connections of human brain cells. These networks can find patterns that may not be obvious to the human eye and can detect and perceive correlations among hundreds of variables, whereas humans can consider only two or three variables at a time.

9.10.1. Neural Networks Process

A generic neural network is illustrated in Fig. 9.3. It is made up of interconnected processing elements (PEs), which are self-adjusting units that are firmly connected with other PEs in the system. A PE receives inputs from the user; each input has a certain weight assigned to it. The weights influence the way the input is processed by the PE, and the PE is capable of automatically adjusting the weights of the inputs based on its past experiences. Each PE processes the input and generates a *single* output signal to other PEs in the network. The system observes the overall *pattern* of outputs generated by PEs; this pattern forms the basis for information, analysis and retrieval. Thus, unlike other computers, which are *programmed* to perform a task, neural computers are *trained* to perform a task. By controlling and fine tuning the type and flow of information among PEs, the software gradually changes the connections between them, and in this way new information is 'learned'. For example, one neural network learned overnight to pronounce 20,000 words.

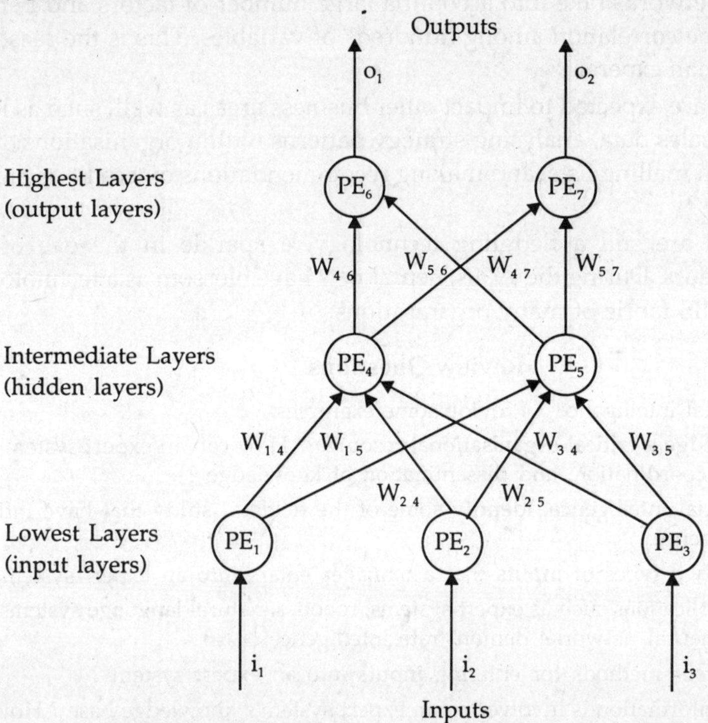

Legend : PE = processing element; W_{ij} = weight of connection between processing elements; i_j = input sources; and o_j = neural network outputs.

Fig. 9.3 Main Elements of a Neural Network

One of the biggest advantages of neural networks is that they do not require any special hardware and can easily be integrated with existing applications and technologies, such as spreadsheets and expert systems. Successful use of neural networks requires only a good understanding of the organisation, its data, the business processes that generate the data, and the business implications of the data.

9.11. APPLICATIONS OF NEURAL NETWORKS

Neural networks is one of the emerging computer technologies in the U.S., Europe, and Japan. Many organisations have started to invest in this technology because it provides a way to recognise complex patterns.

The applications of neural networks include detection of credit card fraud; a diagnostic tool, called Neuroscope, developed by researchers at IBM, France, which runs on a PC and provides early warnings of failure in industrial machinery such as motors, cleaning tools, and pneumatic robots, thus making 'predictive maintenance' a reality. Neural networks are used extensively in financial forecasting. By studying factors such as changing patterns in debt level, cash flow, earnings estimates, and other financial variables that measures the health of an organisation.

Neural networks also perform real estate appraisals by taking into account variables such as location, interior layout, and building materials. The appraisals of the neural networks are more consistent and accurate than those of human appraisers, because the system also compares and studies data on similar houses in similar markets. While human beings are capable of taking into account only a few factors and analysing their correlations, neural networks take into account a large number of factors and perform a detailed analysis of the correlation among hundreds of variables. This is the reason they often outperform human experts.

Neural networks are expected to impact other business areas as well, such as looking for trend patterns in sales data, analysing strategy patterns within organisations, looking for duplicate names in mailing lists, and making recommendations on credit or mortgage applications.

Neural networks are still a fledgling technology, a sparkle in the eye of many technology entrepreneurs. During the 1990s, neural nets have blossom as a technology and are woven into the MIS fabric of many organisations.

Review Questions

1. What is artificial intelligence ? Provide some examples.
2. Why is knowledge a critical organisational resource ? How can an expert system help in the collection, coordination, and dissemination of knowledge ?
3. Describe artificial intelligence. Identify some of the fields of study that have influenced artificial intelligence.
4. What are the two types of inputs that a manager enters into an expert system ?
5. How do AI applications such as expert systems, robotics, natural language systems, vision systems, and neural networks demonstrate intelligence.
6. What are the *four* methods for entering inputs into an expert system ?
7. What type of information is involved in an expert system's knowledge base ? How many relationships between facts be represented ?
8. What is the difference between forward and backward chaining ?
9. Explain briefly the expert system shell.
10. What is the purpose of a knowledge acquisition subsystem ?
11. What is the difference between a computer program that uses expert systems and a conventional computer program.
12. What special skills does the systems analyst need in order to work with the expert in developing an expert system ?
13. What are the two types of explanations produced by an expert system ?
14. Outline the merits and demerits of an expert system.
15. List out the business applications of expert systems.
16. What are the criteria for adopting an expert system ?
17. Describe the major characteristics of neural networks. How many of these be implemented ?
18. How do neural networks 'learn' to recognise patterns ?
19. Identify several applications of neural networks.
20. What is a neural network and how does it differ from more familiar software ? Give two examples of neural networks.

10

Office Information Systems

10.1. INTRODUCTION

Computer technology, during the past 30 years, has helped to enhance productivity in the office. The movement towards automation in office work is often called *office automation* (OA). Office automation includes the new hardware and software technologies — word processors, spreadsheet packages, electronic mail and so on — that make office workers more productive, in addition to the attendant situations created by OA technologies and the people that use these technologies. These combinations of information technologies that have a dramatic impact on day-to-day office operations are called **office information systems** (OIS).

Automation began in the factory and spread to the office in the form of office automation. Originally OA was intended to assist secretarial and clerical workers, but its ability to facilitate both formal and informal communications with people both inside and outside the organisation attracted managers and professionals as users. All of these users use OA to increase their productivity.

There are many OA applications. Some require the use of the computer, some do not. All, however, can provide problem-solving information. OA can be tailored to the communication needs of each manager. A particular manager's OA mix is influenced by the type of organisation, the manager's personal preference, and the OA resources available to him. OA appeals to managers at all levels because it not only supplements their traditional interpersonal communications media but offers new communications capabilities as well.

10.2. OFFICE AUTOMATION

The origin of office automation can be traced back to early 1960s, when IBM coined the term *word processing* to describe the activity of its electronic typewriter division. The term expressed the concept that office activity is centered on the processing of words. The intent was to draw the same attention to office products that had been lavished on computers and *data processing.* Since the debut of word processing, other technologies have been applied to office work. It includes all formal and informal electronic systems primarily concerned with the communication of information to and from persons both inside and outside the organisation.

10.3. OFFICES AND OFFICE SYSTEMS

The fundamental nature of office work has changed drastically over the past 30 to 40 years. At one time, virtually the only role of equipment in the office was to help workers become more efficient. Until the mid-1960s, only the typewriter, phone, copying machine, and electronic adding machine were standard office equipment. Now, as computer technologies have a strong presence in offices, office workers have powerful tools that make them more effective.

10.3.1. Nature of the Office

In general, an *office* is a place where staff and line professionals, secretaries, and clerks perform management and administrative tasks. The work performed by office workers is often called white collar work.

Office workers. Generally, *five* types of workers can be found in the office :

1. *Managers* — Managers generally spend most of their time in planning, coordinating, and controlling the activities of other people. Some examples are examination controller, chief executive officer, operations manager, head of marketing research, and the principal of the college.

2. *Staff professionals* — Staff professionals support the activities of managers. These professionals have no direct line responsibility, *i.e.*, their role is mostly one of planning, analysing, and informing management of their findings.

3. *Line professionals* — Line professionals include sales persons and purchasing agents. They typically interact daily with such outside groups as the organisation's customers and suppliers.

4. *Secretaries* — Secretaries are normally assigned to one or more knowledge workers in an office. They perform such support tasks as typing, filing, answering phones, and keeping appointment calendars.

5. *Clerical personnel* — Clerical personnel are usually not assigned to anyone in particular. Generally, they support the entire department/section/division. Typical tasks of clerks are filing, typing, and assisting in report preparation.

OA professionals. In many organisations, a separate support group is responsible for promoting and managing office system technologies. The OA personnel often perform a variety of representative office tasks on test or demonstration equipment and for product demonstrations within the organisation by OIS hardware and software.

Office work. The various management and administrative tasks performed in the office can be divided into following *five* categories :

- Decision making
- Data manipulation
- Document handling
- Communication
- Storage

All of the office systems applications fall into at least one of these categories.

10.3.2. Evolution of Office Systems

Until the mid 1960s, information technologies in the office were typewriters, phones, copying machines and electric adding machines. In 1964, a seemingly modest typing, called **word processing**, appeared. Since then, information processing in the office has never been the same. The introduction of microcomputers and small business computers in the late 1960s and early 1970s also contributed to the alteration of the office's technology. Smaller computers made it possible to decentralise computing down to regional offices and individual offices. It was not unusual for large offices to own their computers. This trend towards decentralisation was called *distributed data processing* (DDP).

Owing to inexpensive microcomputer systems, quality microcomputer software, electronic mail, internet, LAN, and gateways to mainframe systems, office technology is changing yet again. The proliferation of computing technologies into office life has been so pervasive that computer-illiterate knowledge workers have problems in most of today's offices. Two terms are associated with the computerisation of offices in the 1980s and 1990s: office automation and departmental computing. Here, office automation is preferred because it is more widely accepted.

Of all the areas currently under the MIS domain, the office information systems area is probably the hardest to define because it is composed of many different technologies and overlaps considerably with the end-user computing, discussed in a later chapter, and DSS areas.

The primary purpose of office information systems is to facilitate communication among members of an organisation and between the organisation and its external environment. Ideally, an office information system allows individuals and group members to create, store, and exchange messages through a variety of communications media, including data, documents, images, voice (audio), and video. OA is moving towards the realisation of these ideals. The electronic office of today looks entirely different from the mechanised office of just a few years ago. Even more dramatic changes are in store. Now, we are beginning to witness the **virtual corporation,** which gives people the ability to work from any place without being confined by physical boundaries. Fig. 10.1 shows the major components of an office information system.

Various kinds of office automation tools and equipment needed to support these tools are given in Table 10.1.

Table 10.1 Office Automation Tools and Equipment Needed for OIS

Tool	*Type of Data*	*Computer*	*Description*	*Technology*
Word Processing	Written	Yes	Programs that make it easy to create and alter documents.	Computer, printer
Desktop Publishing	Written	Yes	Programs with extensive word processing and graphic capabilities.	High-resolution computer, printer
Imaging	Written, grpahics	Yes	Imaging converts paper, microfilm, microfiche, and electronic data into digital images that can be printed, faxed, or viewed on a computer screen.	Scanner, optical disks, workstation
E-mail	Written	Yes	Programs that allow individuals, who are linked through a network, to electronically communicate with each other, any time, anywhere in the world.	Computer, network

contd. ...

Tool	Type of Data	Computer	Description	Technology
Fax	Written	No	Uses telephone lines to transmit documents.	Fax machine, telephone
Groupware	Oral, written, visual	Yes	A broad term given to communication tools such as E-mail, voice, fax, and videoconferencing, that foster group decision making.	A multitude of tools are used in groupware. The nature of the tool depends on the kind of application
Multimedia	Written, audio, visual	Yes	A computer-based tool that uses a graphical and interactive interface and combines two or more media types, such as text, graphics, animation, audio, and video. Today, many computers have multimedia capabilities which include a sound card and a video card.	Multimedia computer and printer
Voice Mail	Oral	Yes	The sender's voice message is processed by a modem and stored in a server at the receiver's end. When the receiver is ready to receive the message, the digitized message is retrieved from the server and reconverted into analog signals.	Telephone, server, network
Videoconferencing	Oral, visual	No	A type of electronic meeting system that uses telephone, television, computers and communication links to allow geographically separated decision makers to hear and see each other.	Telephone, television, network

Virtual Corporation. The concept of virtual corporation was popularised by William Davidow a few years ago. It is a group of employers and employees who are not bound by a physical work environment, but instead use technology to come together temporarily and communicate to achieve a shared business goal.

In a virtual corporation, employees don't come to a place called work; instead, they can work from anywhere, at any time; thus businesses need not invest in office space, furniture, and other amenities. Mobile computing will allow workers at remote locations to dial up the office, retrieve messages and urgent documents via touch-tone phones or voice recognition systems, and give directions to their co-workers in the organisation as easily as if they were in the same building. Evidently, the virtual office will create a different kind of knowledge worker and pose new challenges for the management.

Successful managers will know how to differentiate when it is appropriate to use technology to share resources and when a face-to-face meeting is called for. Perhaps the greatest challenge will be the culture shock and the lack of control that managers may feel when they face quiet corridors and invisible employees. The personal lives of employees will also be affected, because the virtual office guarantees around-the-clock electronic access to any employee, any time, anywhere in the world, thus increasing the potential for employee burnout. Since the access of the virtual office depends to a large extent on technology and its applications, technology decisions and failures will be critical to organisational success.

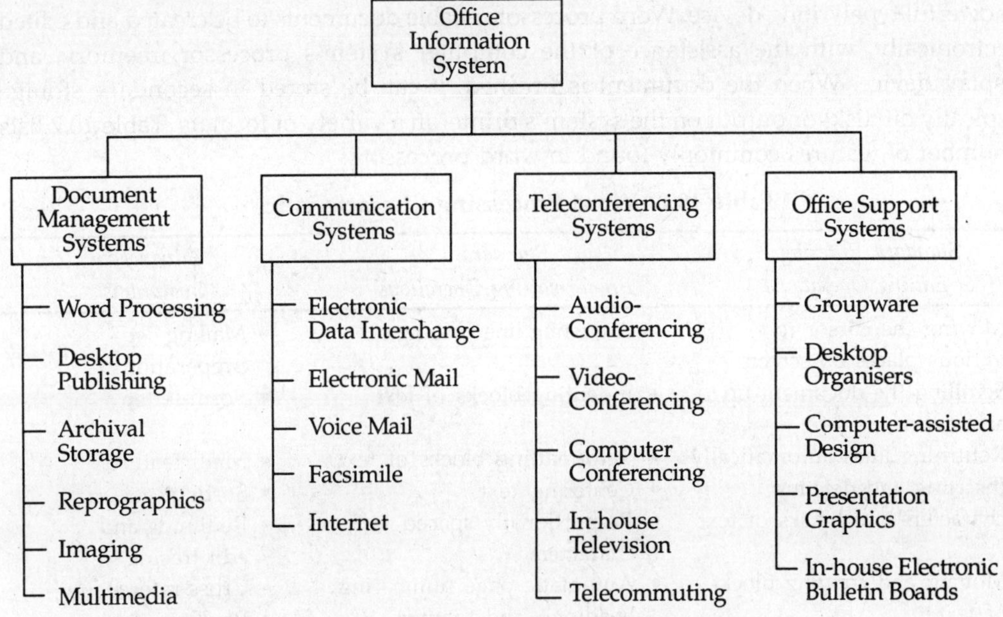

Fig. 10.1 Major Components of an Office Information System

In essence, any discussion of office automation must be based on the understanding that tremendous change is on the way and that new approaches to information sharing will principally change the way knowledge workers receive, process, and disseminate information.

10.4. TYPES OF OFFICE AUTOMATION SYSTEMS

There are *four* major types of office automation systems (Fig. 10.1). These are:

- Document management systems
- Communication systems
- Teleconferencing systems
- Office support systems

The applications of these systems are shown in Fig. 10.1.

10.4.1. Document Management Systems

Document management systems are computer-based tools that provide access to repositories of data, regardless of their form (text, graphics, or images) or location. The retrieved documents can be displayed in different formats, edited, distributed, and integrated using other communication systems. These communication systems include word processing, desktop publishing, archival storage, reprographics, imaging and multimedia. Such systems enable knowledge workers to better control, coordinate, and manage the myriad electronic documents used in decision making. Some of the applications fall under document management systems are discussed.

Word Processing

The most widely used and recognised office-system technology is word processing. It involves hardware and software tools that allow the computer system to become more than a powerful typewriting device. Word processors enable documents to be created and edited electronically, with the assistance of the computer system's processor, memory, and display device. When the document is finished, it can be stored in secondary storage (typically on disk) or output on the system's printer in a variety of formats. Table 10.2 lists a number of features commonly found in word processors.

Table 10.2. Word Processing Characteristics

Standard Entering & Editing Operations	*Standard Pre-formatting Operations*	*Advanced Operations*
• Moving the cursor to various places on screen	• Adjusting line spacing	• Mailing list preparation
• Scrolling the document up and down	• Indenting blocks of text	• Form-letter
• Returning lines automatically	• Reformatting blocks of text	• Math feature
• Inserting and deleting characters and blocks of text	• Centering text	• Sorting
	• Proportionally spaced characters	• Redlining and edit tracing
• Moving and copying blocks of text	• Automatic page numbering, headings, and footings	• Cross-referencing
• Searching for text strings	• Multiple columns per page	• Preparing index and table of contents
• Replacing text strings	• Selection of fonts	• Desktop publishing features
• Spell check	• Orphan and widow elimination	• Integrated with spreadsheet program
• Thesaurus feature		• Embedded typesetting codes

Today, word processing packages that run on general purpose computers is in the microcomputing area, where such packages as WordPerfect, Microsoft Word, WordStar, MS-Office are among the current leaders. Many of these packages are recently released versions for the Windows operating environment. Newer versions of these packages incorporate numerous graphics and desktop publishing features that were not included in earlier versions.

With the popularity of computer networking, 'shared' word processing systems are designed to share the resources of a communication network, *e.g.*, LAN, WAN.

Desktop Publishing

Desktop publishing (DTP) is the use of a computer to prepare printed output. It consists of a microcomputer configuration, shown in Fig. 10.2. The configuration includes a high-resolution cathode ray tube screen and a laser printer, and is driven by DTP software. The high-resolution screen enables the operator to display the image in a WYSIWYG form. **WYSIWYG** means "what you see is what you get." The screen display looks exactly like the hard copy that will be produced by the laser printer. The DTP software permits the selection of type fonts and sizes, hyphenation and right-margin justification, the addition of horizontal and vertical lines, and layout of pages (including graphics).

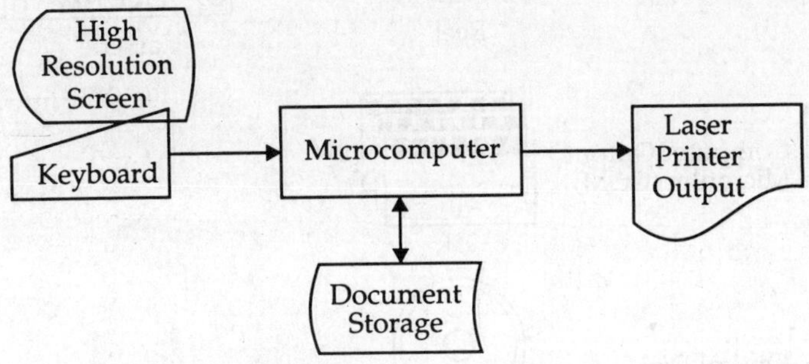

Fig. 10.2 A DTP System

DTP applications fall into three areas :

- *Administrative applications* include documents intended for such internal use as correspondence, reports, and newsletters.
- *Technical applications* include such training materials as slides, overhead transparencies, and manuals.
- *Corporate graphics* include advertisements, brochures, and other documents intended for use outside the firm.

To the MIS organisation, beyond the technology of DTP lie many management-oriented challenges and several opportunities. Educating users and establishing standards for use are among these challenges. The problems of implementing DTP systems are that some users carry DTP to its extreme and also the lack of general knowledge about DTP.

Archival Storage

One of the key functions in an office is storage. To save the expense associated with storage space, handling, and paper costs, archival data was traditionally placed onto various media and stored off-line. Such media are also particularly useful to firms requiring to keep large files available that do not have to be updated, or to firms that need to process large amounts of data but find on-line access too expensive.

Four common technologies used to store archival materials are :

- *Magnetic tape* — It is one of the oldest and most common ways of storing data for archival purposes. Tape is inexpensive, compact, and can store rather large text files.
- *Computer output microfilm* (*COM*) — COM refers to all technologies that either place data onto microfilm media — such as a reel of microfilm or a microfiche card — or that allow those media to be read by humans. Microfilming media are often superior

to magnetic tape because they are better suited to graphic data, easier to handle and use in many situations, and are more rugged.

- *Optical disks* — Optical disks for microcomputers store 650 MB of data on a single 5 $\frac{1}{4}$" platter. Those for midrange and mainframe systems are usually larger in diameter and have storage capacities in the multigigabyte range. It is felt that this medium will encroach seriously on the archival storage niche now occupied by COM.

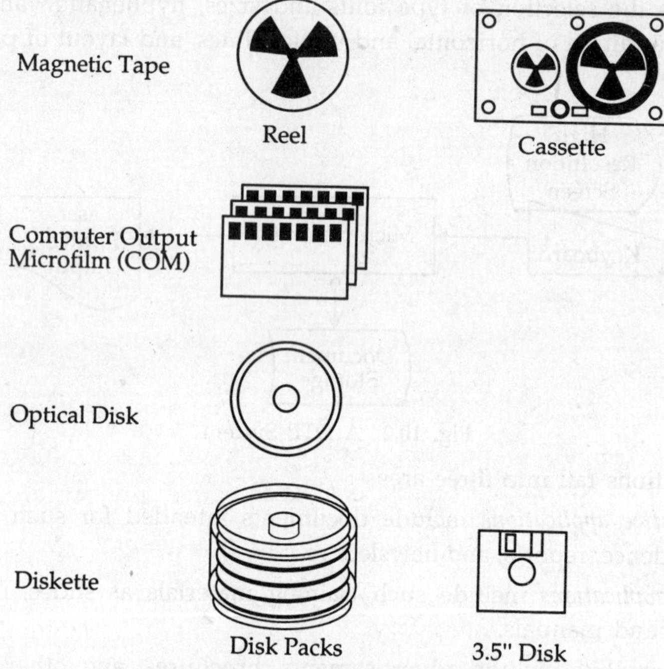

Fig. 10.3 Archival Storage Media

- *Diskettes* — Diskettes are suitable only in those situations in which modest amounts of archival storage are necessary.

These media are shown in Fig. 10.3, and are useful for storing backup copies of documents, programs or data.

Reprographics

Reprographics is the process of reproducing multiple copies of a document. Office personnel are usually reponsible for making more than one copy of a report, letter, and other documents. When documents are widely distributed, either internally or externally, reprographics often includes collating, folding, binding, and related tasks. Most of the time, however, a photocopier is used for multiple copies.

The most sophisticated type of copy equipment currently available is the *intelligent copier system.* Figure 10.4 shows that documents created on microcomputer workstations or display terminals may be electronically transmitted to the intelligent copier. Also, intelligent copiers can transmit documents to other systems.

Imaging

Imaging is a type of document management system that converts paper, microfilm, microfiche, and electronic data into digital images that can be printed, faxed, or viewed on a computer screen. LAN-based image-processing systems (Fig. 10.4), nowadays common in use, include several servers, each dedicated to a specific function such as database management, scanning, or printing.

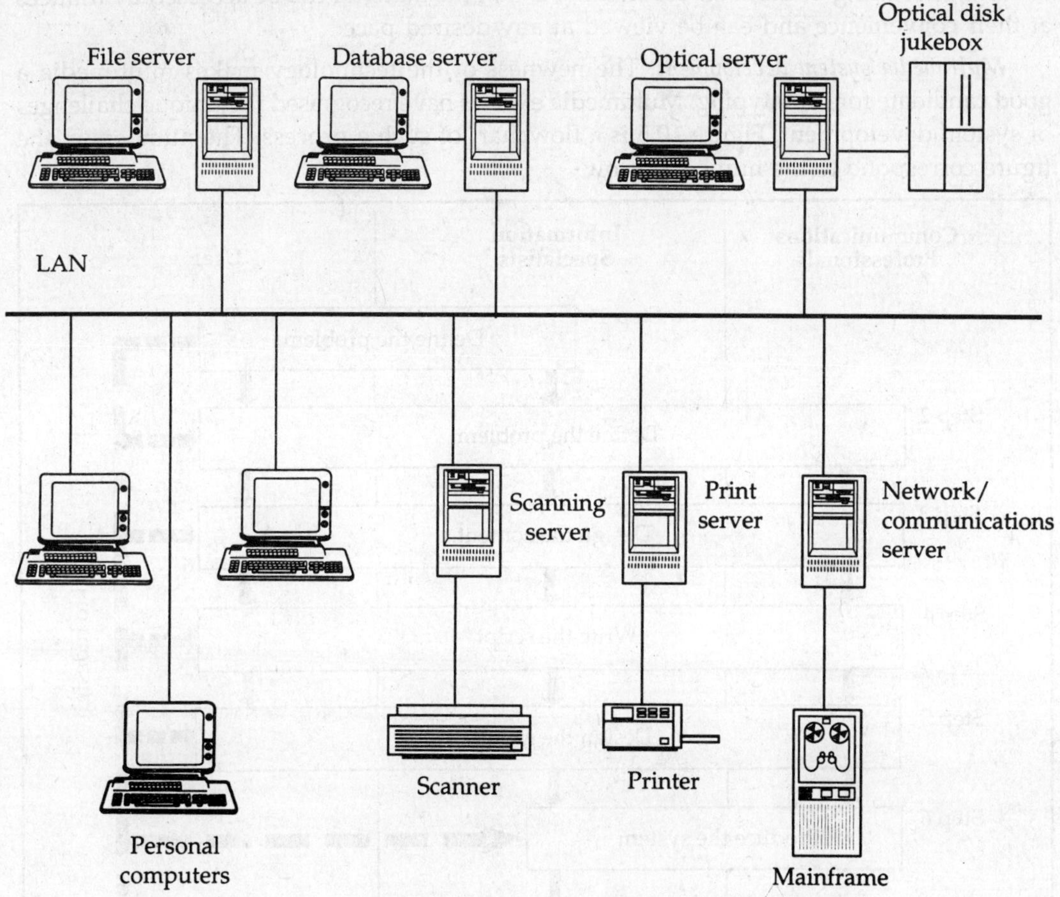

Fig. 10.4 A General LAN-based Image Processing System

The main advantage of imaging systems is the decrease in storage costs. Also, imaging allows more than one persons to view or analyse a document at the same time. Thus, imaging changes the work flow from sequential to parallel, increasing productivity.

Imaging is used in problem-solving when it is required to review historical documents for understanding a problem. An operator accesses the document management system from a workstation and produces a hard copy output for the manager.

Multimedia

Multimedia encompasses a group of computer-based technologies that integrate different types of media, such as text, graphics, animation, audio and video, to generate information. Multimedia is made possible by integrating audio and video capabilities into personal computers. Besides the usual CPU and peripherals, for a computer to have multimedia capabilities it should also have a CD-ROM drive, stereo speakers, a microphone for voice input, a sound card, a video card, and a video compression card. Any problem that requires the integration of text, graphics, sound, and video can be approached by using multimedia. Multimedia, in particular, is very useful in corporate training and business presentations. Besides, multimedia is interactive (allows two-way communication) and provides consistency in the content and the delivery of training material. Another advantage of using multimedia for training is that the material can be accessed by trainees at their convenience and can be viewed at any desired pace.

Multimedia system development. The newness of the technology makes multimedia a good candidate for prototyping. Multimedia experts have recognised the unique challenges of system development. Figure 10.5 is a flowchart of such a process. The numbers in the figure correspond to the numbers below.

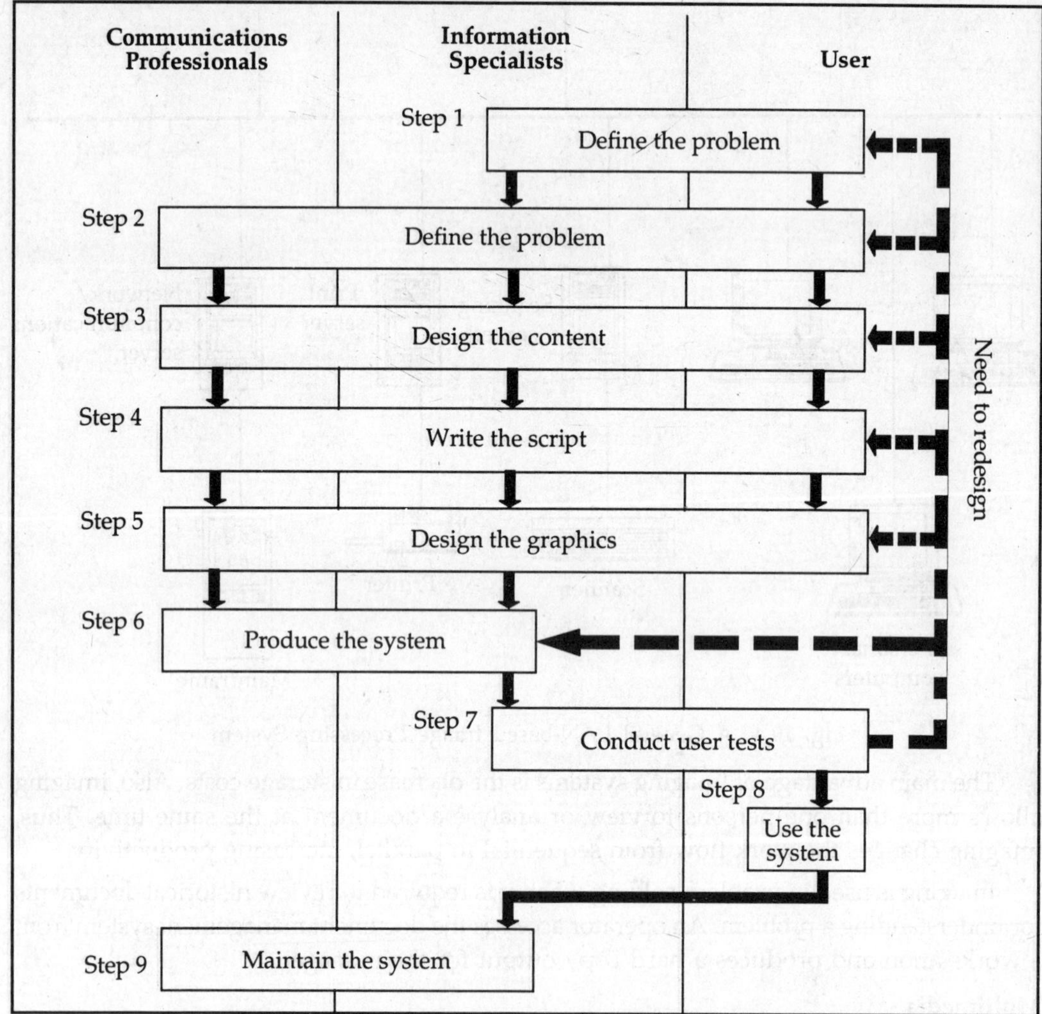

Fig. 10.5 The Multimedia System Development Process

1. Define the Problem. The systems analyst identifies the user's needs and determines that the solution requires multimedia.

2. Design the Concept. The systems analyst and user, possibly working with such communications professionals as producers, directors, and video engineers, engage in *concept design* by determining the overall message and conducting a walkthrough of all major sequences.

3. Design the Content. The developers engage in *content design* by preparing detailed application specifications. This is where the media are selected. It is important to avoid the *christmas tree look* of incorporating too much multimedia and too little system functionality.

4. Write the Script. The dialogue and all of the detailed elements of the sequences are determined.

5. Design the Graphics. Graphics are selected that support the dialogue. Any necessary sets or props to be used in videos are designed.

6. Produce the System. The system developers produce the various parts and integrate them into a system. In addition to development of the application software, the tasks involve such specialised activities as video editing, and authoring. **Authoring** is the integration of the separate elements through the use of special prewritten software.

7. Conduct User Tests. The systems analyst educates the user in system use and gives the user an opportunity to become familiar with all of the features. If the system is satisfactory, the user puts it into use. Otherwise the prototyping process is repeated by reverting back to an earlier step. This iterative process is repeated until the user is satisfied with the system.

8. Use the System. The user benefits from system use.

9. Maintain the System. Just like any other computer-based system, the multimedia system must be maintained. The main difference is that the user cannot be expected to perform the maintenance. This is the task of the specialists and professionals. Multimedia is not an end-user computing application.

In its relatively short life, multimedia has proven itself as a business tool. The potential seems almost limitless, but it is a concept that evolved in much the same way as office automation. Two popular multimedia applications fit into the OA area. One, *workgroup computing*, enables several people to share the same computer workspace at the same time. The participants can carry on a discussion while viewing a common display that may include a complete range of media, including photographs and full motion video. The other OA application is *desktop video conferencing*, which allows participants to conduct a video conference while sitting at their desks, using their microcomputer screens on attached televisions. Thus, multimedia will be an integral part of business computing, but the same type of planning, that was done for office automation, will be necessary for the multimedia technology to be applied in an effective manner.

10.4.2. Communication Systems

Various written communication systems being used in office automation are discussed.

Electronic Data Interchange

Electronic data interchange (EDI) can be defined as :

"The transfer of electronic datza, from one organisation's computer system to another, the data being structured in a commonly agreed format so that it is directly usable by the receiving organisation's computer system."

What distinguishes EDI from other electronic communications between organisations, such as fax, electronic mail, telephone and telex, is that in these latter cases the information is intended for consumption by a human being who needs to understand it before any action can be taken. With EDI the received electronic data can be immediately processed by the receiver's computer system without the necessity for human interpretation and translation before action.

EDI method. EDI may be introduced where a group of organisations wish to ensure that electronic transactions are passed between one another.

EDI groups require EDI services in order to effect the data exchanges. These are often provided by a third-party organisation. The service provided by the third party is more than merely the transmission of the data. It is customary for added facilities, especially mailbox facilities, to be offered. An electronic mailbox for a client is an electronic storage location for messages or data that are sent to the client by other organisations. The client (addressee) can read the data or messages, which are usually held on an identified area of the service provider's disk space. By providing these services the third party adds value to the data transmission and is thus said to run a *value-added network.* One of the earliest EDI groups was set up to allow international airlines to process bookings electronically worldwide (IATA).

A typical configuration for EDI transfer is illustrated in Fig. 10.6. The message produced by the sender's applications software is translated into the agreed EDI format and placed on the network by the network access software. This electronic data is sent

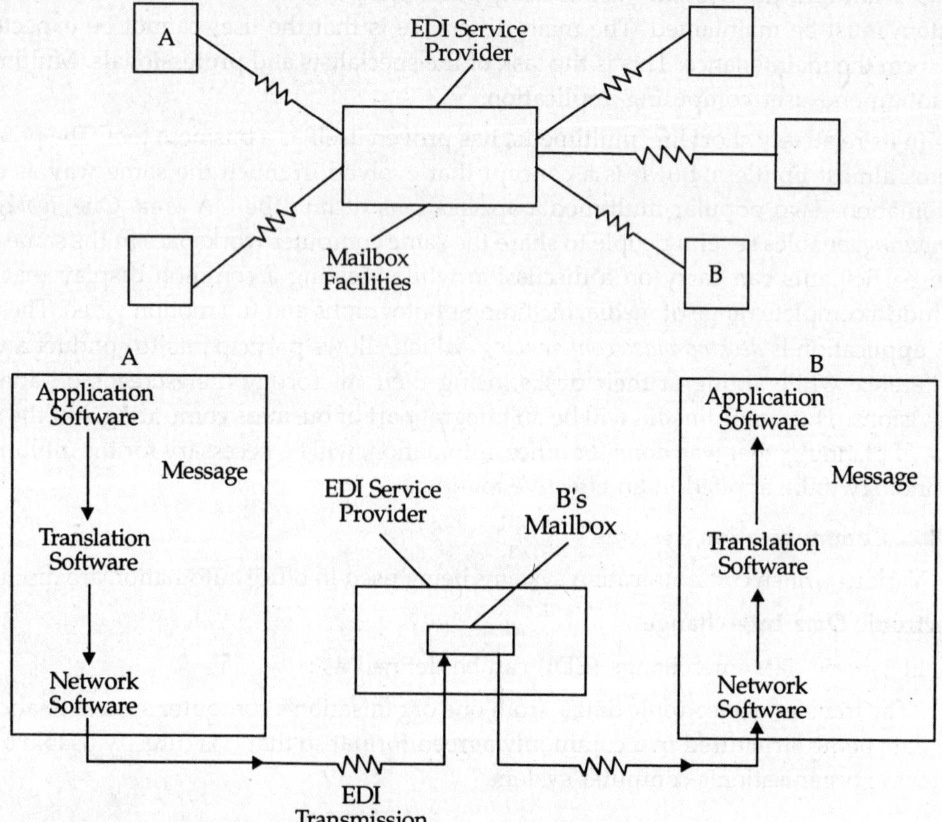

Fig. 10.6 Electronic Data Interchange Network

to the mailbox facility of the EDI service provider. Here it is stored until retrieved by the receiver organisation using the retriever's network access software. The received electronic data, in the agreed format, is then translated by software into a form directly usable by the receiver's applications programs.

Benefits of EDI. EDI ensures:

- The speed with which an inter-organisational transaction is processed, is minimized.
- The paperwork involved in transaction processing is eliminated.
- The costs of transaction processing are reduced, as much of the need for human interpretation and processing is removed.
- Reduced human involvement reduces error.

Electronic Mail

Electronic mail, popularly known as *E-mail*, is a system that allows a person or a group to electronically communicate with others through a network, in written form, at any time, from anywhere in the world. Figure 10.7 shows the system configuration. A user types a message at his/her terminal keyboard; the message is stored in the electronic mailbox of the receiver. The message is retrieved at the convenience of the recipient, using his/her terminal and providing the proper password. The electronic mailbox is usually a file on a server. Electronic mail software controls the process. Users can also edit, sort, save, and classify messages and forward them to other individuals on the network. If two users are logged onto the network at the same time, they can converse through E-mail. Some E-mail systems have multimedia capabilities allowing E-mail users to send not only text, but also voice and still pictures.

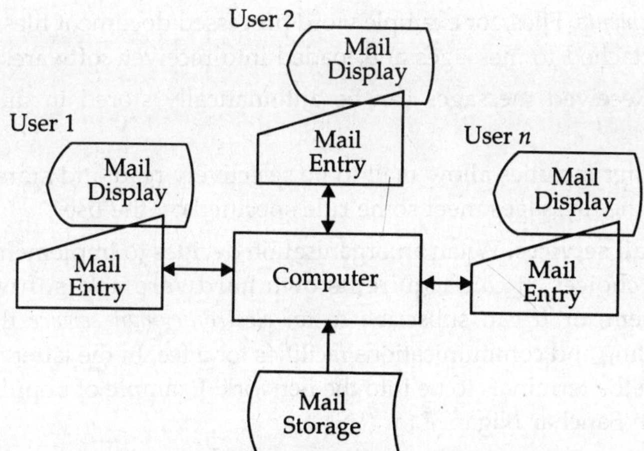

Fig. 10.7 The E-mail System Configuration

Nowadays, E-mail is a popular form of business communication with the majority of organisations possessing an E-mail address. There are a number of windows-based communications software programs for dealing with the sending and receiving of E-mail. E-mail has many benefits. First, it is very cheap. Second, it allows organisations to be responsive to customer needs. Third, it provides instantaneous access to and dissemination of information, thereby eliminating the time lag involved in using the postal service. Fourth, E-mail messages do not get lost or reach the wrong party.

Finally, E-mail systems must be carefully selected, since a poor package may not only deter users from using E-mail but can also result in poor communications. Some factors to consider before selecting an E-mail package are:

1. What hardware and operating system platforms must the mail system support ?
2. How many users do we currently have ?
3. How many users will we have in two years ? In five years ?
4. Will remote users at multiple sites need to use the system ?
5. Can messages be sent between different platforms (say, from a UNIX machine to a Macintosh or an IBM PC) ?
6. Is the package capable of meeting the growing needs of the organisation ?
7. Will the vendor provide training and technical support, if necessary ?

These and other related questions must be carefully addressed for successful working of the E-mail system.

Typically E-mail packages provide following facilities :

1. *Notification of receipt/reading.* On receipt/reading of the E-mail, the receiver's package automatically replies with an acknowledgement. It is often useful to know if a recipient has received and (particularly) read a message.
2. *Mailing and distribution lists.* The E-mail package enables a user to build up several lists of E-mail addresses which can be called up and inserted with one key stroke, for example, all departmental heads, or all client contact names.
3. *Forward or reply.* A message may be forwarded or replied. Typically, this can be accompanied by the reader's comments (editing) and be with or without the original text.
4. *File attachments.* Files, for example word processed document files, or spreadsheets, can be attached to messages and loaded into receiver software.
5. *Folders.* Received messages can be automatically stored in different electronic folders.
6. *Filters.* Filter facilities allow mail to be selectively read and stored depending on whether the messages meet some rule specified by the user.

Electronic mail services. When an organisation decides to implement electronic mail, it has two basic choices. It can acquire its own hardware and software and install an in-house system, or it can subscribe to an *electronic mail service* that provides the necessary computing and communications facilities for a fee. In the latter case, a subscriber need only furnish the terminals to tie into the network. Example of popular E-mail service in India is Videsh Sanchar Nigam Ltd. (VSNL).

Voice Mail

Voice mail facilitates oral communication. In this system, the sender dictates a message by speaking them over the telephone rather than typing them. A special device, called a **codec**, converts the analog signal of the sender's voice into a digital message. The message is transmitted over the network and stored in a server at the receiver's end. A blinking light on the receiver's phone indicates that he/she has a voice message. When the receiver chooses, the digitised message is retrieved from the server, reconverted into analog form, using a codec at the receiver's end, and the receiver receives it over the phone. Figure 10.8 illustrates the voice mail system.

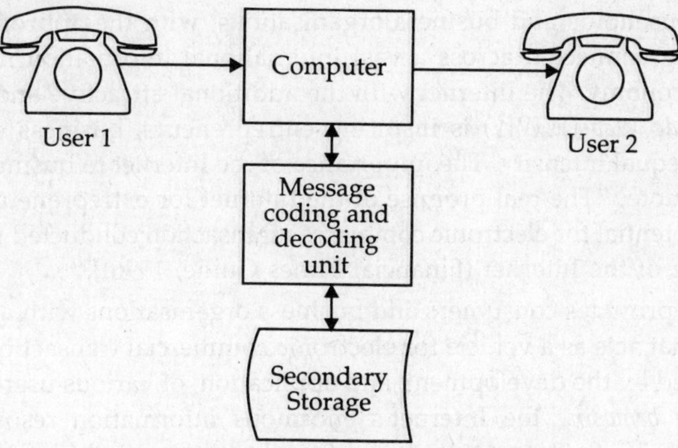

Fig. 10.8 A Voice Mail Configuration

Voice mail eliminates a number of problems such as 'phone tag'. It also ensures that a message reaches the right person even when the person is not available. Some voice mail systems can send the same message to more than one person, reroute a message to another phone, save messages for future reference, and retrieve messages from any telephone, anywhere in the world. In some systems, users need a password to access voice messages, making voice mail a secure medium for confidential messages.

Facsimile

Facsimile, popularly known as fax, systems are commonplace in most organisations today. Fax technology uses telephones, modems, and scanners to transmit text and graphics to an individual or organisation anywhere in the world. The scanner in the fax machine scans the document at one end and at the other end, a built-in modem receives the message, and a printer prints it.

Fax machines can send the same document to multiple users. They can also be integrated with applications such as word processors, so that faxes can be edited without being reentered into the computer. Fax machines can be programmed to send faxes at a time when telephone rates are lowest. A portable fax machine allows users to retrieve documents using a touch-tone phone's keypad. An interesting development is the fax modem, which allows users to send or receive faxes using their PCs.

Another new feature in fax technology is fax-on-demand (FOD), which uses touch-tone phones and prerecorded instructions to provide users with customised information by treating the keypad of the touch-tone phone as a data terminal and the fax machine as a printer. Organisations are actively embracing FOD technology because it can reduce operating costs.

Another new development is LAN-based fax systems, also called **enterprise-wide systems**. Such systems are increasingly becoming popular because they help to centralise the receiving and sending of faxes and thereby monitor and control the cost of fax traffic. In a survey, it is revealed that most of the organisations were not keeping control on fax expenditures.

Internet

The Internet has emerged from the academic research world to become one of the most significant driving forces behind business change and innovation. It is estimated that there will be between 100-200 million users of the Internet by the year 2000; which offers the possibility of households and business organisations, with the appropriate information technology, being connected across a vast international information network that truly offers a global economy. The Internet with the additional attractive and exciting features of the *World Wide Web* (*WWW*) is inspiring entrepreneurs, business organisations and consumers with equal intensity. The importance of the Internet to business practice can be gauged by the quote, "The real promise of the Internet for extrepreneurs and consumers alike lies in its potential for electronic commerce : transaction conducted through computer networks [FT a-z of the Internet (Financial Times Guide, 1996)]."

The Internet provides consumers and business organisations with a global communications facility that acts as a vehicle for electronic commercial transactions. The use of the Internet is assisted by the development, and application, of various user-friendly software for searching or *browsing* the Internet's enormous information resources. The act of searching or browsing the Internet is often referred to as *surfing the net*. It is an appropriate analogy given the vast ocean of information that is available for anyone with a suitable *search engine*. Therefore, it is in the interests of all business organisations to understand and utilise the Internet in order to remain competitive within the commercial business environment.

What is Internet ? The Internet is a global network of millions of smaller computer networks linked by terrestrial and extra-terrestrial communications channels. The most significant business promise of the Internet lies in the potential for global electronic commerce, known as E-commerce, in the shape of transactions conducted through the millions of computer networks that make up the Internet. The Internet is a relatively inexpensive business resource that permits small organisations to compete with large organisations because of the absence of any major cost or competition constraints of using the Web. A web site is a set of linked information pages which forms a unique home location for a user on the Internet. Individuals and organisations can create their own web sites of information to reflect their own business needs.

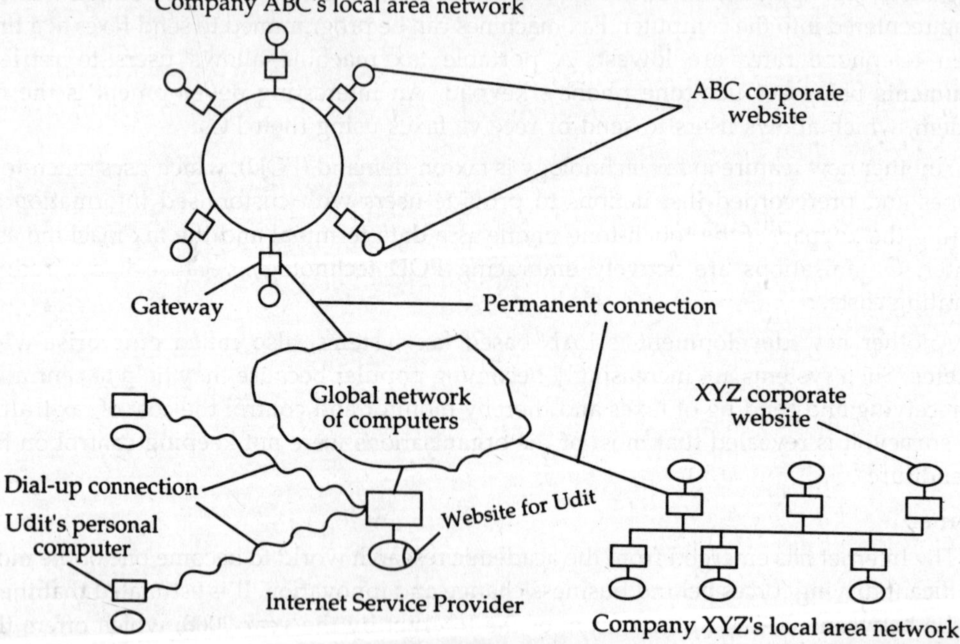

Fig. 10.9 Connections and the Internet

Linking of the Internet. 1. *Connection to the Internet.* A computer may be connected to the Internet and transmit and receive information from the Internet in a number of ways : (*a*) If the computer is part of a local area network, then the computer will be connected through LAN to a gateway which itself will be linked to another network; (*b*) Another method of connection is via a dial-up line to an *Internet Service Provider* (*ISP*). It is usually a commercial organisation which provides access to the Internet for a private user or to a small business. Figure 10.9 illustrates the connections and the Internet. 2. *Addresses and domain names.* Each computer attached to the Internet is given an address. This consists of a 32 bit number. The host computer names are translated into the relevant 32 bit addresses by means of the Domain Name System (DNS). This is a worldwide hierarchical system of assigning names. Each name is allocated by a name server. This server is responsible for allocating all names within its domain. There is a set of two letter domains which correspond to the highest domain in each country on the Internet. Within each country, the domains are broken down into lower level domains. For example, higher level domains are categorised as follows:

Domain	*Area*
com	commercial organisation
edu	educational organisation
gov	governmental organisation
mil	military organisation
org	non-governmental organisation
net	network resource

Now, the trend is to use a two-letter abbreviation of the country name as defined in ISO 3166, *e.g.*, AU — Australia, CA — Canada, IN — India, FR — France, and so on. In fact, a DNS administrator must set up name servers for his/her zone.

3. *Connection through the Internet.* In an Internet connection, the information that passes between one computer and another is divided into packets with different packets taking different routes through the network. There is thus only a virtual circuit connection. In order to ensure that information proceeds from the transmitter computer to the correct receiver computer, and that the information that is received in different packets is assembled in the correct order at the receiving computer, *two* important standard (protocols) are used:

(*a*) *Internet protocol* (*IP*) — It ensures that a packet of data arrives at the correct address (receiver computer) after transfer through the Internet. Transmission of a packet from one network to another is handled by computers known as *routers.* One packet contains the equivalent of only about 1500 characters.

(*b*) *Transmission control protocol* (*TCP*) — It ensures correct transmission of packet from one end to the other.

The combination of IP and TCP occurs so regularly that it is known as TCP/IP. Most operating systems (*e.g.*, Microsoft Windows) contain software to handle these protocols.

If all the data that is being sent can be fitted into one packet, an alternative protocol may be used. This is known as the *User Datagram Protocol.* It has the advantage of being less complex and swifter in operation than TCP.

Some users will be using a telephone connection and modem for the first part of the connection into the Internet. For example, an employee might connect to the Internet from home or whilst travelling on business through the employee's organisation's local area network. The first part of the connection will often be made using a protocol known as *Point to Point Protocol* (*PPP*). This protocol allows a computer to use a modem and telephone line to establish TCP/IP connection to the Internet.

The World Wide Web (WWW). The World Wide Web, which is often referred to as the 'web', was first developed by the European Council for Nuclear Research's (CERN) European Laboratory for Particle Physics in Switzerland as an academic publishing tool to enable scientists to distribute academic papers to fellow colleagues. To achieve this, the web was conceived in 1989. The web's suitability, regardless of the platform or environment in which the user worked, made the web instantly recognisable as a useful communications interface. The main features of WWW are :

- A standard way of providing information on web pages stored electronically on a host computer. This would include text, formatting, graphics, audio and video.
- The use of hyperlinks to direct a web page reader to other web pages on the same website or to a different website.
- Easy-to-use software that would enable users to transfer quickly between pages on a website or between different websites at the click of a mouse.

The National Centre for Supercomputing Applications (NCSA) released a web browser program, *Mosaic*, for easy and powerful access to the web. Its successor software browser, *Netscape*, led to an explosion in the development of websites and the accessing of these by users. Other browsers include Infoseek, Hotjava, and Microsoft Explorer. A user essentially needs to use a **browser** to interact with a Internet. It is a software package that runs on the user's computer.

Individuals and business organisations can register a website which can be available to any one searching or browsing the Internet. Commercial websites range from simple product lists to elaborate multimedia presentations incorporating three-dimensional images, sound and video. In order to achieve the hypertext and multimedia context of the web, the scientists at CERN developed two specialist software language applications known as **hypertext mark-up language** (HTML) and **hypertext transmission protocol** (HTTP). HTML permits users to design web pages, and other documents, with all the necessary hypertext links to other pages and documents. The links can be local or over global networks. The linked documents are retrieved and sent in plain text format to speed the transmission process and the **browser** software program interprets the HTML on the user's screen. The HTTP application deals with the **communication** of documents and overcomes the need for a user to link to other networked computer systems in order to achieve communication with another network.

The tools and techniques of hypertext allow a web user to travel across a global array of networks connected through a set of visually obvious, but not technologically obvious, links on a web page. The user-friendly nature of browser applications has persuaded some organisations to replicate and incorporate the wider techniques of browser technology into the internal information systems of the business domain. For instance, the visually attractive and user-friendly front-end interfaces of browsing software can be duplicated to access the integrated information systems that are internal to a business organisation; such application of web technology into the fabric of a business organisation is known as an **Intranet,** rather than 'Internet', because the scope of the technology is restricted to the physical confines of a business organisation. Such Intranet systems offer the flexibility of browser applications technology with the additional advantage of security; due to the fact that the Intranet is restricted to internal use and control within a business organisation.

Extranets. Extranet is the new buzzword in the arena of Internet. It can be defined as a business-to-business intranet that allows limited, controlled, secure access between a firm's intranet and designated, authenticated users and organisations from remote locations. It allows organisations to communicate faster and more effectively with customers and business partners.

Universal Resource Locator (URL). Each page on the web is on a website which is itself located on a computer attached to the Internet. Each computer attached to the Internet has an address. The URL identifies the location of a resource on the web (type of resource, site and position or path to the resource at the site). It is useful to think of the URL as the web page address. An example is given below:

http://www.un.org/overview/origin.html

This states that information may be retrieved using the HTTP at the website with the address **www.un.org.** Within that website the page retrieved is a subpage, called **origin.html.** of the main page, **overview**. Other URL examples are : http:/www.expressindia.com/net_express/resume.html for the Indian Express site for exploring career options; http://www.lords.org/worldcup for the official website of World Cup 99; http://www.ge.com for General Electric; http://www.employees.org/~hsyed/urdu.html for lovers of urdu poetry. Pages are usually organised as tree structures with the top node known as the **home page.**

Web search engines. It is a program which, when running, makes connection to many thousand of websites a day, retrieving and indexing web pages from these sites. In the course of time, a web search engine will have visited and indexed millions of web pages. This index will be stored at the website associated with the search engine. A user accesses the website at which the search engine is located and enters, via a form on the screen, a word or words, known as the **search string,** of search interest. The web search engine then displays at the user's terminal the URLs of all sites at which the search string is located. An example of a search string might be :

Jackson AND president AND NOT (Michael OR music OR five).

There are several web search engines. Examples are Alta Vista, WebCrawler, Netsearch, Infoseek, Excite, and Easy Searcher. Sites that enable search multiple indexes simultaneously include yahoo and search.com.

Plug-ins. Plug-ins are (usually) small programs that are 'loaded into' a larger program in order to add some function. The plug-in may be produced by an (third party) organisation different from the publisher of the larger program. Web browsers may have plug-ins associated with them that allow to carry out extra functions. The examples of plug-ins for browsers that extend their functionality are : Internet telephone tools; Interactive 3-D viewers; Audio and Video viewers; and Streaming audio and video viewers.

Businesses and other organisations may develop their own websites for a number of reasons. Amongst these are :

- to advertise services and products;
- to sell services and products;
- to promote the corporate image;
- to provide information (especially public services).

It is possible to identify reasons and advantages an organisation might be expected to reap by using a website. These are :

- Reduction in cost of advertising
- Cheaper and easier provision of information
- Ease of update
- Lack of need to maintain a shop front
- The ease of crossing geographical boundaries
- The absence of the middleman
- Reciprocal arrangement
- Web communities
- Commercial advertisement.

Three main areas must be considered in the development and maintenance of a corporate website. These are *connection, publication policy,* and *presentation of materials.*

The following is a list of some of the common business uses of the Internet :

- Information storage and retrieval through the establishment of web pages and the use of Internet search engines.
- The sending, receiving and distribution of E-mail messages to individuals and groups of individuals internal and external to the business organisation.
- The sending and receiving of documents around the globe and responding to suppliers and customers through EDI links on the Internet.
- The acquisition of business intelligence through the establishment of web page links to keep an organisation abreast of competition and social, political and economic developments on a global scale.
- Collecting and collating market research information and publishing tenders for contracts and other competitive bid work.
- Keeping up-to-date in current research and development through the publication and dissemination of research articles via the areas of government, business and academia.
- Acquiring and downloading commercial software applications that are relevant to the business environment and the interrogation of various help and assistance sites.

Rapid, reliable and effective telecommunications are essential to competitive business organisations. Telecommunications are essential for organisations that trade over a wide geographical area or across continents. Business organisations have access to a number of communications applications that speed the transmission of information.

The rules of etiquette are often referred to as *netiquette.* The **netiquette code of conduct** lays out some standards of courteous behaviour that should be commonly acceptable on the Internet as follows :

- Never send any electronic message, or commercial transaction, that you would not want publicised or to be used in the public domain. The rule to acknowledge is that what you would put on a postcard you would not mind being seen in the public domain.
- Never engage in the sending of abusive, threatening, harassing or bigoted electronic messages or creating web pages that threaten another individual or organisation.

- Avoid smearing the reputation of others and avoid the creation of shadow identities on the Internet that besmirch the reputation of an individual or business organisation. Such shadow identities can misinform and mislead the Internet user.
- On a technical level, try to avoid creating web pages that require an enormous amount of memory space to run. This will slow down the transmission rate and may prevent users with inferior technology being able to access the relevant web pages.

E-Commerce — The Future of Business

The new buzzword is E-commerce, the idea of doing business electronically over the Internet. It has many offshoots now, including **E-business** and **E-tailing.** It is being projected as the next wave of the information technology applications. It is expected that the volume of transactions may grow up to $ 1.3 trillion in 2003. Multinational companies are betting their future on E-business.

In E-commerce, the first function is the creation of virtual shops and shopping malls which exhibit the products and services they want to sell. To facilitate selling, there has to be a way of paying electronically, which then calls for security and identification systems. Electronic banks have to be created, which allow people to deposit, withdraw and pay money just by pressing keys on a computer in their home. Then there has to be a system of delivery of goods : either on-line in the case of information products or a physical delivery system in the case of hard products.

The high end of E-business is B2B (business to business) in which firms tie up resources. Some companies are doing business with their dealers electronically. Orders, schedules, receipts, invoices — all can be delivered on-line. Thus, they can save on costs by managing their stocks and inventories properly. As systems of electronic money are perfected, money too will flow electronically. In India, it is essential to develop E-commerce since thousands of man-hours are wasted annually for such day-to-day jobs that should not take at all.

E-commerce can be divided into :

- E-tailing or 'virtual storefronts' on websites with on-line catalogues, sometimes gathered into a 'virtual mall'.
- Collection and use of demographic data through the Internet.
- EDI, the business-to-business exchange of data.
- E-mail and fax as media to reach customers.
- Business-to-business buying and selling.
- The security of business transactions.

Though E-business is growing by leaps and bounds, but the move towards a *digital society* still has to take off. In India, there are objections to implement the technology from different sections of society owing to certain inherent risks. It is still at a nascent stage. There are some bottlenecks in implementing globally the E-commerce successfully. The US government has taken a lead in creating a Global Information Infrastructure (GII).

10.4.3. Teleconferencing Systems

Teleconferencing systems consists of tools and techniques (both computer and non-computer-based) that allow a group of people, separated by time and distance, to exchange ideas using audio, video, and other teleconferencing media. The main feature of this sytem is that they reduce operating costs and increase productivity because decision makers do not have to travel to attend face-to-face meetings. In this section, audioconferencing, videoconferencing, computer conferencing, in-house television, and telecommuting are discussed.

Audio Conferencing

Audio conferencing is the use of voice communication equipment (Fig. 10.10) to establish an audio link between geographically dispersed persons for conducting a conference. The **conference call**, which allows more than two people to participate in a telephone conversation, was the first form of audio conferencing. Some firms install private, high-quality audio communications circuits between conference sites that can be activated with the flip of a switch. It does not require a computer.

Audio conferencing can be made more efficient by following a few simple rules as given below :

- The person who organises the conference should serve as a moderator, making certain that all participants have an opportunity to speak and that the objectives of the conference are achieved.

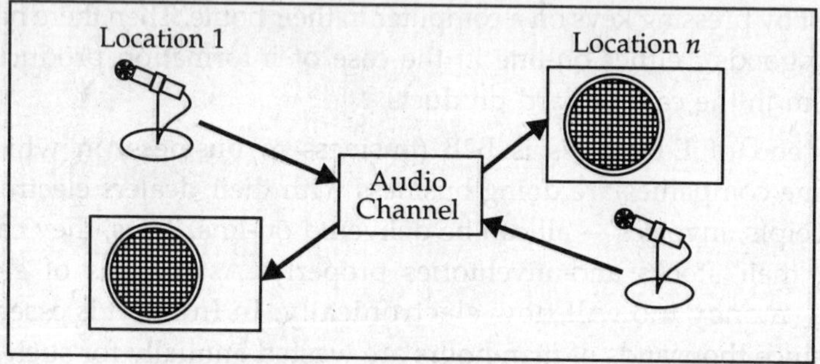

Fig. 10.10 An Audio Conferencing System

- The number of participants should be kept to a manageable size, say not more than 10.
- A copy of the conference agenda should be made available to the participants in advance.
- When participants speak, they should identify themselves.
- A taped record of the conference should be kept.
- A hard copy record should be prepared from the taped record, and distributed to all participants.

Audio conference is best suited to firms that are spread over a wide area.

Video Conferencing

Video conferencing is another type of teleconferencing systems that uses telephones, TV monitors, computers, and networks to link geographically separated decision makers to hear and see each other. Figure 10.11 shows a video conferencing system. A computer digitises sound and video images, then converts them to analog signals and transmits them over the telephone lines to the receiver's computer, which reconverts the analog signals to digital signals. These are then translated into audio and video messages and presented on the TV monitor and sound system.

There are **three** basic types of video conferencing (Mcleod, 1993), based on the signal capabilities :

- *One-way video and one-way audio.* Video and audio signals are sent from a single transmitting site to one or more receiving sites.
- *One-way video and two-way audio.* The two-way audio capability allows people at the receiving sites to talk to people at the transmitting site while everyone views the same video images.
- *Two-way video with two-way audio.* The video and audio communications between all sites are two-way.

Figure 10.11 illustrates the video conferencing systems.

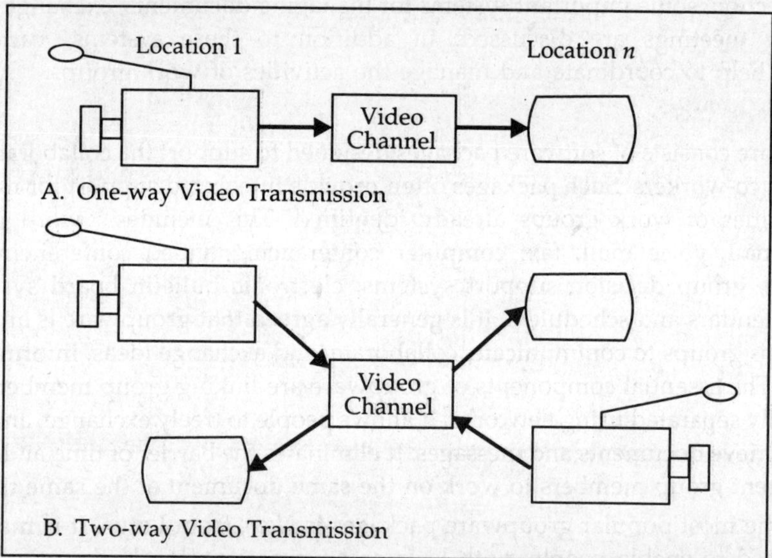

Fig. 10.11 Video Conferencing System

Although video conferencing avoids travel costs, firms are not motivated to use it solely for that reason. Instead, firms regard video conferencing as a way to get more managers involved in decision-making — managers who otherwise would not participate because of their geographical location.

Computer Conferencing

Computer conferencing is the use of a networked computer to allow members of a **problem-solving team** to exchange information concerning the problem that is being solved. In this system, a group can consist of a large number of participants. It differs from audio and video conferencing in that it can be used within a single geographic site. A person can use computer conferencing to communicate with someone in the next office.

Teleconferencing includes all three forms of conferencing — audio, video, and computer.

In-house Television

In-house TV is a relatively new technology. In this system, an organisation invests in a studio, a period of time on a satellite, and a satellite transmitter for broadcasting. Company sites — or even customers — are given satellite dishes so that they can view the broadcast. Scramblers inhibit competitors from gaining access to the transmission. This technology has already shown potential in the areas of competitive advantage, cost cutting, and employee motivation. A good example of this is Indira Gandhi National Open University where this system is working successfully.

Telecommuting

With telecommuting, people use communications technology to work at home or in a remote city — and to avoid the usual physical commute to work. Using a remote communications terminal or a microcomputer workstation, a person can do his/her work at home instead of at the office.

10.4.4. Office Support Systems

In this section, some important systems for managing documents, exchange messages, and holding meetings are discussed. In addition to these systems, various other applications help to coordinate and manage the activities of work groups.

Groupware

Groupware consists of software packages designed to support the collaborative efforts of a group of co-workers. Such packages often provide integrated support for many of the typical activities of work groups already identified. This includes : word processing services; E-mail; voice mail; fax; computer conferencing; video conferencing; project management; group decision support systems; electronic bulletin board systems; and electronic calendars and schedulers. It is generally agreed that groupware is an electronic tool that helps groups to communicate, collaborate, and exchange ideas, information, and knowledge. The essential components of groupware are linking group members who are geographically separated using networks. It allows people to freely exchange, analyse, edit, store, and retrieve documents and messages. It eliminates the barrier of time and space and allows different group members to work on the same document at the same time.

One of the most popular groupware packages is *Note*, from Lotus. It is menu-driven and icon-based to enable people, with little or no programming background, to use it effectively. **Note** is a distributed database that allows users to share a wide variety of documents in different forms and from different sources. Notes operates on IBM-compatible microcomputers and workstations and on Macintosh computers. It runs under a number of operating systems, including Windows, OS/2, and UNIX, and can be loaded on both LANs and WANs.

One of the multinational engineering firms, Asea Brown Boveri, uses Notes to enhance enterprise-wide communications. It helped the firm provide a uniform face to data on a global basis, while at the same time capturing the information needs and preferences of its local business units.

Desktop Organisers

Desktop organisers are software packages that provide users with the electronic equivalent of the organising and coordinating tools found on a typical office desk. Among many features, it includes electronic calendar, card file, notepad, clock, and calculator.

Computer Aided Design

Computer aided design (CAD) refers to computer systems that enable designers to work with a display-screen interface and specifications database to design various products. It is widely used in engineering environments.

Electronic Bulletin Boards

Electronic bulletin boards allow members to post their ideas and elicit responses from other group members. Primary benefits are increased responsiveness to market forces and significant improvement in the quality of business processes such as product development, account management, and customer service.

10.5. INTEGRATED OFFICE

An organisation can acquire separately the necessary hardware, software, or services required to implement any of the applications discussed in earlier section — or it can integrate many of them. Nowadays, integrated office packages can be purchased or leased from software vendors. An integrated office package features word processing, E-mail, and several desktop organising tools. An example of an integrated office is illustrated in Fig. 10.12. This might entail integrating any of the following sets of heterogeneous elements:

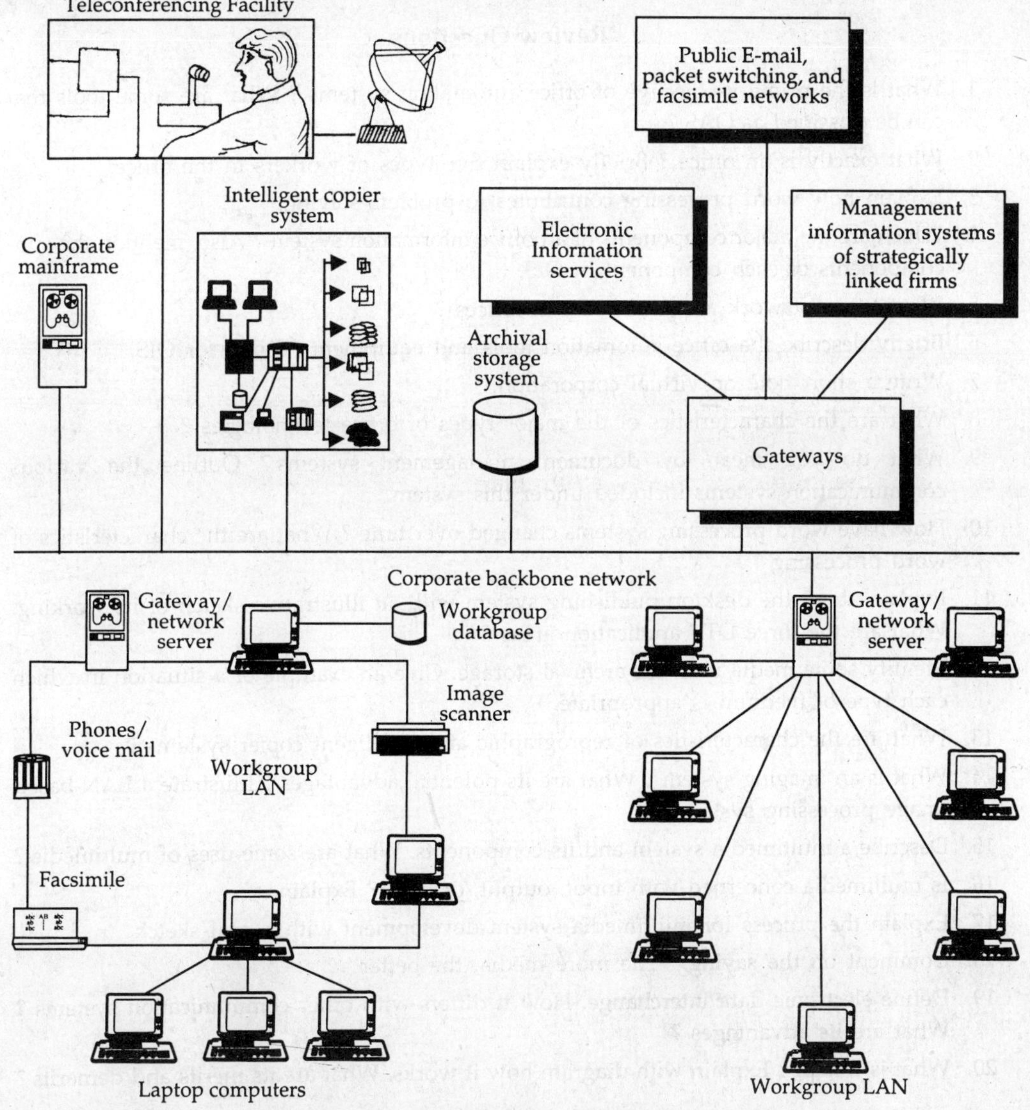

Fig. 10.12 An Example of an Integrated Office

- The hardware and software products of several vendors.
- Various communications protocols.
- Text, graphics, voice and video data.
- Various types of computer networks and network elements, *e.g.*, LAN, WAN, PBX, intelligent copier systems, and gateways to large mainframes and/or remote commercial databases.

Office information systems are successfully implemented in many ways. Most problems with implementation stem from a lack of clear objectives for office systems. Success is more likely when the organisation implements new office technologies after a careful strategy is planned. Individual office automation applications can be implemented through integrated office software packages or through a more comprehensive integrated office strategy. The aim is to achieve full integration in days to come : the office of the future.

Review Questions

1. What is the primary objective of office automation systems ? What are some tools that can be classified as OAS ?
2. What exactly is an office ? Briefly explain five types of workers in the office.
3. Explain how word processing contributes to problem-solving.
4. Which are the major components of an office information system ? Also, mention the sub-components of each component in OIS.
5. What types of work are performed in offices ?
6. Briefly describe the office automation tools and equipment needed for OIS.
7. Write a short note on virtual corporation.
8. What are the characteristics of the major types of office technologies ?
9. What do you mean by document management systems ? Outline the various communication systems included under this system.
10. How have word processing systems changed over time ? What are the characteristics of word processing ?
11. Explain about the desktop publishing system with an illustrative sketch of its working. What are the three DTP application areas ?
12. Identify some media used for archival storage. Give an example of a situation in which each type of medium is appropriate.
13. What are the characteristics of reprographic and intelligent copier systems ?
14. What is an imaging system ? What are its potential advantages ? Illustrate a LAN-based image processing system.
15. Describe a multimedia system and its components. What are some uses of multimedia ?
16. Is multimedia concerned with input, output, or both ? Explain.
17. Explain the process for multimedia system development with a neat sketch.
18. Comment on the saying, "The more media, the better".
19. Define electronic data interchange. How it differs with other communication systems ? What are its advantages ?
20. What is E-mail ? Explain with diagram how it works. What are its merits and demerits ?

21. In what ways are E-mail and voice-mail alike ? In what ways are they different ?
22. What are the characteristics and potential advantages of facsimile system ? What is the difference, if any, between stand-alone fax and fax-on-demand ?
23. What is Internet ? Explain about the connections and the Internet with an illustrative diagram. Briefly describe the working principle of the Internet.
24. What do you mean by World Wide Web ? What are its main features ?
25. Write short notes on the following :
    (*a*) Universal research locator
    (*b*) Web search engines
    (*c*) Plug-ins
    (*d*) Voice mail
26. Outline the common business uses of the Internet. Mention the rules of etiquette to be commonly acceptable on the Internet.
27. What is E-commerce ? How is it useful in business ?
28. What is teleconferencing ? How do video conferencing, audio conferencing, and computer conferencing differ ? Explain how they work.
29. Explain *three* basic types of videoconferencing supporting with an illustrative diagram.
30. What is groupware ? How does it facilitate group decision making ?
31. What is your vision about an integrated office ? What are its heterogeneous elements ? Illustrate your imagination with a neat sketch.
32. In what ways will DTP result in both problems and opportunities in the publishing and typesetting industries ?
33. Which new technologies, in your opinion, have the biggest impact on office work in the years to come ? Justify your arguments.
34. What distinguishes computer conferencing from E-mail ?

11

Information Systems in Business

11.1. INTRODUCTION

The role of information systems in organisational productivity has been extremely challenging. This is partially because the benefits of information systems are often intangible, manifesting themselves in areas such as improved customer service and greater organisational responsiveness. Hence, organisations are developing new measures, such as 'reduce cycle times' and 'delighting the customer', to better measure the impact of information systems on organisational productivity.

The various functional areas in business, including manufacturing, marketing, finance and accounting, quality control, and human resources, have all been influenced by information systems. Earlier the emphasis was on developing standalone functional systems and to create customer-oriented systems. In this chapter, these functional areas, using information systems, to capture new markets, achieve a competitive edge in existing markets, and provide effective customer service, are discussed. Today, most organisations are planning to develop cross-functional systems. Examples of some of them are given.

There are many different types of information systems: transaction processing systems, MIS, and intelligent support systems, consisting of decision support systems, expert system, executive information system, and office automation systems. All of these play a supportive role in a business function, and functional information systems often consist of one or more of the aforementioned systems.

11.2. FUNCTIONAL AREAS OF BUSINESS

Every business consists of several well-defined functions. These functions are often organised into areas or departments. These areas are known as the *functional areas* of business. In each functional area, a set of business functions is performed.

In order to study the impact of information systems on each of the function area, following *five* functional areas in an organisation are detailed :

- Manufacturing
- Quality Control
- Marketing
- Accounting and Finance
- Human Resources

Truly successful systems that have a lasting impact on the organisations are those that are cross-functional, *i.e.*, systems that are not narrowly defined by functional boundaries, but instead address the broad information needs of managers, regardless of their functional specifications.

In each of the functional area, a data flow model portrays the local decision making environment. Figure 11.1 shows the data flow diagram, which consists of the following components:

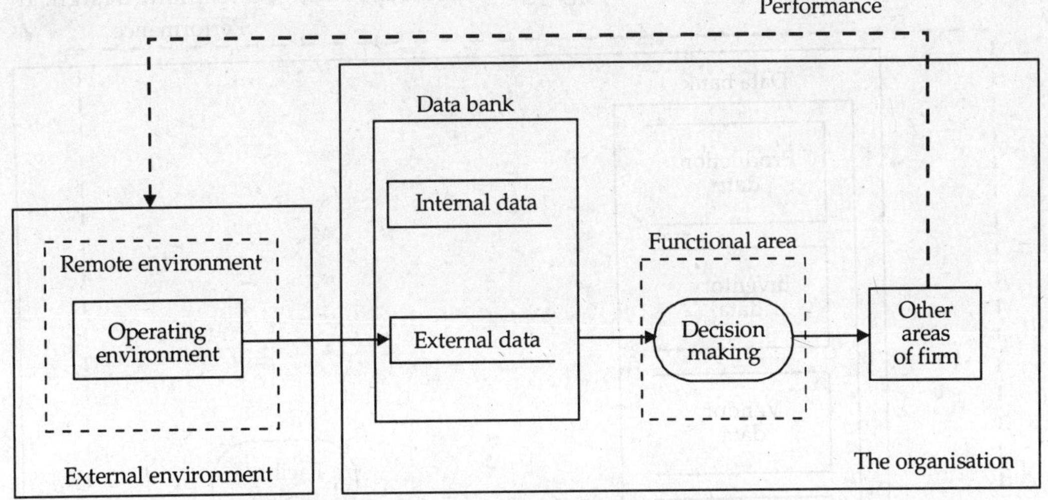

Fig. 11.1 Data Flow Diagram in Basic Functional Areas

External environment. The external environment contains *two* components: the **operating environment**, which consists of consumers, suppliers, competitors, distributors, and the labour supply; and the **remote environment**, which consists of economic, social, political, technological, and industry concerns. These environmental sources generate key external information that flows into the firm, at times informally.

Data bank. The term 'data bank' is used generally to describe the general storage of data. A data bank can include data existing in files and in computer databases. An organisation's data bank consists of **internal data**, such as those generated from the firm's transaction processing system or from internal forecasts, and **external data**, which are collected from monitoring the external environment. Both types of data have information potential.

Decision making. Decision making is the key of each functional data flow model. This process consists of selecting those data needed to make a decision and then making the decision.

Other areas of the firm. Information produced by decision making in one functional area is often used in another. For example, sales forecast prepared by the marketing department is used as data by the finance department to produce the overall financial plan for the firm.

Feedback mechanism. The dotted feedback arrow indicates that decisions made by the firm ultimately affect its performance in the marketplace. The firm's performance, in turn, generates other data that are used by elements in the environment. The firm's performance is often important to the competitor's, consumers, and suppliers in its operating environment, whereas the remote environment is generally not affected. Only a radical change coming from within a big organisation such as a state (or provincial) government, or a corporate giant, like Tata Industries; would cause noticeable change in the remote environment.

11.3. MANUFACTURING INFORMATION SYSTEMS

Manufacturing information system is a system that supports the manufacturing functions of purchasing, receiving, quality control, inventory management, material requirements planning, capacity planning, production scheduling, and plant design. It

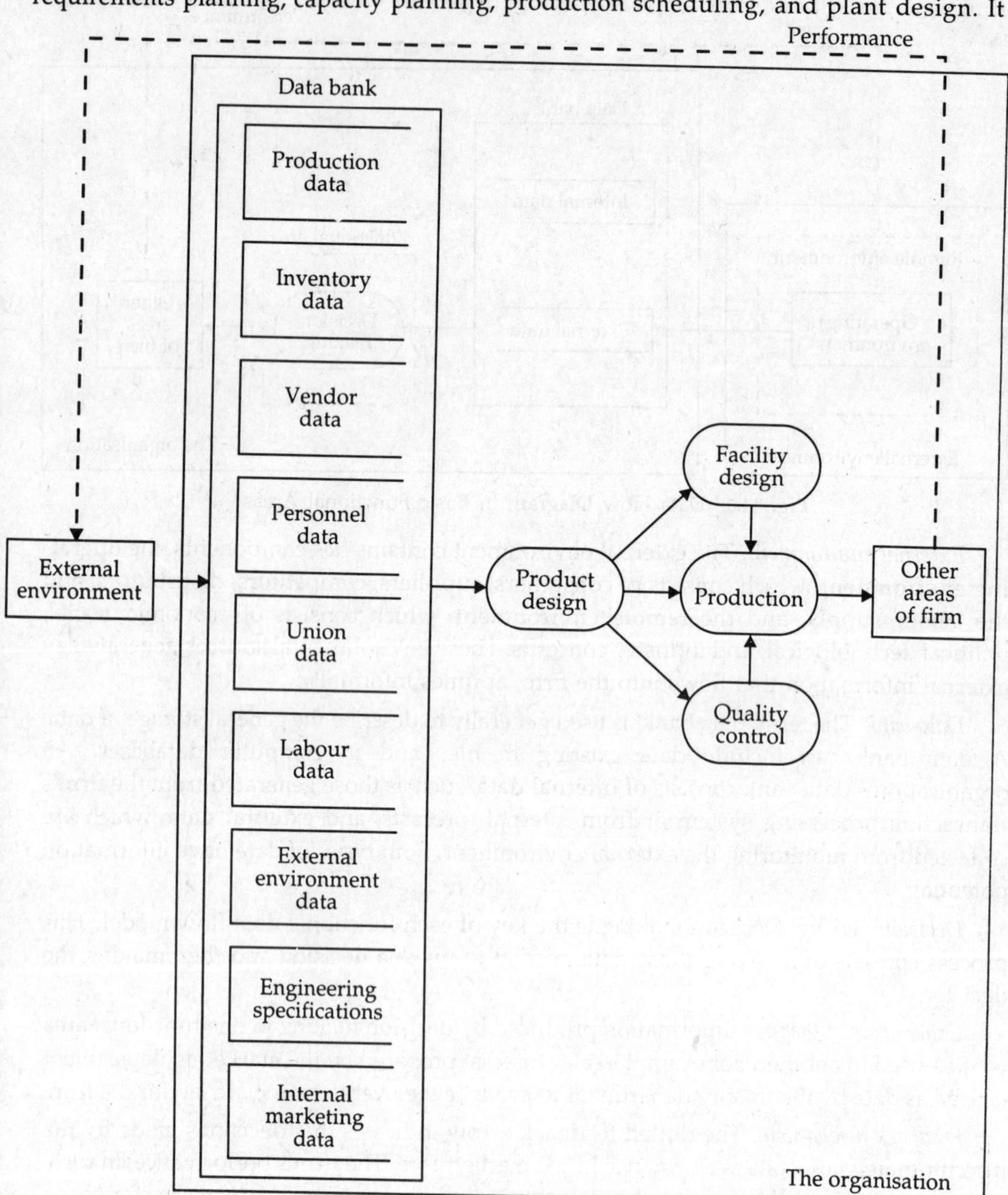

Fig. 11.2 Data Flow Representation of Manufacturing Information System

applies to both manufacturing and service environments. Hence, the term *manufacturing* should be considered in terms of delivering both goods and services. Production systems, a subset of manufacturing information systems, are directly associated with the production of goods and services. It specifically addresses information needs relating to raw materials, equipment, manpower, and other issues directly related to production of goods and services.

Generally, the primary decisions made in the manufacturing include *product design, production, facility design,* and *quality control* (Fig. 11.2). **Product design** is the starting point of the manufacturing process. It is the step in which the design and technical specifications for the product are finalised. Increasingly, product design and engineering are becoming more computerised through approaches such as computer aided design (CAD), computer aided engineering (CAE), and robotics. After a product is designed, the **facilities to manufacture** must be planned. This design may be as simple as changing a few manufacturing stations on the production floor or as complex as designing an entirely new plant. The computer can also model plant layout. Monte Carlo simulation on computers has been used since 1950s to address certain facility layout problems — sometimes with substantial success. **Production** is the process of making new products from raw materials. Generally, the production process consists of many interrelated activities. There are two basic types of production methods : job shop and process. Most production, however, is of the process type. Many computerised approaches are used by firms to model the production process as an integrated system. One successful process production approach, which has been a staple in the automated factory since the early 1980s, is called **manufacturing resources planning (MRP II).** It integrates all the resources required to make a product: personnel, machines and equipment, plant capacity, pricing, distribution, and cost accounting.

Some firms are trying to integrate CAD, CAM and other manufacturing activities, a concept known as **computer-integrated manufacturing (CIM).** Ideally, with CIM, all manufacturing processes concerned with information processing, storage, collection, and distribution are related in a way that optimises performance of the entire enterprise. Integration allows organisations to efficiently manage (and control) manufacturing and engineering information by eliminating barriers across departments and functions — possibly even across organisations. CIM increases a firm's compatibility for planning, productivity, responsiveness, control and innovation.

Agile manufacturing refers to manufacturing environments that are dynamic and flexible enough to instantaneously produce customised goods and services in varying quantities and to effortlessly switch the manufacturing process from one product to another. Agile manufacturing has *four* main characteristics :

1. The ability to thrive on constant change.
2. Recognition by the organisation that people are its main asset.
3. Incorporation of the virtual company idea through the use of telecommunications.
4. A focus on creating products and services with real added value.

Agile manufacturing will also help firms to better integrate their information systems.

Quality control relates to activities which ensure that the final product is of standard quality. Its function is concerned with detecting existing quality deficiencies, as well as with preventing future product quality problems. Quality control is, therefore, both an important area of expense and an important area of opportunity. One group of computerised quality control techniques that has helped in manufacturing operations is known as **statistical process control** (SPC). The objective of SPC is to closely monitor production units at various stages of the production process, identifying potential problems before they result in defects and adjusting the production process accordingly through observations. Another promising role for the computer in quality control is in the area of vision inspection systems, where robotic 'eyes' replace humans in the quality control inspection process.

11.3.1. Sources of Manufacturing Information

Information needed for manufacturing decisions stems from a variety of data sources as shown in Fig. 11.2, and are described as follows :

- **Production data.** By using terminals around the production floor, data on production processes can be quickly gathered and processed. These data are used for billing and in almost every aspect of production control.
- **Inventory data.** Inventory data include inventories of raw materials, goods-in-process, and finished goods. Accurate raw material data are especially important in a manufacturing situation because running out of certain items at critical times can shut down production lines, leaving workers idle.
- **Vendor data.** Vendor data show sources and prices for raw materials. Often, vendor data are maintained by the purchasing department, although sometimes the manufacturing area will personally buy certain items. In any case, manufacturing personnel must be constantly aware of the origination of their raw materials, what new types of products are offered by vendors, and current prices.
- **Personnel data.** Personnel data show various statistics on current manufacturing personnel. Often, in the course of production, people switch assignments, so personnel skills must be reviewed to fit the right person for the right job.
- **Union data.** Many types of labour today are unionised production shops usually have strict regulations regarding such items as pay scales, hiring and firing, promotion, and working conditions.
- **Labour data.** Raw materials and people are at the core of manufacturing a product. While vendors are the source of raw materials, the labour market is the source of people. Data must be kept regarding where new personnel may be obtained as labour shortages occur in the firm.
- **External environment data.** To manufacturing managers, the most pressing information need in the area of external environment data is the outlook for raw material prices and labour availability. For example, if certain raw material prices will skyrocket next month, it may be wise to pad inventories now. Or if labour threatens to strike, manufacturing managers should immediately make decisions regarding how to produce goods in a degraded mode.
- **Engineering specifications.** Engineering specifications data indicate whether something can be built and how. Engineering specifications contain such facts as sizes of screws; whether a certain drill bit is suitable for wood, metal, or masonry;

how to build a sub-assembly of a certain type; and so on. Massive libraries of such specifications are often assembled on magnetic media for retrieval by database management systems. Such technology applications as CD-ROM, hypertext, multimedia, object-oriented databases, and screen publishing (published materials in screen form) have great potential in this area.

- **Internal marketing data.** Marketing ends where manufacturing begins, so marketing output is manufacturing input. Marketing specifies the number of units of goods that must be produced in each time period in order to meet consumer demand. Marketing data are also useful to production personnel as part of the engineering design process.

11.3.2. Advantages of Manufacturing Information Systems

Manufacturing goods and services is the main function of a business. The information generated from the shop-floor (or service floor) drives the rest of the organisation. Hence, the firms that have well-integrated manufacturing information systems are bound to reap significant benefits.

In late 1990, an India-based multinational firm started replacing its PC-based manufacturing system with a new manufacturing information system called *Integrated Information System Architecture.* The main objective was reducing manufacturing costs and cutting down cycle times. The new system, which uses databases, networks, GUIs, and off-the-shelf software, allows 1800 employees distributed throughout the firm to easily access enterprise-wide manufacturing data by integrating a number of core business systems (such as general ledger, accounts payable, and manufacturing). Embedded with decision support capabilities, the system allows managers to be decision makers instead of data collectors.

11.4. MARKETING INFORMATION SYSTEMS

Marketing strategies consist of a mixture of ingredients that has been named the marketing mix : product, promotion, place and price. Collectively they are known as the four Ps. *Product* is what the customer buys to satisfy a perceived want or need. *Promotion* is concerned with all the means of encouraging the sale of the product, including advertising and personal selling. *Place* deals with the means of physically distributing the product to the customer through a channel of distribution. *Price* consists of all the elements relating to what the customer pays for the product.

Kotler (1966) identified *three* types of marketing information :

- *Marketing intelligence* — information that flows into the firm from the environment.
- *Internal marketing information* — information collected within the firm.
- *Marketing communications* — information that flows from the firm outward to the environment.

A marketing information system can be defined as a computer-based system that works in conjunction with other functional information systems to support the firm's management in solving problems that relate to marketing the firm's products. Two elements in the definition make key points. First, all of the functional information systems must work together, and second, the problem-solving support is not limited to marketing managers.

Thus, a marketing information system is a system that meets the information needs of an organisation in sales, distribution, advertising, market analysis, market intelligence, product research, service management, customer profile, and other marketing functions.

Since marketing information systems are primarily customer-oriented information systems, the systems work toward realising the strategic sales plan and the marketing plan of an organisation.

11.4.1. Inputs of Marketing Information Systems

Information used for marketing, decisions arrived at from different data sources, the most important of which are shown in Fig. 11.3, and are explained.

- **Transaction processing data.** *Transaction processing data* show the sales that result from specific mixes of the four Ps. Thus, they provide feedback on the effectiveness of past marketing strategies. They are also useful for appraising performance and controlling marketing expenditures.

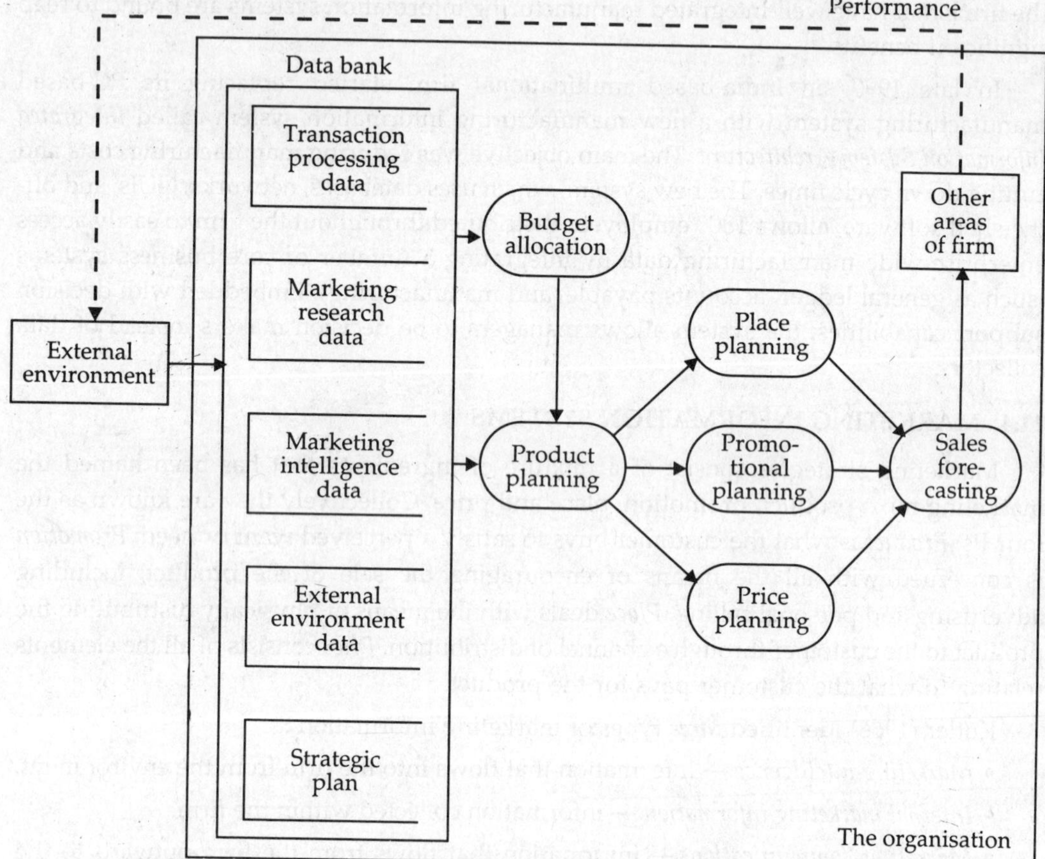

Fig. 11.3 Data Flow Representation of the Marketing Information System

- **Marketing research data.** *Marketing research* is the marketing are responsible for gathering consumer-related data that can be used to support marketing decisions; for example, personal interviews, phone interviews, and mail surveys. Statistical packages are often used by the marketing research staff to analyse these data and to provide useful facts about a product that could not otherwise be obtained from analysing raw sales figures. Often, tests determine if the research findings are statistically significant or if they should be attributed, instead, to chance.

- **Marketing intelligence data.** *Marketing intelligence* refers to information about the strategies of competitors. The term "intelligence" is a carryover from the military, which uses the term to describe data gathered about enemy activities. Most marketing intelligence information is collected in an unstructured or semistructured manner : through word-of-mouth interaction or through observing statistics available in the media and commercial data-base services.
- **External environment data.** In marketing, success is largely attributable to what will happen in the future *external environment*. For example, when a new car is introduced, the firm never knows exactly how consumers will react to it. May be a prototype was built, and the marketing research staff found that, perhaps, 198 out of 235 people who tested the prototype loved it and said they would buy it. But whether they actually do buy the car, in fact, depends on numerous other factors in the external environment. For instance, the economy may be in recession when the car comes out. Or the government may change its policy on imported cars.
- **Strategic plan.** The *strategic plan* is really the starting point of all marketing decisions. It contains the types of products that the firm plans to supply to the consumer marketplace. These broad guidelines define the direction of the marketing effort. The tactical marketing plan addresses what, how, when, and where questions that are appropriate to the implementation of the strategic plan.

11.4.2. Outputs of Marketing Information Systems

Each output subsystem provides information about its part of the marketing mix (four Ps). These are discussed to have the principal decision areas.

- **Product planning.** Product planning is often complicated, unstructured decision. A number of factors contribute to a product's success or failure. Complicating these product planning decisions are the facts that the choice of consumers constantly change and that competitors always develop new products. Most products follow a product life cycle. As its name implies, the product life cycle traces the sales of a product from its introduction to its withdrawal from the market. The four stages in the life cycle are introduction, growth, maturity and decline. A number of techniques have been developed to provide the manager with the information needed for making product-oriented decisions.
- **Place planning.** Place planning refers to the channels of distribution that a firm uses to get its products to the consumer. The resources flowing through a channel includes a supplier, manufacturer, wholesaler, retailer, and consumer. The material flow originates with the supplier and ends with the consumer. The money flow is just the reverse; and an information conduit provides a two-way flow that connects all participants. Information that flow in the direction opposite to the material flow is called *feedback information*, and the flow of information toward the consumer is called *feedforward information*. This includes announcement of new products, sales and promotion aids, and forecasts of demand to the wholesaler and retailer. Feedforward information to the consumer can include instructions for use, safety tips, and warranties.

- **Promotion.** Promotion is composed of two principal areas : personal selling and advertising. Technology is vital to the selling effort in several ways : (*a*) Tying in customers and suppliers; (*b*) Increasing selling time; (*c*) Increasing effectiveness of the client site; (*d*) Identifying selling opportunities; and (*e*) Making salespeople more efficient.
- **Price.** Depending on the firm's pricing policies, the price area can run close to promotion in terms of decision support difficulty. Some firms engage in **cost-based pricing** by determining their costs and then adding a desired mark-up. This approach is a rather cautious one. A less cautious pricing policy is **demand-based pricing**, which establishes a price compatible with the value that the consumer places on the product. The key to this approach is correctly estimating demand. This requires a good understanding of the consumer and also of the market, including the state of the economy and competition.
- **Budget allocation.** Two other important decision making areas, in addition to four Ps, are the allocation of the marketing budget and sales forecasting. Marketing does not have an unlimited source of funds. Thus, a budget must limit the overall size of expenditures. Some computerised allocation models can estimate desirable mixes in this area, but success is limited. This decision is still made largely through manual means and personal judgement.
- **Sales forecast.** The sales forecast reflects estimates by the marketing personnel on future product sales. Since it is the main source of firm's revenue, sales forecast is an important part of the financial plan. Many technology tools are also used in sales forecasting.

The database created for input and output marketing information system should provide answers to the following :

- What is the optimal way to capture data at the point-of-sale ?
- How can one ensures that marketing operations are run smoothly and efficiently ?
- What are the goods and services that customers want ?
- How do customers define customer service ?
- What kinds of services are important to customers ?
- Are customers interested in and willing to use information technology ?
- How much are customers willing to pay for higher quality service ?
- What impact would higher quality customer service have on the profits of the firm ?
- How can customers be attracted and retained ?

11.4.3. Advantages of Marketing Information Systems

A good marketing system provides employees with information that helps firms capture niche markets in highly competitive industries. Marketing information system has a deep and direct influence on the quality of customer service. Hence, it is seen that competitive intelligence is of interest to the firm as a whole. Although the name of a functional information system implies that it is only for managers in that area, the information output can be of value to other managers and executives as well. Hence, marketing information systems play a vital and critical role in helping an organisation achieve its goals.

11.5. QUALITY INFORMATION SYSTEMS

Quality information systems are standalone systems or embedded systems that help an organisation to achieve its quality goals. The quality plan is derived from the strategic information plan.

Figure 11.4 shows how the strategic quality plan is derived from the strategic information plan. In some cases, a firm has no separate quality plan, but instead makes quality a component of other plans, such as marketing, manufacturing, and so on. Table 11.1 provides some do's and don'ts for executives involved in TQM efforts.

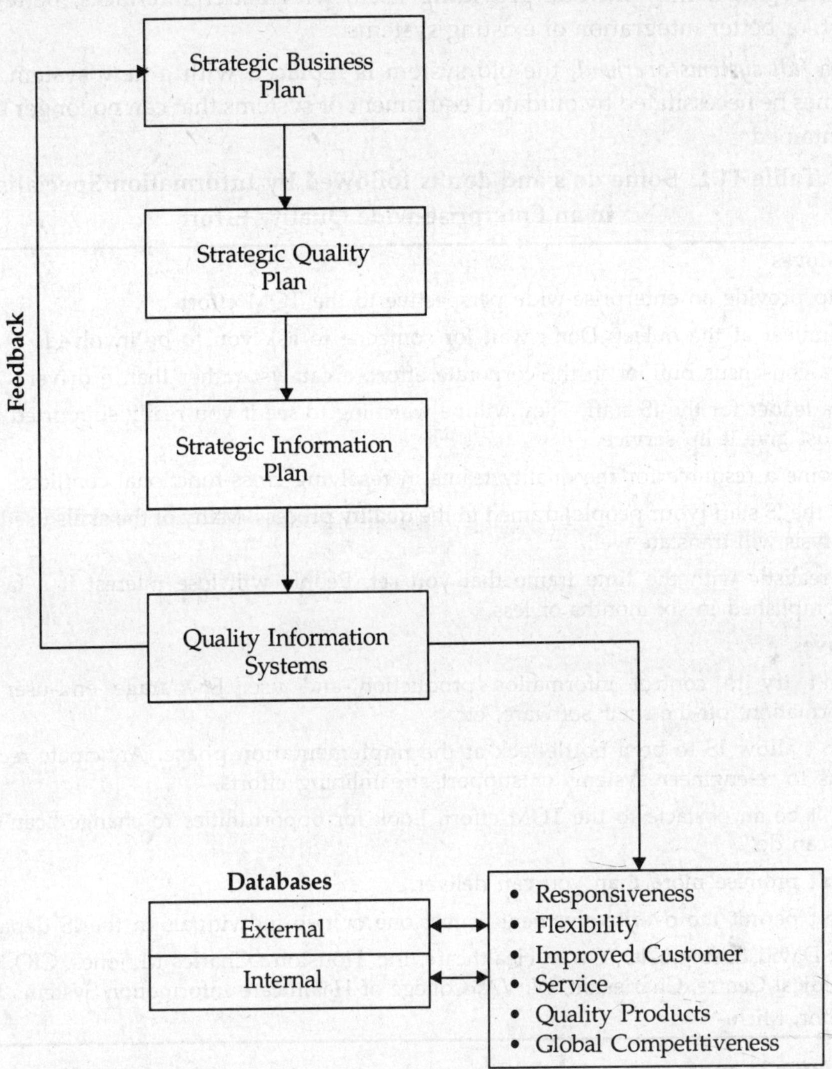

Fig. 11.4 Quality Control Information System in an Organisation

The information systems (IS) department plays a major role in ensuring the success of TQM efforts in an organisation. An information system can promote quality and provide tools and techniques to help the firm achieve its quality goals. Information systems also help firms achieve quality certification. There are many institutions and agencies that certify the quality efforts of an organisation and provide guidelines to firms that plan to instill quality in all aspects of their operations.

The role of IS may vary from one organisation to the next, or even from one program to the next, but there are four major areas where IS plays an important role in the certification process. They are: **partial systems overhaul, full systems overhaul, training,** and **oversight.**

In a *partial systems overhaul*, existing systems are partially revamped in order to update them and make them more responsive to the changing needs of decision makers. Partial systems overhaul may include providing users with better interfaces, better end-user support, or better integration of existing systems.

In a *full systems overhaul*, the old system is replaced with a new system. This may sometimes be necessitated by outdated equipment or systems that can no longer be updated or maintained.

Table 11.1. Some do's and don'ts followed by Information Specialists in an Enterprise-wide Quality Effort

Good Moves

- ☐ Help provide an enterprise-wide perspective to the TQM effort.
- ☐ Volunteer at the outset. Don't wait for someone to ask you to be involved.
- ☐ Be a consensus builder in the corporate effort, a catalyst rather than a driver.
- ☐ Be a leader for the IS staff. They will be watching to see if you really supported the process or just give it lip service.
- ☐ Become a resource for the quality teams in resolving cross-functional conflicts.
- ☐ Get the IS staff [your people] trained in the quality process. Many of the skills used in systems analysis will translate well.
- ☐ Be realistic with the time frame that you set. People will lose interest if a task can't be accomplished in six months or less.

Bad Moves

- ☐ Don't try to control information production and use. Encourage end-user access to information, off-the-shelf software, etc.
- ☐ Don't allow IS to be a bottleneck at the implementation phase. Anticipate recommendations to re-engineer systems or support streamlining efforts.
- ☐ Don't be an obstacle to the TQM effort. Look for opportunities to change "can't be done" to "can do".
- ☐ Don't promise more than you can deliver.
- ☐ Don't permit the overinvolvement of just one or two individuals in the IS department.

Source : David Loebig, CIO, Owen Healthcare, Inc. Houston : Charles M. Jones, CIO, Charleston Area Medical Centre, Charleston, W. VA; College of Healthcare Information Systems Executives, Ann Arbor, Mich.

Training is another area where IS can play an important role in quality certification. Users must be well-trained in systems that are partially or fully overhauled, because this has a direct impact both on quality and on productivity. More important, good data come from well-trained users and good data form the basis of good decisions.

Finally, IS should oversee the entire quality certification process; this is often a time-consuming task. It requires coordination and cooperation among departments; IS can play a facilitating role by ensuring the free flow of information between decision makers. Often, organisational data and information have to be sent to external agencies and IS plays a critical role in getting the right data to the right people at the right time.

11.5.1. Advantages of Quality Information Systems

The aim of most firms all over the world is to produce high-quality goods and services; information is essential to achieve this goal — accurate, timely, and reliable information. Achieving quality also involves being able to develop strategic alliances with suppliers and customers, and information is again essential to this process. A high-quality car manufacturing firm in India has developed a quality information management system (QIMS) to achieve its quality goals. The system highly integrates information generated on the shop-floor, for instance about defective auto parts, so that decision makers can take immediate action to correct the situation. Managers have changed from data collectors to quality enforcers, since now they can take proactive action to keep the firm on the quality track.

11.6. FINANCIAL AND ACCOUNTING INFORMATION SYSTEMS

Financial and accounting information systems (FAIS) is a system that provides information related to the accounting and financial activities in an organisation. It includes budgeting, cash and asset management, capital budgeting, portfolio analysis, general ledger, accounts receivable, inventory control, and payroll systems. Other systems include record keeping, account analysis, cash management, financial analysis, leasing options, insurance claims processing, and investment management. Financial institutions, such as banks, use specialised FAIS, such as commercial loan analysers, credit approval systems, commercial account rating systems, credit application systems, automated teller control, and securities trading. Other institutions and firms may have their own specialised FAIS subsystems. Regardless of the type and number of subsystems, financial and accounting subsystems work together to create, record, generate, and disseminate financial and accounting information vital to good decision making.

Figure 11.5 shows how the financial information plan is derived from the strategic information plan and the strategic business plan. Although most financial and accounting managers operate under the 'tyranny of the urgent', a strategic financial plan and an integrated set of information systems that support the plan are a necessity for the survival and growth of any organisation.

11.6.1. Types of Financial and Accounting Information Systems

Various functions of FAIS are explained briefly.

General ledger systems generate the firm's income statements and balance sheets and are responsible for managing new and old accounts in the firm. **Asset management systems** maintain an inventory of the firm's long-term assets and ensure that accounting practices for firm assets comply with regulatory standards. The output of this system often becomes input to the general ledger system. **Order entry systems** capture and manage different kinds of data relating to a transaction, such as number of units sold, customer billing, credit history, sales tax, and inventory levels. The output of this system is input to a number of other systems, such as accounts receivable and inventory management.

Accounts receivable and *accounts payable* capture and process data, such as creditor and customer billing information, payments received and owed, credit terms, account balances, and payment schedules. The *inventory control system* captures, processes, and manages all data related to the firm's inventory, such as items in inventory, inventory levels and costs, accounting practices related to inventory maintenance, stock balance, and data on lost, damaged, or returned goods. Finally, *payroll systems* capture and process data related to wages and salaries, including central and state taxes, other payroll deductions, employee benefits, overtime, and related data.

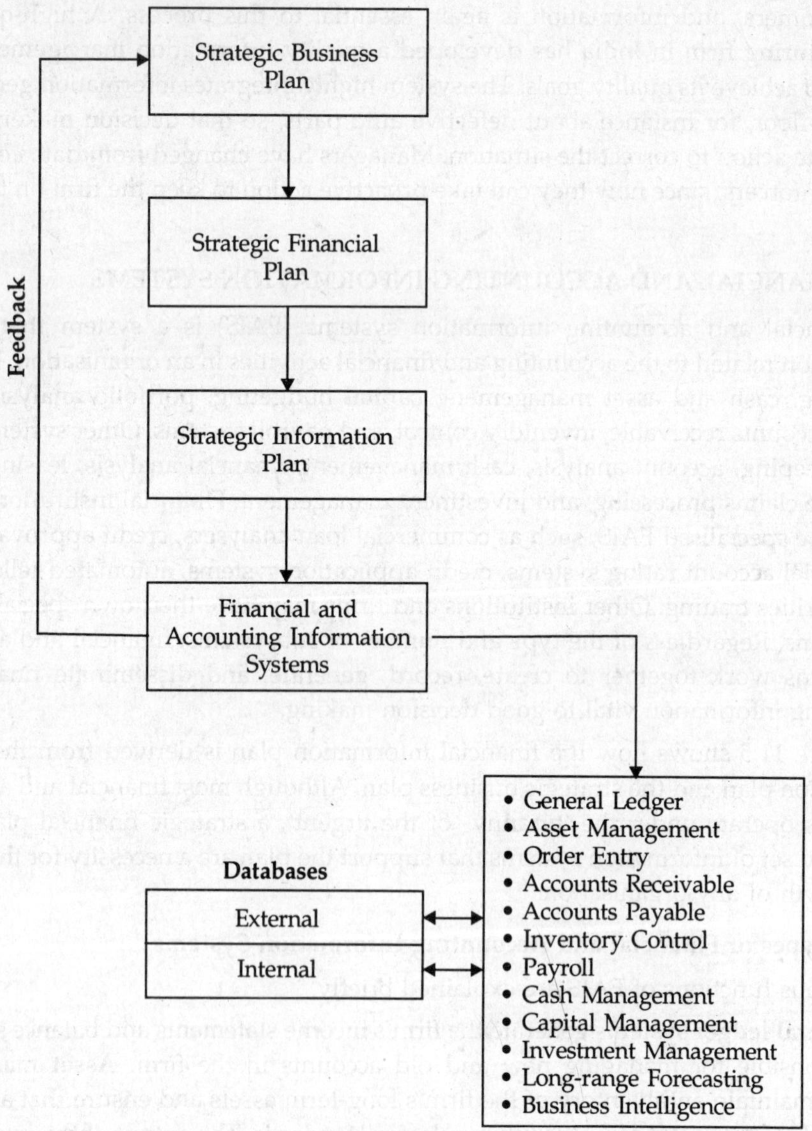

Fig. 11.5 Financial and Accounting Information System with Its Subsystem

These systems are designed to support mostly operational decisions. There are other kinds of FAIS to support tactical and strategic decision making in the organisation, such as the following :

- *Cash management systems.* Systems that ensure that the organisation has enough cash to conduct normal business, to receive the best possible return on its short-term cash deposits, and to leverage its cash flow to achieve good ratings in financial markets.
- *Capital budgeting systems.* Systems that ensure the acquisition and disposal of capital assets, such as land, buildings, and so on.
- *Investment management systems.* Systems that ensure that the organisation gets the best possible returns on its long-term investments.

11.6.2. Integrated Financial and Accounting Systems

FAIS are often integrated with other functional systems in the organisation to facilitate data sharing and team decision making. After all, financial decisions are not made in vacuum; they often involve marketing, manufacturing, and human resources. Thus, a free flow of information among these functional units is vital for good decision making. A radically different form of accounting, called ABC accounting, is helping firms integrate financial information with other systems. The activity-based costing (ABC) accounting system assigns overhead costs based on actual consumption of resources. A key benefit of ABC is that it allows a firm to determine the true cost of a product and the cost of serving a customer. This system is simple but highly information-intensive. Instead of viewing the business as a collection of salaries and machines, ABC views it as a collection of processes or activities, and calculates the cost of each process or activity. These calculations are made by integrating information from different sources, such as the firm's general ledger and time-keeping systems. Determining the true cost of a product is the first step toward increasing profits and a FAIS can help a firm achieve this goal.

For global and multinational firms, integrated financial and accounting systems are simply a necessity.

11.7. RESEARCH AND DEVELOPMENT INFORMATION SYSTEMS

Advances in information technology have spawned specialised information systems in many other business areas. The significant area receiving considerable attention is R&D. R&D has long been recognised as an information-intensive activity that is usually

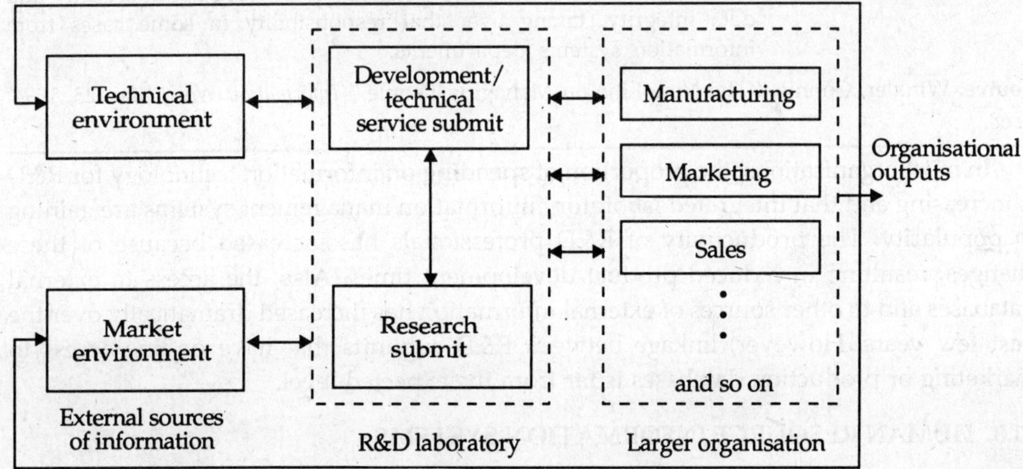

Fig. 11.6 Information Flow in R&D

responsible for evolving a stream of new products and production process innovations for the organisation. R&D is responsible for creating and developing new products or services in order to capitalise on recognised opportunities. R&D may also be responsible for overcoming recognised weaknesses in current organisational production and operation processes in order to make them more efficient, cost-effective, and competitive. Because of this mandate and the potential of R&D to provide the organisation with competitive advantage, many researchers suggest that R&D information systems should be considered to be strategic information systems.

Like many other organisational systems, R&D is an open system that has important information and communications exchanges with the external environment and other organisational subunits. Figure 11.6 depicts the major information flows crucial for R&D effectiveness. This figure suggests that strong linkages should exist between R&D and the external environment; it also suggests that solid links should exist between R&D and the marketing/production subsystems of the organisation.

Table 11.2. Guidelines for Selection at a HRIS

Get advice	Help from a reputable HR consulting firm minimizes the risk. These specialists have been through the process before.
Tests the payroll	High-volume transaction processing is the toughest job for client-server systems. Ask prospective human resources vendors to run your payroll for you.
Play the numbers	Don't ignore the benefits of outside service bureaus — especially in the area of payroll. Tax, retirement, and other legal conditions change. If you've got more than 500 employees, run a cost-benefits analysis.
Get it in writing	Don't be afraid to ask your vendor for a guarantee.
Train, train, train	Provide plenty of project staffing and technology education for your HR staff on the new system.
Be prepared	A merger or acquisition can affect your business at any time. A firm might need to add 5,000 employees to benefits and payroll systems within 30 days.
Act like traditional IS	Today's human resources departments must worry about security and data integrity, taking over that responsibility in some cases from information systems departments.

Source. Winkler, Connie, "The New Line on Managing People." *Information Week*, May 23, 1994, p. 68.

In most organisations, the proportion of spending on information technology for R&D is increasing and that integrated laboratory information management systems are gaining in popularity. The productivity of R&D professionals has increased because of these changes, resulting in reduced product development times. Also, the access to external databases and to other sources of external information has increased dramatically over the past few years. However, linkage between R&D subunits that have on-line access to marketing or production databases is far from the expected level.

11.8. HUMAN RESOURCE INFORMATION SYSTEMS

Human resource information system (HRIS) is a system that supports the planning, control, coordination, administration, and management of an organisation's human resources. HRIS also includes a large number of subsystems that address the information needs of various human resource functions. They provide managers with information, policies, and procedures concerning recruiting, layoffs, employee evaluation, promotion, termination, transfer, salary equity monitoring, job descriptions and responsibilities, training, affirmative action plan (AAP), and equal employment opportunities (EEO). Since HRIS also facilitate vital information on matters such as payroll, central and state taxes, health benefits, child care, grievance procedures, and other personal information that affects employees' personal and professional lives, it is imperative that these systems be highly responsive to employee needs. Figure 11.7 illustrates the variety of HRIS applications.

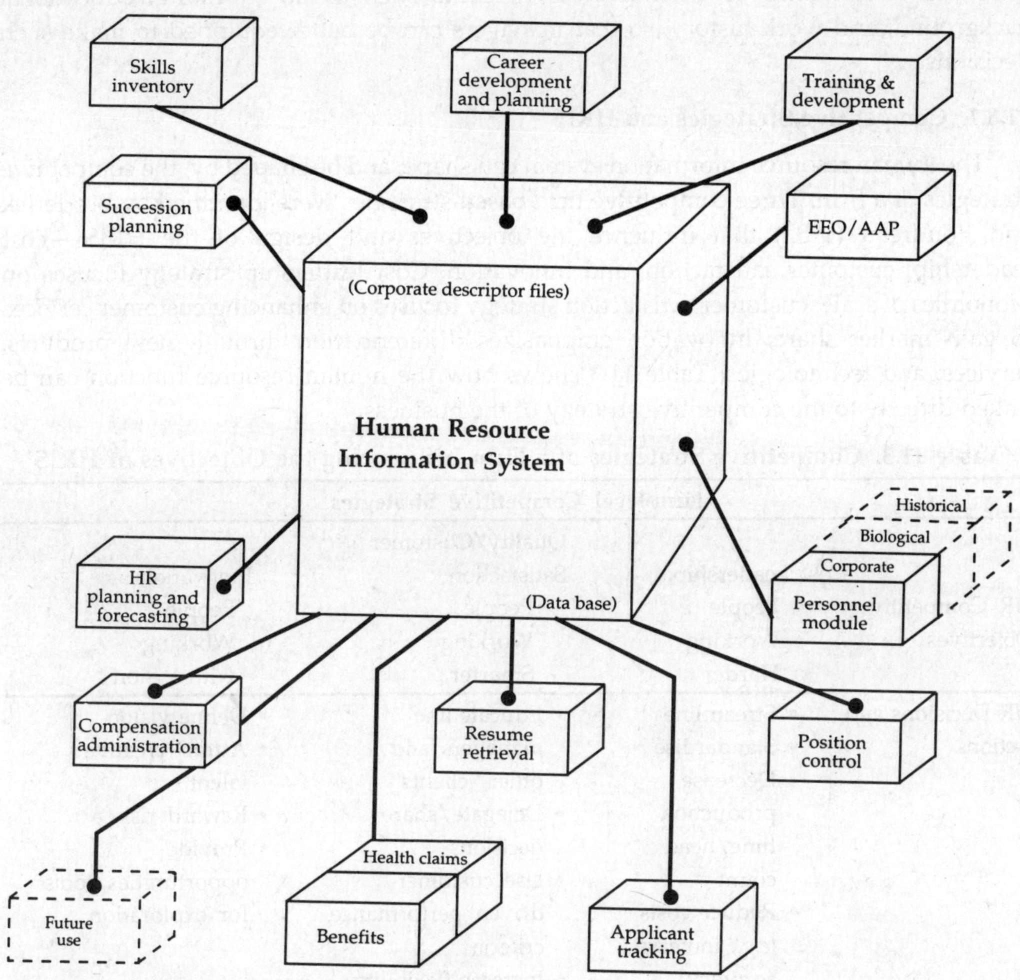

Fig. 11.7 Human Resource Information System Applications Network

Human resource systems were slow to be computerised in 1960s. However, in 1990s, many organisations began to realise the importance of HRIS. It is estimated that by the year 2000, HRIS will be a necessity for most of the big giants if they are to keep up with increasing government regulations and respond to personal information queries about employees. Table 11.2 gives some guidelines for selecting an HRIS.

Although many people believe that HRIS can be used only to enhance HR decisions, in fact they can be used to cut costs, increase efficiency, and achieve a competitive edge in the marketplace. For example, finance and human resource managers of an India-based multinational firm jointly developed a HRIS that determines how hiring and training decisions made by the personnel department can increase sales revenues. Also, the system links the performance of an individual to items such as past training, educational background, and work history, so that managers can be better equipped to make such decisions.

11.8.1. Competitive Strategies and HRIS

The human resource information system can shape, and be shaped by, the competitive strategies of a firm. Three competitive firm-based strategies were identified by Broderick and Boudreau (1987) that influence the objectives and design of the HRIS — cost leadership, customer satisfaction, and innovation. Cost leadership strategy focuses on economies of scale; customer satisfaction strategy focuses on enhancing customer services to gain market share; innovation emphasizes differentiation through new products, services, and technologies. Table 11.3 shows how the human resource function can be linked directly to the competitive strategy of the business.

Table 11.3. Competitive Strategies of a Firm Influencing the Objectives of HRIS

	Firm-level Competitive Strategies		
	Cost Leadership	Quality/Customer Satisfaction	Innovation
HR Competitive Objectives	People Working Harder	People Working Smarter	People Working with Vision
HR Decisions and Actions	• Streamline • Standardise • Decrease production time/head count • Reduce costs (*e.g.*, increase accuracy)	• Educate line managers and other "clients" • Delegate/share decisions • Use customer-driven performance criteria • Increase flexibility	• Define vision • Attract creative talent • Reward risk • Provide opportunities/tools for exploration

Source. Broderick, Renae and John W. Boudreau. "Human Resources Management Information Technology and the Competitive Edge," *Academy of Management Executives*, 1992, vol. 6, no. 2, p. 10.

Regardless of the strategy that drives the firm, HRIS must be integrated with other systems in the organisation. This helps the entire organisation to better plan its manpower and to explore employee-related cost-benefit relationships.

11.8.2. Human Resource Information System Development

The HRIS is derived from the strategic business plan, the strategic human resources plan, and the strategic information plan (Fig. 11.8). Some sub-systems within the HRIS are personnel data, payroll, benefits, administration, equity monitoring, processing job applications, monitoring positions, training and development, safety, workers' compensation, union negotiations, and collective bargaining.

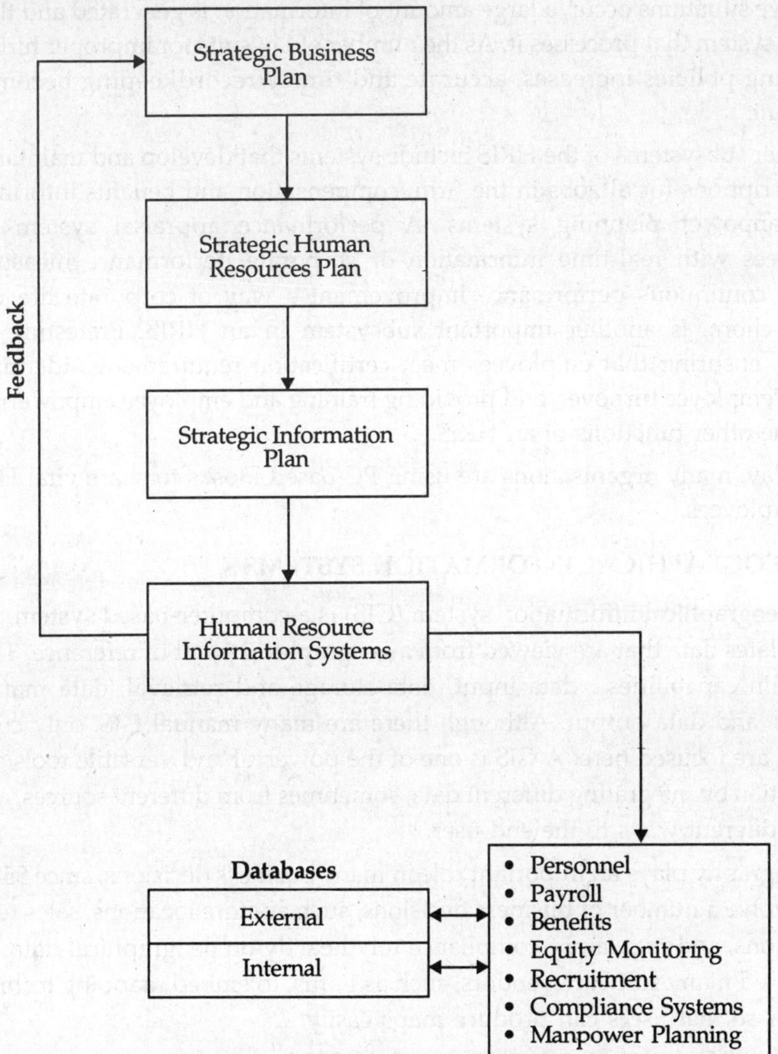

Fig. 11.8 HRIS and Its Subsystems

The core of an HRIS is a database that contains detailed personal and professional information about each employee in the organisation. Personal data include name, age, gender, address, and social security number; professional data include educational level, job title, job description, department code, years of employment, number of promotions, performance evaluations, and so on. All other human resource subsystems derive their information from this core database.

An important subsystem of the HRIS is the compliance system, which closely tracks and monitors the organisation's record of compliance with government laws and regulations, such as affirmative action, equal employment opportunities, and others. In the last two decades, the amount of regulatory paperwork has increased manifold and organisations are actively looking for ways to cut down the time and money they spend on these activities. One way to achieve this objective is through compliance subsystems.

Another vital HRIS subsystem manages records and generates information regarding recruitment, transfer, promotion, layoff, and termination of employees. Often, when any of the above situations occur, a large amount of information is generated and the organisation needs a system that processes it. As the number of lawsuits for improper hiring, promotion, and firing policies increases, accurate and timely recordkeeping becomes even more important.

Other subsystems of the HRIS include systems that develop and maintain job titles and job descriptions for all jobs in the firm, compensation and benefits information systems, and manpower planning systems. A performance appraisal system that provides employees with real-time information or corporate performance measurements, thus making continuous performance improvement a way of corporate life rather than an annual chore, is another important subsystem in an HRIS. Pretesting compensation policies, ensuring that employees meet certification requirements, identifying problem areas in employee turnover, and providing training and employee empowerment programs are some other functions of an HRIS.

Today, many organisations are using PC-based kiosks to share vital HR information with employees.

11.9. GEOGRAPHICAL INFORMATION SYSTEMS

A geographical information system (GIS) is a computer-based system that stores and manipulates data that are viewed from a geographical point of reference. This system has four main capabilities : data input, data storage and retrieval, data manipulation and analysis, and data output. Although there are many manual GIS, only computer-based systems are focused here. A GIS is one of the powerful and versatile tools as it can create information by integrating different data, sometimes from different sources, and display the data in diferent ways to the end-user.

Geography plays an important role in many business decisions, since 85% of corporate data involve a number of business decisions, such as store locations, sales territories, sales promotions, and regulatory compliance rely heavily on geographical data. Awareness of this has led many software vendors, such as Lotus, to embed mapping technology in their products so that users can produce maps easily.

The number of business applications of GIS has grown significantly in the last few years. For example, a GIS allows a bank to compare deposits with loan approvals in a given area and show that loan approvals meet regulatory standards in areas with deposits. In essence, GIS is an excellent decision making tool that integrates geographical data with other business data. For organisations with a customer focus, a GIS provides clear profiles of customers and their needs; hence these tools can be integrated with any of the functional areas of the business already discussed. The ability to integrate different data, analyse their impact on the customer, and integrate the findings in organisational decision making is one of the key factors of GIS.

11.10. CROSS-FUNCTIONAL SYSTEMS

Nowadays, emphasis is given on building cross-functional systems that facilitate the flow of information among all units in an organisation. Decision-making should not be compartmentalised in functional areas, but should instead be viewed in the context of the entire organisation. The close link between information systems and the various functional units in the organisation emphasizes the fact that students, regardless of their area of specialisation, should be well grounded in information systems and technologies. In the coming years, computer skills will be grouped with the basic skills of reading, writing, and arithmetic, and computer-literate individuals with a good understanding of information systems will be eagerly sought after by employers.

What is the relationship between the functional systems and the different *types* of information systems, namely, TPS, MIS, DSS, EIS, ES, and OAS ? The various types of information systems form the backbone of the functional information systems. The type of functional system depends on the nature, scope, and complexity of the task. If the task is routine, structured, involves transactional data, and is related to operational decisions, whether in finance, accounting, marketing, manufacturing, or human resources, the system is likely to be a transaction processing system. Summary and exception reports for different functional areas are likely to be generated by a management information system. For example, a report of the number of people who worked overtime last month (human resources) or the number of machines operated during the night shift last month (manufacturing) are often the output of an MIS.

If a problem is semi-structured or unstructured, requires internal and external data, and is related to tactical decisions, the system is likely to be a decision support system. Strategic decisions made by senior managers that require data and information to be presented in a succinct manner are likely to be supported by an EIS. Capturing and disseminating knowledge in various functional areas of a business often requires an expert system. For example, experience associated with loan approvals in a bank is often modeled by an expert system. Finally, office automation systems facilitate the flow of oral and written communications in the entire organisation, and hence are used by all the functional areas.

Review Questions

1. Explain some of the advantages of information systems to an organisation. Identify *at least three* intangible benefits of information system.
2. Briefly describe the functional areas of business. Explain, with a neat sketch, how the data flow in a functional area.
3. What are the primary decisions made in the manufacturing ? Explain each of them briefly, with an illustrative diagram.
4. What is computer-integrated manufacturing ?
5. Describe agile manufacturing. What are the *four* main characteristics of agile manufacturing ?
6. What is the difference between manufacturing information systems and production systems ? Give an example of a production system.
7. Explain in brief the sources of manufacturing information.

8. How is quality control function important in manufacturing ?
9. What are the advantages of manufacturing information systems ?
10. What do you mean by a marketing information system ? Explain three types of marketing information.
11. Explain various inputs of marketing information system and their usefulness.
12. Briefly describe the different outputs of marketing information system.
13. What should be the essential features of the database created for input and output marketing information system ?
14. Outline the advantages of marketing information systems.
15. How can information systems help an organisation achieve its quality goals ? What type of information a decision maker may collect in the process of monitoring and assessing the overall quality of goods and services.
16. Outline the good and bad moves to be followed by the information specialist in an enterprise-wide quality effort.
17. How is quality information system play a significant role in quality certification ?
18. What are the subsystems of financial and accounting information systems ? Explain each of them with a neat sketch.
19. Explain various functions of financial and accounting information systems.
20. Explain in detail about ABC accounting.
21. What are the characteristics of R&D information systems ? What impacts do these have on the productivity of R&D professionals and on the competitiveness of the firm ?
22. What do you mean by HRIS ? Explain briefly the HRIS application network with an illustrative diagram.
23. Why should a firm's competitive strategies be taken into account before designing a HRIS ?
24. What are the guidelines for selection of an HRIS ?
25. Outline the main features of HRIS development.
26. Explain briefly HRIS and its subsystem with an illustrative sketch.
27. What is a GIS. Identify some uses of GIS. Mention some types of decisions that rely on geographical data.
28. What are the advantages of cross-functional systems ?

12

Systems Analysis and Design

12.1. INTRODUCTION

Systems analysis is an important activity that takes place when new information systems are being built or existing ones are changed. It includes collection of necessary data and developing plans for new systems. For this purpose, it is necessary to set up the right processes to ensure that all the organisation's personnel have all the data needed for their work. Equipment must be chosen and new programs are written to support these processes on the equipment. The systems are often made up of many interrelated tasks. Changes to any one of these tasks or the addition of new tasks can affect existing ones. It is, therefore, necessary to spend considerable time gaining a thorough understanding of the system and its problems. It is only after developing a good understanding that it becomes possible to propose useful changes, which should make the system more useful and should not cause unforeseen effects. The investigation into system operation and possible changes to the system is called **systems analysis**. Once systems analysis is completed, system design commences. People who analyse systems use the understanding of the existing system and its problems to design and eventually build a usable system. In addition, *systems analyst* must determine the requirements of users of a new system so that during analysis they can discuss with users how to design a new system that meets these requirements.

It is known that a system is a collection of interrelated parts that work together to achieve one or more common goals; in particular, an information system is a set of processes and procedures that transform data into information and knowledge. A system has five components — input, processes, output, feedback and control — as shown in Fig. 12.1. These five components are central to any information system. Developing meaningful systems is the joint responsibility of the information system department and the end users. Therefore, it is utmost important that everyone in the organisation should have some basic knowledge of methodologies and other aspects of system development.

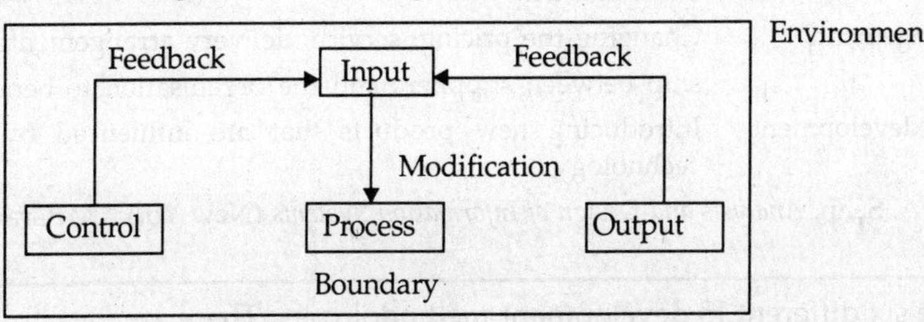

Fig. 12.1 Components of a System

Table 12.1 identifies five 'Cs'— capability, control, communication, cost, and competitive advantage — as possible reasons for system development.

Table 12.1. Five C's : Reasons for Initiating Information Systems Projects

Reasons	*Explanation*
Capability	
Great processing speed	Using the computer's ability to calculate, sort and retrieve data when greater-than-human speed is desired.
Increased volume	Providing the capacity to process a greater amount of activity, perhaps to take advantage of new business opportunities. Often a result of growth that causes business to exceed the capacities and procedures underlying the achievements to date.
Faster information retrieval	Locating the retrieving information from storage. Conducting complex searches.
Control	
Greater accuracy and improved consistency	Carrying out computing steps, including arithmetic, correctly and in the same way each time.
Better security	Safeguarding sensitive data in a form that makes them accessible only to authorised personnel.
Communication	
Enhanced communication	Speeding the flow of information between remote locations as well as within offices.
Integration of business areas	Coordinating business activities taking place in separate areas of an organisation, through distribution of information.
Cost	
Cost monitoring	Tracking the costs of labour, goods, and facilities to determine how actual costs compare with expected ones.
Cost reduction	Using computing capability to process data at a lower cost than would be possible with other methods, while maintaining accuracy.
Competitive Advantage	
Lock in customers	Changing the relationship with, and the services provided to, customers in such a way that they will not choose to change suppliers.
Lock out competitors	Reducing the likelihood that competitors will be able to enter the same market.
Improve arrangements with suppliers	Changing the pricing, service, delivery arrangements, or relationship between suppliers and the organisation to benefit the firm.
New product development	Introducing new products that are influenced by information technology.

Source. James A. Senn. *Analysis and Design of Information Systems* (New York : McGraw-Hill, 1989), p. 53.

There are six different IS development methodologies. These are :

- System Development Life Cycle (SDLC)
- Prototyping

- Rapid Action Development
- End-user Development
- Software Packages
- Outsourcing.

This chapter focuses these system development methodologies.

12.2. SYSTEM DEVELOPMENT LIFE CYCLE (SDLC)

The system development life cycle (SDLC) is a framework for developing computer-based information systems. It is defined and portrayed in slightly different ways by different authors. The SDLC is generally easy to recognise and well-acknowledged. It consists of *five* phases: Problem definition, system analysis, system design and programming, system testing and implementation, and system maintenance. These steps are illustrated in Fig. 12.2.

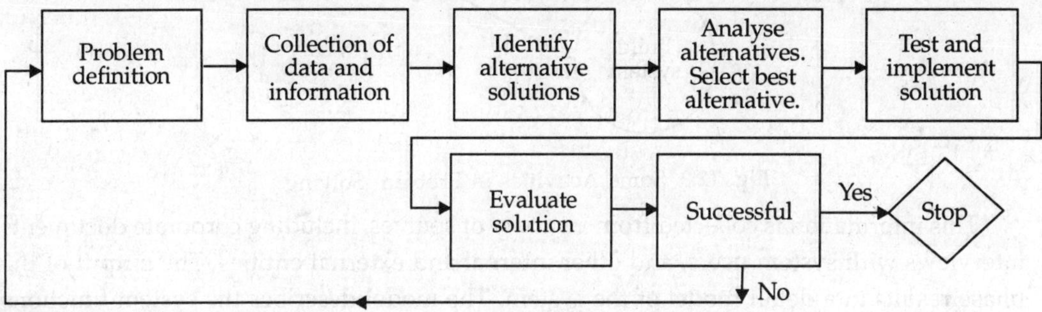

Fig. 12.2 System Development Life Cycle

12.2.1. Problem/System Definition

System definition is the process of defining the current problem, determining why a new system is needed, and identifying the objectives of the proposed system. In this phase, the main aim is to answer 'why do we need a system ?' and 'what are the objectives of the new system ?' The first question identifies the inadequacies of the existing system and elaborates on how these problems can be eliminated by developing a new system. The second question identifies the primary goal(s) of the system and establishes system boundaries, which are necessary to prevent the project from becoming a 'moving target' or growing too large and complex to be successfully completed.

12.2.2. System Analysis

In this phase, a detailed problem analysis is undertaken to better understand the nature, scope, requirements, and feasibility of the new system. Main activities included in this phase are : *Understanding the problem, feasibility analysis,* and *system requirements.*

Understanding the problem. It emphasises the clarification and understanding activities set out in Fig. 12.3. Developers and users should fully understand the existing problems and the strengths and weaknesses of the existing system. Other activities include identifying the overall implications and benefits of the new system for the entire organisation, taking an inventory of existing hardware and software, and identifying the information needs of existing and potential users.

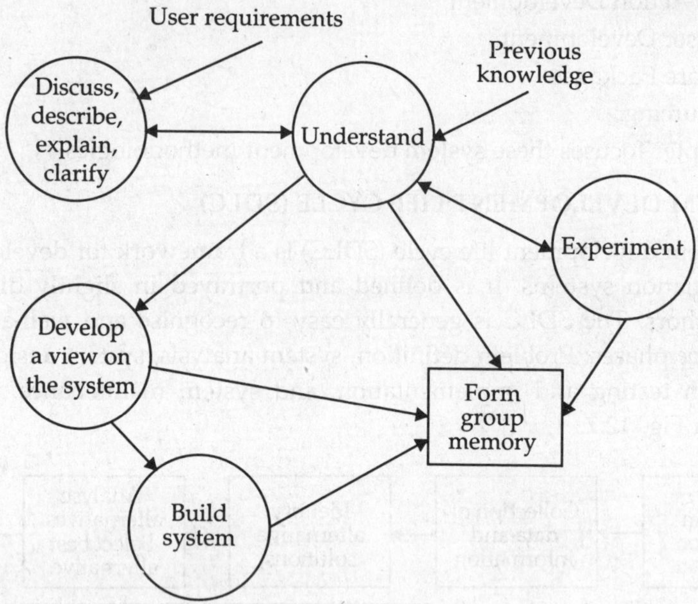

Fig. 12.3 Some Activities in Problem Solving

This information is collected from a variety of sources, including corporate documents, interviews with system users, and other internal and external entities. The output of this phase results in a detail model of the system. The model describes the system functions, system data and system information flows. The phase report contains any revisions to project goals and cost-benefit estimates.

Feasibility analysis. The feasibility analysis carefully examines technical, economic, operational, scheduling, legal, and strategic factors of a system to make sure that the system can be successfully developed. **Technical feasibility** analysis determines whether the proposed system can be developed and implemented using existing technologies or whether new technologies are required. Hardware, software and network requirements are also determined. **Economic feasibility** analysis evaluates the financial aspects of the project by performing a cost-benefit analysis and assessing both tangible and intangible benefits of the system. **Operational feasibility** analysis determines whether there will be any problems in implementing the system in its operational environment, looks at issues such as integrating the new system with existing systems in the organisation, and assess how the system fits with the strategic business plan and the strategic information plan of the organisation. **Schedule feasibility** studies address the time it will take to complete the project, taking into consideration available resources, and additional resources required, if any. **Legal feasibility** takes into account factors such as copyrights, patents, and state regulations. **Strategic feasibility** looks into factors such as the ability of the system to increase market share, give the firm a competitive advantage in the marketplace, enhance the productivity of knowledge workers, and achieve other strategic goals of the firm.

Some guidelines that firms use in project feasibility analysis are given in Table 12.2.

Table 12.2. Some Guidelines Used by Firms During Feasibility Stage

Build Knowledge

Process : Define technology and business issues

Goal : Formulate preliminary goals

Timetable : Can take months

Players : Affected business unit and its IS liaison

Determine Feasibility

Technology : Are current products sufficient ?

Skills : Does present staff have them ?

Time and cost : Are projections workable ?

Risk factor : Is the potential downside acceptable ?

Players : Affected business unit and its IS liaison

Test Practicality

Pilot : Build a prototype of the system

Experiments : Test various tools and technologies

Involvement : Make development interactive

Reviews : Keep business users abreast of progress

Players : Application developers, affected business unit and its IS liaison, central IS

Prove Profitability

Analysis : Do a traditional cost-benefit analysis

Benefits : Predict intangible benefits

Players : Affected business unit and its IS liaison, central IS

Commercialisation

Deployment : Utilise the finished application or system

Source. "Gateways to Innovation," *Computerworld*, October 31, 1994, p. 81.

System requirements. In this phase, systems specifications are identified by asking who, what, where, when, and how. Some questions addressed during this phase are :

- Who needs the system and for what purposes ?
- What are the needs of the user ?
- Who will receive system output ?
- When should the system be delivered ?
- How, or in what type of format, should the output be delivered ?
- Who are the users ? What type of training will they require to become proficient in the use of the system ?
- What are the maintenance requirements of the system ?

System requirements, therefore, establish various functions of the new system so that it can achieve the objectives established in the problem definition phase. **Creeping requirements** — requirements that are not finalised during the system analysis phase but continue to evolve throughout the development life cycle — can seriously jeopardise system development.

12.2.3. System Design and Programming

System design is the determination of the processes and data that are required by a new system. A number of technical, organisational, and managerial considerations, along with user preferences and resource constraints, should be taken into consideration before designing a system. It involves carefully scrutinising each system requirement and converting it into a sequence of detailed procedural steps and system specifications. The system developer must analyse each requirement and determine how to convert system requirements into system features.

Two types of design exist — **logical design** and **physical design**. Logical design identifies the records and relationships to be handled by the system. It focuses on the reasoning by breaking down the system into subsystems, and each subsystem into smaller subsystems, until the process cannot be further repeated. It establishes the relationships among various subsystems, the records and variables in the subsystems, and interrelationships among variables and subsystems. DeMarco (1978) has proposed a method for creating a new logical model from the current one, as shown in Fig. 12.4.

(*a*) Current logical model

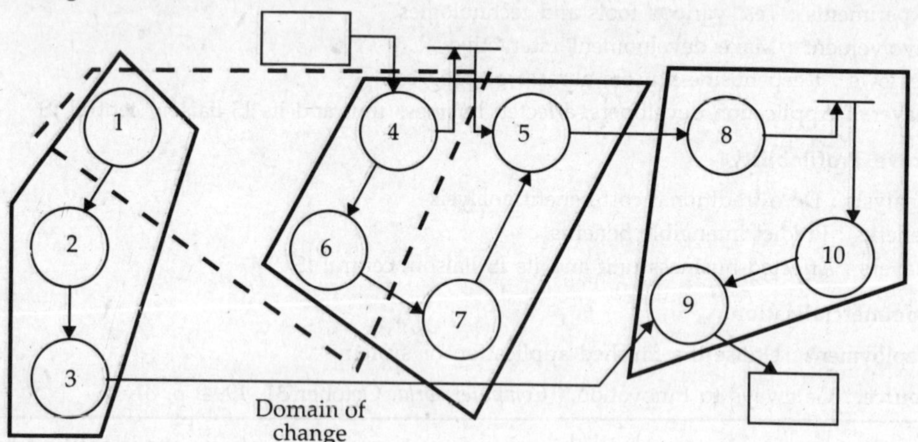

(*b*) New logical model

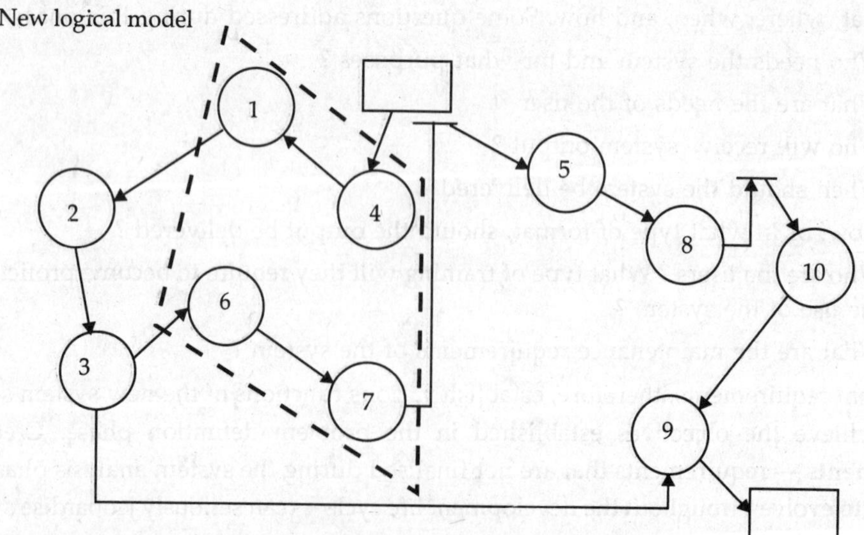

Fig. 12.4 DeMarco Problem-solving Cycle

Physical design proceeds, after logical design is complete, in two steps:

- an initial broad-level design; followed by
- a detailed design.

It addresses the physical aspects of the system, *viz.*, input and output devices, hardware configurations for the network, memory and storage, physical security, etc. It also defines data structures, access methods, file organisation, indexes, blocking, pointers, and other attributes of the system. In particular, physical design involves *three* main activities : (*a*) To know the technology required to implement the system; (*b*) To ensure that the design is rigorous and reliable; and (*c*) To provide detailed specifications and system objectives. The broad design identifies the main architecture of the proposed system. This architecture is verified against the proposed system model and validated against user requirements. **Detailed design** starts only when a broad solution is chosen. In this phase, the database and program modules are designed and detailed user procedures are documented. The interaction between the system users and computers is also defined. These interfaces define exactly what the user will be expected to do to use the system.

System development. The individual system components are built during the development period. Programs are written and tested and user interfaces developed and tried by users. The database is initialised with data.

12.2.4. System Testing and Implementation

Testing is one of the most difficult tasks in system development; it requires creativity, persistence, and a thorough understanding of the system. It involves thoroughly probing the system to ensure that its performance matches system requirements and meets the expectations of end-users.

There are *three* types of testing: **unit testing, system testing,** and **acceptance testing.** In unit testing, a system is viewed as a collection of programs (units), and each program is individually tested, without any assurance that the system is free of errors. In system testing, testing is performed of the entire system to ensure that its component units will function effectively when brought together as a system. In acceptance testing, developers and users test the system under actual or simulated operating conditions to ensure that it is acceptable to users.

A good system prevails when it is implemented without affecting the routine operations of the organisation. This requires careful planning and coordination. In case the system is new, implementation is quite straightforward. If the system is replacing an existing one, implementation becomes critical. In such a case, there are *four* types of conversion strategies: **parallel conversion, direct cutover, a pilot study,** and a **phased conversion.** These conversion strategies are explained briefly in Table 12.3.

Table 12.3. Four Methods for Introducing a New System into Its Operational Environment

Method	*Description*
Parallel conversion	• Old and new system run in parallel till new system becomes reliable • Costly but safe approach • Best suited to critical applications
Direct cutover	• Old system is replaced with new system • Less costly but more risky than parallel approach • Best suited to noncritical applications
Pilot study	• One department or unit is testing ground • Good for systems that are moderately critical
Phased conversion	• New system is slowly phased into the operational environment • Safe and conservative approach • Well suited to critical systems

A post-implementation review helps developers and users to analyse and highlight the successful and not-so-successful parts of a system. This review enables to perform a systematic search for better ways to develop and implement systems, apart from helping the organisations to recap the important lessons it gained from developing the system. Such an audit is normally conducted after the system is fully operational and its performance can be evaluated.

12.2.5. System Maintenance

System maintenance ensures that it continues to meet the growing and changing needs of users through system modifications as and when it requires. System maintenance starts after the system becomes operational, and should last as long as the system is in use. Maintenance is the key to continuing to drive the maximum benefits from a system. User requests for new features or for enhancement of existing facilities, a changing business climate, new technologies, or new information needs within the organisation can accelerate system maintenance. Maintenance costs usually increase with time and when it is more expensive than to develop a new one, the organisation must decide to abandon the existing system and build a new system.

System maintenance is basically performed for three reasons : (*a*) To correct errors; (*b*) To keep systems current; and (*c*) To improve the systems.

In essence, the SDLC is one of the most common and traditional system development methodologies. It is based on a systems approach to problem-solving. Various phases of the SDLC are summarised in Table 12.4.

Table 12.4. Activities in Different Phases of SDLC

System definition and planning	Address the questions: • Why do we need a new system ? • What are the objectives of the new system ?
System analysis	• Gain thorough understanding of the problem • Conduct feasibility study • Determine and establish system requirements
System design and	• Explore different designs and select best design

contd. ...

development	• Provide a detailed roadmap for converting requirements into actual performance • Create logical and physical design specifications • Plan, coordinate, control, and manage technical aspects of the system • Convert design specifications into program code
Testing and implementation	• Perform unit, system, and acceptance testing • Decide on implementation strategy : parallel conversion, direct cutover, or phased conversion • Evaluate system performance
Maintenance	• Make modifications and enhancements to ensure that system continues to meet user needs

12.2.6. Limitations of SDLC

The system development life cycle is appropriate to those systems that are highly structured and routine, such as TPS and MIS. However, it has some inherent limitations for its inflexible, sequential processes. These are :

1. Structured methods are no more applicable, because things done today are fast, cheap and reality checking.
2. Step-by-step approach of the SDLC does not suit the PC-based systems.
3. SDLC assumes that system requirements can be frozen during the system analysis phase. However, in the dynamic real world, user requirements change frequently.
4. The SDLC works better in stable environments, whereas the world of information system today is turmoil. The number and complexity of operating systems, user interfaces, network choices, software languages, and development tools have grown manifold.

Inspite of its limitations, the SDLC continues to be widely used for developing large, monolithic systems. As a way to better respond to users' needs, information analysts have more modifications to the SDLC so that the time required to implement systems is minimised. Of the many modifications attempted, two approaches — *prototyping* and *end-user computing,* which are best suited for PC-based systems, are increasing in popularity.

12.3. PROTOTYPING

Prototyping, also an important component of rapid application development (RAD), is the approach where systems are developed swiftly, without having undergone a complete analysis and specification. The system that is developed is known as the *prototype.* The process relies on the prototype system itself being an aid to the specification — by consideration of the prototype and identification of its weaknesses an improved system can be developed. Prototyping also relies on the presence of software tools to produce prototypes quickly. Typically, users take part in the prototyping process either with or without the aid of the computer centre. The process is thus heavily user-orientated. There are two types of prototypes : discardable prototypes and operational prototypes.

12.3.1. Types of Prototypes

There are two types of prototypes : *Discardable prototype* and *operational prototype.* Discardable prototype serves as the blue-print for the operational system.

Discardable prototype. The steps involved in discardable prototype are as follows:

1. Identify user needs.
2. Develop a prototype, using one or more prototyping tools — integrated application generators and prototyping toolkits. An **integrated application generator** is a prewritten software system that is capable of producing *all* of the desired features in the new system — menus, reports, screens, a database, and so on. A **prototyping toolkit** includes separate software systems, each capable of producing a *portion* of the desired system features.
3. Determine if the prototype is acceptable.
4. Code the operational system.
5. Test the operational system.
6. Determine if the operational system is acceptable.
7. Use the operational system.

Operational prototype. For developing this prototype, the first three steps are the same as for discardable prototype. The next step is as follows :

4. Use the prototype.

This approach is possible only when the prototyping tools enable the prototype to contain *all* of the essential elements of the new system.

12.3.2. Prototyping and SDLC

For small-scale systems, prototyping can replace the system development life cycle. However, for large-scale systems or those that affect large organisational units, prototyping is incorporated into the SDLC. Table 12.5 shows that prototyping can be used in all of the life cycle phases.

Table 12.5. Use of Prototyping in SDLC

Life Cycle Phase	*Step*
Planning	Define the problem
	Set system objectives
Analysis	Define information needs
Design	Prepare the detailed system design
	Evaluate alternative system configurations
Implementation	Specify the hardware resources
	Obtain the software resources
Use	Maintain the system

12.3.3. Advantages of Prototyping

Users and information experts like prototyping for the following reasons :

- Communications between the systems analyst and user are improved.
- The expert can do a better job of determining the user's needs.
- The user plays a more active role in system development.
- The expert and the user spend less time and effort in developing the system.
- Implementation is much easier because the user knows what to expect.
- A system developed through operational prototyping is capable of easy adaptation.

12.3.4. Disadvantages of Prototyping

Following are the potential pitfalls of prototyping:

- Because of prototyping's *iterative* nature, there is no definite deliverable or completion deadline.
- Code inefficiencies may be a drawback in terms of functionality.
- The computer-human interface provided by certain prototyping tools may not reflect good design techniques.

Prototyping is most appropriate for applications characterised by:

1. *High risk.* The problem is not well structured, there is a high rate of change over time, and the data requirements are uncertain.
2. *Considerable user interaction.* The system features on-line dialogue between the user and a microcomputer or a terminal.
3. *Large number of users.* Agreement on design details is difficult to achieve without hands-on experience.
4. *A need for quick delivery.*
5. *An expected short use phase of the system.*
6. *An innovative system.* The system is on the cutting edge, either in the way that it solves the problem or in its use of hardware.
7. *Unpredictable user's behaviour.* The user has had no previous experience with such a system.

Prototyping is least likely to be appropriate when :

- Appropriate development tools are not available and not understood by the users/ computer centre.
- End users are unwilling to commit the necessary development time to prototype development.
- High-volume transaction processing is required.
- Technical efficiency in the use of computer-processing resources is a high priority.

12.4. RAPID APPLICATION DEVELOPMENT (RAD)

A methodology that has the same objective of speedy response to user needs as does prototyping but is broader in scope, is called **rapid application development (RAD).** RAD is a term coined by James Martin, computer consultant and author, for a development life cycle intended to produce systems quickly without sacrificing quality. It is an integrated set of strategies, methodologies, and tools that exists within an overall framework called **information engineering (IE).** Figure 12.5 illustrates the top-down nature of information engineering, involving both data (left face of the pyramid) and activities (the right face). IE starts with the executive level, with strategic information resources planning applied to the entire enterprise. Thereafter, each business unit within the firm is subjected to **business area analysis (BAA)** to define the activities or processes and data that are necessary for the unit to function as intended. With the completion of BAA, RAD can proceed.

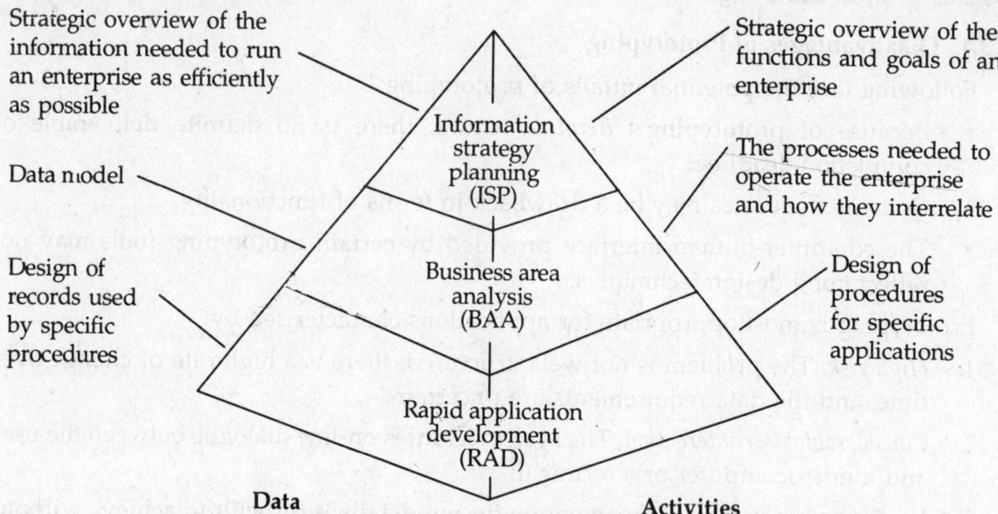

[**Source.** James Martin. *Rapid Application Development* (New York, Macmillan, 1991)]

Fig. 12.5 Rapid Application Development — An Integral Part of Information Engineering

12.4.1. Essential Ingredients of RAD

RAD requires *four* essential ingredients : *management, people, methodologies,* and *tools.*

Management. Management, particularly top management, should be **experimenters,** who like to do things in a new way, or early **adapters,** who quickly learn how to use new methodologies. Management should be fully supportive of RAD and provide a work environment that makes the activity as enjoyable as possible.

People. RAD recognises the efficiencies that can be achieved through the use of several specialised teams. There can be teams for requirements planning, user design, construction, user review, and cutover. Members of these teams are experts in methodologies and tools that are required to perform their specialised tasks. Martin uses the term **SWAT** (skilled with advanced tools) **team** in describing the team.

Methodologies. The basic RAD methodology is the *RAD life cycle,* which consists of *four* phases : (*a*) Requirements planning; (*b*) User design, (*c*) Construction, and (*d*) Cutover. These phases, like the SDLC, reflect the systems approach. Users play key roles in each phase, participating with information experts.

Tools. RAD tools consist mainly of fourth generation languages and computer-aided software engineering tools that facilitate prototyping and code generation. 4GLs enable information experts or users to generate computer code without using a conventional programming language. Examples of 4GLs are Natural, Focus and SQL.

12.5. END-USER COMPUTING

End-user computing refers to a situation in which the end-users of an information and decision support system are involved in the design, development, maintenance, and use of the system and its applications. In end-user computing, users of the system will be expected to play a leading role in most, if not all, of the following :

- Identification of the need for a system or application.
- Specification of the type of system and/or software to satisfy that need.

- Purchase/resourcing of the hardware/software.
- Development of the application according to corporate standards.
- Use of the application for business purposes.
- Management of security/backup for the application.

12.5.1. Types of End-User Computing

End-user computing involves a range of individuals with different types of skills, access to, and relationship with the computer system. If end-user computing is to be managed well within the organisation, then an understanding of the types of end-user is essential so that proper training, control, resourcing and applications development can be undertaken, and an understanding of the stage of development will determine appropriate strategies for management of the process.

Skills of end-users. There are *six* categories and end-users may 'progress' from one category to another. Each is distinguished by a different type of skill and information requirement. Recognition of this will aid end-user management :

1. Non-programming end-user.
2. Command-level end-user.
3. Programming-level end-user.
4. Functional support personnel.
5. End-user support personnel.
6. Data-processing programmers.

Maturity of end-user computing. The model has *five* stages in which the degree of integration of the application is taken as the measure of maturity :

1. Isolation
2. Standalone
3. Manual integration
4. Automated integration
5. Distributed integration.

If organisations are to proceed in their growth towards maturity in end-user computing, then management must plan to move smoothly from one stage to the next. Then it is necessary to emphasize standardisation in order to achieve the integration in the later stages.

12.5.2. Managing End-User Computing

There are three essential activities in managing end-user computing : *Coordination, support,* and *evaluation.*

Coordination. Coordination is vital to develop an integrated information environment within the organisation and to ensure that all end-users follow standard development policies and procedures. For this, hardware, software, networks, applications, personnel, and other resources associated with end-user computing must be carefully coordinated, controlled, and managed.

Support. Supporting end-users involves providing all the resources that they need to develop, manage, implement, and maintain information systems. This includes problems and system selection, providing backup for applications and systems, helping with system development, ensuring that all systems are properly documented, facilitating error resolution, providing information on resources available within organisation, ensuring that systems are properly maintained and secured, and providing necessary training.

Evaluation. Evaluation provides managers with the information needed to resolve the paradox inherent in simultaneously supporting and controlling, facilitating and restricting, enabling and disciplining, nurturing and regulating, and fostering and restraining end-users. All evaluation mechanism must take into account for this purpose.

There are *four* approaches to bring together the elements of coordination, support and evaluation. These are *sink or swim, stick, carrot,* and *support*. In sink or swim approach, any benefits derived from end-user computing are attributable solely to the initiative of the end-users. The stick approach strict policies and procedures to control end-user computing. In carrot approach, end-user is treated as a responsible employee who understands the risks, rewards, and implications of developing systems. In support approach, IS department provides necessary support to enhance the success of these applications.

Clearly, no one approach will work for all organisations; even within one organisation, different approaches may be required to meet the profiles and needs of end-users.

12.6. SOFTWARE PACKAGES

Nowadays, software packages designed for specific tasks, such as word processing, financial analysis, inventory control, scheduling, payroll system, are available to develop information systems. They are the effective tool to quickly develop systems. These software packages range in complexity from very simple to highly sophisticated systems. However, inspite of wide choices, sometimes a program still has to be customised. Customising allows firms to overcome some of the bottlenecks inherent in in-house development, while taking advantage of all benefits of tailor-made software. It reduces system development cost, time, and manpower considerably. However, readymade software is not customised to meet the needs of the organisation. This may require the firm to fit the problem to the tool, rather than finding a tool that fits the problem.

12.7. OUTSOURCING

Outsourcing is the hiring of outside professional services to meet the in-house needs of an organisation. In information systems, outsourcing means using external agencies to create, process, manage, and maintain information systems and to provide the firm with a wide range of information-related services. Organisations outsource for reasons that can be classified into *four* broad categories : *Strategic focus, economies of scale, market forces,* and *technical considerations.* One of the main concerns that managers face when it comes to outsourcing is legacy systems, which are large systems (usually on mainframes) that handle the firm's payroll, inventory management, and so on. There are three main outsourcing options with regard to legacy systems:

1. Outsource the maintenance of legacy systems and use in-house staff to build new systems.
2. Outsource the development of new systems and keep in-house staff to run and maintain legacy systems.
3. Use insourcing for both legacy systems and new systems. This involves treating the IS department as a 'business within the business' and training the systems development staff to meet present and future development needs.

Table 12.6 presents a summary of these three options.

Table 12.6. Outsourcing/Insourcing Options*

Outsource legacy maintenance, keep new development.

+ Investment in internal staff brings state-of-the-art technical know-how in-house and keeps staff motivated.
+ IS management can tap available supply of labour well-versed in older technologies (readily available, cheaper).
– Outsiders must be entrusted with operating key legacy systems that are needed to run business today.
– Internal staff may not be malleable enough to adjust to new technologies and techniques.

Outsource new development, keep legacy maintenance.

+ Enables IS management to make quick progress on new development efforts by using the latest techniques.
+ Staff members work on what they know best (*i.e.*, the legacy systems).
– The company may end up with new systems that cannot be supported by its own staff.
– Internal staff may feel neglected and become discontented or quit the organisation.

Insource the development.

+ Insourcing promotes a "business-within-a-business" atmosphere to focus and professionalise the group.
+ Economies of scale are leveraged to provide development personnel with training and tools.
– Lack of familiarity with the approach may confuse IS staff and distract them from user needs.
– IS may be pressured to offer new services that are not within its capabilities.

*Eliot, Lance B. "Legacy Systems, Legacy Options," *Computerworld*, July 11, 1994, pp. 86, 88.

Outsourcing has both advantages and disadvantages. The main advantage of outsourcing is that the responsibility of developing and delivering high-quality information systems is on the outsourcing vendor, not on the organisation. Reputable outsourcers provide state-of-the-art technologies, which help a firm to be responsive and competitive. However, outsourcing to the wrong vendor may result in loss of control over the quality and reliability of the IS function. It often results in job losses; when it does, fewer employees end up carrying a higher workload. This can be demoralising and unproductive, and can result in high employee turnover. Therefore, a firm must carefully analyse and balance the pros and cons of outsourcing, and take into account not only its information needs, but also the organisational culture, the managerial style, and the strengths and weaknesses of its IS personnel.

12.8. COMPARISON OF IS DEVELOPMENT METHODOLOGIES

Six different methodologies are discussed for developing information systems and their advantages and disadvantages. Each methodology has its own strengths and weaknesses, and all should be equally weighed and assessed carefully before selection of any one methodology. Table 12.7 shows the comparison of IS development methodologies.

Table 12.7. Comparison of Six IS Development Methodologies

	Characteristics	*Advantages*	*Disadvantages*
SDLC	Traditional development approach Sequential step-by-step approach Five phases	Suitable for large projects Provides structure and control	Expensive Time-consuming Inflexible Limited role of users
Prototyping	Iterative methodology Based on building a working model	High user emphasis Promotes teamwork Reduces wastage Flexible	Sometimes used as an excuse for poor development methods High levels of stress
Rapid Application Development	Speed response to user needs and is broader in scope	Involves management, people, methodologies and tools. Involves both CASE and prototyping.	The system is delivered in modules, not all at once. Goals are set by end-users instead of management.
Application Software	Off-the-shelf packages used to develop applications Can be customised	Eliminates some development problems Reduces overhead costs Speeds up development	Fitting the problem to the tool Allows only limited customisation
End-User Movement	End users assume full responsibility for system development	Speeds development Reduces IS backlog Users become sponsors	Lack of control results in laxity, security and stan-dards
Outsourcing	Outside vendors provide full or partial IS related services	Business can focus on strategic areas Cost-effective Reduces obsolescence	Eliminates jobs Can cause morale prob-lems Loose control over quality of systems

Nowadays, there is a strong movement in many organisations to shift the focus from right methodology to the needs of the customer. Hence, the primary focus of IS projects should be to meet the customer needs.

12.9. OTHER TOOLS FOR INFORMATION SYSTEMS DEVELOPMENT

Modeling tools play three important roles in system development: Communication, experimentation, and prediction. *Communication tools* help end-users and developers communicate effectively with each other and are specially useful in representing system specifications. *Experimentation tools* allow developers to experiment with different design and development approaches and learn by trial and error. *Prediction tools* are designed to help users and developers predict the impact of a new system on a firm, including the system's financial and human resource implications and its effect on competition.

12.9.1. Structured Tools

Structured tools are tools and techniques that support traditional development methodologies in SDLC. Figure 12.6 shows the tools used in each phase of the SDLC.

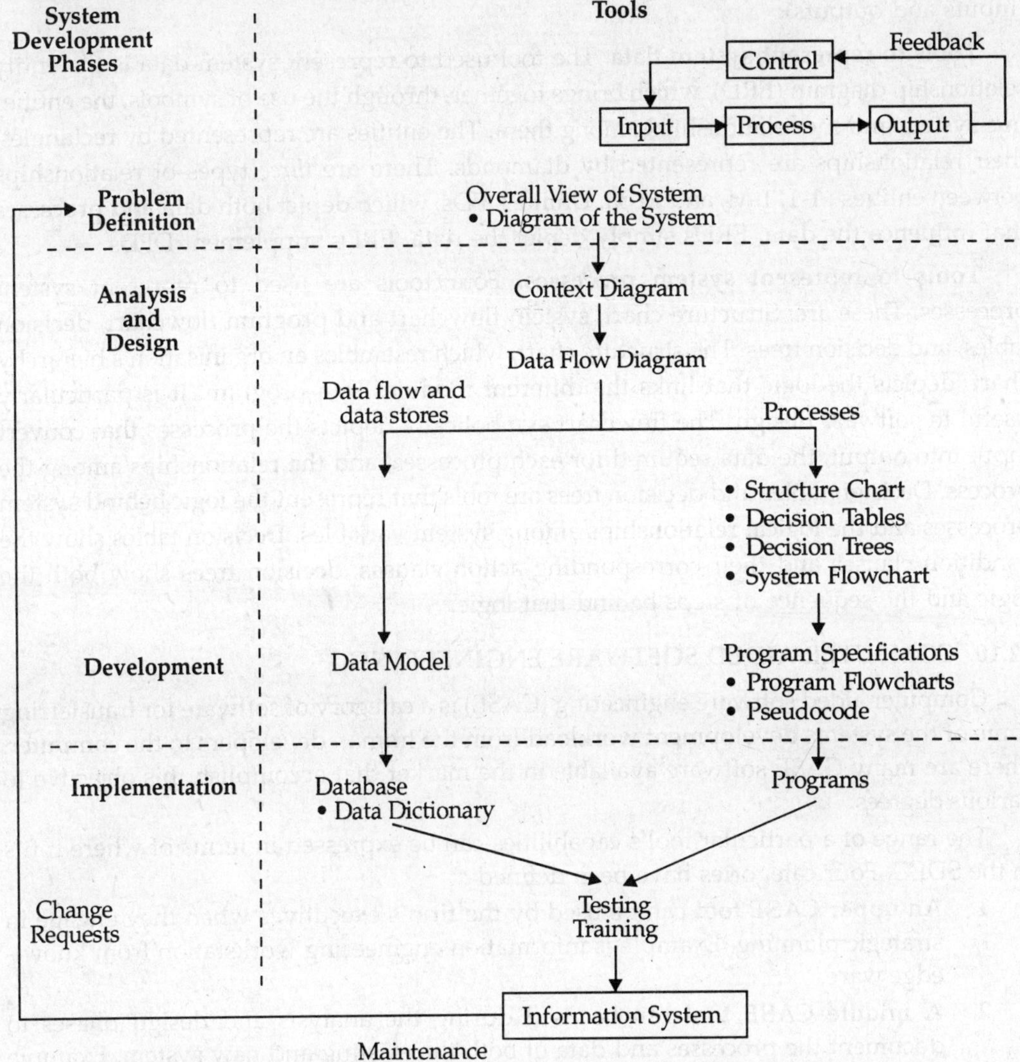

Fig. 12.6 Structured Tools and Techniques used in Different Phases of SDLC

In the problem definition phase, the aim is simply to gain an overall understanding of the system and its major components: the input, processes, output, feedback, and control.

Tools supporting system analysis and design. The *two* tools that facilitate system analysis and design are the *context diagram* and the *data flow diagram.*

The **context diagram** gives a broad overview of the system and identifies the major inputs, processes, and outputs in the system. It allows users and developers to view the 'big picture'.

The **data flow diagram (DFD)** identifies the inputs, outputs, processes, and data stores of subsystems within the overall system, providing a layered, or hierarchical, view of the context diagram. The DFD uses four symbols: the data flow symbol, the process symbol, the data store symbol, and the external entity symbol (an entity is a person, place, thing, or concept about which data are collected). The DFD depicts the flow of data in a system (inputs and outputs).

Tools to represent system data. The tool used to represent system data is the entity relationship diagram (ERD), which brings together, through the use of symbols, the entities in a system and the relationships among them. The entities are represented by rectangles; their relationships are represented by diamonds. There are *three* types of relationships between entities : 1-1, 1-M, and M-M. Unlike DFDs, which depict both data and processes that influence the data, ERDs simply depict the data. ERDs supplement DFDs.

Tools to represent system processes. Four tools are used to represent system processes. These are: Structure chart, system flowchart and program flowchart, decision tables, and decision trees. The structure chart, which resembles an organisation's hierarchy chart, depicts the logic that links the different modules in a program. It is particularly useful in software design. The flowchart symbolically depicts the processes that convert input into output, the data required for each processes, and the relationships among the process. Decision tables and decision trees are tools that represent the logic behind system processes and the logical relationships among system variables. Decision tables show the condition clauses and their corresponding action clauses; decision trees show both the logic and the sequence of steps behind that logic.

12.10. COMPUTER AIDED SOFTWARE ENGINEERING

Computer aided software engineering (CASE) is a category of software for transferring some of the systems development workload from the human developers to the computer. There are many CASE software available in the market that accomplish this objective to various degrees.

The range of a particular tool's capabilities can be expressed in terms of where it fits in the SDLC. Four categories have been defined :

1. An **upper CASE tool** can be used by the firm's executives when they engage in strategic planning. Example is information engineering workstation from knowledge ware.
2. A **middle CASE tool** can be used during the analysis and design phases to document the processes and data of both the existing and new system. Example is Visible Analyst from Visible Systems.
3. A **lower CASE tool** is used during the implementation and use phases to help the programmer develop, test, and maintain code. These tools are often referred to as **code generators.**
4. An **integrated CASE tool** offers the combined coverage of the upper, middle and lower CASE tools.

Most of the activity has concentrated on the middle CASE level, where the need was initially recognised to free systems analysts from the drudgery of documenting existing and new system designs. Subsequently, system maintenance expanded the scope of CASE to enclose the entire SDLC.

With the help of information engineering facility (IEF), the concept of a model, an encyclopaedia of design information, and SDLC methodology can be worked out. Also, a subject area diagram, an Entity Relationship Diagram (ERD), a process action diagram, and a screen design diagram can be drawn. Being a graphics-oriented tool, it can automatically create charts, matrices, data flow diagrams, structure charts, etc. It also automatically converts program specifications into program code and automates some of the tasks associated with coding, testing, and maintaining information systems.

CASE brings discipline to a highly complex process by coordinating a multitude of activities that take place during system development. It enhances the quality and reliability of the overall system by minimising the possibility of human error.

12.11. CHALLENGES IN DEVELOPING INFORMATION SYSTEMS

There are two major challenges in system development in most of the organisations:

1. Backlog
2. Runaway projects

A **backlog** occurs when the development of an information system has been delayed because of lack of resources. In many organisations, backlog continues to grow at a rapid rate. **Runaway projects** are the projects that are behind schedule and over budget. It is a universal problem. Often runaway projects are the result of poor management than of technological complexities. In order to regain control of runaway projects, sometimes the best alternative is to abandon the project. However, many organisations are reluctant to do for fear of losing face. Another alternative is to recruit users as system sponsors so that they have a personal stake in the success of the system. A third alternative is to hire managers with good planning and project management skills. Finally, good reporting systems and tracking systems can give early warnings of deadline slippage and cost overruns.

A survey found that *five* main reasons for success of developing IS projects are :

- User involvement
- Executive management support
- Clear statement of requirements
- Proper planning
- Realistic expectations.

Major *five* reasons for failure of developing IS projects are :

- Lack of user input
- Incomplete requirements and specifications
- Changing requirements and specifications
- Lack of executive support
- Technological incompetence.

Review Questions

1. Explain the five components of an information system with illustration. Discuss the suitability of these components in other systems.
2. What are the reasons for initiating information system projects ? Explain each of them in detail.
3. What are the five different system development methodologies for information systems ? Why is it essential for knowledge workers to know these methodologies ?
4. Discuss the five phases of SDLC. Explain the type of system for which SDLC is appropriate.
5. 'Analysis' is the *what* of the system whereas design is *how* of the system. Comment.
6. What are the various system analysis tools and why more than one tool is needed at a time ?
7. What is the difference between analysis and design ? Can one begin to design without analysis ?
8. What activities make up system design ? How does system design simplify implementation ?
9. A number of activities are carried out in implementation. Elaborate.
10. What is system development ? Outline the activities involved in system development.
11. Systems analysis involves a multifaceted role. Explain and illustrate situations where the roles might be best applied to the SDLC.
12. What is structured analysis ? Briefly review the tools used.
13. In your own words, describe the process of system design.
14. What design methodologies are used in system design ? Be specific.
15. Identify and briefly describe the three primary activities in the systems analysis phase. What are some types of feasibility analysis that are conducted in this phase ?
16. Explain the two types of system design ? Identify three main activities in the system design phase.
17. What is prototyping ? Identify any two strengths and two weaknesses of this methodology.
18. Explain the uses of prototyping in SDLC.
19. What do you understand by rapid application development ? Explain with an illustrative diagram.
20. Explain briefly the essential ingredients of rapid application development.
21. What is end-user computing ? Discuss the main features of end-user computing required for implementation.
22. Identify three essential activities required for managing end-user computing. Explain each one in detail.
23. Identify and explain some reasons why organisations choose to outsource their information systems.
24. Explain the outsourcing/insourcing options.
25. What are the merits and demerits of outsourcing ?
26. How is computer aided software engineering helpful for systems development from the human developers to the computer ?
27. Identify two major challenges that organisations face in developing information systems.

13

Strategic Management Information System

13.1. INTRODUCTION

Strategic management information system (SMIS) is the set containing systems considered critical to the current or future business competitiveness, and hence survival, of an organisation. An SMIS also supplies an organisation with business intelligence. In other words, if an information system is used in creative ways to achieve the goals and fulfill the mission of the organisation, it can be viewed as an SMIS, whether it is a TPS, an MIS, or any other type of system.

Strategic management information system can be external or internal systems. **External strategic systems** are used mainly by external entities in the business environment, such as customers, suppliers, and distributors, and have a value-added component that gives developers some time to reap the benefits of system innovation. Some benefits of external strategic systems are two-fold: (*a*) *Benefits to the customer* — increased customer satisfaction, increased customer control, and reduction in transaction costs; and (*b*) *Benefits to the organisation* — increased market share, reduction of processing costs, ability to charge higher prices because of value added components, and increase in profit margins. **Internal strategic systems,** on the other hand, are used by employees within the organisation and do not have a value-added component. The employees focus on issues such as improving the quality of products and services and enhancing the decision-making capabilities of managers. Such systems are often used at all levels in the organisation; they have long-term implications for the firm and for the business processes within the firm.

In general, strategic information systems can be divided into three categories:

1. Systems that focus on innovation for competitive advantage.

2. Systems that use information as a weapon.

3. Systems that increase productivity and lower the costs of goods and services.

Table 13.1 shows some strategic systems that fall into each of these categories.

Table 13.1. Strategic Information Systems Supporting Innovation, Information Services and Productivity

Innovation

Customer Service Systems
Order, order inquiry, service systems
Marketing Planning Systems
Forecasting, sales analyses

Information Services

Financial Planning Systems
Systems with mathematical models to aid financial planning
Executive Information Systems
Systems that allow top management to retrieve internal and external data and information directly from the computer
Logistics
Vehicle routing, freight rate management, shipment tracing, performance measurement
Electronic Data Interchange (EDI)
Electronically sending bills, payments, or orders to suppliers and customers
Access to External Databases
Compustat, Compuserve, *Dow Jones*, and so on.
Expert Systems
Computerised "consultant" systems for specialised situations

Productivity

Transaction Processing
Accounting, billing, payroll
Inventory Management
Raw materials, finished products, work-in-process
Centralised DBMS
Software systems to facilitate access to all organisational data and information
Production Planning
Materials and capacity requirements planning, scheduling, due-date setting
Personnel System
Skills inventory and personnel performance tracking
Statistical Systems
SAS, SPSS, Minitab, and so on.
Factory Floor Control
Robotic islands, automated guided vehicle systems, automated storage and retrieval

Source. Hagmann, Constanza and Cynthia S. McCahon. "Strategic Information Systems and Competitiveness," *Information and Management*, vol. 25 (1993), pp. 183-92.

13.2. CHARACTERISTICS OF SMIS

There are *three* common characteristics in all strategic management information systems. These are :

1. Telecommunications as a central part of SMIS.
2. Reliance on a number of vendors for providing information technologies.
3. Cooperation among a number of organisations.

Telecommunications is a vital part of SMIS; the successful organisations transcended traditional organisational boundaries and eliminated the barriers of time and space through the use of telecommunications. However, developing and implementing information systems that rely heavily on telecommunications is a challenging task and is often becomes one of the bottlenecks for development of SMIS.

For integration of complex technologies to develop an SMIS, *a number of vendors* are needed in many cases. Therefore, one of the ingredients of an SMIS is the ability to identify, coordinate, and manage transactions with a number of vendors and effectively bring together diverse technologies to achieve a goal.

Interorganisational systems are those systems which are shared by more than two organisations, in terms of cooperation and collaboration rather than the competition. Such ventures often result in powerful systems enhancing productivity, reduction in operating costs, increased market share, and create new partnership, especially for organisations that conduct business transactions in global markets.

Nowadays, interorganisational systems are proliferating because the trend towards globalisation continues to accelerate. With the result, managers are expected to quickly access and disseminate large volumes of information across national and international boundaries. Second, interorganisational systems are the lifeline of multinational firms relying mainly on free flow of information between business units and head-offices. This often requires collaboration among diverse units. Third, creating interorganisational systems have become less expensive because of continued decline in hardware costs and advances in technology become commonplace.

Another type of interorganisational system is *electronic data interchange* already discussed in detail in one of the chapters earlier.

13.3. STRATEGIC PLANNING FOR MIS

An organisation's IS strategy, and the plan that document it, must be consistent with :

- Its corporate plans
- Its management's view of the role of IS in the organisation
- Its stage of maturity of use and management of IS.

For strategic planning of MIS, following five questions should be addressed :

- Where does an IS strategy fit within the wider set of strategies ?
- What has been the history of IS strategy planning ?
- What circumstances demand major re-assessment of IS strategy plans ?
- Who might be employed to do the actual planning ?
- What might an IS strategy plan contain ?

Two slightly different terms with slightly different meanings of strategy planning are encountered in the literature of MIS :

- **IS strategy planning.** It is the *process* of planning that will *deliver* a 'document' that defines what the IS strategy is, *i.e.*, the posture to the use and management of IS; this could be a fairly pedestrian portfolio of applications that best suit the needs of the organisation.
- **IS strategic planning.** It implies that the *process* of planning has, as its *purpose* and time horizon, strategic levels of importance. This means that either it is performed by executives at the strategic, as opposed to tactical or operational, level; or it is of significant business importance.

When one is talking of the process, the first term is used, only when implying business importance will one use the second.

13.3.1. Business Goals and Objectives

Identifying business goals and objectives should lead to articulating an overall business strategy. Figure 13.1 represents where an IS strategy fits in context. It shows the system hierarchy and does not imply a fixed *sequence*. The corporate level strategy will often establish the framework that deals with:

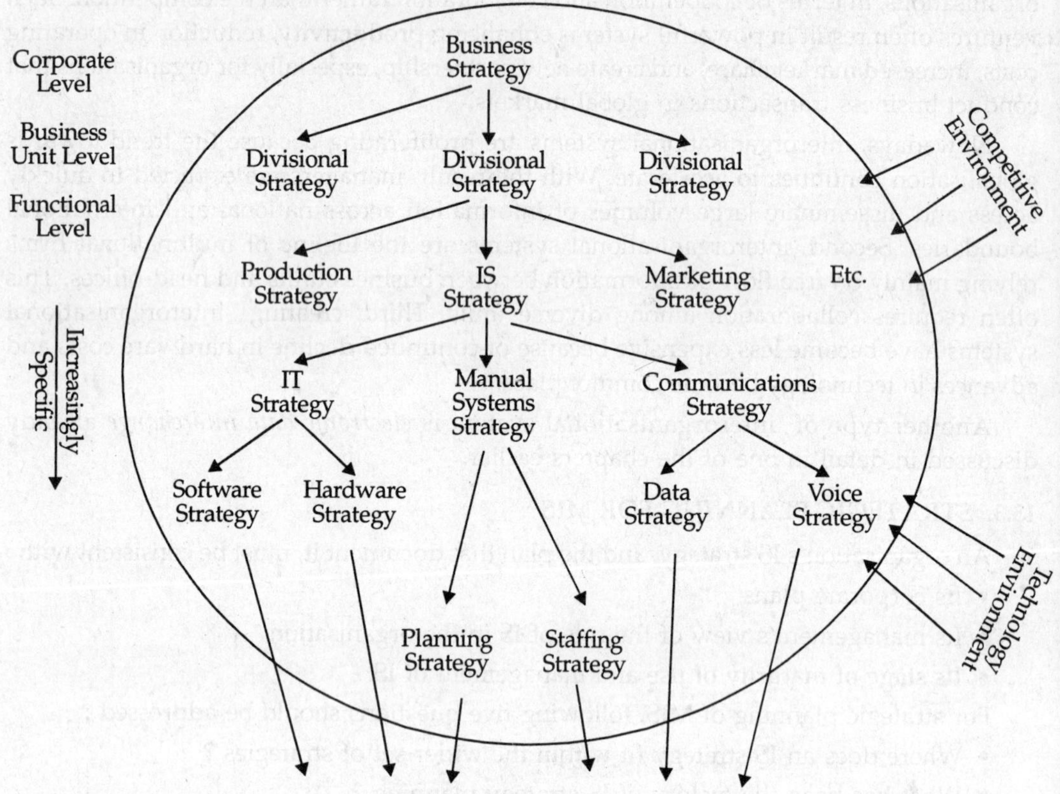

Fig. 13.1 Hierarchy of Strategies

- Corporate level information needs.
- Common systems architectures to get maximum benefit from internal expertise and to establish good relations with vendors.
- Organisational arrangements to ensure that business units strategies support and perhaps enhance the corporate strategy.

The current fashion, however, is for a minimalist corporate IS, and business, strategy that gives only overall direction and leaves maximum autonomy and freedom of interpretation to the business units.

13.3.2. Past History of IS Strategic Planning

IS strategy planning is a relatively recent phenomenon and it is still often not done or done badly. MIS are of major importance to modern business; they are either valuable tools when correctly aligned with business needs or a heavy cost burden when in- appropriate or managed incorrectly. Therefore, strategic planning for IS arrived with the primary objectives of the planning effort broadening to encompass the desire to improve communication with users, to increase the degree of top management commitment, to still allocate resources of course, but to find more opportunities for improving the IS function and spot the new, higher business payback, MIS application. Organisations tend to make two to five years of experimenting with their process for formulating IS strategies. By learning how to plan effectively and strategically, organisations find that IS and business strategies align and interact to give real business benefits. However, perhaps the most significant benefit for the majority of organisations is that the process and its resultant strategies produce a better understanding throughout the organisation and its business.

13.3.3. Reasons for Re-assessments of IS Strategic Plans

Three common circumstances that alter the objectives of an IS plan are :

- Major corporate changes
- External competitive opportunities or threats
- Evolutionary change in IS maturity.

13.3.4. Personnel involved in Strategic Planning

Planning teams can be formed primarily of specialist planning staff. They then will probably hold responsibility for co-ordinating, if not actually developing, many other planning efforts.

A second approach is to make the production of the IS strategy and the responsibility of 'general' IS staff.

The third route is to use a coalition team drawn from a number of business functions, certainly including IS and perhaps including some specialist planning staff. When making the choice of planning approach, an organisation is in something of a chicken-and-egg situation. There must be some concept of the likely scope of the delivered plan to establish an appropriate planning team.

13.3.5. Contents in IS Strategic Plan

Despite the possible variety of formats, it is possible to identify the necessary core elements to the IS strategy plan. They are :

1. A clear statement of the IS objectives, that give a clear sense of direction, *i.e.*, where the organisation wishes to be.
2. An inventory and assessment of both the current organisational capabilities and problems resulting from current practices, *i.e.*, where the organisation is now.
3. A concrete implementation plan that translates the sense of direction and knowledge of the start point into a navigable route map, *i.e.*, how to get from (1) to (2). The plan must identify both long-term and short-term actions and resource allocations. Additionally, the IS strategic plan must acknowledge that organisational change is an almost inevitable corollary to the planning process.

A relationship between different planning elements is shown in Fig. 13.2. Thus, key concerns of strategic planning for MIS are two-fold:

1. From the perspective of those destined to be consumers of IS service, the key concern of IS strategy planning is that they are able to interpret IS developments and services in terms of their business strategy and hence business needs.

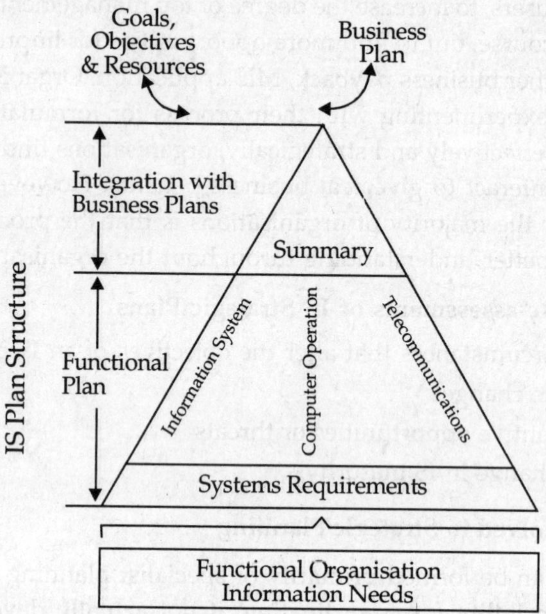

Fig. 13.2 Interconnection between Planning Elements

2. From the perspective of those destined to provide and manage IS services, the overriding objective is to provide service levels and styles that are appropriate to the business needs. Thus, IS are concerned to reconcile and satisfy user requirements to identify, plan for, and so manage, the IS resources and technologies needed. They are concerned to fill the technical, probably advisory, role in identifying and exploiting opportunities to use information to improve business performance.

13.4. DEVELOPMENT OF SMIS

An organisation should ask two questions before developing a SMIS. 'Is the project financially feasible' ? and 'Is the project technically feasible'. Strategic systems require substantial resources over an extended period of time, often with little or no guarantee of success. The primary reason why strategic systems are risky financial ventures is that they are often ground-breaking systems with few or no precursors, so they must be justified on the basis of the business strategy they support. Justifying SMIS primarily by financial standards is often futile.

Technical feasibility of the project. Strategic systems require well established technologies, which are also widely accepted by users. Sometimes the complexity of the technology can hinder the success of the system. State-of-the-art technologies and untested technologies can add a new and unexpected twist to the development of strategic systems. Technical failures of strategic systems can even place the organisation at a strategic disadvantage.

Key factors to success of SMIS. Following are the *five* factors that contribute to the success of a strategic system:

- Technology decisions should be grounded in a clear understanding of the processes that drive the technology.
- Strategic systems should be driven by strategic alliances between trading partners.
- Continuous improvement and investment in strategic systems are essential for their long-term success.
- The organisational culture should encourage some risk-taking.
- Users must be fully trained if the full potential of the strategic system is to be aimed.

Apart from these factors, there is a growing awareness, driven by the recession, that having an IS strategy focuses actions and hence *lowers* costs. Therefore, management attention has moved from the debate about competitive advantage to one of the competitive survival.

Information systems has devised three techniques for applying business process redesign (BPR) to the computer-based information systems. These techniques are known as three **Rs** — reverse engineering, restructuring, and re-engineering. These components can be applied separately or in combination.

13.4.1. Reverse Engineering

Reverse engineering had its origin in business intelligence. Firms keep current on their competitors' products by purchasing samples and taking them apart to see what makes them sick. The design specifications of the competitors' products are derived from the products themselves, reversing the normal pattern, where the design comes first.

As used in computing, *reverse engineering* is the process of analysing a system to identify its elements and their interrelationships, and to create documentation in a higher level of abstraction than currently exists. Reverse engineering is applied to a system when little or no documentation exists and there is a need to prepare new documentation.

The starting point in reverse engineering a system is the program code, which is transformed into such program documentation as structured English and program flowcharts. This documentation can, in turn, be transformed into more abstract descriptions such as data flow diagrams and system flowcharts. The transformation can be accomplished manually or by business process redesign software.

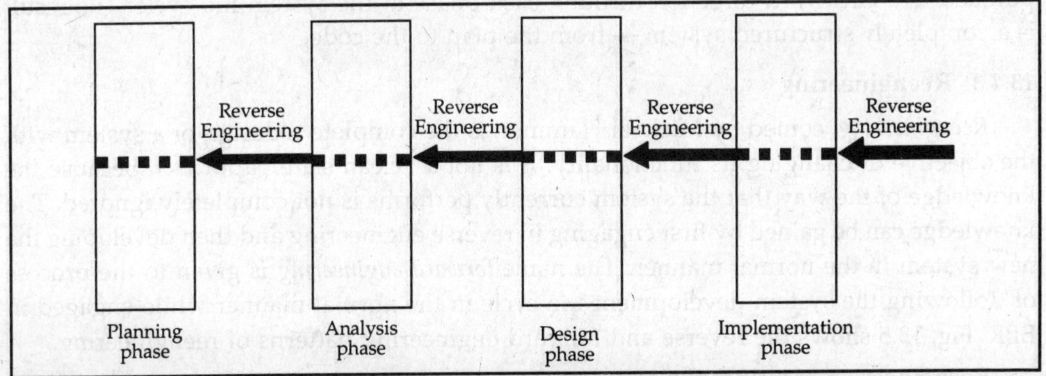

[**Source.** E.J. Chikotsky and J.H. Cross II. 'Reverse Engineering and Design Recovery : A Taxonomy.' *IEEE Software* 7, January 1990, page 14.]

Fig. 13.3 Reverse Engineering Process

Reverse engineering therefore follows a backward path through the system life cycle, as illustrated in Fig. 13.3, reconstructing the system design and planning that went into the original development effort.

The result is a thoroughly documented system. However, the system still does exactly what it was originally designed to do. Reverse engineering does not change the *functionality* of a system — the job that it performs. Rather, the objective is to better understand a system so as to make changes by other means, such as restructuring or reengineering.

13.4.2. Restructuring

Restructuring is the transformation of a system into another form without changing its functionality. A good example of restructuring is the transformation of a program written in "spaghetti code" into one in a structured format. Restructuring is pursued as a means of updating systems that were developed prior to the advent of structured techniques.

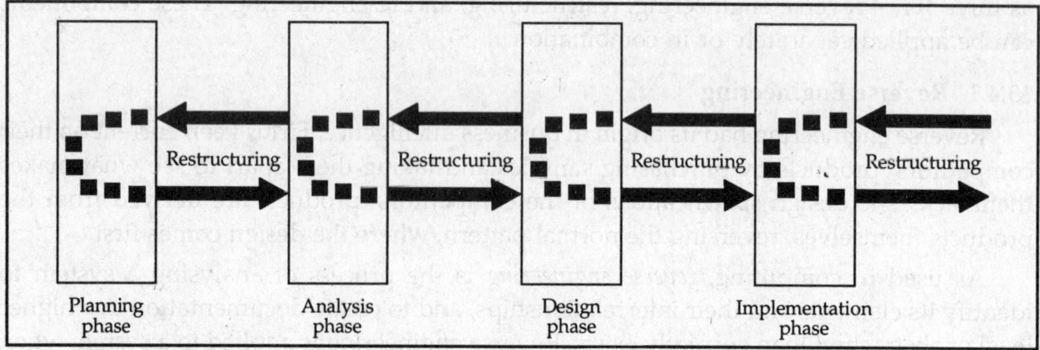

[**Source.** E.J. Chikotsky and J.H. Cross II. 'Reverse Engineering and Design Recovery : A Taxonomy.' *IEEE Software* 7, January 1990, page 14.]

Fig. 13.4 Restructuring Process

As soon as a program has been restructured it is put back into use, producing the looping pattern shown in Fig. 13.4. As with reverse engineering, restructuring can be pursued in a backward direction through each phase of the system life cycle. The result is a completely structured system — from the plan to the code.

13.4.3. Reengineering

Reengineering, coined by Michael Hammer, is the complete redesign of a system with the objective of changing its functionality. It is not a "clean slate" approach because the knowledge of the way that the system currently performs is not completely ignored. The knowledge can be gained by first engaging in reverse engineering and then developing the new system in the normal manner. The name *forward engineering* is given to the process of following the system development life cycle in the normal manner while engaged in BPR. Fig. 13.5 shows the reverse and forward engineering patterns of reengineering.

Reengineering identifies the essential elements of a core business process right across the organisation and sometimes beyond its boundaries. Davenport (1993) suggests a staged approach for process redesign :

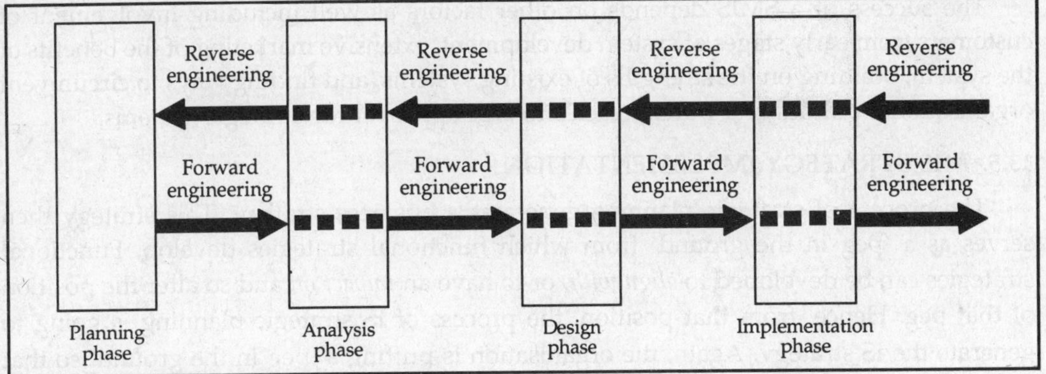

[**Source.** E.J. Chikotsky and J.H. Cross II. 'Reverse Engineering and Design Recovery : A Taxonomy.' *IEEE Software* 7, January 1990, page 14.]

Fig. 13.5 Reengineering Process (consists of reverse engineering to understand the existing system, and forward engineering to construct the new one

- Identify the process of innovation
- Identify the change levers
- Develop the process vision
- Understand the existing processes
- Design and prototype the new process.

This approach allows the organisation to concentrate upon the most *critical* processes, create a 'vision' of how they should be, and in doing this they challenge *all* the old assumptions about work flows, job definitions, management procedures and organisational structures; and all the, often implicit, rules must be tested for validity. The organisation will need to focus upon *outcomes* rather than *tasks* and use IS to empower one person to achieve that outcome. Whilst the re-design may demand an entirely new IS infrastructure, the process is even more about change management. In other words, the development of a strategic information system is never really complete; instead, it is an evolutionary system that must be frequently updated and enhanced if it is to continue to benefit the organisation.

The ability to continue to reap the competitive benefits of a strategic system long after it is developed is referred to as *sustainable competitive advantage.* An SMIS can provide sustainable advantage to an organisation under any one of these conditions:

- Competitors cannot duplicate the system and its advantages.
- Competitors cannot derive the benefits of the system even if they duplicate it.
- Competitors do not wish to duplicate the system.

Hence, it is necessary that continuous investment in strategic systems is vital to staying ahead of the competition. The organisational culture should encourage top managers to be 'champions' and 'passionate sponsors' who are willing to play a key role in the development and implementation of the SMIS and encourage its use and acceptance by employees and customers. Finally, the organisation should have a pool of talented people with technical skills and a good understanding of the business for the development of complex and sophisticated information systems. The organisation must also be willing to invest in training, since strategic systems often fundamentally alter the way business is done.

The success of a SMIS depends on other factors as well including involvement of customers from early stages of system development, extensive marketing of the benefits of the system, building on the strengths of existing systems, and finding ways to circumvent organisational politics and bureaucracies to win approval for strategic systems.

13.5. MIS STRATEGY IMPLEMENTATION

The process of strategic planning generates a business strategy. This strategy then serves as a 'peg in the ground' from which functional strategies develop. Functional strategies can be developed to *align with,* or to have an *impact on* and so alter the position of that peg. Hence, from that position, the process of IS strategic planning is going to generate the IS strategy. Again, the organisation is putting a 'peg in the ground' so that the *process* of getting this far can move from centre stage. The IS strategy forms a benchmark against which policy decisions can be judged. There are *five* major strategy implementation issues :

1. Information system resource structure
2. End-user computing
3. Information systems management and hybrid managers
4. Information value and information systems investment
5. Selection and acquisition.

Each of these strategies involves a range of potentially suitable actions. The IS strategy gives a 'template' against which to test the implications of a given decision. Figure 13.6 shows the relationship between an IS strategy and IS policies. The IS strategy defines, for those able to read and understand it, the weight to be attached to each factor.

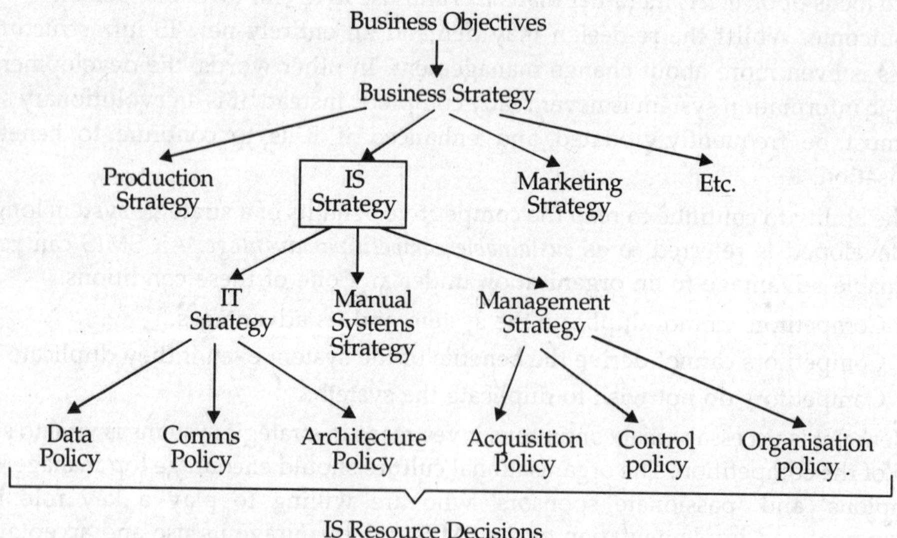

Fig. 13.6 Relationship between IS Strategy and IS Policy

academics and practitioners. These are given in Table 13.2. Dixon and John (1989) strongly emphasize that there is a difference between the management of the technology of IS and the management of its use. Silk (1990), a UK writer, considers that the key issues arise from the business needs, the technology trends and the barriers that exist to successfully use technology to meet business needs. Hunt (1990) places the blame for the failure to effectively use IS upon senior management's reluctance to take responsibility for IS as a critical business element. Finally, organisations must carefully study and improve their business processes before investing in strategic systems; they should be driven by strategic alliances with trading partners; and they must continue to invest in their strategic systems if they are to sustain their competitive advantage.

Table 13.2. Key Issues Involved in Strategy Formulation Process

Dixon and John (1989) categorise key issues as:	*Silk (1990) identifies and ranks the top 20 issues in the management of IS as:*	*Hunt (1990) lists key difficulties as:*
1. Management and organisation	1. The impact of IS on users	1. Business led use of IS
	2. Security of information	2. Value for money from IS
2. Hybrid partnerships	3. The need for an information strategy	
3. Managing the infrastructure	4. Justifying the cost of new systems	3. Open systems
	5. Managing the IS function and IS development	4. Standards
4. Macro-financial and planning issues	6. Defining requirements adequately	5. Choice of solutions
	7. Integration of data and databases	6. Third party supply
	8. Ensuring systems meet manager's requirements	
	9. Standards; flexibility; being locked-in	
	10. Back up and reliability of vital systems	
	11. Changing data into useful management information	
	12. Keeping informed about IT developments	
	13. Problem of updating large systems	
	14. Judging when to get into new technology	
	15. Involvement of senior managers; political factors	
	16. The attitude of IT professionals	
	17. Getting tangible business advantage from IS	
	18. Complying with legal and audit requirements	
	19. Distraction of staff and PCs	
	20. Assessing expert systems	

13.6. BARRIERS TO DEVELOPMENT OF SMIS

Two researchers, Chris Kemerer and Glenn Sosa, both of the Sloan School of Management, identified 12 barriers to the successful development of SMIS. These barriers fall into three categories : *Problem definition, implementation,* and *maintenance of strategic systems.*

Development (definition) barriers

- Generating workable ideas requires leadership and team work.
- Many innovative ideas are technically infeasible.
- Many innovative ideas are prohibitively expansive.
- Many ideas die because they lack a sufficient market.

Implementation barriers

- Telecommunications increases the complexity of implementing SMIS.
- Multiple systems are difficult to integrate.
- SMIS systems often require interorganisational cooperation.
- State-of-the-art technologies are difficult to implement.

Maintenance barriers

- Competitors can copy SMIS.
- Unanticipated demand can overwhelm the usefulness of an SMIS.
- Applications can be expensive to maintain or enhance.
- High exit barriers can cause devastating losses.

Organisations with limited financial resources, technological sophistication, and organisational flexibility will likely face one or more of these barriers.

Review Questions

1. What is a strategic management information system ? 'An information system is classified as a strategic system based on how it is used.' Discuss.
2. Outline the difference between external and internal strategic systems ? Give an example of each system.
3. What are the *three* different categories of strategic information systems. Explain each of them in detail.
4. What are the three common characteristics of SMIS. Briefly explain each characteristic.
5. Define IS strategy planning and IS strategic planning.
6. Illustrate with a neat diagram the hierarchy of strategies. Explain the framework for establishing the corporate level strategy.
7. Identify the primary objectives of strategic planning.
8. What are the three common circumstances that alter the objectives of an IS plan.
9. What are interorganisational systems ? Give some reasons why interorganisational systems are on the increase.
10. Identify the core elements to the IS strategy plan. Illustrate the interconnection between planning elements.
11. Why should the SMIS planning be closely aligned with the strategic business plan ? Discuss.
12. Identify some strategies for developing and implementing successful strategic systems.
13. What are the *five* key factors to success of SMIS ?
14. What do you understand by reengineering ? Explain the stepwise approach for process re-design.
15. What is meant by sustained competitive advantages ?
16. Identify some barriers to the successful development of strategic systems.

14

Information Resources Management

14.1. INTRODUCTION

The study of managing information and its allied components is referred to as information resource management (IRM). It requires a broad perspective on information, its uses, and its impact on the goals and the mission of the organisation. Various entities that influence, and are influenced by, information, such as people, policies, procedures, products, and internal and external business entities, must collaborate for IRM to be effective. Following are the three perceptions that are shaping the way IRM is viewed by the organisation.

1. Information technology is growing and changing rapidly. Expectations as to what information systems can do for an organisation have increased considerably in the last few years.
2. Top management is dissatisfied, increasingly, with the poor returns and inadequate performance of information systems. As corporate resources become tighter, there is increased pressure to put existing resources to better use.
3. Information systems are no longer regarded as just an operational tool. Managers realise that if utilised creatively, IS can provide a strategic advantage that competitors find hard to overcome.

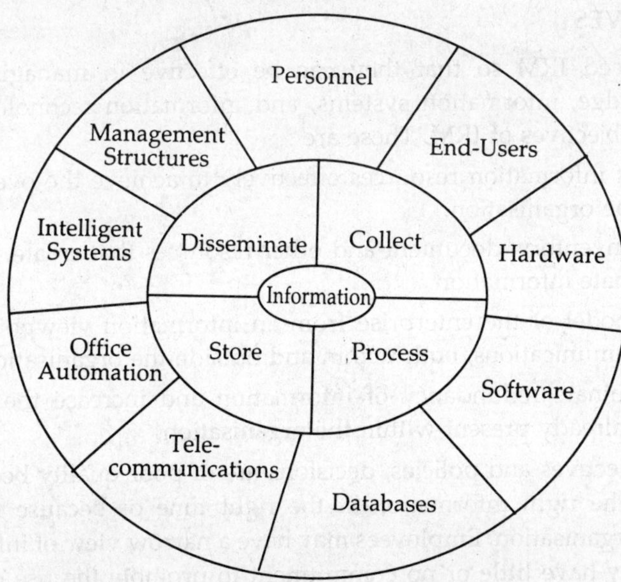

Fig. 14.1 Components of IRM

In essence, information resource management refers to policies, principles and procedures that effectively manage all components of an organisation that collect, store, process, retrieve, and disseminate information. IRM can be defined as 'the planning, budgeting, organising, directing, training, and controlling of information systems and its associated elements. The term encompasses both information and its resources, such as personnel, equipment, funds, and technology.' It is a multidisciplinary approach closely linked to the overall mission and objectives of the organisation and permeates all aspects of the organisation's culture.

Figure 14.1 shows some information-related components that must be managed in an organisation. These include software, hardware, databases, telecommunications, office automation, intelligent systems, management structures, IS personnel, and end-users.

An IRM model is presented in Fig. 14.2. It provides the setting for discussing the chief information officer's (CIO) responsibility for managing information technology. The model shows the CIO as a member of the executive committee and as the manager of one of the firm's main functional areas — information services.

14.2. PRINCIPLES OF IRM

The organisations successful in using information, information systems, and information technologies follow well-established policies and principles. In particular, such organisations share the following *four* principles :

1. The IS department should be managed like any other department of the business.
2. The main purpose of information systems is to help the organisation meet its goals and objectives.
3. IRM is the responsibility of all managers, regardless of their discipline/function.
4. The commitment of the top management is the key to realising the full potential of information resources.

14.3. IRM OBJECTIVES

Organisations need IRM so that they can be effective in managing their data, information, knowledge, information systems, and information technology. There are basically *four* main objectives of IRM. These are :

1. Utilisation of information resources effectively to achieve the overall goals and mission of the organisation.
2. Monitoring inventory, document and other resources that create, process, store, and disseminate information.
3. Develop a model of the enterprise from an information viewpoint in order to improve communications, both within and outside the organisation.
4. Aims to eliminate redundancy of information and increase the reusability of information already present within the organisation.

Without IRM objectives and policies, decisions are of poor quality because decision makers do not get the right information at the right time or because information is undervalued in the organisation. Employees may have a narrow view of information, and top management may have little or no commitment to promote the use of information systems and technologies to achieve the overall goals of the organisation. Other problems include information mismanagement, acquiring technology for technology's sake, obsolescence, hostile relations between the IS department and end-users, and projects with cost overruns and missed deadines.

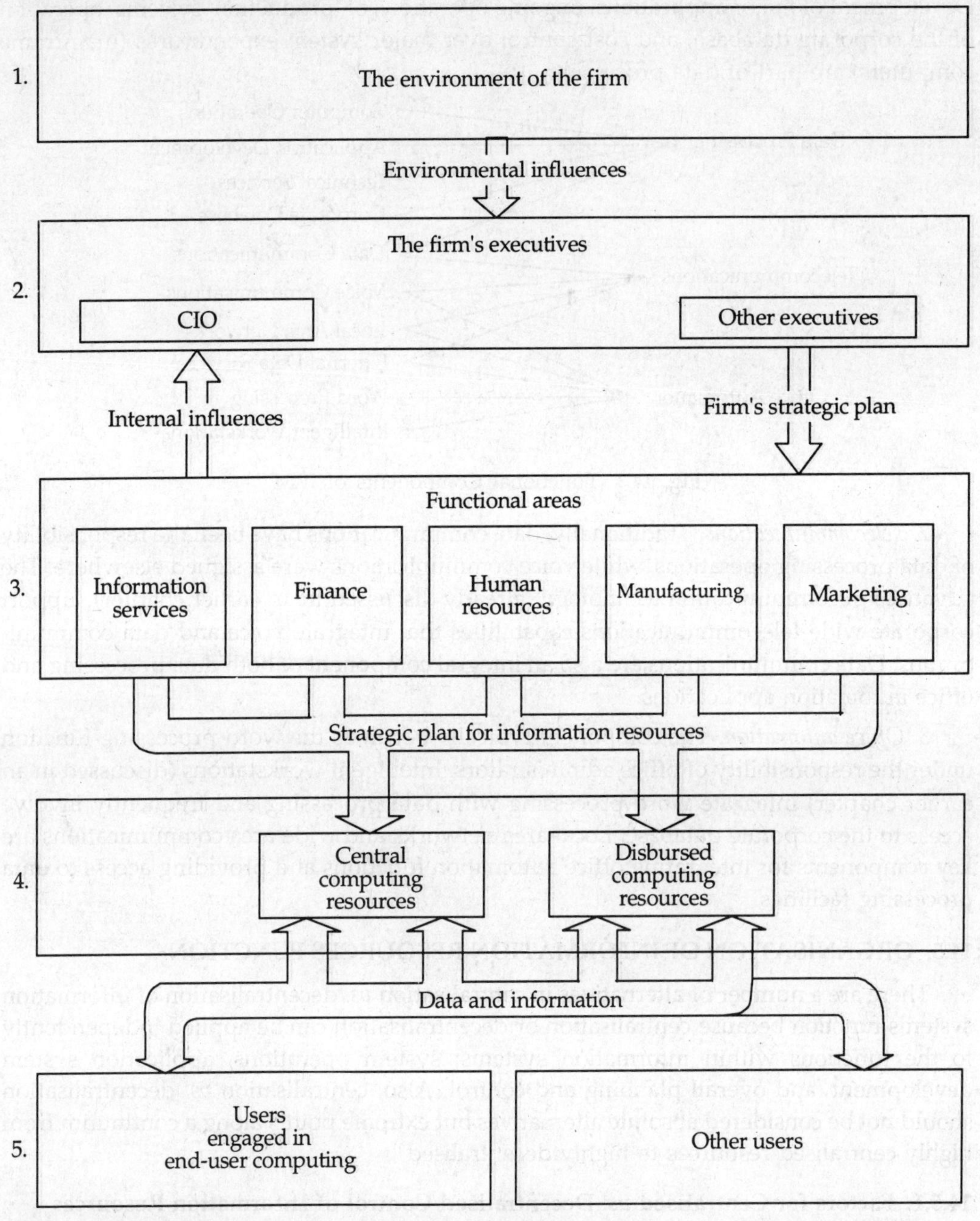

Fig. 14.2 An IRM Model

14.4. FUNCTIONAL COMPONENTS OF IRM

The component activities that make up the overall information resources function are shown in Fig. 14.3. The *three* general components are as follows:

1. *Data Processing.* In a traditional information system environment, information resources are synonymous with data processing. In organisations where information systems have a broader charter, data processing continues to play a significant role. Development of major applications, ongoing operations of 'production' systems, operation of the corporate database, and cost control over major system expenditures (mainframe computers) are part of data processing.

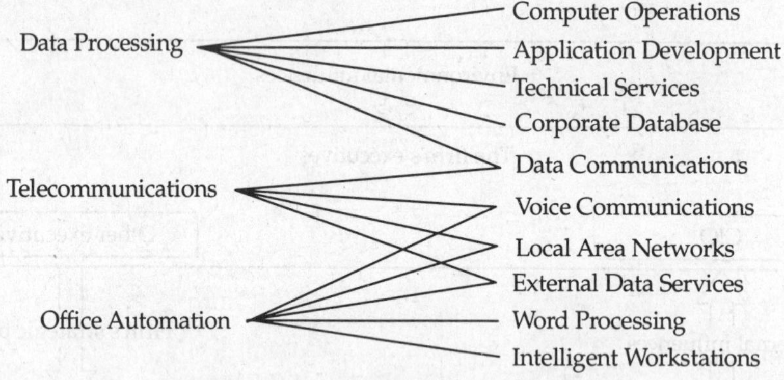

Fig. 14.3 Functional Components of IRM

2. *Telecommunications.* Traditionally, data communications have been the responsibility of data processing operations, while voice communications were assigned elsewhere. The advances in communication technology (already discussed in an earlier chapter) support corporate-wide telecommunications capabilities that integrate voice and data communications. Data communications are also an integral component of both data processing and office automation applications.

3. *Office automation.* The component typically began as the word processing function under the responsibility of office administrators. Intelligent workstations (discussed in an earlier chapter) integrate word processing with data processing and frequently involve access to the corporate database. Local area networks and wide area communications are key components for integrating office automation functions and providing access to data processing facilities.

14.5. ORGANISATION OF INFORMATION RESOURCES FUNCTION

There are a number of alternatives in centralisation *vs.* decentralisation of information systems function because centralisation or decentralisation can be applied independently to the functions within information systems: system operations, application system development, and overall planning and control. Also, centralisation *vs.* decentralisation should not be considered absolute alternatives but extreme points along a continuum from highly centralised resources to highly decentralised.

14.5.1. Factors for Centralised *vs.* Decentralised Control of Information Resources

Many organisational units requiring information resources tend to prefer to have those resources directly under their control, thus encouraging decentralisation. However, there are other factors favouring a centralised authority.

Factors for decentralised control. Following factors attributed to decentralised control of information resources:

— Availability of low-cost technology
— Backlog of development work
— User control over operations
— Organisational behaviour
  • Psychological value of unused information
  • Information is often collected and communicated to persuade.
  • Information use is a symbol of commitment to rational choice.

Factors for centralised control. Following factors attributed to centralised control of information resources:

— Staff professionalism
— Corporate database control
— Technical competence and research
— Comparative cost advantage.

14.5.2. Other Organisational Forms for Information Systems

The organisational forms (functional, product, and matrix) are also applicable to the organisation of information resources. Each of these forms may be implemented in a centralised environment; modified forms may be appropriate in a decentralised environment, depending on the size of each organisational setup. Nonetheless, there can be various combinations of centralisation or decentralisation.

14.5.3. Distributed System Operations

In system operations, there are *three* elements that may be centralised or decentralised. These are : *hardware location, processing control,* and *location of data.* For hardware location and control, a number of alternatives exists. These are presented in approximate order from highly decentralised to highly centralised:

1. Distributed computer hardware with no central control over configurations and no communications.
2. Distributed computer hardware with central control over equipment configurations.
3. Distributed computer hardware with communications network for communicating between hardware at different locations.
4. Distributed computer hardware for local processing and a central computer for large jobs.
5. Distributed computer hardware with communications network controlled by a central computer that allocates jobs to local computers.
6. Centralised computer hardware with remote job entry stations for input/output.
7. Centralised computer hardware with remote terminal access to specify jobs to be executed.
8. Centralised computer hardware with remote terminal access only for input/output.

Another important aspect of system operations for centralisation/decentralisation is *storage of and access to data.* Again, there exists a number of alternatives for achieving central/local storage and control. These are also presented in approximate order from decentralised to centralised:

1. Each distributed computer has its own files, and there is no interchange or central control.
2. Each distributed computer has its own files, but there are organisation-wide standards on naming, integrity checks, etc.
3. Each distributed computer has its own files, but the data can be accessed by other computers.
4. There is a centrally controlled network of distributed files and databases. A file or database is assigned to a local computer, and data records are transferred to other computers as needed.
5. There is a central database with subfiles downloaded to local computers for local use; file changes and transaction data are sent to the central computer for updating of the database.
6. A central computer has all files and databases.

The ultimate decentralisation is for each user to have a microcomputer and files. However, individual users require data developed by transaction processing. These data may be downloaded from the computer used for transaction processing.

14.5.4. Distributed System Development

System development is achieved by centralisation-decentralisation of its application through the organisational location of systems analysts and programmers or other control mechanisms. In general, systems analysts/programmers within the organisation can design applications and interact with operating personnel much better than systems analysts from outside. In such a case, managers tend to be more responsive to information processing. The advantages are reduction in communication difficulties between project phases. Having a user as a member of the project team is commonly suggested as a way to increase user input and user responsibility for the final product.

Another common mechanism for maintaining a centralised development group while improving responsiveness to user needs is the role of a *user liaison*. A person in this position typically reports to a centralised function having responsibility to the user group for which he/she is responsible. The reverse is also possible. The user liaison's most important task is translation and communication of user requests into data processing specifications and of data processing 'jargon' into terms understandable to the user.

14.6. APPLICATION OF SCARCE INFORMATION SYSTEM RESOURCES

An important management task is the allocation of scarce resources. In particular, there are more demands for information resources than can be provided in case of information systems. This will often be a part of the information system planning process, but allocation often takes place outside of formal planning.

14.6.1. Centralised *vs.* Decentralised Resource Allocation

The centralised approach to resource allocation is to assign the allocation to a central person or body. The central person can, for example, be the chief information officer (CIO). The CIO has a broad information resources view and may be able to make allocations that improve overall organisational information resources. However, there are many political factors in such allocations and coalitions of managers within the organisation may not be recognised by the CIO. The centralised approach is consistent with a service/profit centre concept for information systems. Users are not permitted to turn to outside services. The significant advantage of this approach is that it facilitates integration and an overall balance of development of information system applications; it also facilitates close adherence to an overall MIS master plan.

An alternative approach is to provide users with the basis for making such decisions. This requires a *chargeback system* that makes users responsible for their own information system costs. In order to serve decentralised planning and control, a chargeback system should have the following characteristics :

- *Understandability* — Users should be able to associate costs with specific activities.
- *Controllability* — Charges should be under the conrol of the user.
- *Accountability* — Costs and utilisation of information system costs should be a factor in user employee performance evaluation.
- *Cost/benefit incidence* — The user receiving the bill for services should also receive the benefits of those services.

However, different goals of chargeback system may be in conflict and cannot be met by the same method. In keeping with the profit centre strategy, all decisions regarding system development priorities are decentralised to users, and they have responsibility for cost-justifying their decision to management.

One disadvantage of the profit centre approach is the difficulty of accommodating it to a corporate database or corporate telecommunications requirements. In fact, the development of non-integrated divisional databases should be expected. In addition, it is difficult to reconcile user-controlled decisions to an information system master plan. Finally, users must be considerably sophisticated about information systems in order to determine their own information system needs and evaluate competitive alternatives for meeting them.

14.7. MANAGEMENT OF INFORMATION SYSTEMS PERSONNEL

Based on the growth rate in data processing and information systems jobs, one of the most difficult responsibilities of information systems managers has been to attract and retain competent employees. While some of the work of systems professionals may be shifting to users, recruiting and retention of technically trained employees is still a major management task. For management of information systems personnel, different job positions, range of skills, training, aptitude required, motivation of information systems personnel, career path planning, and job design must be considered.

14.8. MANAGEMENT OF END-USER COMPUTING

The trend to end-user computing represents a significant shift to decentralisation of information systems resources. The organisation of end-user computing can be highly decentralised or somewhat centralised. Responsibilities can be allocated to fit the organisational philosophy. Following are examples of allocations of responsibility and authority (ranging from highly decentralised to somewhat centralised):

1. Decentralised end-user computing with no central coordination or control.

2. Decentralised end-user computing with centralised responsibility for overall planning, major resource allocation, and enforcement of standards. Selection and training of technical specialists may also be centralised.
3. The operation of an information centre that provides analysts who go to users to work with them.
4. The operation of a centralised information centre to which users come as needed for training and assistance.
5. The operation of a centralised information centre for end-users in conjunction with a centralised computer and centralised databases. Access to the facilities of the information centre and the databases of the central computer is subject to centralised standards and procedures.

Three organisational issues important in the context of end-user computing are : *organisational policy and procedures for acquisition and use of microcomputers, end-user software support*, and the *organisation of the information centre.*

14.9. A PROACTIVE CIO STRATEGY

In most firms, the CIO can exert much influence over his/her future based on the strategy that is followed. The CIO can face the challenges head-on, and provide quality information support by following a strategy that consists of the following elements :

1. *Emphasize quality management of information resources* by identifying the quality needs of both external and internal information users. The external users exist in the environment of the firm in the form of the firm's customers, suppliers, stockholders, etc. The internal users consist of both management and non-management personnel within the firm.
2. *Achieve strong user ties* by ensuring that IS objectives are compatible with those of users, and applications of strategic value to the firm receive the highest quality support, and emphasizing joint application development.
3. *Strengthen executive ties* by becoming expert in the business of the firm and providing information support for the firm's executives.
4. *Assemble an IS management team* that has the technical and managerial competence necessary to integrate information resources in user areas so that they form a smooth functioning network.
5. *Assemble competent IS staff in leading-edge technologies and methodologies* to provide user support superior to that which can be obtained anywhere else.
6. *Build an information services information system* that enables the CIO and IS management to manage information resources in a dynamic, distributed environment.

Review Questions

1. Define information resources management. Explain how it can help an organisation to better manage its information resources.
2. What are the components of IRM ? Explain each component briefly.
3. What is the role of CIO in the area of information services of the firm ? Explain with an illustrative diagram.

4. What are the four principles of IRM ?
5. Explain the objectives of IRM.
6. The area of data processing, telecommunications, and office automation, traditionally separate, now require integrated coordination and control. Explain with a neat diagram.
7. Describe an information systems function with the following :
   (*a*) Centralised operations and decentralised development
   (*b*) Decentralised operations and centralised development
   (*c*) Decentralised operations and development.
8. How has the introduction of personal computers occurred in large organisations ? How could personal computers be introduced under central control ? Under decentralised control ?
9. The procedures of allocating scarce information resources should reflect the organisation and management philosophy of the organisation. Explain the allocation mechanism that best fits the following organisations :
   (*a*) A highly centralised organisation in which budget allocations are made by the owner-manager.
   (*b*) A highly decentralised organisation in which each business unit is a profit centre.
   (*c*) A moderately decentralised organisation in which committees are used to resolve many issues.
10. How do information centres improve service levels for users of information system services ?
11. As a user, would you welcome or resist the distribution of information system functions to user areas ? Why ?
12. As a user, what would you expect in chargeback system whose purpose was to help you control costs of system operations for your division.
13. Outline the three organisational issues for management of end-user computing.
14. Explain the responsibilities that can be allocated to fit the organisational philosophy in the management of end-user computing.
15. Which of the six elements in the CIO's proactive strategy to chart his/her own future course do you believe is the most important ? Explain.

15

Enterprise Resource Planning

15.1 INTRODUCTION

Enterprise resource planning (ERP) is a software architecture facilitating the flow of information among different functions of an organisation. It is an area which has revolutionised the business environment. Many organisations have re-engineered the processes and adopted ERP. It encompasses a broad set of activities supported by multi-module application software, and includes product planning, purchasing, maintenance inventories, vendor/customer service, and tracking orders. ERP uses a client/server environment, supported by GUI (Graphic User Interface) technology. It is an integrated system of commonly designed applications and consolidating all business operations into uniform system environment. Following are the main features of ERP :

- A software architecture integrating all functions of a business.
- Integration is seamless. This is achieved through (a) common database; (b) instant sharing of information which is common and simultaneous; and (c) one time entry being sufficient for the whole enterprise to get updated.
- Powerful, user-friendly GUI technology.
- Supported by client-server architecture for communication at different levels of the system.
- Uniform system environment.

15.2 ENTERPRISE MODELLING

Enterprise modelling is the most important prerequisite before the selection/ implementation of an ERP system. It encompasses complete understanding and detailed mapping of the firm's business functions and decision-making process, both independently and interactively. Enterprise integration leads to:

- More agile enterprise.
- Helps in eliminating redundant or non-value added activities.
- More efficient system after being enabled by information technology.
- Streamlines *five* important flows in an enterprise:
  (a) Information;
  (b) Material;
  (c) Money;
  (d) Control; and
  (e) Intangibles, such as customer satisfaction and quality improvement.
- Empowerment of employees to take action.

Based on Hansen (1991), there are *five* reasons which help in building the employees motivation due to integration:

- When people understand the vision, or larger task of an enterprise, and are given the right information, the resources, and the responsibility, "they will do the right thing".

- Empowered people—and with good leadership, empowered grous—will have not only the ability but also the desire to participate in the decision process.
- The existence of a comprehensive and effective communications network must distribute knowledge and information widely, embracing the openness and trust that allow the individual to feel empowered to affect the "real" problems.
- The democratisation and dissemination of information throughout the network in all directions, irrespective of organisational position, ensures that the integrated enterprise is truly integrated.
- Information freely shared with empowered people, who are motivated to make decisions, will naturally distribute the decision-making process throughout the entire organisation.

The integration of the enterprise helps in building an efficient and effective information network across the enterprise. Hoffman (1992) identified following reasons for integration:

- Identification of the major functions to be included in a program management organisation.
- Defining the scope and content of the information systems' architecture and related metrics as a management guide.
- Providing guide and/or roadmap through the process of developing such an organisation to manage a large-scale integration program.

15.3 ROLE OF INFORMATION TECHNOLOGY IN ENTERPRISE MODELLING

Advancement in information technology (IT) has transformed the business process in an extended-enterprise system by enabling seamless integration at the interfaces of functions and hierarchies. Table 15.1 gives the indication of shifting paradigms during recent years which have been triggered and supported by integration of enterprise and support of IT.

Table 15.1 Role of IT in Changing the Enterprise System

Old System	*Intervening Trend*	*Emerging Paradigm*
Role of information is very limited.	Information system designs, computerisation of major activities, automation	Seamless integration of enterprise through IT support
Manual analysis of data MRP	Computerisation and net working MRP II.	Integrated network of systems Openloop MRP ERP
Information appears at and accessed from only one place, at one time.	Shared databases, electronic mail, client server architecture	Simultaneously one can access same information at any place and whenever needed.
Only an expert can perform complex work	Expert systems, neutral computing	Novices can perform complex work.
Business must be either centralized or decentralized.	Telecommunication and networks : client/server	Business can be both centralised and decentralised.
Managers make all decisions.	Decision support systems, enterprise expert systems, support systems.	Decision making is part of everyone's job.

contd....

Old System	*Intervening Trend*	*Emerging Paradigm*
Field personnel need offices to receive, send, store, and process information.	Wireless communication and portable computers, information highways, electronic mail	Field personnel can manage information from any location.
Personal contact is the best contact with potential buyers.	Interactive video disk, desktop teleconferencing, electronic mail	The best contact is the one that is most cost-effective.
One has to locate items manually.	Tracking technology, groupware, workflow software, client/server	Items are located automatically.
Overall plans get revised periodically.	High performance computing systems	Plans get revised instantaneously whenever needed.
All must come to one place to work together.	Groupware and group support systems, telecommunications, electronic mail, client/server	People can work together while at different locations.
Customized products and services are expensive and take a long time to develop.	CAD-CAM, CASE tools, on-line systems for JIT decision making, expert systems	Customized products can be made fast and inexpensively (mass customisation).
A long period of time is spanned between the inception of an idea and its implementation (time-to-market).	CAD-CAM, electronic data interchange, groupware, imaging (document processing)	Time-to-market can be reduced by 90 per cent.
Information-based organisations and processes.	Artificial intelligence, expert systems	Knowledge-based organisations and processes.
Move labour to countries where labour is inexpensive (off-shore production).	Robots, imaging technologies, object oriented programming, expert systems, geographical information systems (GIS)	Work can be done in countries with high wages and salaries.

Source: Compiled in modified form from Hammer and Champy (1993).

15.4 FLOW OF INFORMATION

Information mapping is the key indicator by which an enterprise can be modelled. It requires careful analysis of what, when and how, in terms of information, that every entity needs. If this is done properly, half of the battle related to enterprise modelling is won. The capability of ERP/IT and their organisational impact is shown in Table 15.2.

Table 15.2 IT/ERP Capabilities and their Organisational Impacts

Capability	*Organisational Impact/Benefit*
Transactional	IT/ERP can transform unstructured processes into routinized transactions.
Geographical	IT/ERP can transfer information with rapidity and ease across large distances, making processes independent of geography.
Automational	IT/ERP can replace or reduce human labour in a process.
Analytical	IT/ERP can bring complex analytical methods to bear on a process.
Informational	IT/ERP can bring vast amount of detailed information into a process.
Sequential	IT/ERP can enable changes in the sequences of tasks in a process, often allowing multiple tasks to be worked on simultaneously.
Knowledge Management	IT/ERP allows capture and dissemination of knowledge and expertise to improve the process
Tracking	IT/ERP allows detailed tracking of task status, inputs, and outputs.
Disintermediary	IT/ERP can be used to connect two parties within a process that would otherwise communicated through an intermediary (internal or external).

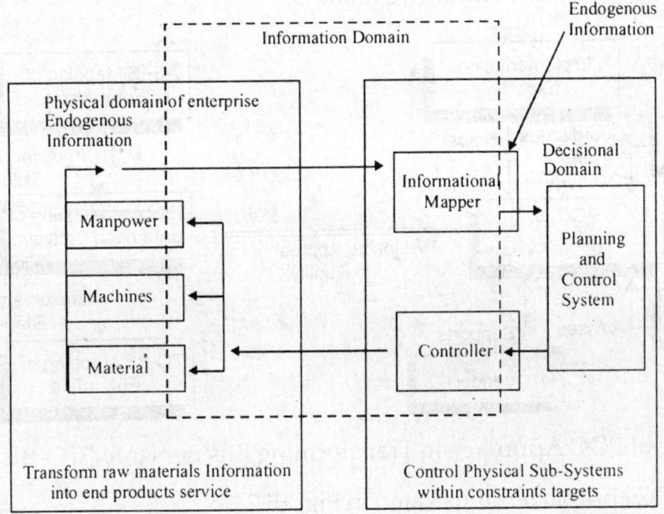

Fig.15.1 Display of Different Domain of Information

The information domain of the enterprise should be looked into two sub-domains: physical and decisional. Physical domain is the information-linking of the enterprise entities. It is mostly influenced by endogenous information. The decisional domain pertains to the planning and controls aspects of the physical sub-system of the enterprise. Its representation is shown in Fig. 15.1. Shankar (1998) and Shankar and Vrat (1999) have extensively identified reasons for considering vagueness in the information input at the design stage of a system. The recognition of information domain, related characteristics of information, and sharing of information without conflicts are the three key ingredients in an enterprise-modeling endeavour.

15.5 ROLE OF COMMON/SHARED ENTERPRISE DATABASE

The integrated enterprise system is supported by a central database, which is also called as enterprise databases. It works as the heart of the enterprise's model. Information is stored, updated, retrieved and managed in this portion. It draws data from and feed data into various enterprise applications, that support different functions. Single database reduces information time-lag, reduce distortion in information, instant updating, enhanced reliability and streamlined flow of information.

15.6 SELECTION OF ERP

Selection of appropriate ERP package involves careful evaluation of existing ERP alternatives and the needs/profile of the enterprise. Proof of concept (POC) approach is a comprehensive and real-time selection approach for ERP solution. In this approach, the organisation is provided with the ERP software for few months. The aim is to get confidence on the software before a final selection is made. Following stages are incorporated in the POC approach:

1. Preparation of project and constitution of ERP team.
2. Analysis of key business requirements.
3. Selection of system.
4. Team agreement on product to prototype.

15.7 APPLICATION OF POC APPROACH

The decision regarding final choice of one ERP-solution is extremely difficult. Many of the available alternatives would be capable of serving the requisite function. Therefore, a considerable level of confidence is needed before going for trial or final stage of procurement. The confidence may be achieved by an actual trial in the organisation environment for a reasonable period of time, say, one or two months.

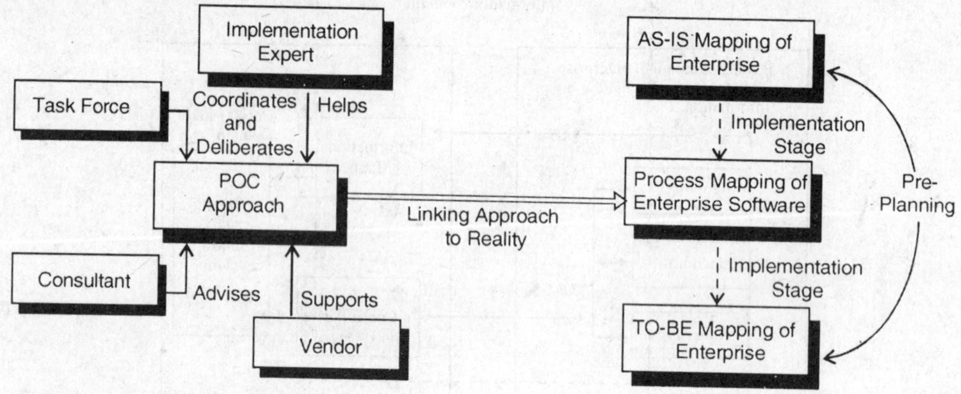

Fig. 15.2 Use of POC Approach in Transforming Business into "TO-BE" Situation

The use of POC approach is illustrated in Fig. 15.2.

The POC approach and its implementation is supported by vendor, who should be willing to extend his facilities. Consultants, if hired till this stage, advise regarding efforts needed for the change. Help of some body, who has hands-on experience on previous implementation, is very useful. The role of the task force is to coordinate and organise the business activities and make an indepth deliberation on various issues.

Next aspect would be linking the approach to reality. For this, some pre-planning is needed. To start with, the enterprise should prepare the present scenario in the minutest detail. This is called. "AS-IS mapping of enterprise". Next step is to visualise scenario, which may emerge after the implementation. This is called. "TO-BE mapping of the enterprise".

Now, the POC is applied to map the processes of the enterprise on the software. The objective would be how to transform the enterprise from an "AS-IS" situation to "TO-BE" situation. At this level, the help of implementation expert and support of vendor are crucial.

15.8 MATERIAL REQUIREMENTS PLANNING

In the early 1960s, Joseph Orlicky of the J.I. Case Company devised a new approach to materials management called *material requirements planning* (*MRP*). MRP is a proactive materials strategy. Rather than wait until it is time to order, MRP looks into the future and identifies the materials that will be needed, their quantities, and the dates on which they will be needed.

Figure 15.3 illustrates the major components of an MRP system. The numbered systems below correspond to the numbers in the figure.

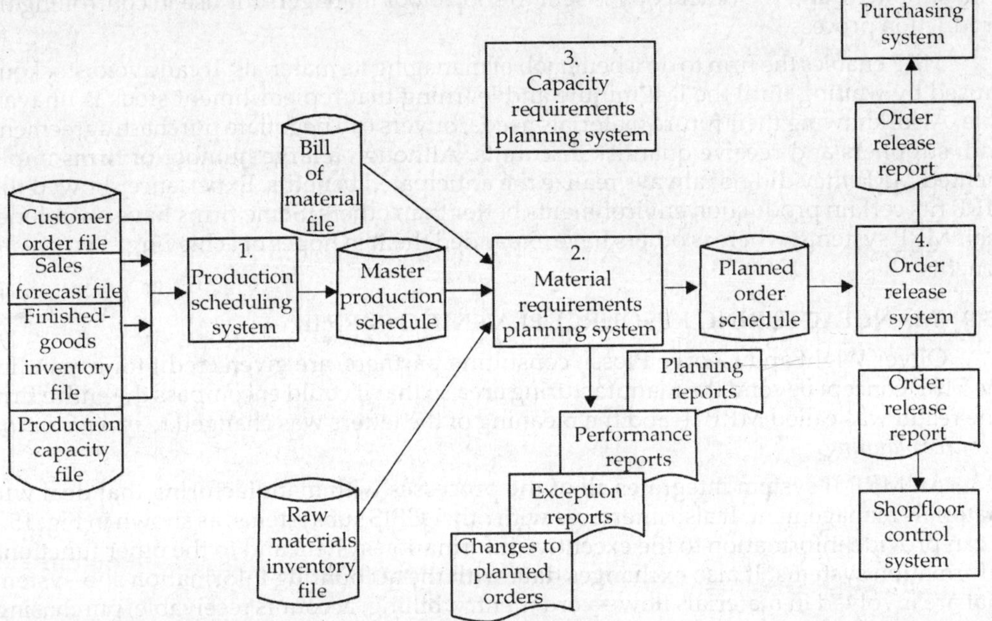

Fig. 15.3 An MRP System

1. The *production scheduling system* uses four data files in preparing the master production schedule. The input data include Customer Order file, the Sales Forecast file, the Finished-goods Inventory file, and the Production Capacity file. The *master production schedule* projects the production far enough into the future to accommodate the production process that accounts for the longest combination of supplier lead time and production time. Production schedules can look more than a year into the future.

2. The *material requirements planning system* determines how much material will be needed to produce the desired number of units. The Bill of Material file is used to *explode the bill of material* for each item scheduled for production by multiplying the quantities on the bill of material times the number of units to be produced. The purpose of the explosion is to determine the total material requirements, called the *gross requirements*, that will be needed to produce the scheduled products. Next, the Raw Materials Inventory file is used to determine which of the materials are already on hand. The materials on hand are subtracted from the gross requirements to identify the *net requirements* – the items that must be purchased in order to meet the production schedule.

3. The material requirements planning system works in conjunction with the *capacity requirements planning system* to ensure that the scheduled production will fit within the plant capacity. After that determination has been made, the material requirements planning system produces several outputs. The main output is the *planned order schedule*, which lists the needed quantities of each material by the time period. Other outputs include :

- Changes to planned orders that reflect cancelled orders, expedited orders, and modified order quantities.

- Exception reports that flag items requiring management attention.
- Performance reports that indicate how well the system is performing in terms of stockouts and other measures.
- Planning reports that can be used by manufacturing management for future inventory planning.

4. The *order release system* uses the planned order schedule for input and prints an *order release report*. One copy is sent to buyers in the purchasing department for use in negotiation with suppliers, and the other copy is sent to shop-floor managers for use in controlling the production process.

MRP enables the firm to do a better job of managing its materials. It can avoid stockouts caused by waiting until the last minute and learning that replenishment stock is unavailable. Also, knowing their future materials needs, buyers can negotiate purchase agreements with suppliers and receive quantity discounts. Although a large number of firms implemented MRP, they did not always realize the anticipated benefits. Experience showed that MRP fits certain production environments better than others. Some firms have abandoned their MRP systems, whereas others have expanded them in hopes of achieving even greater benefits.

15.9 MANUFACTURING RESOURCE PLANNING (MRP II)

Oliver Wight and George Plossl, consulting partners, are given credit for expanding the MRP concept beyond the manufacturing area so that it could encompass the entire firm. The result was called MRP II, and the meaning of the letters was changed to *manufacturing resource planning*.

An MRP II system integrates all of the processes with manufacturing that deal with materials management. It also interfaces with other CBIS subsystems, as shown in Fig. 15.4. It can provide information to the executive information system and to the other functional information systems. It also exchanges data with the accounting information sub-systems that are involved in materials flow — order entry, billing, accounts receivable, purchasing , receiving, accounts payable, and general ledger.

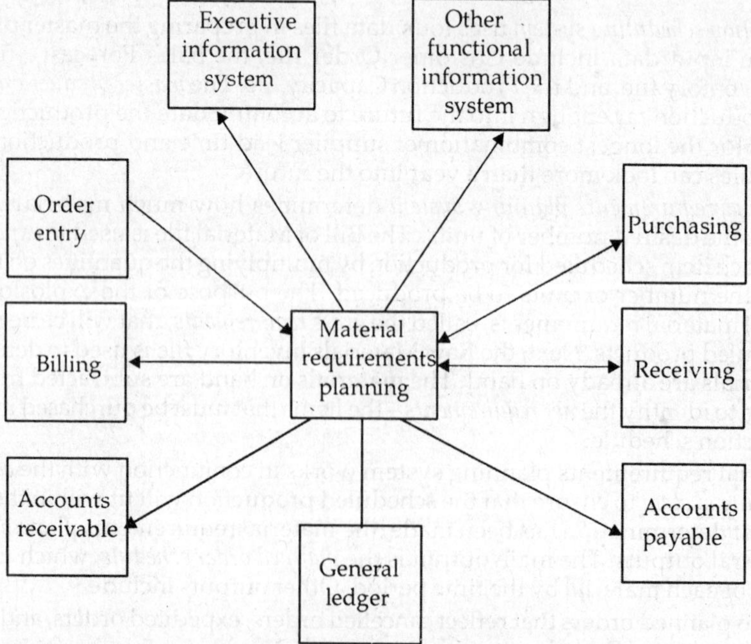

Fig. 15.4 An MRP II System

Benefits of MRP II

When top management commits to MRP II, the firm can expect benefits in one or more of the following areas.

- *More efficient use of resources.* Reductions can be anticipated in both work-in-process and finished- goods inventories, plant equipment can be better utilized, bottlenecks in work centres can be spotted, and equipment maintenance can be better scheduled.
- *Better priority planning.* The amount of time required to get jobs into production can be reduced, and the production schedule can be more easily modified to reflect changing customer needs.
- *Improved customer service.* The ability of the firm to meet promised delivery dates can be enhanced, and the opportunity exists for improved quality and reduced prices.
- *Improved employee morale.* Employees can gain confidence in the system, resulting in improved co-ordination and communication between departments.
- *Better management information.* Management can use the system output to gain an improved insight into the physical production system and to measure the performance of that system. In addition, the firm's executives and managers from all functional areas can do a better job of long-range planning.

The MRP family of systems represents the mainstream activity of North American and European manufacturers in applying the computer as an information system. However, during recent years, the Japanese have popularized a new approach that is given credit for much of their manufacturing success. Nowadays, MRP-II system is very popular in India due to emphasis on manufacturing sector.

15.10. BUSINESS PROCESS RE-ENGINEERING (BPR)

ERP is a result of modern enterprise how the information system is to be configured to the challenging environment of new business opportunities. However, merely putting in place an information system is not adequate. Every organisation that intends to implement ERP has to re-engineer its processes in one form or the other. This process is known as Business Process Re-engineering (BPR). Table 15.3 illustrates some typical processes of BPR.

Table 15.3 Some typical processes with descriptions

Process	*Description*
Forecasting	Shows sales, fund flows, etc. over a long period of time, say, next two years
Fund management	Necessity of funds and the way to raise these funds. Uncertainty and risk factors to be considered. Simulation with 'what if' type analysis.
Price planning	Determines the price at which products are offered. Involves application of technology to pricing support such as commercial database services. Also, feedback and sensitivity analysis.
Budget allocation	Using computerised algorithms to estimate desirable mix of funds allocated to various functions.
Material requirement planning	Process of making new products from raw materials

	and include production scheduling, requirement planning. Also, activities for monitoring and planning of actual production,
Quality control	Take care of activities to ensure that the products are of desired quality.

15.10.1 What is BPR ?

Business process re-engineering is defined by Hammer and Champhy as "the fundamental rethinking and radical redesign of processes to achieve dramatic improvement in critical, contemporary measures of performance such as cost, quality, service and speed". Radical redesign means BPR is reinventing and not enhancing or improving. In a nutshell, a "cleansiate approach" of BPR says that "Whatever you were doing in the past is all wrong", do not get biased by it or reassemble your new system to redesign it afresh. Fundamental rethinking means asking the question "why do you do what you do", thereby eliminating business process altogether if it does not add any value to the customer. There is no point in simplifying or automating a business process which does not add any value to the customer. There is no point in simplifying or automating a business process which does not add any value to the customer. A class example is that of asking for an invoice from the supplier for payment when the firm has already received and accepted a particular quantity of materials physically and at an agreed price. Receiving, processing, and filling of invoices add no value to customer and makes only the supplier unhappy for delayed payments. Thus, BPR aims at major transformation of the business processes to achieve dramatic improvement. Here the business objectives of the enterprise (e.g., profits, customer-satisfaction through optimal cost, quality, deliveries, etc.) are achieved by "transformation" of the business processes which may, or may not, require the use of information technology.

15.10.2 Business Engineering

Business engineering is the rethinking of business processes to improve speed, quality and output of materials/services. The emphasis of business engineering is the concept of process-oriented business solutions enhanced by the client-server computing in information technology. The main point in business engineering is the efficient redesigning of firm's value added chains. Value added chains are a series of connected steps running through a business which when efficiently completed add value to enterprise and customers. Information technology helps to develop business models, which assist in redesigning of business processes. Business engineering is the method of development of business processes according to changing requirements.

15.10.3 Business Management

ERP merges well with common business management issues like BPR, total quality management, mass customization, service orientation, and virtual corporation, etc. The basic objective of implementing an ERP program is to put in place the applications and infrastructure architecture that effectively and completely support the enterprise's business plan and business processes. When an enterprise does not have optimized business processes, the ERP implementation needs a process re-engineering which enable to capture knowledge of the experts into the system, thus gaining considerable benefits in productivity.

The first step in implementation of ERP is the development of a business process model showing business process as one large system and the interconnection and sequence of business sub-systems or processes that drive it.

15.10.4 Business Modelling

The approach of ERP implementation is carried out using MIS planning. First, a model consisting of core business processes or activities of the business is to be developed. This is the diagrammatic representation of business as a large system with interconnection of sub-systems/processes that it comprises of. The planning to arrive at the process is from top down, whereas the MIS implementation is done from bottom up.

One can model business as a system making the processes managing their facilities and material as their resources. Information is treated as a vital resource managing other resources.

The data model consists of following two elements.

- A diagram describing various business processes and their interactions.
- An underlying data model.

The reference model can be used by various organisations to list their processes and data entities and, if required, can be subsequently modified to suit specific nature of requirements. Some typical examples are shown in Table 15.4.

Table 15.4 List of some entities forming a data model

Entity	*Description*
External data	Entities outside the firm that interact with it such as customers, suppliers, competitors and distributors. Also, includes predictive data regarding economy and future events in external environment.
Internal data	Data generated from the firm's transaction processing system, internal forecasts or parameters monitored.
Funding data	Includes information on specific sources of funds as well as availability terms and conditions, etc.
Marketing research data	Mainly consumer-related data that can be used to support marketing decisions and result of surveys.
Production data	Shop-floor data on production processes including standards and actual of time and material resources concerned.
Inventory data	Includes inventories of raw materials, goods in progress and finished goods.
Personnel data	Mostly includes profiles of employees, their skill levels, experience and past performance on various assignments.
Sales forecast	Product-wise and period-wise forecast for various products sold by the firm.
Payroll data	Data about salaries, tax deductions, statutory forms and other deductions.
General ledger	Integrated transaction data from pay roll and account receivable. It is the basis for budgeting and planning data.

The general principles of business process analysis and classification and methodology of looking at a business information system to support a series of interlocking subsystems are universally applicable.

15.10.5 Business Modelling in Practice

Most of the ERP packages available today enable flow charting business processes using standard flow chart symbols. By connecting symbols used for users, events, tasks/functions, and other organisational information, complex business information can be analysed. For example, SAP, which is a popular ERP package, uses event-driven process chain methodology to model business process. All ERP packages provide standard template for each of the processes so that actual processes can be compared and deviations analysed. With the help of a business model, it is possible to check as to how well the model fits into the application so that the degree of suitability of the ERP package can be assessed. Business modelling is the basis by which one can select and implement a suitable ERP package.

15.11 ERP IMPLEMENTATION METHODOLOGY

The implementation of ERP is generally done in close association with the vendor, who supplies the package. Many organisations go for hiring professionals/consultants to facilitate the implementation process. Within the organisation, there is a need to form an ERP-team. This team comprises of people with high calibre and motivation. They are from different streams. Process engineer, industrial engineer, HRD personnel, financial executive and works manager are sure to find a place in this team. The role of the top management is crucial, as the commitment and required flow of finance are the two major ingredients without which any effort whatsoever is futile.

A general methodology for the implementation of ERP is presented in Fig. 15.5 as a flow chart. The identification of the need for ERP should be developed through a feasibility report. In this report, the present enterprise should also be evaluated along with much needed future capabilities. Then comes the stage of selection and evaluation of ERP. If the ERP solution is acceptable, then the strategy for business process re-engineering (BPR) is decided.

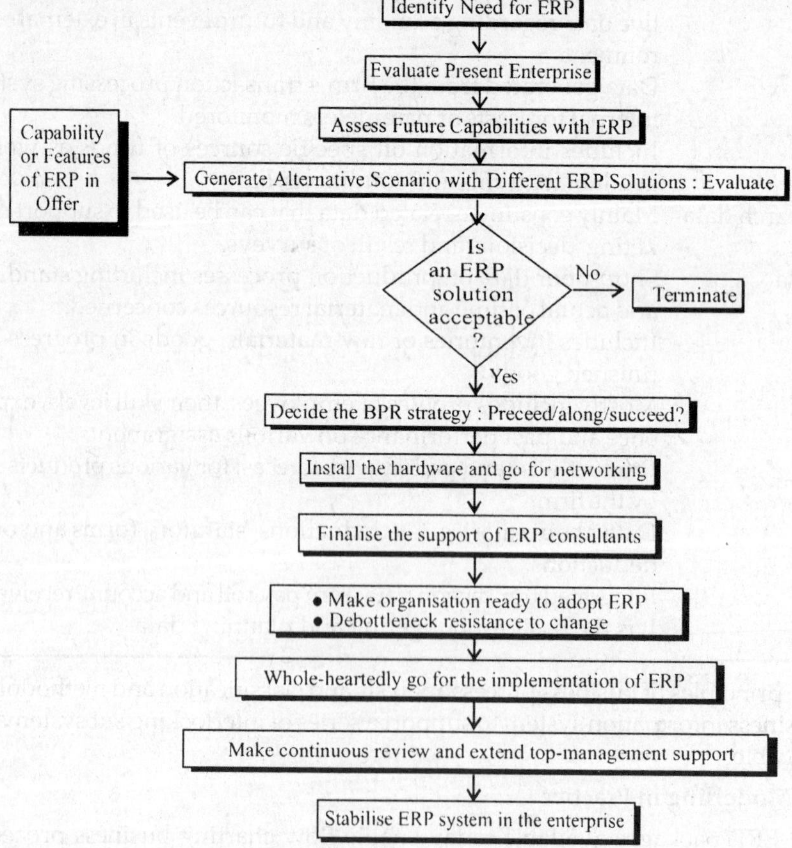

Fig. 15.5 Methodology for ERP Implementation

15.12 PRINCIPLE FOR ERP IMPLEMENTATION

Some of the typical failures of ERP implementation have revealed that most of these organisations have started the ERP implementation process by first focussing on automation effort. Studies have also revealed that automation in an enterprise for productivity improvement,without understanding and simplifying the process, is one of the major reasons for failure of the ERP implementation. This leads to the USA principle for implementation of the ERP system (Fig. 15.6).

USA stands for a sequential approach : Understand-Simplify-Automate. The USA approach calls for dedicated effort towards understanding the business process. Without this, any effort for implementation of ERP is likely to fail. Second step is to go for simplification of the process. Final step is to go for the automation of the procedure.

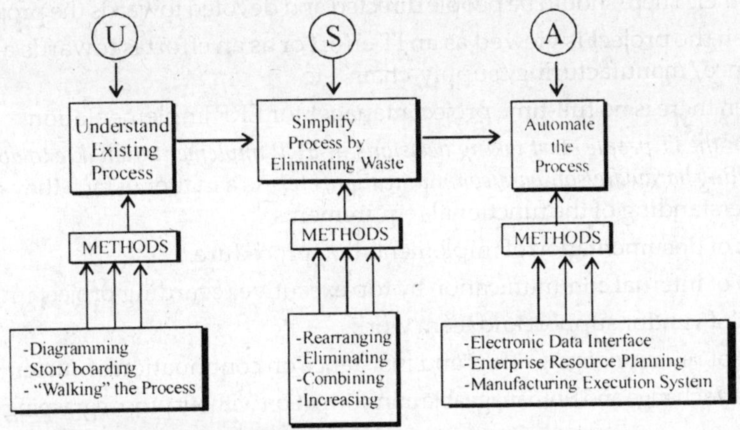

Fig. 15.6 The USA Principle : Implementation Flow

15.13 GUIDELINES FOR ERP IMPLEMENTATION

Based on experiences from the successful ERP projects, following useful guidelines are available in literature:

1. Understand the needs of the enterprise and feeling for corporate culture in the context of readiness for change.
2. The message should come from the top regarding adoption of the project.
3. Continuous and frequent communication from top regarding usefulness and mindset for the project.
4. Initiate with a feasibility report.
5. Start with changes in the business processes in the early stages of the project. Make everybody aware of this. Keep them informed : it will reduce resistance for change.
6. Decide phases of project implementation. Hold consultative meetings. Try for consensus.
7. Top executive should play the role of champion and set the project as the ultimate goal in all efforts.
   A total dedication and mission is needed at this stage.
8. Hire experienced consultants.
9. Visit sites of your vendors. See how the ERP solution is functioning. Extract useful tips from the existing users.
10. Carefully study the documentation of the vendor.
11. Make a balanced implementation team, which should include IT, HRD, works, financial and top executives. Other experienced functional managers should also be included.

12. Hold regular training and appraisal sessions in the organisation.
13. Ensure that the problems arising out of changes are handled carefully. Such problems are inevitable.
14. Ensure good feedback mechanism to evaluate the results due to implementation.
15. Decide whether to go for modular or complete ERP solution.
16. Look into the future capabilities of the enterprise when it is armed with ERP. Take radical decisions for transformation, if need arises.

15.14 CAUSES OF FAILURE IN ERP IMPLEMENTATION

The ERP implementation fails to succeed due to following reasons:

1. *Absence of an executive sponsor* : Since ERP crosses functions within a company, the implementation needs someone with an authority to bring various functional executives together. There should be people directed and devoted towards the project.
2. When the project is viewed as an IT effort or as an effort is towards automating finance/ manufacturing/ supply-chain, etc.
3. When there is no full-time project manager for ERP implementation.
4. *When the IT people start taking decisions in ERP implementation due to dominant role in handling hardware/software/communication, etc.* As a matter of fact, they generally lack understanding of the functional requirements.
5. Lack of documentation of implementation procedure.
6. Lack of internal communication by top executive regarding project implications.
7. Lack of vendor support and team work.
8. Lack of re-engineering effort and insistence on continuation of current practices.
9. Massive change and unmanageable transformation without proper grasping by employees.

15.15. POST-IMPLEMENTATION

To start with, many post-implementation problems can be traced to wrong expectations and fear. Expectations and fear that corporate management have from an ERP are outlined.

A few of the popular expectations are :

- Improvement in process.
- Enhanced productivity in all fronts.
- Total automation and disbanding of all manual processes.
- Improvement of key peformance indicators.
- Elimination of manual record keeping.
- Actual information system available to concerned people on requirement basis.
- Integration of all operations.

A host of fears in respect of ERP implementation are :

- Job redundancy
- Loss of importance as information is no longer an individual prerogative
- Change in job profile
- Loss of proper control and authorization
- Increased stress due to greater transparency
- Fear of loss of authority by individuals.

Hence, it is almost essential to balance the expectations and fear in the implementation process.

Some realities that any organisation must keep in mind are :

- For organisational change, strategic, business process and change and consequential organisational change are involved.

- Change in mindset is essential for organisational change.
- Measuring key performance indicators is necessary to bring a new culture in the organisation. However, it is seen that this aspect is not taken care of by most companies in India because either the company did not feel it necessary or lacked the tools to do so.
- Some of the processes are better to be done manually.

In essence, a successful ERP implementation is not the end of the road. Continuous improvements are required to derive the maximum benefit.

15.15.1. Tasks after ERP Implementation

The effective use of ERP is the process at communication in all forms – written, oral, workshops, meetings, etc. The process should start early by educating all layers of the management on the particular ERP product, its relevance, functionality, limitations and benefits.

At the start of the project, critical success factors (CSFs) or the organisation as a whole should be listed. These should be drilled down to CSFs for respective functionalities of each department/section of the organisation. From these CSFs, performance measures required to address these CSFs should be culled out. Numeric figures against these performance measures can be classified as key performance indicators (KPIs). The process of firming up is usually done through workshops.

Envisioning the processes to be configured on an ERP is the critical portion to ensure user buy-in during the post implementation phase. The important end-users should be involved in evolving the process. This should be done keeping the ERP functionality, KPIs derived from the organisational goals and CSFs in mind.

Having evolved the processes during configuration, construction and implementation stage, some of the tasks required to be performed in past-implementation period are :

- Develop new job descriptions and organisation structure to suit the post-ERP scenario.
- Determine the skill gap between existing and envisioned jobs.
- Assess training requirements, plan and implement the training for the required staff.
- Develop and amend human resources, financial and operational policies to suit the future ERP environment.
- Develop a plan for workforce logistics adjustment.

15.15.2. Post-Implementation Blues

It is generally seen that in most Indian organisations, monitoring KPIs and taking corrective business decisions to improve them do not exist. Therefore, it is necessary to follow a stretched target to be achieved in phases. Certain KPIs, although exist in the system, are better monitored and controlled after the ERP system attains maturity.

During post-implementation phase, it is necessary to change the system requirements many times. It may be because of the following reasons :

- A change in the business environment requires a change in CSFs, resulting in a new or changed set of KPIs necessitating re-configuration.
- A review indicates the need for change in some processes.
- Vision changes in the ERP and improvements in hardware and communication technology necessitate changes.
- New additions in the business require extra functionality.

At present, trend is to outsource the activity of maintenance and upgradation to enable the organisation to concentrate on its core business activity. ERP audit, an emerging trend, is to correct its course as and when required. It could be general in nature or very specific. One of the specialised areas is to evaluate the security, authorisation and controls. Hence, a periodic independent audit is essential for an organisation to ensure that it gets the best return on investment.

15.16. SAMPLE LIST OF ERP VENDORS

A sample list of ERP Vendors is given :

Bann (The Baan Company). In 1994, a Boeing order catapulted Baan into the global ERP vendor league. Baan has held and built keeping in mind for simultaneously addressing manufacturers from the largest global player to the smallest ERP user. Baan has a sound technology base and broad functional scope. It offers credible tools for business process analysis linked to implementation of its software, and is launching work flow capabilities.

Business Planning & Control System (BPCS). It remains the market-lending manufacturing ERP solution in terms of sites. It offers good functionality for process, discrete and Kanban manufacturing, but not for project management. It lags in the area of process-oriented implementation tools and work flow. However, there are signs that it has turned the corner.

Mapics XA (Marcam Corporation): Mapics is a suite of 40 modules with good functionality. Many users report that Mapics offers more functionality than they need. It offers robustness, easy implementation and reasonable value for money.

MFG/Pro (QAD). This package is strong in competitive manufacturing. It was originally designed to meet MRP II criteria published by Oliver wright. It is known for reliable manufacturing functionality and straightforward implementation.

Oracle Applications (Oracle). It is internet-enabled, network-centric computing. As a one-stop shop, it offers the database, tools, implementation, applications and UNIX operating systems running on a wide choice of hardware.

Prism (Marcam Corporation). It is a specialist process manufacturing solution for AS/400. Its production model, which is akin to a flow chart, handles process industry problems elegantly.

R/3 (SAP). It is the market leader with excellent philosophy of matching business process with its modules. It offers a wide range of functions and covers almost all business segments.

System 21 (JBA). Its software license revenues are small compared to offer major ERP methods. It offers a rugged, reliable manufacturing solution. It does not offer leading-edge technology.

15.17. ERP SOFTWARE PACKAGE (SAP)

SAP AG has developed an ERP package called SAP. It is a unique system that supports nearly all areas of business in a global scale. SAP has a number of applications modules in the package. Some of these modules are :

- Financial
- Controlling
- Investment management
- Treasury
- Integrated enterprise management
- Sales and distribution
- Production, planning and control
- Materials management
- Human resources management
- Internet and intranet

Each of these modules has a number of components, each taking care of specific functionalities of any normal business.

15.17.1. Financials

It covers all aspects of financial accounting and complies with international accounting standards such as GAAP and IAS. It also fulfils the local legal requirements. It mainly covers:

- Financial accounting
- General ledger
- Accounts receivable and payable
- Fixed asset accounting.

15.17.2. Controlling cost

It covers the following :

- Overhead cost control
- Cost centre accounting
- Overhead orders
- Activity-based costing
- Product cost control
- Cost-object controlling
- Profitability analysis

15.17.3. Investment Management

Investment management has the following important aspects :

- Corporate wide budgeting
- Appropriation requests
- Investment measures
- Automatic settlement to fixed assets
- Depreciation forecast

15.17.4. Treasury

It includes

- Cash management
- Treasury management
- Market risk management
- Funds management

15.17.5. Integrated Enterprise Management

It enables accounting data prepared by subsidiaries for corporate reporting which are automatically prepared simultaneously within the local books of each subsidiary. The data is then transferred to a module called Enterprise Controlling (EC).

Enterprise Controlling consists of **three** modules :

* EC-CS : For statutory financial and management consolidation and for complex investment structures.

* EC-PCA: It allows to work with internal transfer prices as well as to have right values from company, profit centre, and enterprise perspectives in parallel. It is also possible to take data directly from EC-PCA to EC-CS. This provides the management with a consistent view of external and internal financial management reports.

* EC-E15 : Executive information system deals to take financial data from EC-PCA,

EC–CS or any other application and combine with any external data from non–SAP applications to build a organisation–specific comprehensive enterprise information systems.

EC, therefore, can work with data from SAP and non–SAP sources.

15.17.6. Sales and Distribution

The system's sales and distribution application offers access to real–time, on line information from sales support to the billing process. The sales support component has easy to use tools to manage information on sales leads, sales calls, inquiries, quotations, marketing campaigns, competitors, and their products.

Sales and distribution supports a wide range of contracts from general to more specific contracts. The features of this module are :

(a) Specify delivery quantities, delivery dates and prices;

(b) Scheduling agreements and more complex requirements, such as just–in–time delivery schedules, are supported; and

(c) Products can be followed up with the service management components with functions such as call management, warranty management, service and maintenance contract processing.

Other aspects of sales and distribution includes

- Shipping management system
- The transport module
- Foreign trade processing
- Billing
- Sales information system

15.17.7. Production Planning and Control

Production planning and control (PPC) module covers the complete production process starting from creation of master data, production planning, MRP, capacity planning, production control and costing. PPC covers the following :

- Sales and operation planning (SOP)
- Production control
- Quality management
- Project system
- Project information system

15.17.8. Materials Management

This module contains all functions required to simplify business processes in requirements planning, purchasing, inventory management, warehouse management and invoice verification. It also introduces a high degree of automation into standard procedures. Materials management module has the following features : Purchasing; Inventory management; Warehouse management; Invoice verification; Inventory control using purchase information system; Quality management; Plant maintenance; Service management.

15.17.9. Human Resource Management

This module provides comprehensive process-driven solutions that can address organisation's needs for human resources. It covers the following :

- Personnel administration
- Employee master data
- Recruitment management
- Open positions
- Selection and hiring

- Travel management
- Benefits administration
- Personnel cost planning
- Shift planning
- Training and event management

15.17.10. Internet and Intranet

It offers a special internet functionality for large number of business processes. SAP business workflow enables to create work routines. All users automatically receive a list of their tasks in their mail system in box. Once the work is completed, the work flow starts the next predefined work-step and sends relevant messages. A range of work flow techniques, such as optical archiving mailing and office communications, can be used at every stage.

In essence, the success of any organisation today depends on its ability to look at business in totality without being influenced by strict departmental boundaries. ERP, which is an integration of components such as business models, operating processes, control processes, and changing strategic business processes, enables the organisation to realize its vision and objectives in a systematic and feasible manner.

Review Questions

1. What do you understand by ERP? Explain its main functions.
2. Explain the purpose of modelling an enterprise. How does ERP fit in the enterprise modelling endeavour?
3. Discuss in detail the role of information technology in enterprise modelling.
4. Discuss the role of centralised/shared enterprise database.
5. What do you understand by PoC approach? Discuss the use of PoC approach with an illustrative example.
6. Explain the methodology adopted in implementing ERP.
7. Explain the USA approach in the selection of ERP.
8. What are the factors involved in ERP implementation? What should be done to avoid failure in ERP implementation?
9. Outline the expectations of an organisation during past-implementations at ERP package.
10. 'ERP package ends up with job redundancy, change in job profile and increased stress due to greater transparency'. Comment on this statement with reasons.
11. Why are continuous improvements necessary for a successful ERP implementation ? Explain with valid reasons.
12. What are the critical success factors ? How can these be listed ?
13. What are the key performance indicators ? Explain the process of their measurement.
14. Explain in detail why is it necessary to change the system requirements many times during post-implementation phase.
15. List out **any five** ERP vendors. Explain about each one of them in brief.
16. Mention different application modules of ERP software package (SAP). Explain ***any three*** of them in detail.
17. What are the major components of an MRP system ? Explain each one of them in detail.
18. Explain manufacturing resource planning (MRP II). Outline the benefits of MRP II.
19. What is business process re-engineering (BPR) ? How will you interface BPR with ERP effectively ?

16

Supply Chain Management

16.1 INTRODUCTION

Supply chain management (SCM) is a management concept integrating the management of supply chain processes. It integrates supplier, distributor, and logistic requirements of the customer into one cohesive process to reduce time, effort and inventory costs. For SCM solutions, necessary and clear understanding of ERP is necessary as many ERP vendors provide SCM solutions.

16.2 DEFINITIONS

Supply chain and supply chain management reveal the common theme of material, information and financial flows coordinating among suppliers, manufacturers, distributors and customers of products and services. The supply chain may be defined as "a network of autonomous and semi-autonomous business entities involved through upstream and downstream linkages in different processes and activities that produce value in the form of physical products and services in the hands of ultimate customers." Supply chain consists of the network of organisations that connects suppliers and end users. It provides the route through which raw materials is converted into finished products and reaches into the hands of customers. Supply chain management, in turn, covers the "flow of goods from suppliers through manufacturing and distribution chains to the end users". In the context of an ERP solution, SCM is defined as "a part of ERP software solution, internal business practices, and tightly managed trading partner relationships, that allow an enterprise to provide more efficient services to the customers by better organising and coordinating internal and partner activities".

16.3 CONCEPT OF SCM

The concept of supply chain management provides a framework for integration of information, material and finance of an enterprise, right from the suppliers to the customers. The elements of coordination are shown in Fig. 16.1.

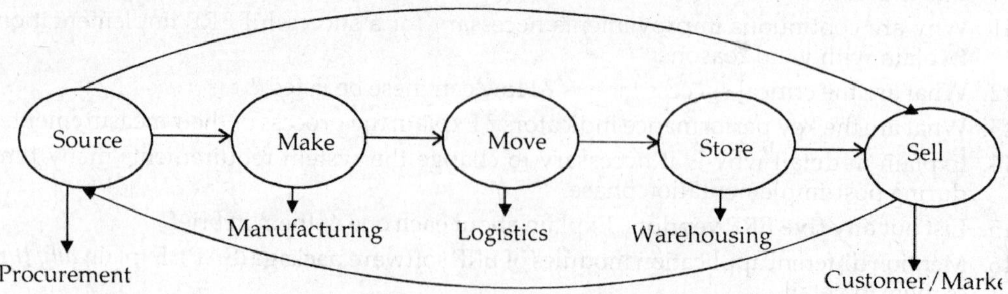

Fig. 16.1 Scope of Supply Chain Management

16.4 SCM PROCESS

Supply chain management encompasses management of all elements and activities of the supply chain (Fig. 16.2). This includes material suppliers, production facility, distribution, services and customers; linked together via the feed-forward flow of information and the feedback flow of materials. 'Supply chain' term is common in industries having global customer/supplier base, e.g., textile, electronics, automobile, pharmaceuticals, etc. The inclusion of distribution as a key link of the supply-chain make its scope wide and extended. Distribution may incorporate many stages such as warehouse, C & F (Carry and Foraward) agents or third party freight-forwarders, wholesalers, retailers and servicing units. The involvement of this link of the supply-chain with the end-user (customer) makes it extremely vital in the context of present day focus on customer satisfaction.

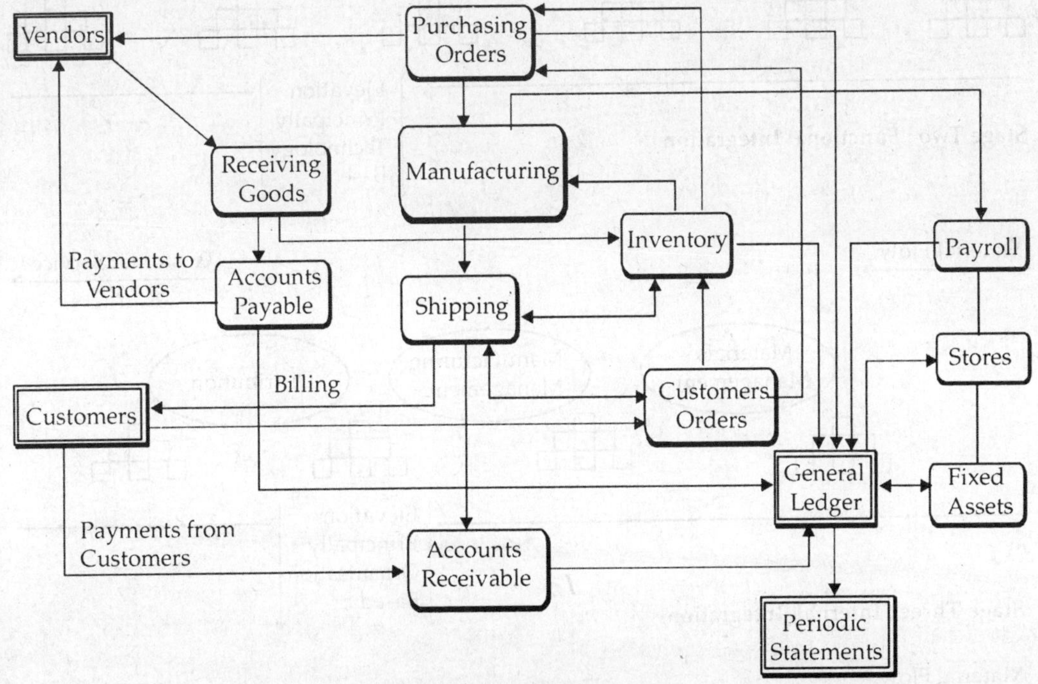

Fig. 16.2 SCM Process

16.5 STEVAN'S MODEL OF SUPPLY CHAIN INTEGRATION

Stevans (1989) and Stevans, et./al. (1995) have provided a simple model to understand supply-chain integration. It involves transforming of an enterprise from an inward looking to a flexible outward looking in an efficient manner. The transformation can be performed incorporating the technological, organisational and attitudinal attributes as shown in Fig. 16.3. Integration of the supply chain is a four stage process involving the following :

- *Base - line* : Understanding of material flow from purchasing to distribution.
- *Functional integration* : Understanding the functionality of material management, manufacturing management, and distribution.
- *Internal integration* : Internal integration of material management, manufacturing management and distribution.
- *External integration* : Integration of suppliers, internal supply chain and customers.

There are two common approaches for evolving a SCM environment :

- **Internal Integration**
  - Integrated system, e.g., ERP solutions such as SAP R/3.

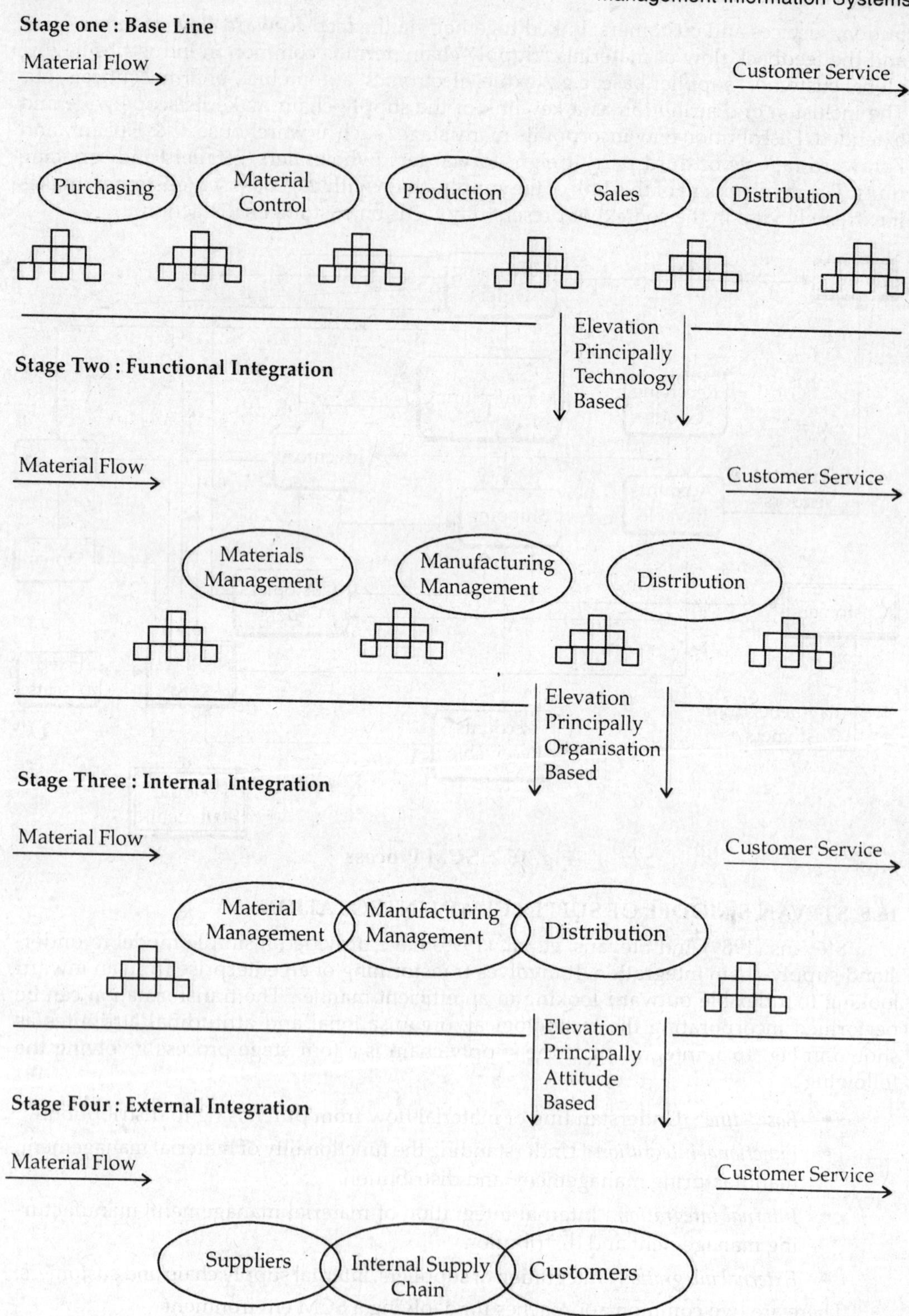

Fig. 16.3. Stevan's Model of SCM

  - Link-functions such as purchasing, manufacturing, inventory, finance, marketing, etc.
  - Shared data and integrated processes.
- **Intra-firm Integration**
  - Inter-organisational information system such as extranet.
  - Link firm's system with external entities– suppliers, distributors, retailers, etc.
  - Shared data and integrated processes.

16.6 GOAL/COMPONENTS OF SCM

The goal of SCM is to cut costs, increase profits, improve performance in relationships with customers and suppliers, and develop value-added services that give a firm a competitive edge. SCM has mainly *three* business objectives :

1. Get the right product to the right place at the least cost.
2. Keep inventory as low as possible and still offer superior customer service.
3. Reduce cycle times. SCM seeks to simplify and accelerate operations that deal with how customer orders are processed through the system and ultimately filled, as well as how raw materials are acquired and delivered for manufacturing processes.

Components of SCM are explained below :

- **Supplier management**. Use electronic commerce to help reduce the number of suppliers and get them to become partners in business in a win/win relationship.
- **Inventory management**. Shorten the order-ship-bill cycle with electronic commerce processes, and keep inventory levels to a minimum.
- **Distribution management.** Use electronic data interchange to move documents related to shipping (bills of lading, purchase orders, advanced ship notices, and so on).
- **Channel management**. Use E-mail, bulletin board systems, and newsgroups to quickly disseminate informations about changing operational conditions to trading partners.
- **Payment management**. Use electronic funds transfer to link the company and systems suppliers and distributors so that payments can be sent and received electronically.
- **Financial management.** Use electronic commerce systems to enable global companies to manage their money in various foreign exchange accounts.
- **Sales force management.** Use sales force automation methods to improve the communication and flow of information among the sales, customer service, and production functions.

SCM relies on information technology and management practices to optimise information and product flows among the processes and business partners within the supply chain. All the constituents of supply chain have their own short-term and long-term objectives. Their operating decisions are based on these objectives. It is very common that the decisions of the constituents may not be aligned to the overall strategic goal of the entire supply chain.

16.7. PERFORMANCE OF SUPPLY CHAIN

To judge the performance of supply-chain is important for two reasons : one, it gives idea regarding the current position. Second, it is helpful in identifying gaps for improvements. There are initial types of measures of performance : Resources ; Output; and flexibility. These are explained in Table 16.1. Considerations regarding potential of ERP implementation suggest that these performance measures will improve considerably once ERP is operational across the supply-chain.

Table 16.1 Performance measures of supply chain

Performance Measure Type	*Goal*	*Purpose*	*Example List*
1. Resource	High level of efficiency	Efficient resource management is critical to profitability	• Total cost • Distribution cost • Manufacturing cost • Inventory cost • Return on investment (ROI)
2. Output	High level of customer service	Without acceptable output, customers will turn to other supply-chains.	• Number of items produced • Time required to produce a particular item or a set of items • Number of on-time deliveries • Customer satisfaction • Product quality • Total revenue (sales) • Profit (total revenue less expenses) • Fill rate (proportion of order filled immediately) • On-time deliveries • Back order (stockout) • Customer response time • Manufacturing read time (total time required to produce a particular item or batch • Shipment error • Customer complaints
3. Flexibility	Ability to respond to a changing environment	In an uncertain environment, supply-chains must be able to respond to change.	• Volume flexibility (ability to change the output level of products) • Delivery flexibility (ability to change planned delivery dates, • Mix flexibility (ability to change variety of products produced) • New product flexibility (ability to introduce and produce new products and ability to introduce modification in existing products)

In ERP perspective, SCM provides a completely different solution as compared to classical material management and control of manufacturing system. Following reasons establish the answer:

- SC is an integrated system. It is not like an interfaced system as commonly seen in conventional enterprise.
- SCM is focussed and directed towards the end-supply to the customer. It is a domain of strategic decision making rather than operational decision in conventional enterprise. All elements of the chain share a common platform and have common objective of overall reduction in cost, increase in market share, customer satisfaction, etc.
- SC negates the fragmented responsibility of each functional unit such as suppliers, manufacturing, purchasing, distribution, and sales. It has been observed that the effectiveness of any element of the supply-chain is greatly affected by the performance of the total chain. Sometimes back, the Japanese car manufacturers went for the takeover of the distribution activities (Stalk and Hout, 1990). The reasons were the following :

  (a) More responsive to market demand,

  (b) Enable manufacturer to smooth production by varying sales capacity using surplus upstream labour, and

  (c) Obtain more reliable sales data on which manufacturing capacity can be decided.

  It is easy to understand now why ERP solution for SCM is so important. A common information sharing platform, which ERP provides, solves most of the problems faced in the above case.
- Inventory is closely linked with information or data-flow in the chain. Integration of enterprise through networking and common information-access, facilitates prudent decision regarding inventory management, logistics, purchasing, supply and customer service.
- Enterprise these days gets more involved in the operation and policies of its suppliers. Vendor audit, open costing, vendor development/training, on-line monitoring of scheduling and delivery of vendors, sharing technological capabilities, providing services of quality team to vendors/suppliers, etc. are few measures which may not be cost-effective in short run. But, in long run, this union is bound to prove beneficial, cost-effective and reliable.
- Several suppliers to a common unit (say, manufacturing) may collaborate in the logistic arrangements for deriving the benefits of economy of scale. Subcontracting among themselves may also be beneficial in many instances. However, all is effectively well with mutual trust, only when there exists a common enterprise-wide integration of information along the supply -chains.
- Supplier is linked with the inputs from the end-user regarding specifications, timing and quality. Integration facilitates quick response time. Secondly, their interaction improves cost reduction effort through value engineering technique. Supplies input is upgraded through better manufacturability of supplied items, quick response time and better preparedness.
- The era of multi-supplier-enterprise network is gradually phasing out. The new paradigm is "dependable, mutually-developed, partner-type, single sourcing". The potential benefits in single sourcing are more evident when integration, data-sharing, technology transfer and vendor development effort are accounted.

- Visibility of full supply-chain provides executives the ability to see problems before they arise.

The study of supply chain is critical due to its influence on the following :

- Timing
- Configuration
- Location
- Environment
- Technology
- Cost
- Flexibility
- Performance
- Integration
- Use of information technology
- BPR and benchmarkers
- Quality and customer, etc.

The market is competitive. Therefore, the chain is expected to operate faster.

16.8 COMPARISON BETWEEN ERP AND SCM

A Comparison between ERP and SCM is given below:

ERP	SCM
Primary function of ERP is to generate data	SCM provides capability to the date enterprise so that it can make sense out of data to help to make decisions.
ERP is the body of the enterprise	SCM is the brain of the enterprise.
ERP systems are linear and interactive	SCM is constraint-based and optimised.
ERP generates data	Data generated in ERP are used in the best possible way by optimising the system in a SCM
ERP excels in the transaction management	SCM affords forecasting and the decision-support.
ERP links processes only within the organisation	SCM goes beyond the conventional boundaries of the organisation and spans in the entire supply chain.

16.9. ERP IMPLEMENTATION : A CASE OF DISTORTION OF DEMAND

'Distortion of demand' along the supply chain is a common problem. While explaining the law of industrial dynamics, Burbidge (1984) postulated that the variation in demand for product increases as it passes through a series of transfers in a supply-chain, and stock-control ordering is used.

A 'flywheel effect' in the supply-chain is explained and shown in Fig. 16.4. Uncertainty in economy, market being in-and-out of recession, tendency of management to over-react to periodic economic swings, which are very common, and creating a safety-net in material planning are few reasons for "amplification of demand" in a supply-chain (Fig. 16.4). The effect of amplified demand-distortion is evident in a factory (factory E), which is a down-stream link of the chain. This may be due to time-delays, planning, distortions and inventory movements in the preceding links of the chain.

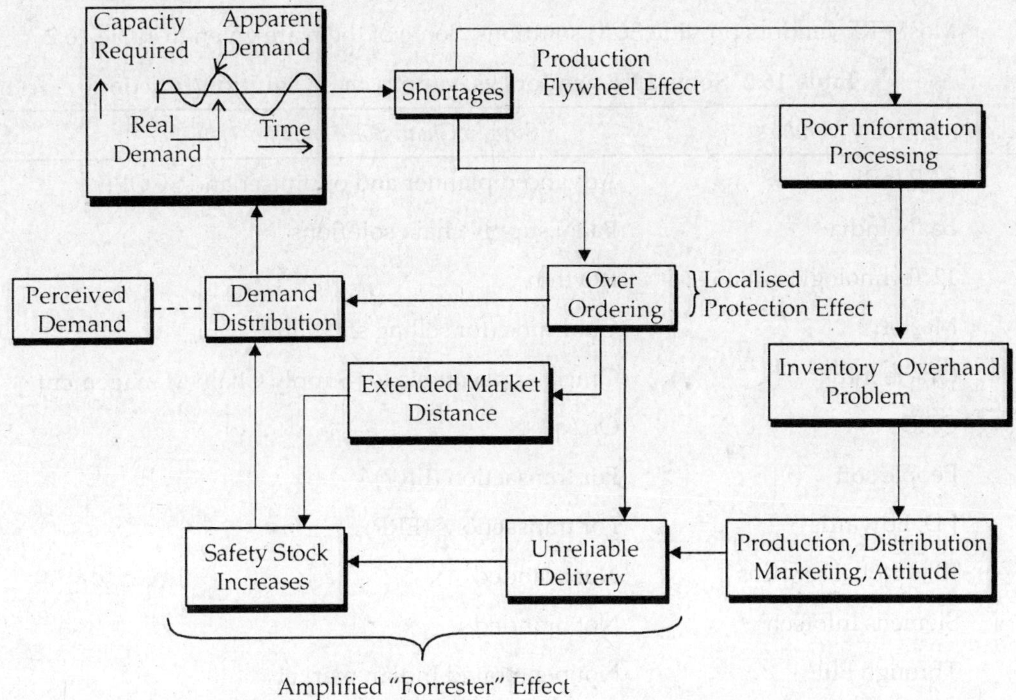

Fig. 16.4. Some General Causes of Demand Amplification

Internally this behaviour is seriously present all throughout the chain. The classic case is the "marketing-manufacturing conflict". The demand forecast is initial by marketing so as to obtain longer allocation from the manufacturing units. This saves them from being caught in short-supply situation under an upward market swing. Manufacturing and distribution are also smart people. They make a second guess apparently to nullify, which creates further distortion in demand. Similarly, other elements of the chain contribute to the inventory building measures. Decisions regarding required-capacity of the enterprise lag behind the changes in demand. This causes further building-up of a safety net for inventories or lost sales due to under-production. The amplification in perceived demand is shown in Fig. 16.4.

The integration of supply-chain through SCM solution of an ERP package is a suitable preposition to reduce, if not completely eliminate, many of the reasons for distortion in demand. If this is minimized, the inventory build-up will go down. Using SCM solutions of ERP domain, single point data entry and simultaneous-common sharing of information across the supply-chain facilitate the reduction in demand distortion. SCM solution reduces the outward complexities, which need to be handled at the exterior of the supply chain. This saves excess capital investment in inventory and capacity. The vulnerability of the supply chain is further minimized by better management of functional objectives and policies. Table 16.2 presents some of the SCM solutions available in the market. Due to regular updates coming into the market, most of these supply-chain solutions are undergoing through major changes. Capabilities of new vendors and recent updates must be considered before adoption.

16.10. SUPPLY CHAIN SOLUTION VS ERP VENDORS

Most ERP vendors provide SCM solutions. Some of them are given in Table 16.2.

Table 16.2 Some ERP vendors vs. supply chain solution/function

ERP - Vendors	*Supply Chain Solution/Function*
SAP India	Advanced planner and optimiser and SCOPE
BaaN India	BaaN supply chain solutions
12 Technologies	Rhythm
Mastek	Goldmine (for selling software)
Oracle India	Oracle applications for Supply Chain Management
QAD	On/q
People soft	For transaction (ERP)
J.D. Edwards	For transactions (ERP)
IBM global services	Not branded
Siemens Infotech	Not branded
Through Put	Not penetrated Indian market
Geologistics LEP	Yet to come to India
Red Pepper	For resource planning, strategy
Manugistics	For operational, tactical response
Paragon	—
Numetrix	Transactions support, ATP, CTP

16.11 BENEFITS OF SCM

The benefits of SCM can be harnessed by better integration of supply-chain in terms of information, material and money flows. Better coordination of different functions is possible through ERP implementation/SCM solution. Some of the benefits of SCM are :

- Integrated view of enterprise resources & constraints
- Improved channel efficiency by sharing information between suppliers and customers
- Reduced inventory levels and production costs
- Extension of organizational control beyond firm boundaries
- ROI (Return on Investment) : typically 10 times the cost of developing and implementing the system

16.12 DISADVANTAGES OF SCM

- Poor implementation due to enlargement of scope
- Information access and security

- Supply-chain interruptions
- Undirectional loss of bargaining power
- Training and change management
- System maintenance
- Challenge of developing trust and managing interorganizational dependencies

Review Questions

1. What do you understand by supply chain and supply chain management ? Explain the concept of supply chain, with an illustrative diagram.
2. Discuss in detail the supply chain management process, and its interlinking with other major functions.
3. Explain the Stevan's model of supply chain integration, illustrating all the four stages diagrammatically.
4. What are *three* business objectives of SCM ? Explain different components of SCM in the context of E-commerce.
5. How is performance of supply chain evaluated ? Explain the measures of performance with some typical examples.
6. Outline the reasons `where SCM provides better solution in terms of ERP perspective.
7. Enumerate the influencing factors for effective supply chain management. How is SCM a better solution than ERP.
8. How is SCM implemented ? Discuss with a case of distortion of demand.
9. Mention the names of ERP vendors providing SCM solutions.
10. Discuss the advantages and disadvantages of SCM.

17

Applications of Information Technology in Business

17.1 INTRODUCTION

A new revolution is in the making, similar to the industrial revolution that took place at the turn of the last century. Many economists, management experts and futurists agree that the world has entered the new age of information. Alvin Toffler's *third wave* or Peter Drucker's post-industrial society—the new era is being increasingly referred to as the *Information Age*.

The primary drivers of this information age—technology and markets—are well known. Marketing, enterprise, entrepreneurship are some of the other drivers. According to Professor Tom Cannon, the new industrial revolution surrounding us requires profound change; profound change in the way enterprise is being considered, develop businesses, the way we manage and the structures within which we manage. He foresees not just a change in the market but a fundamental change in the economic relationships between people, between economies, and between societies. Information and information technology (IT) are the new drivers of this age.

The continuous strife of businesses to increase productivity and efficiency, reduce the costs of their products and services, and use technology to continually innovate in order to expand and create new markets is not new. Technology is an enabler of change and a catalyst, but change itself has to be driven by business drivers that take advantage of the technology. The globalisation of the market place, and the means of accessing the same through the national and global information superhighways have given a new dimension to the concept of information. Information and knowledge are critical to manage change, which is one critical aspect that will be permanent during the foreseeable future for businesses.

The key business characteristics of industrial age and information age businesses have been compared by Tjaden.

Industrial Age	*Information Age*
1. Mass production.	1. Mass customisation.
2. Labour serves tools	2. Tools serve labour.
3. Labour performs repetitive tasks	3. Labour applies knowledge.
4. Command and control structure.	4. Common control structure.
5. Capital intensive.	5. Knowledge intensive.
6. Capitalists own production means.	6. Labour owns production means.
7. Capital is primary driver.	7. Knowledge is primary driver.

Information age is thus *knowledge-based industrial revolution*. The firms would be `learning organisations', i.e., the organisations where people continually expand their capacity to create the results they truly desire, where new and expansive patterns of thinking are nurtured, where collective inspiration is set free and where people are continually learning how to learn together.

In order to combat the competitive edge, electronic commerce is the outstanding value addition for businesses in the marketplace. The Internet, which was the exclusive preserve of the academic and research community ever since its creation in the 1960s, was allowed for commercial use in the 1990s. Suddenly a large pool of information is available on the World Wide Web at no charge. The seamless merging of data, information and entertainment electronics has opened up new vistas for businesses. Organisations, with networking and completely decentralised methods of working, with totally new reengineered work processes are expected to make this happen. The Internet, intranets and extranets through the tools of E-Commerce (EC) have begun to transform industries in many fundamental ways.

The free flow of information which is enabled by the Internet without any geographic and national barriers comes forth with a myriad security and privacy problems. There are legal issues with respect to patents, trademarks, copyrights, responsibility of ownership of data, contracts and so on. This calls for fundamental changes in the legal, commercial and economic frameworks.

The EC tools are also being used to change the methods of governance. Electronic governance, as it has come to be known, uses the Internet and other proprietary networks to deliver services to citizens, bring in transparency between governments and citizens and between business organisations and consumers. Therefore, it is in the interests of all business organisations and the government to understand and utilise the Internet in order to remain competitive within the commercial business environment.

17.2 E-COMMERCE (EC)

The Internet and the Web have revolutionised commerce and created new paradigms. The new business paradigm is based on the virtual corporation paradigm which has come into being through the combination of intranets and extranets. The following three types of EC, supported by networks, have emerged:

- Consumer to business
- Business to business
- Intranet procurement.

Consumer-to-business EC. Electronic malls, virtual storefronts allow individual consumers to browse for products and shop using credit cards. This form of EC is Internet based, with unrestricted access to consumers. Credit-card payments have to be secured against unauthorised access by intruders on public networks.

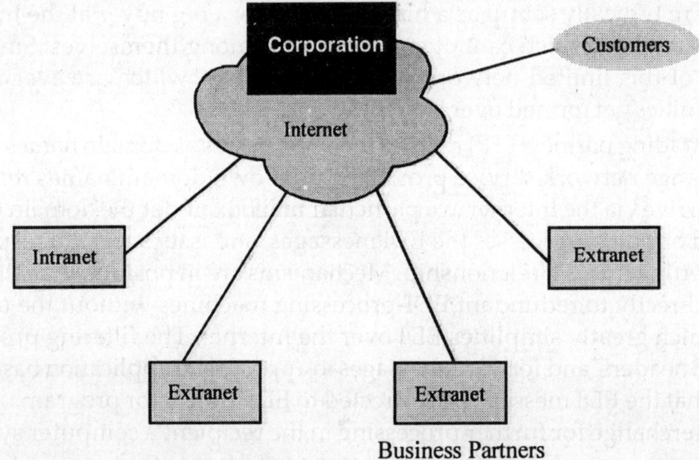

Fig. 17.1 Extranet-Intranet-Internet relationship

Business-to-business EC. In this case, bulk of commerce, as much as 70%, is conducted over networks. Business-to-business procurement and fulfillment including financial transactions has traditionally been conducted over private networks. This segment of EC is driving extranets. It is restricted to business partners and uses secure procedures based on firewall, encryption and authorisation level, with payment by predetermined credit terms.

Intranet procurement. Business transactions, which are internal to an organisation, across its departments and subsidiaries also comes under EC. Internet sales, order processing, intracompany charging and billing, fund transfer for accounting purposes are some of the transactions which can be very large and voluminous depending upon the size and nature of an organisation. This can span the entire globe in case of multinationals. Intranets are responding to this challenge.

E-commerce on the Internet, intranets and extranets uses the common standard, i.e., TCP/IP on the internetworked information infrastructure that spans the whole world. Typical commercial EDI transactions on sale-purchase is now being integrated into Web commerce servers launched by companies like Netscape, Microsoft, IBM, Open Market, Sun Oracle, and others. Even ERP system vendors are trying to integrate EC solutions into their products. This includes Baan, Oracle and SAP. A extranet-intranet-internet relationship is shown in Fig. 17.1.

17.3 COMMERCE OVER THE INTERNET

Commerce over the Internet is conducted essentially in two ways : EDI over the Internet and Web-based EDI.

17.3.1 EDI over the Internet

Internet mail is used as a means for transmitting EDI messages. The IETF-MIME specification is used to envelope the EDI data within the E-mail message. With this arrangement, the Internet replaces the proprietary VANs for exchange of EDI messages between trading partners. While the cost of transmitting EDI messages gets substantially reduced this way, there are other problems related to security and integrity of transactions, as also reliability of the Internet which become dominant issues. These issues are being addressed, and cost-effective solutions have been created by a number of organisations.

EDI over the Internet is more flexible, since there is no need for a prior network connection. This way more and more firms, including smaller firms, can exchange EDI messages. EDI networks are typically set up as a hub with spokes; a big buyer at the hub dictating its suppliers at the spokes, which cannot communicate among themselves. Since the Internet replaces much of this limited network with its own links, which are everywhere, virtual trading communities get formed over it.

Individual trading partners (TP) register their businesses as domain names on the Internet. Even if they change network service providers, their own domain names remain the same. EDI messages arrive via the Internet in a particular mailbox under the domain name. Filtering software, based on rules, processes the EDI messages, and issues an auto response for information about setting up a TP relationship. Mechanisms are in position that allow delivery of EDI messages directly to redundant EDI-processing machines without the usual store and forwarding, which greatly simplifies EDI over the Internet. The filtering programs analyse values in MIME headers, and forward messages to appropriate application bases. It is through this approach that the EDI messages get directed to EDI Translator programs, which retrieve the business interchange for further processing in the recipient's computer system.

The standard E-mail model of Mail Transfer Agent/User Agent is used to transfer EDI messages via standard exchange protocols. The MIME-encoded EDI message has the following parts (Table 17.1).

Table 17.1

Headers :	Author & Recipient Addresses
	Subject Summary
	Creation Date
	Handling Node Name, etc.
Body :	Structured Body Parts
	Conforming to MIME
	(Text, different types e.g. voice, graphics)

These are transmitted using SMTP protocol over the Internet. A typical MIME-encoded EDI message transaction on the Internet, is illustrated in Fig. 17.2.

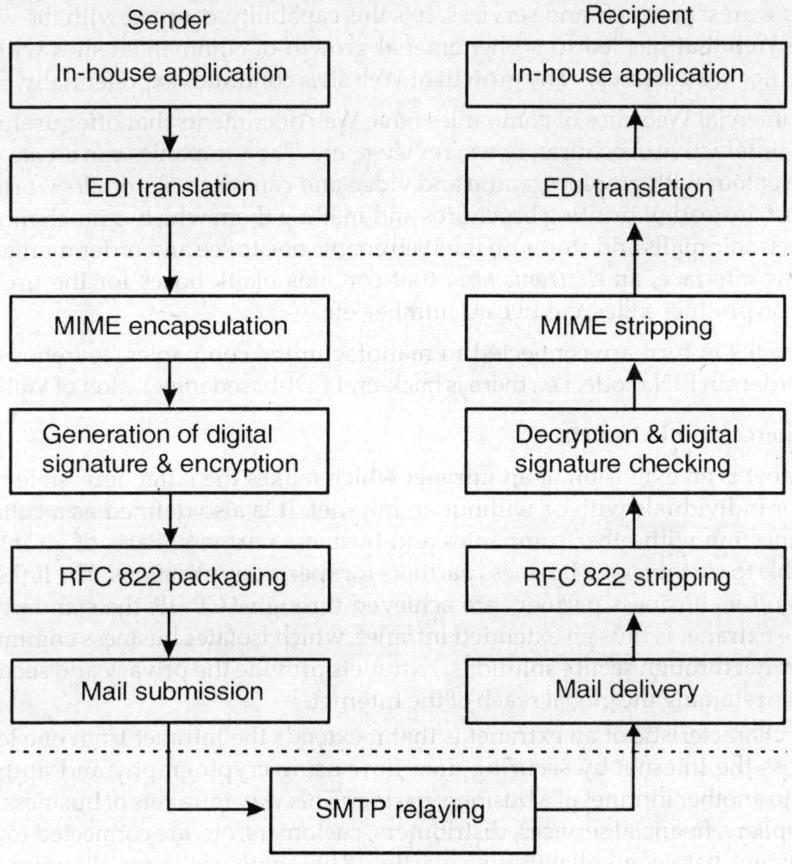

Fig. 17.2 EDI over Internet

Table 17.2

Business Data from Database
EDI Translator
MIME Encapsulation
RFC 822 Packaging
Mail Submission
SMTP Relaying
Mail Delivery
RFC 822 Stripping
MIME Stripping
EDI Translator
Business Data Recovery.

The IETF-EDI specifications define the security standards for EDI messages. The implementation will require secure E-mail software as a layer between the mailer and the mail processing program, which will perform security functions such as decryption, digital signatures, receipts, problem handling, etc.

17.3.2 Web-based Commerce

Web-based commerce on the Internet has taken the world by storm. It is a new way of conducting commerce. The Web, with its capability to play audio, display graphics, pictures and video, enables Internet users to request information and order products instantly. This is possible in interactive mode making it an excellent choice for companies and organisations to display their wares: products and services. It is this capability, coupled with the worldwide reach of the Web that has led to a phenomenal growth of commercial sites with Internet registrations (.com addresses). The growth of Web sites continues exponentially.

The commercial Web sites of companies have Web documents that offer useful product information, interactive brochures, news, reviews, etc. The companies can create electronic brochures in colour with graphics, audio and video and can reach customers worldwide for very little cost, instead of printing brochures and mailing them which is much more expensive. The electronic malls and stores on the Web enable one to see and order merchandise by using a forms interface, an *electronic form* that contains blank boxes for the user to enter information on product codes, credit card number, etc.

The websites in turn are connected to manufacturers' companies/warehouses which receive the orders in EDI mode, i.e., there is back-end EDI-based integration of Web stores.

17.3.3 Commerce over Extranets

An extranet is an extension of an intranet which makes the latter accessible to outside companies or individuals with or without an intranet. It is also defined as a collaborative Internet connection with other companies and business partners. Parts of an intranet are made available to customers or business partners for specific applications. The links between an intranet and its business partners are achieved through TCP/IP, the standard Internet protocol. The extranet is thus an extended intranet, which isolates business communication from the Internet through secure solutions. Extranets provide the privacy and security of an intranet while retaining the global reach of the Internet.

The key characteristic of an extranet is that it extends the intranet from one location to another across the Internet by securing data flow using cryptography and authorisation procedures, to another intranet of a business partner. This way intranets of business partners, material suppliers, financial services, distributers, customers, etc. are connected to extranets by an agreement between collaborating parties. The emphasis is on allowing access to authorised groups through strictly controlled mechanisms. This has led to the true proliferation of EC. It is the combination of intranets with extranets which has established the virtual corporation paradigm. This business paradigm is turning out to be critical for EC, allowing corporations to take advantage of any market opportunity anywhere, anytime, and offering customised services and products. E-Commerce is perceived to be a business avenue for reducing cost of sales and time of marketing, as well as providing more targetted marketing.

Business-to-business EC is growing on extranets. Companies gain competitive advantage through speedier transactions and access to newer markets, as also by simplified and faster distribution of information, products and services.

Finally, it is worth noting that extranets are not a new technology. Businesses have been trying to develop secure links with trading partners and customers for years. The use of IP to support secure intercompany virtual private networks has led to the creation of extranets.

This does not mean creating any new physical networks. Instead, access privileges and routing tables and overlayed on existing intranet and the Internet infrastructure. Security of transactions with permitted corporate websites and databases is then enabled on the extranet. In addition to simple commercial transactions of sale-purchase, collaborative activities between business partners on the extranet are enabled at much lower costs than over VANs.

17.3.4 Security Issues in Electronic Transactions

The main issues that confront in relation to securing electronic transactions are:

- Confidentiality
- Integrity
- Availability
- Authenticity/non-repudiability
- Auditability

Confidentiality: Information should be protected from prying eyes of unauthorised internal users, external hackers and from being intercepted during transmission on communication networks by making it unintelligible to the attacker. The content should be transformed in such a way that it is not decipherable by anyone who does not know the transformation algorithm.

Integrity: On retrieval or receipt at the other end of a communication network the information should appear exactly as was stored or sent. It should be possible to generate an alert on any modification, addition or deletion to the original content. Integrity also precludes information 're-play'—i.e., a fresh copy of the data is generated/re-sent using the authorisation features of the earlier authentic message. Suitable mechanisms are required to ensure end-to-end message content and copy authentication.

Availability: The information that is being stored or transmitted across communication networks should be available whenever required and to whatever extent as desired within pre-established time constraints. Network errors, power outages, operational errors, application software errors, hardware problems and viruses are some of the causes of unavailability of information. The mechanisms for implementation of counter-measures to these threats are available but are beyond the scope of end-to-end message security for implementing Electronic Commerce.

Authenticity: It should be possible to prevent any person or object from masquerading as some other person or object. When a message is received it should therefore be possible to verify whether it has indeed been sent by the person or object claiming to be the originator. Similarly, it should also be possible to ensure that the message is sent to the person or object for whom it is meant. This implies the need for reliable identification of the originator and recipient of data.

Non-repudiability: After sending/authorising a message, the sender should not be able to, at a later date, deny having done so. Similarly, the recipient of a message should not be able to deny receipt at a later date. It should, therefore, be possible to bind messages and message acknowledgements with their originators.

Auditability: Audit data must be recorded in such a way that all specified confidentiality and integrity requirements are met.

Implementing a security solution in an Electronic Commerce environment, therefore, necessitates a risk analysis of the business scenario. In some cases, confidentiality might be an extremely critical issue whereas in others it may only be data integrity that is of paramount importance. All possible threats should be considered and a security requirements policy drawn out for the organisation based on a combination of some or all of the services listed above.

17.3.5 Technology Solutions for Security Services

Implementation of technology solutions for all the security services listed above are based on *cryptographic* techniques. Cryptography comprises *encryption*—the process of making information unintelligible to the unauthorised reader—and *decryption*—reversing encryption to make the information readable once again. Conventional cryptography uses a secret code or key to encrypt information. The same secret key is used by the receiver to decrypt the information.

A simple encryption scheme could be one in which all alphabetic and numerical characters are shifted by a fixed number of positions in the encrypted text. If the characters are to be shifted by, say, 5 places then the result would be as follows:

Character	*Represented as*
A	F
B	G
C	H
V	A
W	B
X	C
Y	D
Z	E

Using this encryption scheme, where the key is a 5-character shift, the plaintext message 'THIS IS A BOOK' would be encrypted to read 'YMNX NX F GTTP' which would not be very easily decipherable to the casual reader.

Over time, many complicated encryption systems have developed and with the increased availability and advancement of computing resources, the level of sophistication of these systems has also increased. While the most obvious application of these processes is in ensuring confidentiality of information, advances in the science of cryptography have also made possible the provision of other security services such as integrity, authentication and non-repudiation.

There are two basic types of cryptographic systems or cryptosystems—*symmetric* and *asymmetric*. The symmetric system is based on a single secret key which is shared by the parties engaging in secure communication. The asymmetric system hinges on the possession by these parties of a pair of keys—one private and the other public.

The RSA Algorithm

One of the most popular and widely used public key cryptosystems is the RSA algorithm—developed in 1978 by Ron Rivest, Adi Shamir and Len Adleman of the Massachusetts Institute of Technology, USA.

Two large prime numbers p and q are randomly chosen and their product $N = p \times q$ is computed. From the product $(p-1)\times(q-1)$, a number e is chosen such that e is relatively prime to $(p-1)(q-1)$, *i.e.*, both $(p-1)$ and $(q-1)$ do not have any common factors with e. Similarly, d is chosen such that d satisfies:

$$de = 1 \ mod \ (p-1)(q-1), \qquad \text{i.e., } de-1 \text{ is divisible by } (p-1) \text{ and } (q-1).$$

The public key is then (N, e), while the private key is (N, d).

To encrypt a message *M* using the public key (*N*, *e*), the value of M^e mod *N* is calculated to produce the encrypted message *E*. For decrypting, calculation of E^d mod *N* yields the original message *M*.

Digital Signatures

Digital signatures are used not only to verify the authenticity of the message and the claimed identity of the sender, but also to verify message integrity. The recipient, however, should not be able to use the received digital signature to falsely `sign' messages on behalf of the original sender.

Using the RSA cryptosystem, a message is encrypted with the sender's private key to generate the `signature'. The message is then sent to the destination along with this signature. The recipient decrypts the signature using the sender's public key, and if the result matches with the copy of the message received, the recipient can be sure that the message was sent by the claimed originator and that the message has not been modified during transmission, since only the originator is in possession of the corresponding encryption key. Figure 17.3 illustrates the implementation of digital signatures.

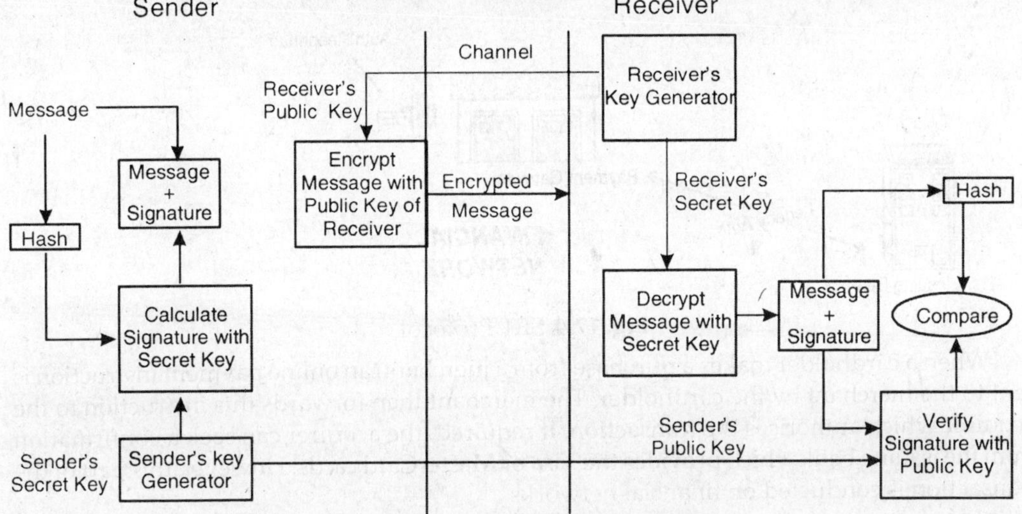

Fig. 17.3 Implementation of Digital Signatures

Though this is a highly secure way of digitally signing messages, it generates a large processing overhead. The size of the signature is the same as that of the original message, thereby resulting in a 100% increase in the data that is to be processed. To reduce this processing load, a *hash* function is employed. Hash functions operate on large messages and generate *message digests* of fixed but of much smaller length. These functions have the property that any change in the original message will cause the message digest to be different.

Processing overheads for implementing digital signatures can, therefore, be reduced by creating message digests and encrypting this digest with the private key to generate the signature. At the receiving end, the message digest is recalculated and compared with that generated by decrypting the received encrypted message digest using the sender's public key. If the two are the same, then the recipient is assured of the identity of the sender as well as the integrity of the message.

The RSA algorithm is widely used to implement digital signatures. The other popular algorithm is the Digital Signature Algorithm (DSA) developed by the US National Institute of Standards and Technology. The basic algorithm which provides the security features is different in DSA as compared to RSA, but the method of implementing digital signatures is essentially the same.

The hashing functions being used include algorithms such as Secure Hash Algorithm (SHA) in conjunction with DSA and MD4 and MD5 Message Digest Algorithms from RSA Data Security Inc.

The Secure Electronic Transaction (SET) Protocol

The SET protocol was developed by Visa and Mastercard to provide security for credit card based payment transactions on the Internet. It is shown in Fig. 17.4.

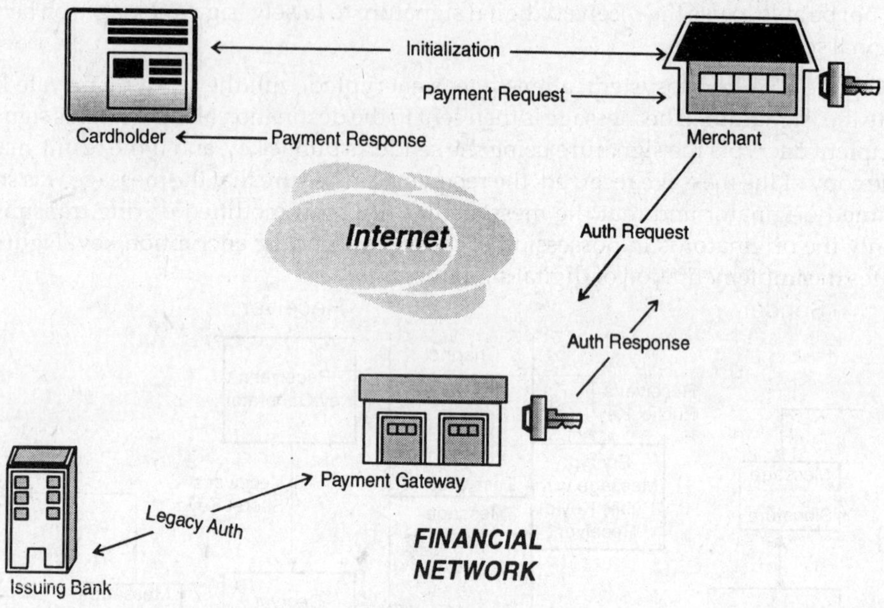

Fig. 17.4 SET Protocol

When a cardholder makes a purchase from a merchant, an online payment instruction is sent to the merchant by the cardholder. The merchant then forwards this instruction to the acquirer which authorises the transaction. If required, the acquirer can seek a confirmation from the issuing bank which provides the Visa or MasterCard cards. However, this part of the transaction is conducted on financial networks.

Within SET, public key cryptography is extensively used. Payment instructions are encrypted so that credit-card numbers are not intelligible to anyone. Cardholders, merchants and acquirers are authenticated to each other and integrity of the data contained in the payment instruction is maintained.

A Verisign digital certificate serves as an electronic substitute for a sealed envelope containing the certificate holder's signature for sending messages across the Internet. The digital certificate resides securely in the browser on the client machine or in its e-mail software and allows digital signing and encryption of messages.

17.4 ELECTRONIC CASH OVER THE INTERNET

Electronic or Digital Cash (e-cash) is a new concept to execute cash payments using computers connected over networks. To make it a reality with security and privacy of transactions, a number of solution providers have come into being.

Using software on the customer's own computer, the customer can withdraw e-cash from his/her own account in a bank. The e-cash is stored in the hard disk of the customer's computer in an electronic wallet which can be spent by the customer for purchase of items from any shop accepting e-cash.

Digital cash can be used for making/receiving payments between customer and merchant or persons or for any money transaction.

The customer can use a browser to see products offered for sale on the web. He scans the sale pages and identifies the products available in different shops along with their sale prices. In doing so, the customer browses through the Web pages on the merchant/shopowner's servers.

After identifying the products the customer wants to buy, he sends a request to the customer's bank server for sending electronic cash from his account to his own system. The message is in enciphered form. The bank server (after checking authenticity, balance, etc.) sends back a secure e-cash packet which is stored in the electronic wallet of the customer's hard disk.

Having obtained e-cash from his own computer, the customer sends an order to the merchant/shop owner's server along with billing and shopping address, quantity ordered and the exact e-cash required for the purchase (from the electronic wallet in the customer's computer).

The merchant (after receiving the order along with e-cash) issues a receipt electronically to the customer and sends the e-cash to his account in the merchant's bank. The merchant takes the desired steps for delivery of items to the customer. The merchant's bank sends the e-cash packet to the customer's bank. The customer's bank after using the customer's public key along with the secure packet received, verifies and remits the actual fund to the merchant's bank who transfers this money to the account. The customer gets the items despatched by the merchant at the shipping address.

As the e-cash can reach the destination site using any computer network or Internet which has an open architecture, the security of the system is very important. Security is provided using encryption, digital signatures and passwords. As e-cash is digitally signed by the customer, there is no room for dispute over payment. The implementations vary from one to another solution provider.

While paying in the form of e-cash, the customer has the option to reveal or conceal his identity. If the customer wants to conceal his identity, the merchant cannot know it. When clearing, the payee is identified by the bank but the merchant does not know of him.

17.4.1 Elements in Electronic Cash Flow

Client Software

Software available from various solution providers works on latest versions of Windows 98, Windows 3.1, Macintosh and Unix. Some of them make use of web browsers and e-mail reader and some require dedicated software for browsing encrypted information. In most of these cases, the software at the customer site is provided free. Almost all solutions require a TCP/IP network connection.

Merchant Server Software

Some solution providers design custom application software for the merchant, others integrate functions with web servers. In another solution, the server must have the Netscape Commerce Server whereas some provide a software library for free.

Payment by the Customer

The customer can make payment using a credit-card number, by e-cash from a participating bank, or through an Automated Clearing House (ACH). The option depends again on the solution being provided by the service provider.

Payment to Merchant

In debit-based transactions, the merchant gets payment immediately, from the customer's bank in his account, through ACH, through a bank transfer, or, within a day of the clearing period. In credit transactions, the merchant gets paid through a bank transfer or through a normal credit-card processing cycle.

A few tools provide this feature of subscription accounting, cumulative billing, etc. In the other cases, the merchant's server has to support these functions.

Transaction Cost

The cost per transaction varies for credit and debit transactions and with the service provider. In some cases, there is a fixed amount per transaction, whereas others charge a percentage of the amount of transaction.

Risk

In most of the solutions provided, the risk is the merchant's for fraudulent transactions. In case of disputed debit transactions or if after payment a merchant is unable to deliver, the customer loses.

As e-cash works like traveller's cheques, in case the customer loses the e-cash, the bank has to be provided with details on serial numbers of lost e-cash so that the bank can refund the money, otherwise the customer loses the money.

Applications

Electronic cash applications include debit cards, vending, telebanking, teleshopping, phone cards, parking systems, public transit systems and automatic toll collection, etc.

17.5 INTERNET SECURITY

For the purposes of business document exchange via EDI, end-to-end security mechanisms are crucial and have to be implemented. In the larger context of Electronic Commerce, it is extremely important to secure internal information systems from being attacked from outside. With client machines on an organisation's internal LAN routinely accessing the Internet, they become targets for attack by unscrupulous elements.

Firewalls are built to protect the internal network of an organisation from attacks originating from the Internet. Firewalls can be implemented in many ways. Some of these are:

- Establishing rules to decide which packets, depending on the originating IP address, should be allowed to pass into the organisation's network.
- Establishment of proxy servers, so that internal client requests for accessing external services are routed through the proxy server. This ensures that the client and the external server are not in direct communication with each other.
- Establishment of an additional network as a buffer between the internal and external networks.

Web communications also require additional levels of security to protect against situations such as compromise of credit-card numbers when transmitted across the network. Client-server authentication mechanisms must also be installed to guard against business malpractices.

The Secure Sockets Layer (SSL) protocol was developed by Netscape Communications to provide security during a communications session. SSL operates above the TCP layer and provides protection to applications such as FTP, TELNET and HTTP. This includes services such as client and server authentication, data integrity and confidentiality.

Secure HTTP (SHTTP) was developed for Commerce Net—a consortium of companies promoting the establishment of Electronic Commerce on the Internet. SHTTP provides security to individual transactions.

17.5.1 Guidelines for Cryptography Policy

Though technology solutions have been developing for the provision of a variety of security requirements, deployment of these technologies by companies and organisations can often turn out to be in disagreement with the security rules as laid down by national governments for their own countries.

In March 1997, the Organisation for Economic Cooperation and Development (OECD) adopted the guidelines for cryptography policy identifying eight principles for national legislation. These are:

- The cryptography methods should be trustworthy in order to generate confidence in their use.
- Users should be free to choose any cryptography method based on their security re-quirements.
- Cryptography methods should be developed in response to the needs of businesses, individuals and governments.
- Technical standards and protocols for cryptography should be developed and promulgated at the national level.
- Fundamental rights of individuals to privacy should be protected.
- National policies may allow lawful access to plaintext, cryptographic keys and encrypted data.
- Liabilities of individuals and entities that offer cryptographic services should be clearly stated.
- Governments should cooperate in coordination of cryptographic policies.

Although the guidelines recognise the need for some state controls over the use of cryptography, it is stressed throughout that these must respect user choice to the greatest extent.'

Similar considerations exist in the framework for providing Electronic Commerce services on the GII. The requirements have evolved from the use of EC over the Internet, which has been the forerunner of the NII and the GII.

According to the framework for Global Electronic Commerce, a secure GII requires:

- Secure and reliable telecommunications networks.
- Effective means for protecting the information systems attached to those networks.
- Effective means for authenticating and ensuring confidentiality of electronic information to protect data from unauthorised use.
- Well-trained GII users who understand how to protect their systems and data.

Accomplishing this goal requires a range of technologies such as encryption, authentication, password controls, firewalls, etc. and consistent use of these technologies. All this should be supported by trustworthy key and security management infrastructures.

17.6 ELECTRONIC BUSINESS (E-BUSINESS)

E-business is about using Internet technologies to transform the way key business processes are performed. Its most visible form is online purchasing, both wholesale and retail. Every day, more companies and people gain access to the Web, and every day, more purchases are transacted electronically. Online purchasing became popular in 1996, when over 100,000 tickets for the Summer Olympics were ordered through the official Olympic Games Web site, which was created by IBM. By the end of 1996, business being conducted over the Web was running at the rate of US$60 billion annually. The pace is quickening: it is estimated that the value of goods that will be ordered or purchased online by 2005 will be one trillion US dollars.

17.6.1 Opportunities

There is a range of e-business opportunities that depend on the nature of the business and the customers it serves. Here are some opportunities of online business:

- Retail sellers on the Internet can sell high-quality, specialized products that appeal to an audience of affluent, well-educated, and well-informed people.
- Companies that sell their goods through catalogs and expand their reach to additional global customers at a low marginal cost.
- Wholesalers, distributors, or service providers can sell to businesses that have embraced e-business and that demand the convenience and efficiencies of buying from a Web site.
- Companies holding comprehensive sets of digital assets (logos, image libraries, inventory information, and so forth) can sell and distribute their products electronically.
- Business-to-business sellers, the majority of whose customer base is already on the Internet, can build a closer relationship, electronically.
- Companies that already have a corporate Web site and an efficient network operation can establish subsidiary sites for related, ancillary, or consumable products.
- Businesses selling products that can readily be distributed over the Internet (for example, software, market research, industry and financial reports, news about local events, sports, travel and so on) can expand their customer bases.
- Businesses selling products that can be sampled on the Web (for example, books, magazines, and recorded music) can promote them economically.
- Businesses selling products that are subject to frequent changes (for example, airline tickets, financial instruments) can reduce production and obsolescence costs because they offer only current products on the site. They can also adjust pricing in real time in response to fluctuations in demand.
- Businesses that configure products to customer measurements or specifications (for example, custom-tailored garments, configured PCs, food shopping and delivery services or other just-in-time products) can expand made-to-order services to new markets.

17.6.2 Benefits

The primary benefits of e-business are global accessibility and sales reach, the prospect of increased profits from new markets and electronic channels, improved customer service and loyalty, shorter time-to-market, and supply chain integration.

Global Accessibility and Sales Reach

An e-business can receive orders from just about any country in the world. The global reach of local companies that have become e-businesses may startle some firms that thought they were established in their markets.

For example, the Lehigh Valley Safety Supply Company in Pennsylvania distributes heavy-duty safety shoes to businesses. Direct sales to individual consumers are restricted to a specific geographic area under the terms of its agreement with the manufacturer. Mail order sales, however, are unrestricted, so using IBM Net. Commerce, Lehigh placed 50 items on the Web for sale. It began getting orders from all over the world and realised a 150 percent increase is revenue. Lehigh is now expanding its IBM Net. Commerce-based Web site to include safety shoes for a variety of other markets.

Market Base Expansion

An e-business can open its critical information systems to entirely new groups of users, including employees, customers, suppliers, and business partners, who formerly did not have timely access to them. This ability enables companies to redesign and Web-enable their core business processes and extend them to anyone of their choosing, inside or outside a company, at any time of the day or night.

Increased Profits

With e-business, companies reach more and different customers and gain exposure in new markets not covered by existing physical channels. Since the Internet is both a sales channel and a distribution channel (for example, for information, software, music, graphics, etc.), companies can sometimes leverage their existing customer relationships to offer new products and services.

By fully implementing e-business, a company can make every process that leads up to, surrounds, and follows an actual transaction more efficient and convenient. Companies are using the Internet to do the following:

- Advertise and create awareness for their products
- Promote and offer special deals that generate demand for their products
- Provide detailed information about their products
- Inform and influence the customer's choice

Build brand loyalty by offering immediate and convenient service after the sale.

What's more, businesses can cut selling costs by using the electronic channel and at the same time, free their sales personnel to focus on higher value activities, such as providing expert advice concerning a potential purchase or opening a new account.

Improved Customer Service and Loyalty

E-business enables a company to be open for business whenever a customer needs it. This level of convenience is a differentiation today, but eventually it will be expected by customers. Up-to-date information about products can be offered on the Web, making it easier and more convenient for customers to serve themselves. In addition, combining the interactive nature of the Web with a proper understanding of a customer's needs helps a merchant to provide products and services built to order for each customer, and thus to build long-term relationships, increase loyalty, and sustain a competitive edge.

Furthermore, customers with questions about products can locate information themselves and solve their own problems, thereby reducing support headaches and costs. Better yet, they can select, configure, and order products themselves, from choosing safety shoes for hazardous work environments, to trading securities based on the underlying company's performance, to selecting electrical components to meet functional requirements, to configuring PCs for specific tasks.

Shorter Time-to-Market

E-business makes for fast and flexible execution and response to market opportunities. The Web enables a company to introduce a new product into the market, get immediate customer reaction to it, and refine and perfect it, all without incurring huge investments in a physical distribution infrastructure or "buying" shelf space at a retailer or distributor. When the product is right, the company can launch it through traditional channels with much greater assurance of its success.

Supply Chain Integration

E-business enables the full integration of a business, making the entire supply chain more efficient from the point of customer contact all the way back through physical distribution, warehousing, manufacturing, resource management, and purchasing. The resulting efficiencies reduce expenses, increase margins, facilitate flexible pricing strategies, and reduce costs by keeping inventories more in line with demand.

17.6.3 e-business Strategy

Following are the e-business strategies:

The Impact of Extending the Enterprise

It is estimated that the number of worldwide business establishments with Web access will grow to 8 million by the year 2002. A substantial portion of these businesses will be interconnected over the Internet or private networks and will have two or more categories of electronic connections: selling to customers over the Internet (or to other businesses over a private network), and buying from suppliers over the Internet, private networks, or both. The typical business will extend out to encompass its supply chain, with goods and services moving towards end consumers and payments moving towards suppliers.

An e-business strategy should address both sides of the supply chain, because the company's total return can be more easily maximized when its linkages with business partners are efficient and swift. The combination of business process automation and Internet-enabled communications helps the business to compete on a higher level and gain share even in an established industry. For example, one start-up company with 35 employees made a very successful entrance into the European insurance industry by concentrating on its core competencies—product development and marketing—and obtaining policy administration, asset management, actuarial services, and other support from world-class companies online. Linked online to independent brokers, it has gone from zero market share to 17 per cent, with a cost structure that is 50 per cent less than those of its competitors.

Updating Operational Habits and Reducing Costs

The Internet is already profoundly influencing the structure of established companies through supply chain integration. By linking to suppliers through a Web-based network, major manufacturers can save the money spent on materials by shopping for better prices on standard components. They can also save on inventory and administrative costs for custom-designed components by integrating their purchasing systems with their suppliers' order processing systems. By integrating suppliers more closely for efficiency and cost savings, companies are giving rise to virtual enterprises in which it is difficult to tell where one organisation ends and the next begins.

Pressuring Resellers

The Internet's integration of the supply chain is pressuring resellers now that producers have a direct channel to the buyer. (And the Internet is a tempting channel indeed, when a bank, for example, can conduct a transaction online instead of conducting it through a teller). Likewise, local distributors will feel more and more competitive pressure from online brokers who can operate independently of time and place. Resellers and distributors will have to find new ways of adding value to the supply chain if they are to survive—perhaps by delivering customization, configuration, and integration services.

Transferring Power to Buyers

The Internet is transferring power to the buyer. Armed with information on price, quality, and availability, the customer now can easily compare items from a world of suppliers. With their competitors only a mouse click away, many businesses will have to rethink the value proposition they offer customers to ensure that it differentiates them from the rest of the field.

Personalization

Among all the Internet-generated changes in commerce, the most exciting is the growing degree of personalization facilitated by this new medium. In the past, businesses focused on the product, designing it to appeal to a mass market. Now, using the information and processing power available to an e-business, they can gain a far more comprehensive knowledge of their clientele and use this knowledge to tailor their products and services specifically to the needs of the individual. Instead of the relationship with the customer ending after the transaction, it can span a lifetime because e-business technologies can help design goods and services that are uniquely relevant to that individual's needs and wants. With growing personalization, suppliers will begin to differentiate their brands as much on an understanding of the customer as on price and quality.

Trust and Privacy

This new relationship with the customer and a thriving online commerce depend on the willingness of people to trust suppliers with large amounts of information about themselves, some of it very personal. People are enthralled by the prospect of buying and selling online, but at the same time, they are very conscious of the increased potential for their personal information being mishandled. Now that technology permits the gathering and analysis of so much information about so many millions of people, the creators of this new world of electronic commerce must act with a passionate respect for individual privacy. Anything less would open the way for consumer distrust and its consequent burdensome government regulation, undermining the most promising advance in global commerce since the Industrial Revolution.

Requirements for e-business Platforms

Consider the trajectory of a successful Internet-based business. It may begin as a place for prospective customers to look up product information; progress to an online store; and from there evolve into a hub for business cycle automation, supporting Web-accessible transactions for a community of consumers or businesses. Because no one can reliably predict how quickly the site will grow or what future integration will be required to support it, technologies underlying e-business site need to be extensible to encompass future requirements. They need flexibility to integrate with business-critical applications and suit a variety of operational configurations. They need the robustness to handle complex transactions reliably. They need scalability to grow with the business and transaction volume. Finally, they need the availability of technology in multiple national languages. The ideal e-business platform should also offer the following:

Quick Startup

Merchants need to be able to get their sites up and running very quickly, either on their own systems or through a development and hosting service, without sacrificing long-term functionality or flexibility.

The key software components of an e-business Web site should be able to run on the same or different servers, which helps reduce expenses while matching capacity to the load. Specifically, merchants should have the flexibility to run the commerce server, the Web server, the payment server, the catalog server, the database, and a firewall on the same or different machines, depending on capacity required.

Scalability and Variety of Upgrade Paths

Companies serving small markets or that are prototyping their sites should be able to set up a commerce system in a hosted environment (renting a storefront from an ISP) or on a small server (on Windows NT) for pilot purposes, and then, depending on performance requirements and availability of assets, migrate it to a variety of industrial-strength platforms such as UNIX servers (RS/6000 or Solaris), departmental or small business systems (AS/400), or mainframes (System 390). Net Commerce is compatible with IBM load-balancing and system-clustering offerings, which provide both scalability and very high availability.

Staff Familiarity

The underlying technologies should be already proven and well known, which allows the business to devote its existing staff (with their experience of the business) to develop the e-business site, while reducing the need to hire and train new staff for Internet-specialized technologies. Examples of operating system technologies familiar to many organisations include AIX (RS/6000), OS/400 (AS/400), and MVS (System 390). Familiar database technology includes relational DB2 with SQL access. Familiar integration technologies include Net Data. MQ Series, and software development workbenches that generate executable code for dynamic link libraries (DLLs).

Availability of End-to-End Service

Timely business development sometimes requires supplemental skills (design, programming) or services (data preparation, conversion, hosting). It is important to know that skills and services surrounding the chosen e-business platform are available if needed to ensure swift achievement of objectives.

Flexible Purchasing Processes

The purchasing process itself varies naturally from market to market, country to country, business-to-business, and merchant to merchant, as well as by type of product. The underlying purchasing process needs to be able to provide purchase orders, order lists, buyer groups, flexible pricing rules, variable discount rules, configurable shipping charges, and multiple tax rates—all at the same site or store.

Strong Search and Product Selection Capabilities

It is easier to sell when customers can find what they want quickly and easily. Customers who are unfamiliar with a product line need sales assistance; customers who know what they want need to be able to compare features of candidate products. These capabilities simplify a "buy" decision and foster repeat business.

Open Architecture

In some scenarios, Internet commerce necessitates connectivity with the business's other applications as well as with trading partner systems. As a result, the e-business systems need to be readily integrated with other systems and architectures at the level of programming calls, operating system commands, transactions, database queries, and files.

17.7. APPLICATIONS OF E-COMMERCE IN INDIA

In India, E-commerce is still in its early stages. Companies have taken a long-term perspective and are looking at one to three years' time for its implementation. Smaller companies lag behind in e-commerce implementation. Sectors like logistics services and metals are relatively ahead of other sectors as far as e-commerce adoption is concerned. Some of the important findings include :

- E-commerce is primarily internally driven.
- Cannot sell everything over the Internet.
- Selling on the Net may take time, but buying on the Net is on, e.g., car manufacturer, Maruti Udyog Ltd, for e-commerce-based supply chain management systems.
- Revenues from e-commerce are yet to take off.

The level of implementation of Electronic Data Interchange (EDI) projects in the govt. regulatory agencies and other sectors with a view to make them EDI capable is as follows:

17.7.1 Customs

In Indian customs, EDI System (ICES) was one of the first EDI projects in India. It was started as a pilot project in May 1995 at Delhi Custom House, Indira Gandhi International (IGI) Airport. Since then this project has come a long way. Custom houses have been made fully EDI-capable with electronic submission of documents over NICNET. ICES has been designed, developed and implemented by National Informatics Centre (NIC). Reengineering has been largely achieved through workflow automation. The customs operations have become nearly paperless.

17.7.2 Reserve Bank of India

It can accept the trade declarations which are forwarded by customs after due processing.

17.7.3 Airport Authority of India (AAI)

AAI has created its Cargo Management System at IGI Airport, Delhi. Also, it is fully linked with its user community, with air cargo agents and airlines.

17.7.4 Apparel Export Promotion Council (AEPC)

AEPC is attempting to fully automate its functions so as to accept the documents appropriately and process them automatically.

17.7.5 Banks

In India, implementation of EDI for banks was first taken up by the Indian Banks Association (IBA) under the aegis of the Financial Message Development Group set up by the EDI Council of India. Initially five participating banks were selected for the Delhi-Mumbai segment of IBA's pilot project. These were the State Bank of India, Union Bank of India, Punjab National Bank, Corporation Bank and Bank of India. The documents selected for exchange over NICNET between branches of participating banks—for both inter-bank as well as intra-bank requirements—were the demand draft advice, caution advice, cancellation advice, and the inter-city credit advice. These messages were converted to EDIFACT and routed through NICNET's EDI mail boxes to the destination branch. Subsequently, these services were extended to other banks as well. At present, these advices not only serve a statistical function but also provide a cross-checking facility before payments are made for the demand draft presented for encashment.

At present, many banks have started an ATM (all time money) network, called the Shared Payment Network System (SPNS). SPNS permits inter-ATM transactions, i.e., the ATM of one bank can be used by an ATM user of another bank. Personal Identification Numbers (PIN) are used for verification and authorisation of bank transactions. This facility is extended further to other cities in India.

The ICICI (Industrial Credit and Investment Corporation of India) Bank sometime back launched INFINITY—its Internet Banking Service. It provides remote banking facilities such as:

- Information about all the accounts of the user at any branch of the bank, over the Internet.
- Account details and statement.
- Financial modeling tools which allow simulation of various deposit options to arrive at an optimum combination.
- Communication with the bank using a messaging facility. Funds transfer between accounts is also possible.

17.7.6 Directorate General of Foreign Trade

This organisation is at present capable of processing import licence applications automatically through its offices in India. The organisation is thus EDI capable.

17.7.7 Port Authorities

Different ports in India are at different levels of automation for their functions, particularly Jawaharlal Nehru Port Trust, Mumbai has a high degree of internal automation, including container tracking.

17.7.8 Ford India Ltd—A Giant in Automobile Company

Ford India has divided its e-business initiative into *four* segments : B-to-B, which connects the company with their suppliers; B-to-C, which is meant for customer relationship, since all their products are being sold through distributors only; B-to-D (business-to-dealers), which connects the company to the dealer network; and B-to-E (business-to-employees) that communicates the activities of the company and other information to their employees.

Ford, along with other major international automobile companies, has formed an e-marketplace called covisint.com. This is an e-marketplace for sourcing materials for its products. But B-to-B is also done in conventional methods. The services of covisint are used mostly for high-value and competitive prices for major raw materials. E-commerce is the responsibility at Ford India on business departments and not on the IT departments.

Ford India is not worried about online payments, being fully aware that people will not spend Rs 5 lakh over the Internet. There are some security aspects to be looked into and the sites have to be certified by an authority, like Verisign, which helps build confidence about a site.

E-commerce in the auto component sector would be primarily driven by:

- E-commerce implementation by automobile firms as there is a gradual migration from extranets and EDI systems to e-commerce. The automobile firms put pressure on component markers to adopt online order processing and e-commerce.
- Need for more efficient channel/dealer management to serve the increasingly competitive replacement market.

17.7.9 Building and Construction Materials Industry

The Rs 210,000 crore building and construction industry in India offers unique challenges and opportunities for e-commerce initiatives. At present, the industry mainly uses the Internet for communication and information exchange rather than for actual sales transactions. Paperwork has been considerably reduced since the documentation processes were computerised. However, payments are being made only by offline channels. Most of the companies in this sector are using their own Web sites for e-commerce transactions.

E-commerce adoption in this sector would be driven by factors such as:

- Improving brand-building and customer service to serve an steadily maturing market.

- Need to widen the distribution and reach significantly, penetrating markets in the semi-urban and rural pockets.
- Improved dealer management, ensuring timely supplies and service.

17.7.10 Metal Industries

The metal industry in general, and certain sectors like the steel industry in particular, has been one of the early movers in e-commerce adoption. The most important rationale for implementing e-commerce was 'customer-driven', following by 'internally-driven'. With the worldwide trading of the product, minimal differentiation, and the need to retain customers through better service and faster transactions makes e-commerce attractive.

In this sector, payment issues and security are seen as critical risks. Also, high cost of e-commerce implementation is also considered an impediment.

E-commerce adoption in the metal sector would be primarily driven by:

- Working with lower inventories and adopting just in time (JIT) techniques, and catering to customers who have adopted/are adopting JIT procurement systems.
- Increased market coverage and widened distribution reach.
- Controlling costs in every stage of the value chain.

Metals industry provide considerable scope for online tendering and auction applications. Online auction models enjoy a relatively higher preferance.

17.7.11 Office Automation Industry

E-commerce in the office automation sector would be driven by:

- Improved customer service as a key differentiator.
- Increasing market coverage, which is critical to serve the geographically scattered market and target the fast growing segment.
- Customisation, important in certain segments.
- Control procurement and marketing overheads by bypassing non-critical channels.
- Major issues required to be addressed are lack of information technology (IT) knowledge and IT infrastructure, and general reluctance to invest in e-commerce.

17.7.12 Packaging Industry

The Rs 10,500-crore Indian packaging industry has developed rapidly in recent years. In India, packaging industry is highly fragmented, and characterised by the presence of a large number of unorganised manufacturers and a few very large players. The companies in this sector are confident that their ware could be sold online. It is believed that if customers standardised the product package, it could be transacted on the Internet. While face-to-face negotiations and interaction is a must for the first time, subsequent orders and processing for the same product could be e-commerce enabled. The demand would be driven by:

- The need for operating with lower inventories, and just-in-time deliveries.
- Widening marketing and procurement reach, identifying opportunities for export.

17.7.13 Indian Engineering Industry

The Rs 116,500 crore Indian engineering industry views e-commerce as a platform for interaction and information exchange. The most important benefit of e-commerce is the likely expansion in marketing reach. The secondary benefits stemming from the widened reach include pre-transaction and post-transaction issues involving interaction and information exchange.

In the long run, it will become imperative for the engineering industry to adopt e-commerce technologies. The challenge before the heavy engineering sector will be to develop sales-oriented Web sites with a global reach, and to reduce transaction costs in order to exploit the export potential and stay cost-competitive. For the light engineering equipment sector, the pressure is to improve the supply chain efficiency and to enhance channel management in order to empower the foward chain and to strengthen distribution. The priorities of the consumable manufacturers would be to sustain their market position and margins by enhancing the front-end chains and the cost equations through e-CRM initiatives and other e-commerce technologies.

E-commerce benefits in the engineering industry are shown in Fig. 17.5.

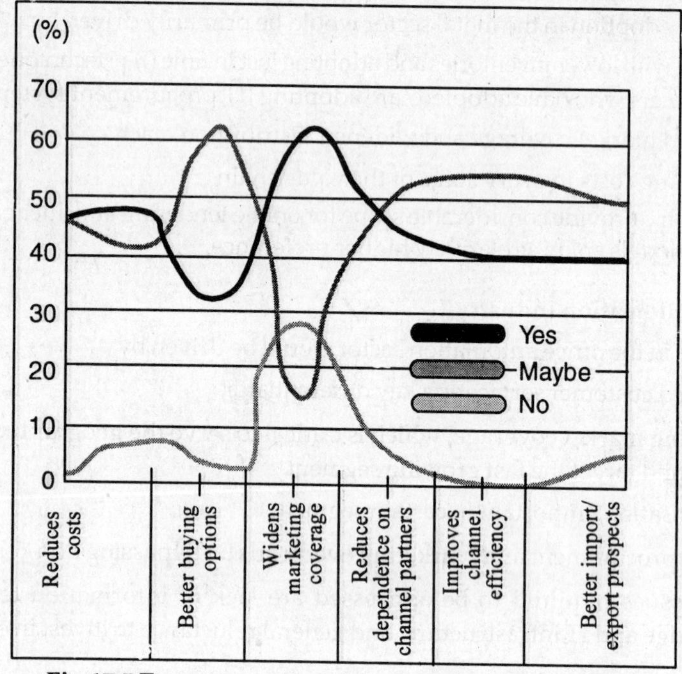

Fig.17.5 E-commerce Benefits in Engineering Industry

17.7.14 The Logistics Industry

Logistics companies have been affected by the coming of age of the Internet as time-to-order and time-to-market became shorter and more efficient. With more transactions taking place through the Internet, it also meant that companies became more customer-oriented and their services more efficient. The Internet is also used for internal exchange of information through EDI.

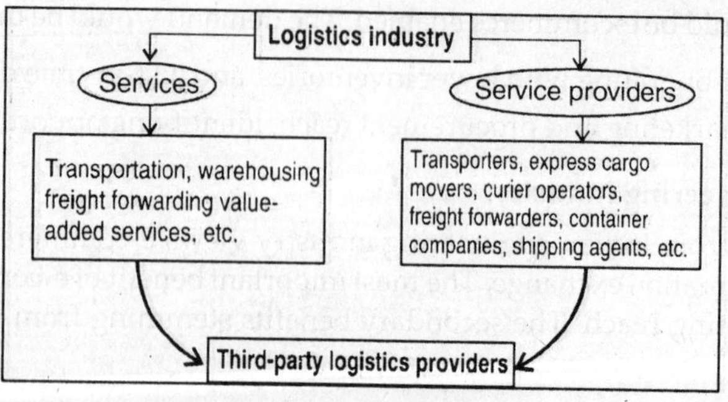

Of the two most common logistics activities, transportation primarily includes road, rail, shipping and airways; while warehousing entails storage and inventory management. In most logistics companies, the documentation process is online, payments are offline. Most logistics firms prefer their own portals for e-commerce transactions.

To be amenable to e-commerce activities, logistics firms need to bolster their distribution system through higher investments on infrastructure. They also need to be price competitive, and should be prepared to provide state-of-art network optimisation and services, which will help their customers simplify their supply chain processes.

The benefits from e-logistics are:

- Faster delivery from suppliers (78%)
- Increased market share (62%)
- Low-cost supplies (58%)
- Greater customer satisfaction (20%)
- Increased productivity (58%)
- Increased profitability (50%)
- Better service from suppliers (80%)
- Serving overseas customers (22%)
- Better awareness of business (58%)
- Effective information collection (30%).

17.8 SUCCESSFUL E-COMMERCE

In order to remain successful in today's Internet-driven marketplace, established enterprises have to be able to function as e-businesses. e-businesses are extended organisations, with lean, core business models, supplemented by outsourcing arrangements and business alliances. They are tightly integrated with customers, suppliers, partners, and remote employees via intranets, extranets and the public Internet. In addition, enterprises need to enhance the functionality of existing applications and/ or develop new applications to meet the new demands for information. They must find the way to deal with the security and management issues that surround, providing extended access to large groups of new users.

17.9 MOBILE COMMERCE

Mobile commerce, commonly referred to as M-commerce, means to pay for merchandise services or information through a mobile phone. Wireless application protocol (WAP) is enabling technology to bring the Internet content and services to mobile phones and other wireless terminals. Today, mobile is a obiquitous, always reachable, highly convenient and supremely secure device for any kind of transaction. Coupled with localisation of services and applications, the enhanced services, the increasing availability of bandwidth, the *always on* Internet connectivity, it is not hard to see while mobiles are redefining communication scope for ever. Experience to date suggests that mobile banking and brokerage services are relatively high on most users wish list. Some of the important aspects of M-commerce are:

WAP : WAP provides a much-needed medium to connect in a secure, fast, nimble, online, interactive way with services, information and other users.

WAP applications : Wireless applications have a major role to play in easing business processes in every situation where information exchange is a critical need. WAP is being used to develop enhanced forms of existing applications and view versions of today's emerging applications.

17.10 E-GOVERNANCE

The advent of new information and communication technologies have made electronic governance as tool to enhance the following relationship:

- Government to Government
- Government to citizen
- Citizen to Government
- Government to private and other sectors
- Private and NGOs to Government.

While e-government is defined as a mere delivery of government services and information to the public using electronic means, e-governance allows citizens to communicate with government, participate in the government's policy-making and citizens to communicate each other. It truly allows citizens to participate in the government decision-making process.

17.10.1 Models of E-Governance

There are four models of e-governance. The models are explained as follows:

Broadcasting/Wider Dissemination Model

This model is based on dissemination of governmental information, already available in public domain, into the wider public domain through the use of ICT and convergent media. This model could be applied in the following possible ways:

— Placing government laws and legislations online.

— To make available online the names, addresses, fax numbers, e-mails, etc. of local/regional/state/national government officials.

— To make available online information relating to government plans, budgets, expenditures, and performances.

— Placing key judicial decisions online, which are of value to general citizens and create a precedence for future actions.

Critical Value Information–Flow Model

This model is based on the principle of dissemination/channelising of information of critical value to target audience or in wider public domain through the use of ICT and convergent media. Possible applications of this model are:

— To make available online corruption-related data about a particular ministry/division/officials

— To make available online research studies, enquiry reports, reports of the various commissions.

— To make available online human rights violations of the government or allied authorities for access to judiciary, NGOs and concerned citizens.

— To make availabel critical environmental information to local inhabitants.

Comparative Analysis Model

This model can harness the potential and capacity offered by latest communication technologies and aims it towards better governance. This model could be applied in the following possible ways:

— To learn from historic policies and actions and derive learning lessons for future policy-making.

— To evaluate effectiveness of current policies and identify key learnings in terms of strengths, flaws in policies.

— To effectively establish conditions of precedence, especially in case of judicial or legal decision-making, and use it to influence/advocate future decision-making.

Interactive Service Model

This model opens up avenues for direct participation of individuals in the governance processes. The model could be applied in the following possible ways:

— To establish an interactive communication channels with key policy-makers and members of planning commission.

— To conduct electronic ballots for the election of government officials and other office bearers.

— To conduct public debates/opinion polls on issues of wider concern before formulation of policies and legislative frameworks.

— Establish decentralised form of governance.

— Performing governance fuctions online such as revenue collection, governmental procurement, payment transfer, etc.

Review Questions

1. 'Information technology is an enabler of change and a catalyst'. Elaborate this statement in detail with one or two live examples.
2. List out the key business characteristics of industrial age and information age businesses, with brief explanation.
3. Establish the relationship between extranet, intranet and internet, with a logical diagram.
4. Explain different types of E-commerce, supported by networks.
5. Discuss in detail EDI over the Internet, supported with a illustration.
6. What is web-based commerce on the Internet? Explain its different aspects in brief.
7. What do you understand by extranets? Explain in detail, with its key characteristic.
8. Discuss the key security issues in electronic transactions.
9. Discuss the RSA algorithm, the most widely used public key cryptosystems.
10. What do you mean by digital signatures? How can digital signatures be implemented effectively. Draw a flow diagram to justify your answer.
11. Explain in brief the secure Electronic Transaction protocal, with a neat diagram.
12. What is electronic/digital cash over the Internet? How can it be used for making/receiving payments.
13. Discuss various elements involved in electronic cash flow. Mention some eletronic cash applications.
14. Discuss the ways to secure internal information systems.
15. List out the guidelines for cryptography policy. Discuss the basic principles for national legislation.
16. What do you understand by electronic business? Discuss the opportunities and benefits of electronic business.
17. Explain in detail the various electronic business strategies.
18. What is E-commerce? Discuss practical applications of E-commerce in banks,engineering industries, logistics industries in India.
19. What do you understand by mobile commerce? How is it useful in business? Discuss some important aspects of mobile commerce.
20. Explain the term 'E-Governance'. Discuss its different models and applications thereof.

18 E-Enterprises

18.1 INTRODUCTION

In the pre-industrial revolution, managing business and ownership were not separated. In the nineteenth century, there was a separation of ownership and control. This resulted in recruiting managers to monitor day-to-day operations of the enterprise and owners (shareholders) gave risk capital. During the industrial era, the enterprise started to adopt mass production which led to focus on productivity and led to turn to task-based specialisation. In the late twentieth century, all earlier factors have changed such as reducing task-based specialisation, fewer levels of hierarchy, and moving from managing physical resources to managing knowledge.

Nature of the enterprise has been changing due to digital development. New coordinating technologies led to the decline of centralised decision-making and bureaucracy. Though the new technologies return to the pre-industrial organisational model, but with a difference that electronic networks help microbusinesses to tap into the global reservoirs of information, expertise and finance. This means future business enterprises are not stable and permanent but temporary.

Earlier, economic eras had long periods of stability followed by short periods of change. This is known as **punctuated equilibrium.** The digital information creates a business environment of constant change known as **punctuated chaos.** Business decisions have to keep pace with electronic markets.

This chapter describes the transformation from e-business to the e-enterprise.

18.2 FROM THE PC TO THE WEB

Information technology has become a global force. The PC era resulted in a homogeneous front-office product. The Web era is moving towards homogeneity of Internet products such as routers, browsers, modems, and many types of Web server hardware and related software. The five elements of evolving information technology are :

- Communication bandwidth has replaced microprocessor speed as the major IT technology. However, communication technology is fragmented such as PCs and satellite, and telephone-based networks, e.g., digital subscriber line (DSL) and integrated service digital network (ISDN).
- Different end-user devices exist such as cable TV setup boxes, PCs or a Web/TV-type device for net access.
- As different from PCS, network computers may vary.
- There are different standards for wireless networks. Europe uses GSM while the US has fragmented standards.

- The PC era had consistent applications such as spreadsheets, word processing, presentation graphics, groupware, databases, file and print, etc, whereas web applications are e-mail, search, audio, video, telephony, etc.

Earlier, information technology was focused on PC hardware, PC software, PC LANs and PC/mainframe communications. This is changed to the Internet or Web such as Internet access, Internet pricing, Web servers, Web sites, etc.

The differences between the global technologies and applications of the PC era to the Web-based era are given in Table 18.1.

Table 18.1 Differences between global technologies and applications of PC era to Web-based era

PC Era	*Web Era*
Microprocessors	Cable TV
Operating Systems	Fibre Optics
RDBMS	XDSL, ISDN
LANS	Carriers/ISPs
Servers	On-line services
Disc drives	ATM/gigabit Ethernet
Laser printers	Satellites/wireless
Word processing	News/entertainment
Spreadsheets	Shopping/finance
Database	Health care
Graphics	Government
File and print	Education/training
	On-line expertise classified ads chat/personals

Source : Papows, 1999, page 179.

18.3 THE INFORMATION AGE

There has been evolution of the infotech usage in e-Enterprise. The phases of development have been Brochureware (1995), e-commerce (1997), e-Business (1999) and e-Enterprise (2000). In e-enterprise, entire value chain, both from the supply side and demand side, is integrated.

This is a complex combination of tradition and infotech, a competitive virtual organisation and an extension of BPR movement of late 1980s and early 1990s. E-enterprise applications consist of not only customers, suppliers and internal processes, employees, and back-office functions, but also external partners.

In 1995, scientists considered as **physical value chain** changes to **virtual value chain.** The physical value chain comprises :

In bound logistics → Operations → Outbound logistics → Marketing and Sales → Service = Value

Contrarily, virtual value chain comprises :

Gather → Organise → Select → Synthesise → Distribute → Value

In the latter case, information is captured at all stages of the physical value chain, and the same is used to increase performance. It was viewed that every business is information business. Without information, business cannot succeed.

There is a difference between information system (IS) and information technology (IT). It is concerned with **how** (the technology infrastructure or platform) while IS focuses on **what** (identification and prioritisation of systems). Information management has many domains in addition to how and what. They are **who** (information management strategy), **why** (organisation strategy) and **where** (information resource strategy). A movement from data to knowledge, distinguishing between data, information and knowledge, is shown in Table 18.2.

Table 18.2. Movement from data to knowledge

	Data	*Information*	*Knowledge*
Content	Events	Trends	Expertise
Form	Transactions	Patterns	Learnings
Information task	Representation	Manipulation	Codification
Human element	Observation	Judgement	Experience
Organizational Intent	Automation	Decision-making	Action
Value test	Building block	Uncertainty reduction	New understanding

Enterprises are required to maximize their know-how. This means a new culture of information discovery, distribution, and application. However, networks are more valuable. There are interdependencies, organisational collaboration, and industrial convergences.

18.3.1 The Network-Centric Era

The network-centric era has produced two distinct type of E-enterprises. Old economy companies have followed the evolutionary changes, while new type companies, based on information technology, have come to be known as dotcom enterprises. The evolution of the era started in 1984 with the introduction of collaborative network-based software and moved to the PCs revolution. Then 'File Server' or 'host' mainframe computer was introduced connected to LAN linking any number of PCs or workstations. In the 1980s and 1990s, the relational database technology started to emerge. Back-office systems were most structured information, while front-office systems dealt with unstructured information.

There was an emergence of collaborative network solutions by groupware which supported the exchange of information among workgroups (whether physical or virtual, formal or informal). The tools were e-mail, electronic calendars, and on-line document repositories. Then there was a development of on-line discussion groups via intranets within the organization. The e-mail became a tool for managing workflow. In the networking era, the labour intensive system was replaced by the 'applicant tracking system' (ATS).

The nature of management improved along four dimensions : asynchronous communications, authentication, information dissemination, and mobility. Asynchronous communications technologies allowed for both voice mail and e-mail connections. These can be saved and official authentication provided. Technologies facilitated rapid information dissemination and increased mobility (time and place irrelevant for messages receiving or answering).

Inside the enterprise. Four layers are distinguished :

- Empowered individual means knowledge access and workflow integration. The former consists of specialized knowledge and expertise of individuals, while the latter consists of using information and knowledge tools in work processes.
- Second layer is automated workgroups. This consists of group collaborations such as team facilitation solutions, electronic discussion solutions, departmental reference system solutions, departmental scheduling solutions and document authorising solutions.
- Third layer is the integrated enterprise. This comprises enterprise data systems, enterprise-wide communication, enterprise knowledge management, and enterprise process innovation.
- Fourth layer in the extended enterprise consists of extranet and electronic commerce. This also consists of customer and supplier transactions, marketing and communications, ecosystem development, and market-facing systems.

The market-facing enterprise depends on computers for defining and managing business environments. There have been three stages of enterprise development. The basic stage came during 1980s to mid-1990s. The intermediate stage was achieved by 1998.

The advanced stage came when IT users integrated and developed competitive advantages internally (managing knowledge assets), externally (market-facing systems), and innovatively (process innovation).

There is a trend of IT industry convergence of four Cs—computers, communications, consumer electronics, and content. All these have one thing in common, that is, digital foundation. The hardware development will have the convergence of PCs and consumer electronics. The communications will have both voice and data. The content will have multiple media—text, image, audio, and video. The industry will have five main elements—hardware, communications, software, content, and services.

Success factors . There are five success factors :

- Application agility/flexibility
- Creation/improvement/integration
- Overcoming political obstacles
- Application and data integration
- Putting the CEO in charge

18.4 BUILDING E-ENTERPRISE

Building e-enterprise has to consider several factors. Major considerations are technological components, technical standards and the nature of architechure used. The architecture required for e-commerce, e-business and e-enterprise varies. Depending on the architecture, various factors change.

18.4.1 Technology Components

Several components for e-enterprise are required. They are :

- Client components
- Server components
- Application servers
- Application frameworks
- Enterprise application integration

18.4.2 Technology Standards

The standards are UML (Unified Modelling Language) for object modelling; PKI (Public Key Infrastructure), digital certificates, and digital signatures for security; WFMC (Workflow Management Coalition) and SWAP (Simple Workflow Access Control) for workflow; and XML (Extensible Markup Language) for messaging. There are following **five** consortia working for establishing the standards for e-enterprise architectures:

- Commercenet (www. commerce. net) started in April 1994.
- Rosetta net (www. rosettanet. org) founded in 1998.
- The Open Buying Initiative (www. openbuy. org) founded in October 1996.
- Open Financial Exchange (www. op x. net) founded in 1997.
- Internet Content and Exchange (ICE) started in late 1998.

A comparison of e-commerce, e-business and e-enterprise in respect of culture, people, business model, organisational model, application model, management processes, and technology is shown in Table 18.3.

Table 18.3. Building e-enterprises

	e-Commerce	*e-Business*	*e-Enterprise*
Culture	Chaos, **COM Mania, Reactive**, individualistic Control, **Hype**	Business **Model** Focus **Practice**, Process Creation, Cooperation, **Branding**	Enterprise Focus, **Iterative**, Process Integration, Empowerment, **Mission Critical**
People	**Technology & implementation Focus,** Hot Skills	**Process/Design Focus**, Core Competence	**Analysis/ROI Focus,** Strategy Orientation, Knowledge-based
Business Model	**Content Aggregation**, VC Funded, Pure Net Play, IPO	**Process Aggregation**, F 1000 Spin-Offs, Hybrid, Consolidation	**People Aggregation**, Inter-enterprise integration, Competition, Virtual Corporations

Organizational Model	Function Focus, Isolated, **Founder Driven,** In-Sourcing	Cross-organizational Focus, Federated, **e-Business Czar Driven**, **Out sourcing**	Extended Enterprise Focus, Collaborative, **CEO Driven, Partner-Sourcing**
Application Model	**B-to-C** Focused On-line Marketplaces for Hard Goods	**B-to-B** Procurement, B-to-B Communities, Soft Goods, B-to-C Auctioning	Mission critical **Inter-Enterprise** applications for unique business processes
Management Processes	**Situation Driven**, Project Orientation, Disconnected	**Process Driven**, Programme Orientation, Connected	**Method/Model/ROI Driven**, Enterprise Solution, Orientation Integrated & Extended
Technology	**Catalyst**, Client Driven **Unique**	**Driver** Server Driven, **Accepted**	**Enabler**, Network Driven & Distributed **Commodity**

18.4.3 Architecture

Net led to the transition from e-commerce to e-business to e-enterprise. This transformation affected all aspects of the business. Changes are significant in several aspects such as culture, management processes, technology, etc as given in Table 18.3. Implications of these aspects and its varying inpact on the type of enterprise are also indicated.

e-enterprise architecture aims at bringing technology and business together. Architecture has to have an integrative approach. Different issues and focus are given in Table 18.4.

Table 18.4. E-enterprises—issues and focus

Issues	*Focus*
e-Business models	Target market analysis, Financial modelling, inter-enterprise touch point, ownership, and resource analysis
e-Process models	Business entities, use-cases, inter-organizational processes, reusable business process, and business components
e-Application models	User-interface mockups, application specification and business rules
e-Application rules	A rules engine, application framework component software
e-Distribution/integration	Distributed object architecture, technology components, middleware, and Enterprise application Integration (EAI) software

contd.....

e-Data	Data management systems, data warehouses, legacy data, and ERP/MRP data repositories
e-Network	Network security solutions, encryption, connectivity tools, a Network Operating System (NOS) and system analysis and management tools.

18.4.4 Customers

All the technologies used are meant for developing business. This depends on customers. The strategy for getting and retaining customers is important. A five-step approach is given hereunder.

- Set strategy (make it easy to deal)
- Focus on the end customer
- Redesign customer-facing business processes
- Wire company for profit
  - — brochureware, i.e., giving the company and product information
  - — providing customer support and enabling interactions
  - — support electronic transactions
  - — personalizing interactions with customers
  - — fostering community
- Faster customer loyalty.

Critical success factors : Eight critical success factors have been identified for best practices. These are :

— Target the right customers

— Own the customer's total experience

— Streamline business processes that have impact on the customer

— Provide a 360-degree view of the customer relationship, i.e., providing one-stop shopping

— Let customer helps themselves

— Help customers do their jobs

— Deliver personalised service

— Faster community-creating common interests and reinforcing common values.

18.4.5. Virtual Office

A virtual office is an alternative work arrangement. Information technology replaces direct contact with co-workers and/or a physical office location. Following are the range of alternative work arrangements, which differs in the degree of presence outside a physical office :

— **Telecommuting :** Fixed offices but one day a week they work at home.

— **Tethered in office :** This arrangement has some mobility and expect workers to report to an office on a regular basis, but they do not have any fixed office and fixed location.

— **Hotelling :** Works have no fixed office space and can reserve a hotel 'room'. Here they can receive and make phone calls and link their laptop computers to the network. This is popular among professional service firms.

— **Home :** The workers have no office and work at home. The work is mostly performed on the computer and the telephone. Some companies have equipped such workers with furniture, computing and high-speed phone lines. This helps in work flexibility and reduce office space costs.

— **Fully mobile :** These workers do not have even home offices. They are on the road or at customer sites during the working day, e.g., representatives of pharmaceutical companies.

There are both benefits and problems with virtual offices. The benefits are cost-saving and worker convenience on a voluntary basis. There are several problems of virtual office. Some of them are :

- Corporate culture
- Loyalty
- Communication
- Access to people
- Managerial control
- Access to materials

As a corollary of virtual office, there can be virtual corporations. Virtual products or services are produced instantaneously and customized in response to demand. It is customer-driven and managed market research, product design, distribution, and internal organization. In order to succeed in virtual corporation, it has to have long-term business relationships with customers and suppliers. All employees, contractors, suppliers, and customers have to be full-time learners. The role of managers is to facilitate the smooth functioning of processes not just by giving orders. It also has the implication that a CEO can give up control but stay in command.

e-CEO. e-CEO has to operate in real time business where nothing can wait for tomorrow. As the e-world moves fast, the e-CEO has to be of a different breed. The differences between traditional CEO and e-CEO are given in Table 18.5 :

Table 18.5 E-CEOs are a Brand New Breed

Traditional CEO	e-CEO
encouraging	evangelizing
alert	paranoid
cordial	brutally frank
infotech semi-literate (at best)	infotech literate (at least)
clearly focused	intensely focused
fast moving	faster moving
hates ambiguity	likes ambiguity
suffers from technology confrontation anxiety	suffers from brandwidth separation anxiety
a paragaon of good judgement	a paragaon of good judgement
age : 57	age : 38
rich	really rich

e-CEO runs companies built on faith which means evangelizing. He has to have the ability as a real-time decision-maker. He has to spend a lot of time in recruiting since his company is growing fast and depends on brainpower. He is paranoid and proud.

18.5 DIGITAL STRATEGIES

The emergence of the Web has given the opportunity for developing a market-facing system. Technology-enabled enterprises are moving towards integration. An enterprise's connection to the outside world is its World Wide Web site. These are the new-breed enterprises.

The merging of technologies is making the marketplace to move into the cyberspace. Now, strategic planning is replaced with **digital strategy.** Internet is eliminating conventional intermediaries, but creating infomediaries. With the advent of the web, it is important to know which countries are already selling to whom, and which countries are sufficiently online to attract clients.

18.5.1 Network-based Business

Some of the businesses such as banks, telephone companies, airlines, and railroads use networks. The distinction is that these networks transport people, goods, or information for customers and do not do mere own distribution. There are three usage patterns :

- **Zero Concentration :** when customers use a network randomly.
- **Zone Concentration :** when customers concentrate their usage on some portion of the network
- **Lane Concentration :** customers use heavily the individual links in a network.

Organizations should handle the natural business unit and make profit-and-loss assessments at that level. In case it is zero concentration, then the company should use the entire network. The concentration usage patterns allow the company to have either the zone or the lane instead of the entire network.

Bill Gates' book *Business @ the speed of thought* gives 12 rules to make the digital information flow an intrinsic part of the company. They are :

For Knowledge Work

- Insist that communication flows through e-mail
- Study sales data online to share insights easily
- Shift knowledge workers into high-level thinking
- Use digital tools to create virtual teams
- Convert every paper process into a digital process.

For Business Operations

- Use digital tools to eliminate single-task jobs
- Create a digital feedback loop
- Use digital systems to route customer complaints immediately
- Use digital communications to redefine the boundaries.

For Commerce

- Transform every business process into just-in-time delivery
- Use digital delivery to eliminate the middle man
- Use digital tools to help customers solve problems for themselves.

While Gates gives twelve rules, Brown tries to find success factors through the examples of successful companies. This is described next.

18.5.2 Nine Ways

e-enterprises have been classified into nine groups. They are the patterns for success in dot.coms. They are :

1. Selling to business, direct-sales practices.
2. Corporate intranet.
3. Streamlining the supply chain.
4. Recruiting online.
5. Winning and keeping web surfers.
6. Direct marketing.
7. Selling to consumers
8. Customer service
9. Coordinating finance

The difference between the Web success and Web failure is how people shift through details and fine-tune plans.

Review Questions

1. What are e-enterprises ? Discuss the nature of work these enterprises are expected to perform.
2. Explain five basic elements of evolving information technology for a homogeneous front-office.
3. Outline the differences between global technologies and applications of the PC era to the web-based era.
4. What is the difference between information system and information technology. Distinguish between data, informaticn and knowledge.
5. Explain the four layers inside the enterprise.
6. Discuss the technology components for building e-enterprise.
7. Explain the issues and focuses of e-enterprises.
8. Define virtual office and the range of alternative work arrangements.
9. What is digital strategy ? Explain in detail network-based business.
10. How are e-enterprises classified ? Discuss in brief.

19

Information Security, Ethics, and Society

19.1 INTRODUCTION

Information is a critical strategic resource for organisations. Therefore, information systems must be closely guarded and protected from accidents, intentional mischief, and natural disasters. For control of the quality and performance of information systems in the business unit, computer hardware, software, networks, and data need to be protected by built-in controls to ensure their quality and security. Hence, computer security can be defined as a set of policies, procedures, tools, and techniques, to protect computer assets from accidental, intentional or natural disasters. It covers all components of an organisation's environment. It is a complex and pervasive problem that often stumps many organisations, which struggle to balance proper security against the cost and inconvenience of providing it. It cannot be achieved through automation or sophisticated equipment alone, it also requires the active participation of employees with common sense, good judgement, and high moral values, because security is ultimately the responsibility of an individual using the computer. Therefore, it is not surprising that organisations that promote creativity, innovation, trust, and high ethical standards appear to be more successful in enforcing computer security than organisations with stifling cultures.

Effective controls provide information system security, i.e., accuracy, integrity, and safety of information system activities and resources. Controls can also minimize errors, fraud, and destruction in the internetworked information systems that interconnect today's end users and organisations. Effective controls also provide *quality assurance* for information systems.

Ethical questions are involved in many strategic decisions such as investment in human resources, modernisation, product development and service, marketing, environmental decisions. Often strategic issues are threats/opportunities that may significantly affect the firm's performance and are characterized by their novelty, complexity, and speed. Such threats/opportunities may involve a large ethical component. Since we are in the midst of an *information revolution*, it is important to understand the ethical dimensions of working in business and using information technology. For example, whether employees' work activities and electronic mail are monitored electronically or employees are permitted to use their work computers for private business/personal use or employees' personal records or workstation files are accessible electronically. These are the few examples of the types of decisions one will have to make that have a controversial ethical dimensions.

19.2 CHALLENGES OF SECURING COMPUTER SYSTEMS

The challenges of securing computer systems in an organisation are as given below:

1. *Intentional breach by employees*. A primary source of security breach is the intentional/unintentional actions of employees.

2. *Increased system complexity*. Open, integrated, mission-critical, and real time systems are highly complex and difficult to monitor and manage.

3. *System components choices are many*. The number of hardware, software, and network configurations has increased tremendously.

4. *Increased network vulnerability*. Networks have become increasingly complex and difficult to manage.

5. *Sophisticated hackers/crackers/cyberpunks/phone freaks*. They are the people who violate computer security. They are better educated and more technically skilled, making it easier for them to break into computer systems.

6. *Complacent top management*. Top managers often feel that security violations happen at other organisations, not at theirs.

19.3 TYPES OF COMPUTER SECURITY BREACHES

19.3.1 Accidental/Unintentional Errors

Accidents in the workplace can cause security breaches. At times the cost of unintentional damage exceeds the cost of computer crime. Accidental security violations can be reduced by education and training, and by establishing and communicating security policies and procedures. Sometimes hardware components accidentally fail — memory, keyboards, terminal emulators, LAN cards, network cabling, network servers, routers or bridges in networks, WANs, mainframe front-end processors, and a multitude of peripherals and accessories — causing a security breach. Cables, modems, fax machines, and cellular phones are particularly prone to failure. Software errors — in input, processing, output, or storage — can also cause security violations.

19.3.2 Intentional Errors

Intentional errors may take the form of illicit entry to a system, access to valuable property, corporate data, stealing passwords, in order to snoop around, reading E-mail, or destroying important files. They may go undetected for days, weeks, or even months, particularly if the violator has intimate knowledge of the workings and the critical elements of a system.

Cracking passwords. Cracking, or decoding, passwords which are the Achilles' heels of computer security, is one of the most common security violations, since hackers (who has the knowledge to illegally break into a computer system/facility, although he/she does not cause any harm to the system) and crackers (a computer thief who breaks into a system with the intent of stealing passwords, files, and programs, either for fun or for profit) can easily guess passwords or capture them as they travel over the network. Once the password is cracked, the perpetrator has full control of the system and can set up accounts, use the system to uncover more passwords, and gain access to vital information, all without even being detected.

Breaking into computer hardware. Modems, fax machines, and cellular phones are particularly vulnerable to this type of damage. Experts recommend that one should not discuss proprietory information over fax/cellular phones/modems, etc. and strongly urge callers to use code words when discussing confidential matters.

Software virus. There are two primary sources of intentional software security breaches: initial and 'sniffer' programs. The greatest threat to software is *computer virus*, a program that causes systems to behave in unexpected and undesirable manner. Some signs of a computer virus include unexplainable loss of free memory, unusually long time for program loading/execution, changes in file or program size, print routines' that stop working, computers 'freezing up', strange beeps/messages, computer reboots in the middle of a process, and corrupted files. When the virus program is executed, it makes copies of itself and spreads from one system/application to another, either through networks or through shared diskettes. Because of this reason, many firms strongly discourage the sharing of diskettes between systems. Use of 'sniffer' programs explore the system to collect data about network users, their passwords, their access codes, and the nature of their work. These programs, very useful for network administrators, can be dangerous in the hands of a hacker, who stealthily monitors data transmissions.

19.3.3 Natural Disasters

Natural disasters are hurricanes, earthquakes, tornadoes, and floods. These can be so devastating that firms, even a entire city, take a long time to recover from them. Some less damaging natural disasters are those affecting power supplies, cooling systems, communication networks, alarm systems, lightning protectors, building structures, and other facilities that support computer systems. Power outages are another common cause of computer downtime and lost productivity. Inspite of the alarming statistics about disasters and their adverse effect on a business, very few firms consider disaster avoidance and disaster recovery in their risk management plans.

19.4 SECURITY CONTROLS

Three major types of controls must be developed to ensure the quality and security of information systems — Information system controls, procedural controls, and facility controls. These are explained.

19.4.1 Information System Controls

These are the methods and devices that attempt to ensure the accuracy, validity, and propriety of information system activities. Controls must be developed to ensure proper data entry, processing techniques, storage methods, and information output.

Input controls. Input controls are needed for the proper entry of data into a computer system. The phrase *garbage in, garbage out* (GIGO) means that entry of inaccurate data/late update/unreadable data, etc. will give the undesirable results. A data entry program can check for invalid codes, data fields, and transactions. Also, the computer can be programmed to conduct 'reasonableness checks' to determine if input data exceed certain specified limits or are out of sequence. This includes the calculation and monitoring of selected *control totals.* Batch totals (the sum of a specific item of data within a batch of transactions) and hash totals (sum of data fields that are added together for control comparisons only) are other forms of control totals. For example, employee number could be added to produce a control total in the input preparation of payroll documents.

Processing controls. Processing controls can include *hardware* and *software controls*. Examples of hardware checks include (a) malfunction detection circuitry, (b) redundant components. and (c) special purpose microprocessors and associated circuitry. Similarly, some software controls ensure that the right data are being processed. Another major software controls is the establishment of *checkpoints* during the processing of a program. *Checkpoints* are intermediate points within a program being processed where intermediate totals, listings, or 'dumps' of data are written on magnetic tape/disk/listed on a printer. These minimise the effect of processing errors/failures. They also help build an *audit trail,* which allows transactions being processed to be traced all of the steps of their processing.

Output controls. Output controls are developed to ensure that information products are correct and complete, and are available to authorized users in a timely manner.

Storage controls (data security). First, control responsibilities for files of computer programs and organisational databases may be assigned to data centre specialists and database administrators for maintaining and controlling access to the program libraries and databases of the organisation. Second, many databases and files are protected from authorized/accidential use by security programs that require proper identification before they can be used. Account codes, passwords, and other security codes are frequently used to allow access to authorized users only. Typically, a *multilevel password* system is used. Many firms also use backup files, which are duplicate files of data/programs. Master files from several recent periods of processing (known as *child, parent, grandparent files* , etc.) may be kept for backup purposes.

19.4.2 Facility Controls

Facility controls are the methods that protect an organisation's computing and network facilities and their contents from loss/destruction. Computer networks and computer centres are subject to such hazards as accidents, natural disasters, sabotage, vandalism, unauthorised use, industrial espionage, destruction, and theft of resources. Therefore, various safeguards and control procedures are necessary to protect the hardware, software, network, and vital data resources of an organisation. This is especially vital as more and more organisations engage in electronic commerce on the Internet. Table 19.1 outlines the security requirements that organisations must establish to provide secure electronic commerce using the Internet, intranet and extranets.

Table 19.1 Security requirements for electronic commerce

Privacy:	Ability to control who sees (or cannot see) information and under what terms.
Authenticity:	Ability to know the identities of communicating partners.
Integrity:	Assurance that stored/transmitted information is unaltered.
Reliability:	Assurance that systems will be available when needed and will perform consistently at an acceptable level of quality.
Blocking:	Ability to block unwanted information/intrusions.

Network security. Security of a network may be provided by specialised system software packages known as *system security monitors.* These are the programs that monitor the use of computer systems and networks and protect them from unauthorized use, fraud, and destruction. Such programs provide the security measures needed to allow only authorised users to access the networks. Security monitors also control the use of hardware, software, and data resources of a computer system.

Encryption. Encryption of data has become important to protect data and other computer network resources especially on the Internet, intranets and extranets. It involves using special mathematical algorithms, or keys, to transform digital data into a scrambled code before they are transmitted, and to decode the data when they are received. The most widely used encryption method uses a pair of public and private keys unique to an individual.

Fire walls. Another important method for control and security on the Internet and other networks is the use of *fire wall* computers and software. It is a 'gatekeeper' computer system protecting the firm's networking system from intrusion by serving as a filter and safe transfer point for access to and from the Internet and other networks. It screens all network traffic for proper passwords/other security codes. Fire walls can deter, but not completely prevent, unauthorised access (hacking) into computer networks.

Physical protection controls. The organisation's computer and network resources requires many types of physical protection controls such as identification badges, electronic door locks, burglar alarms, security police, closed-circuit TV, and other detection systems.

Biometric controls. These security measures provided by computer devices measure physical traits that make each individual unique. This includes voice verification, fingerprints, hand geometry, signature dynamics, keystroke analysis, retina scanning, face recognition and genetic pattern analysis. These devices use special-purpose sensors to measure and digitize a biometric profile of an individual's fingerprints, voice or other physical trait. The digitized signal is processed and compared to a previously processed profile of the individual stored on magnetic field. If the profiles match, the individual is allowed entry into a computer facility or given access to information system resources.

Computer-failure controls. Computer systems fail for several reasons–power failure, electronic circuit malfunctions, telecom network problems, hidden programming errors, computer viruses, computer operator errors, and electronic vandalism.

19.4.3 Procedural Controls

Procedural controls are methods that specify how an organisation's computer and network resources should be operated for maximum security. Some of the procedural controls are:

- Standard procedures and documentation.
- Authorization requirements.
- Disaster recovery.
- Controls for end user computing.

19.5 AUDITING INFORMATION SYSTEMS

There are two basic approaches for auditing information systems:

- Auditing around the computer system
- Auditing through the computer system.

19.5.1 Auditing around Computer System

This approach involves verifying the accuracy and propriety of the input of data and output produced without evaluating the software that processed the data. Since the process does not test the accuracy and integrity of the software used, it is recommended only as a supplement to other auditing methods.

19.5.2 Auditing through Computer System

This approach involves verifying the accuracy and integrity of the software that processes the data, as well as the input of data and output produced by the computer systems and networks. It requires a knowledge of computer system and network operations and software development. Some firms employ special EDP auditors for this assignment. They may use special test data to test processing accuracy and the control procedures built into the software. Another important objective of such auditing procedures is to test the integrity of an application's *audit trail*.

An initial can be defined as the presence of documentation that allows a transaction to be traced through all stages of its information processing. This process starts with a transaction's appearance on a source document and may end with its transformation into information on a final output document/report. In computer-based information systems, auditors must know how to search electronically through magnetic disk and tap files of past-activity to follow the audit trail of most business systems. Such an audit trail helps auditors check for errors or fraud, and helps IS security specialists trace and evaluate the trail of hacker attacks on computer networks.

19.6 CYBER LAWS AND IT ACT 2000

In order to facilitate e-commerce and have legal recognition of electronic records and digital signatures, Information Technology Act came into existence in August 2000 and known as Information Technology Act, 2000. Cyber laws are contained in this Act. The Act aims to provide (a) legal infrastructure for e-commerce in India and would have a major impact for e-businesses and the new economy in India, and (b) legal framework under which legal sanctity is accorded to all electronic records and other activities carried out by electronic means. The Act states that unless otherwise agreed, an acceptance of contract may be expressed by electronic means of communication and the same shall have legal validity and enforceability.

19.6.1 Objectives of the Act

The objectives of the Act are :

- To grant legal recognition for transactions carried out by means of electronic data interchange and other means of electronic communication commonly referred to as 'electronic commerce' in place of paper-based methods of communication.
- To give legal recognition to digital signature for authentication of any information or matter which requires authentication under any law.
- To facilitate electronic filing of documents with Government departments.
- To facilitate electronic storage of data.
- To facilitate and give legal sanction to electronic fund transfers between banks and financial institutions.
- To give legal recognition for keeping books of account by bankers in electronic form.
- To amend the Indian Penal Code, the Indian Evidence Act, 1872, the Bankers' Book Evidence Act, 1891 and the Reserve Bank of India Act, 1934.

The Act is for the whole of India and, unless otherwise provided in the Act, it also applies to any offence or contravention thereunder committed outside India by any person.

The Act initial to the following:

- A negotiable instrument as defined in Section 13 of the Negotiable Instruments Act, 1881.
- A power of attorney as defined in Section 1A of the Powers-of-Attorney Act, 1882.
- A trust as defined in Section 3 of the Indian Trusts Act, 1882.
- A will as defined in Section (h) of Section 2 of the Indian Succession Act, 1925, including any other testamentary disposition by whatever name called.
- Any contract for the sale or conveyance of immovable property or any interest in such property.
- Any such class of documents or transactions as may be notified by the Central Government in the official Gazette.

The Act consists of 94 sections spread over 13 chapters and four schedules to the Act. The Schedules to the Act contain related amendments made in other acts as outlined in the objectives of the Act. The chapters of the Act are :

1. Scope of the act and definitions. (Sections 1 and 2)
2. Authentication of electronic records using digital signatures. (Section 3)

3. Electronic governance. (Sections 4 – 10)
4. Attribution, receipt and dispatch of electronic records. (Sections 11-13)
5. Secure electronic records and secure digital signatures. (Sections 14-16)
6. Regulation of certifying authorities. (Sections 17-34)
7. Digital signature certification. (Sections 35-40)
8. Duties of subscribers. (Sections 41-42)
9. Penalties and adjudication. (Sections 43-47)
10. Cyber regulations appellate tribunal. (Sections 48-64)
11. Offences. (Sections 65-78)
12. Network service providers not to be liable in certain cases. (Section 79)
13. Miscellaneous. (Sections 87-94)

19.7 ETHICAL FOUNDATIONS

Persons hold *ethical values* that guide them in ethical decision making. For example, four basic ethical philosophies are : egoism, natural law, utilitarianism, and respect for persons. These alternative ethical philosophies are :

Egoism. What is best for a given individual is right.

Natural law. Humans should promote their own health and life, propagate, pursue knowledge of the world and God, pursue close relationships with other people, and submit to legitimate authority.

Utilitarianism. Those actions are right that produce the greatest good for the greatest number of people.

Respect for persons. People should be treated as an end and not as a means to an end; and actions are right if everyone adopts the moral rule presupposed by the action.

Ethical values are more specific ethical concepts that people hold, and are heavily influenced by one's cultural background. There are many *ethical models* of how humans apply their chosen ethical philosophies to the decisions and choices they have to make daily in work and other areas of their lives. For example, one theory focuses on people's decision-making processes and stresses how various factors of our perceptions affect our ethical decision-making process. Another example is *a behavioural stage theory*, which says that people go through several stages of moral evolution before they settle on one level of ethical reasoning. In this model, if one reaches the final stage of moral evolution, one's actions are guided by self-chosen ethical principles, not by fear, guilt, social pressure, and so on.

19.8 BUSINESS ETHICS

Business ethics can be sub-divided into two separate areas. The first concerns the illegal, unethical, or questionable practices of managers/organisations, their causes, and their possible remedies. The second is concerned with the numerous ethical questions that managers must confront as part of their daily business decision making. The issues of employee privacy, security of the firm's records, and workplace safety are highlighted because they have been major areas of ethical controversy in information technology. Several important alternatives based on theories of corporate social responsibility can be used :

- *The stockholder theory* holds that managers are agents of the stockholders, and their only ethical responsibility is to increase the profits of the business without violating the law or engaging in fraudulent practices.
- *The social contract theory* states that organisations have ethical responsibilities to all members of society, which allow them to exist based on a social contract. The first

condition of the contract requires organisations to enhance the economic satisfaction of consumers and employees. They must do that without polluting the environment or depleting natural resources, misusing political power, or subjecting their employees to dehumanizing working conditions. The second condition requires organisations to avoid fraudulent practices, show respect for their employees as human beings, and avoid practices that systematically worsen the position of any group in society.

- *The stakeholder theory* maintains that managers have an ethical responsibility to manage a firm for the benefit of all of its stakeholders, which are all individuals and groups that have a stake in or claim on a company. This usually includes the organisation's stockholders, employees, customers, suppliers, and the local community. Sometimes the term is broadened to include all groups who can affect or be affected by the organisation, such as competitors, government agencies, special interest groups, and the media.

19.9 ETHICAL AND SOCIETAL DIMENSIONS OF INFORMATION TECHNOLOGY

It emphasizes that the use of information technology in business has major impacts on society, and thus raises serious ethical considerations in areas such as privacy, crime, health, working conditions, individuality, employment, and the search for societal solutions through IT. However, one should realize that information technology can have a beneficial effect as well as a negative effect in each of these areas. For example, computerizing a production process may have the adverse effect of eliminating jobs, and the beneficial effect of improving the working conditions and job satisfaction of employees that remain, while producing products of higher quality at less cost. As a managerial end user, one should involve managing his or her work activities and those of others to try to minimize the negative effects of IT and maximize its beneficial effects. It would represent an ethically responsible use of information technology. Table 19.2 lists four ethical principles that can serve as guidelines in the implementation of any form of technology.

Table 19.2 Ethical Principles

Proportionality. The good achieved by the technology must outweigh the harm or risk. Moreover, there must be no alternative that achieves the same or comparable benefits with less harm or risk.

Informed Consent. Those affected by the technology should understand and accept the risks.

Justice. The benefits and burdens of the technology should be distributed fairly. Those who benefit should bear their fair share of the risks, and those who do not benefit should not suffer a significant increase in risk.

Minimized Risk. Even if judged acceptable by the other three guidelines, the technology must be implemented so as to avoid all unnecessary risk.

Mason summarizes these four ethical issues with the acronym PAPA - privacy, accuracy, property, and accessibility.

Privacy. What information about one's self or one's associations must a person reveal to others, under what conditions, and with what safeguards? What things can people keep to themselves and not be forced to reveal to others ?

Accuracy. Who is responsible for the authenticity, fidelity, and accuracy of information? Similarly, who is to be held accountable for errors in information and how is the injured party to be made whole ?

Property. Who owns information ? What are the just and fair prices for its exchange ?

Who owns the channels, especially the airways, through which information is transmitted ? How should access to this scarce resource be allocated?

Accessibility. What information does a person or an organisation have a right or a privilege to obtain, under what conditions, and with what safeguards ?

In answering these questions, Mason proposes the development of a new social contract, where information technology will help ensure everyone's right to fulfill his or her human potential. Mason's ideas could serve as the basis for many proposals being debated concerning privacy, censorship, and accessibility of the Internet. In this new social contract, information systems should be designed to ensure accuracy and not invade a person's privacy. Channels of information should be protected and information made accessible to avoid information illiteracy or deprivation. Finally, information systems should be designed to protect an individual's intellectual capital from unauthorized exposure, loss, or damage. Developing, protecting, and enforcing this social contract then become the responsibility of end users, managers, and IS professionals.

19.10 COMPUTER CRIMES

Computer crime is the threat caused by the criminal or irresponsible actions of computer users who are taking advantage of the widespread use of computer networks in the society. It thus presents a major challenge to the ethical use of IT. Computer crime poses serious threats to the integrity, safety, and quality of most business information systems, and thus makes the development of effective security methods a top priority.

19.10.1 Types of Computer Crimes

The mode and type of misuse of computer systems are given in Table 19.3.

Table 19.3 Types of Computer Crimes

Mode	*Type of Misuse*
External	
1. Visual spying	Observing of keystrokes or screens
2. Misrepresentation	Deceiving operators and users
3. Physical scavenging	Dumpster-diving for printout
Hardware misuse	
4. Logical scavenging	Examining discarded/stolen media
5. Eavesdropping	Intercepting electronic or other data
6. Interference	Jamming, electronic or otherwise
7. Physical attack	Damaging/modifying equipment, power
8. Physical removal	Removing equipment and storage media
Masquerading	
9. Impersonation	Using false identities of external to computer systems
10. Piggybacking attacks	Usurping communication lines, workstations
11. Spoofing attacks	Using playback, creating bogus nodes and systems
12. Network weaving	Masking physical whereabouts or routing
Pest programs	Setting up opportunities for further misuse
13. Trojan horse attacks	Implanting malicious code, sending letter bombs
14. Logic bombs	Setting time or event bombs (a form of Trojan horse)
15. Malevolent worms	Acquiring distributed resources
16. Virus attacks	Attaching to programs and replicating

contd......

Bypasses	Avoiding authentication and authority
17. Trapdoor attacks	Utilizing existing flaws
18. Authorization attacks	Password cracking, hacking tokens
Active misuse	Writing, using with apparent authorization
19. Basic active misuse	Creating, modifying, using, denying service, entering false or misleading data
20. Incremental attacks	Using salami attacks
21. Denials of service	Perpetrating saturation attacks
Passive misuse	Reading, with apparent authorization
22. Browsing	Making random or selective searches
23. Inference, aggregation	Exploiting database inferences and traffic analysis
24. Covert channels	Exploiting covert channels or other data leakage
Inactive misuse	Willfully failing to perform expected duties, or committing errors of omission
Indirect misuse	Preparing for subsequent misuses, as in offline pre-encryptive matching, factoring large numbers to obtain private keys, autodialer scanning

Examples of computer crime are :

- Crime on the Internet
- Money theft
- Service theft
- Software theft
- Data alteration/theft
- Malicious access
- Computer viruses

19.11 HEALTH AND ERGONOMICS

The use of information technology in the workplace raises a variety of health issues. Heavy use of computers is reportedly causing health problems like job stress, damaged arm and neck muscles, eye strain, radiation exposure, and even death by computer-caused accidents. For example, computer monitoring is blamed as a major cause of computer-related job stress. Workers, unions, and government officials criticize computer monitoring as putting so much stress on employees that it leads to health problems.

People who sit at PC workstations or visual display terminals (VDTs) in fast-paced, repetitive keystroke jobs can suffer a variety of health problems known collectively as *cumulative trauma disorders* (CTDs). Their fingers, wrists, arms, necks, and backs may become so weak and painful that they cannot work. Many times strained muscles, back pain, and nerve damage may result. In particular, some computer workers may suffer from *carpal tunnel syndrome*, a painful, crippling ailment of the hand and wrist that typically requires surgery to cure.

Prolonged viewing of video displays causes eye strain and other health problems in employees who must do this all day. Radiation caused by the cathode ray tubes (CRTs) that produce most video displays is another health concern. CRTs produce an electromagnetic field that may cause harmful radiation of employees who work too close for too long in front of video monitors.

Solutions to some of these health problems are based on the science of ergonomics, sometimes called *human factors engineering*. The goal of ergonomics is to design healthy work environments that are safe, comfortable, and pleasant for people to work in, thus increasing employees morale and productivity. Ergonomics stresses the healthy design of the workplace, workstations, computers and other machines, and even software packages. Other health issues may require ergonomic solutions emphasizing job design, rather than workplace design. For example, this may require policies providing for work breaks from heavy VDT use every few hours. Ergonomic job design can also provide more variety in job tasks for those who spend most of their workday at computer workstations.

19.12 SOCIETAL SOLUTIONS

Information technology can have many beneficial effects on society. One can use information technology to solve human and social problems through societal solutions such as medical diagnosis, computer-assisted instruction, governmental program planning, environmental quality control, and law enforcement. For example, computers can help diagnoses an illness, prescribe necessary treatment, and monitor the progress of hospital patients. Computer-assisted instruction (CAI) allows a computer to serve as tutor, since it uses conversational computing to tailor instruction to the needs of a particular student. This is a tremendous benefit to students, especially those with learning disabilities.

Information technology can be used for crime control through various law enforcement applications. For example, computerized alarm systems allow police to identify and respond quickly to evidences of criminal activity. Computers have been used to monitor the level of pollution in the air and in bodies of water, to detect the sources of pollution, and to issue early warnings when dangerous levels are reached. Computers are also used for the program planning of many government agencies in such areas as urban planning, population density and land use studies, highway planning, and urban transit studies. Computers are being used in job placement systems to help match unemployed persons with available jobs. These and other applications illustrate that information technology can be used to help solve the problems of society.

Review Questions

1. Explain challenges of securing computer systems in an organisation.
2. What are different types of computer security breaches? Discuss *any one* of them in detail.
3. Discuss the role of hackers and crackers.
4. Why are information system controls necessary ? Explain input controls in detail.
5. Discuss the security requirements an organisation must establish to provide secure electronic commerce using the internet, intranet and extranets.
6. Why is encryption of data became important ? Explain the role of public and private keys.
7. Write in brief about (a) fire walls, and (b) biometric controls.
8. Explain *any one* approach for auditing information system. Define the term 'audit trail'.
9. What are the aims of IT Act, 2000? Explain the objectives of the Act.
10. Discuss *four* basic ethical philosophies. Explain ethical values.
11. 'There are *three* important theories of corporate social responsibility'. Name them and explain each one of them in brief.
12. Name and brief *four* ethical principles for implementation of any form of technology.
13. What do you understand by computer crime ? Discuss various modes and types of computer crimes.
14. 'People working for long on computers suffer cumulative trauma disorders'. Comment on the statement and suggest prevention of such hazards.
15. What are the impacts of information technology on the society ?

Appendix A

Structured Analysis and Its Tools

Structured analysis is a set of techniques and graphical tools that allow the systems analyst to develop a new kind of system specifications that are easily understandable to the user. It specifies the following :

1. Use graphics wherever possible to help communicate better with the user.
2. Differentiate between logical and physical systems.
3. Build a logical system model to familiarise the user with system characteristics and interrelationships before implementation.

Structured analysis essentially illustrates the use of following tools :

1. Context diagram
2. Data flow diagram (DFD)
3. Data dictionary
4. Entity relationship diagram
5. Decision tree
6. Decision table
7. Structured English
8. Flowchart
9. Layout chart.

Context Diagram

A context diagram provides a broad, abstract, top-down view of a system by identifying the major inputs, outputs, processes and entities in the system. An entity is a person, place, thing, event, or concept about which data are gathered. A context diagram, which illustrates the overall system, can be splitted into subsystems, each of which, in turn, is shown using a data flow diagram.

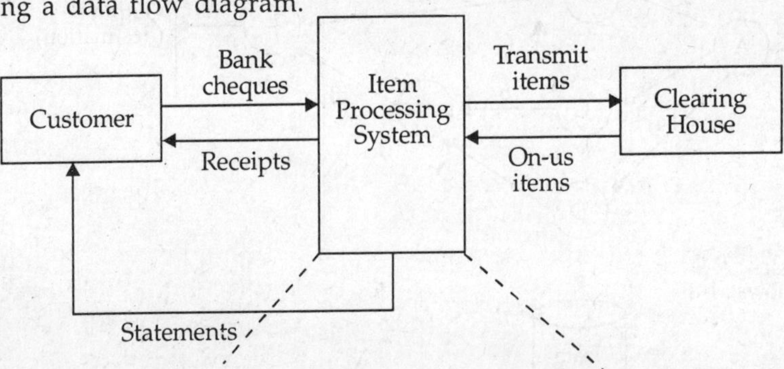

Fig. A1 Context Diagram for a Bank

Figure A1 shows a context diagram for a bank processing system with two entities (shown in rectangular boxes) : customers with a check clearinghouse. The input and output flow are indicated as arrows; for example, bank cheques are inputs to the processing system and transmit items are outputs. Similarly, on-us items (bank cheques, drafts, etc. that have been drawn on the sending bank) are inputs from the clearing house to the processing system, whereas receipts are outputs from the processing system to the customer. The context diagram summarises all the subprocesses in the bank processing system and depicts them as a single process. This is always the case in a context diagram.

Data Flow Diagram (DFD)

The DFD was first developed by Lary Constantine as a way of expressing system requirements in a graphical form; this led to a modular design. A DFD, also known as a 'bubble chart' consists of a series of bubbles joined by lines. The bubbles represent data transformations and the lines represent data flows in the system.

In the DFD, there are four symbols (Fig. A2) : (*a*) A *square* defines a *source* (coriginator) or *destination* of system data; (*b*) An *arrow* identifies *data flow* — data in motion. It is a pipeline through which information flows; (*c*) A *circle* or a 'bubble' represents a *process* that transforms incoming data flow(s) into outgoing data flow(s); and (*d*) An *open rectangle* is a data store — data at rest, or a temporary repository of data.

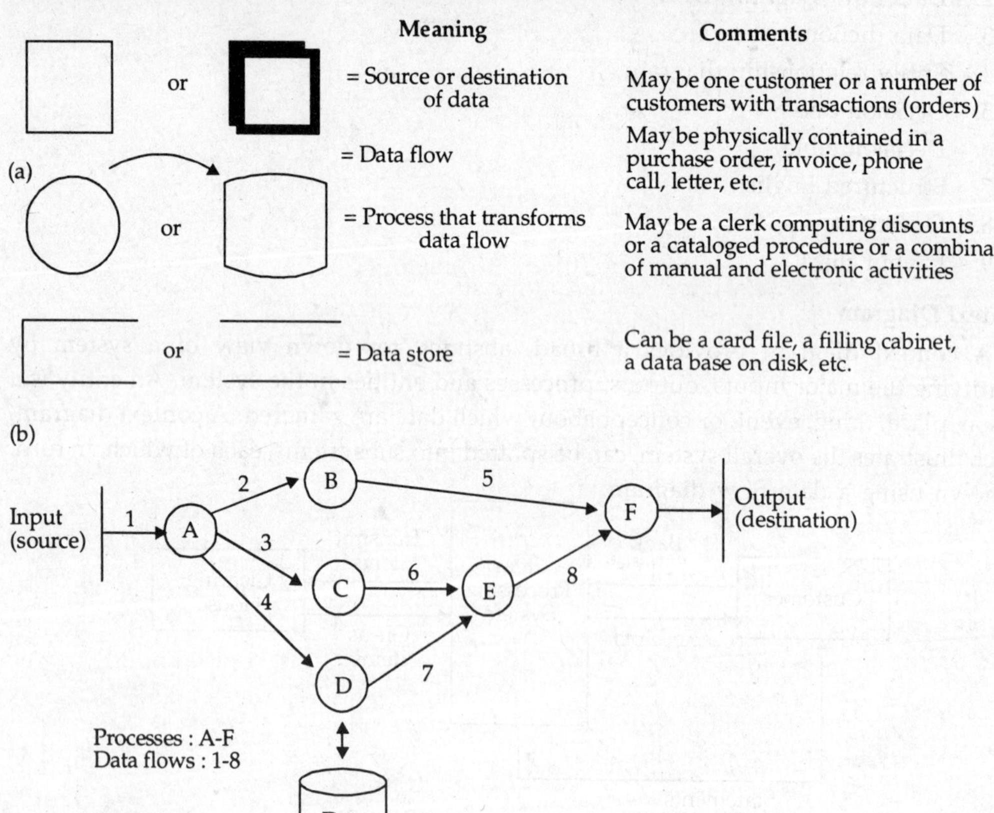

Fig. A2 Data Flow Diagram : (a) Basic Symbols, and (b) General Format

A DFD describes *what* data flow (logical) rather than how they are processed. Therefore, it does not depend on hardware, software, data structure or file organisation. The key question is what major transformations must occur for input to be correctly transformed into output ?

Several thumb rules are used in drawing DFDs : (*a*) Processes should be named and numbered for easy reference. Each name should be representative of the process; (*b*) The direction of flow is from top to bottom and from left to right. Data traditionally flow from the source (upper left corner) to the destination (lower right corner), although they may flow back to a source. An alternative way is to repeat the source symbol as a destination. Since it is used more than once in the DFD, it is marked with a short diagonal in the lower right corner (Fig. A3); (*c*) When a process is exploded into lower-level details, they are numbered; and (*d*) Names of data stores, sources, and destinations are written in capital letters. Process and data flow names have the first letter to each word capitalised.

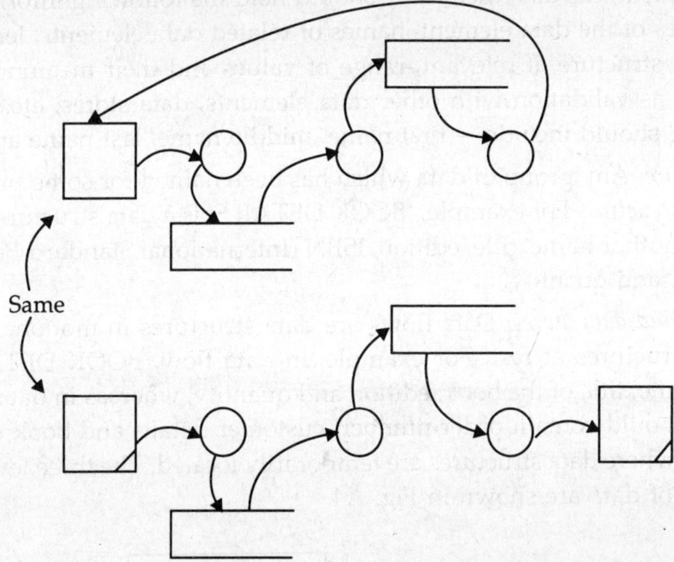

Fig. A3 Alternative Use of Source/Destination Symbols

How detailed should a DFD be ? The DFD is designed to aid communication. If it contains dozens of processes and data stores, it gets too unwieldy. The thumb rule is to explode the DFD to a functional level, so that the next sublevel does not exceed 10 processes. Beyond that, it is best to take each function separately and expand it to show the explosion of the single process.

A DFD typically shows the minimum contents of data stores. Each data store should contain all data elements that flow in and out. The DFD methodology is quite effective, especially when the required design is unclear, and the user and the analyst need a notational language for communication. The DFD is easy to understand after a brief orientation. The main problem, however, is the large number of iterations that often are required to arrive at the most accurate and complete solution.

Data Dictionary

A *data dictionary* is a structured repository of data about data. It is a set of rigorous definitions of all DFD data elements and data structures.

A data dictionary has many advantages. The most obvious is documentation; it is a valuable reference in any organisation. Another advantage is improving analyst/user communication by establishing consistent definitions of various elements, terms, and procedures. During implementation, it serves as a common base against which programmers who are working on the system compare their data descriptions. Also, control information maintained for each data element is cross-referenced in the data dictionary. For example, programs that use a given data element are cross-referenced in a data dictionary, which makes it easy to identify them and make any necessary changes. Finally, a data dictionary is an important step in building a data base. Most data base management systems have a data dictionary as a standard feature.

If words are chosen that represent the general thinking of common vocabulary, there are three classes of items to be defined :

1. *Data elements.* The smallest unit of data that provides for no further decomposition. For each data element, the data dictionary should hold the following information: name, description, aliases of the data element, names of related data elements, length and data type, codification structure, if relevant, range of values and their meaning, and editing information such as validation with other data elements, data stores, etc. For example, AUTHOR NAME should include — first name, middle name, last name and alias.

2. *Data structure.* Any group of data which has been named for some purpose will be defined as a *data structure.* For example, 'BOOK DETAILS' is a data structure consisting of data elements — author name, title, edition, ISBN (International Standard Book Number), publisher's name, and quantity.

3. *Data flows and data stores.* Data flows are data structures in motion, whereas data stores are data structures at rest. For example, in data flow, BOOK DETAILS should contain author name, title of the book, edition and quantity, whereas in data store, BOOK STORE-ORDER should contain order number, customer details and book detail. A data store is a location where data structures are temporarily located. The three levels that make up the hierarchy of data are shown in Fig. A4.

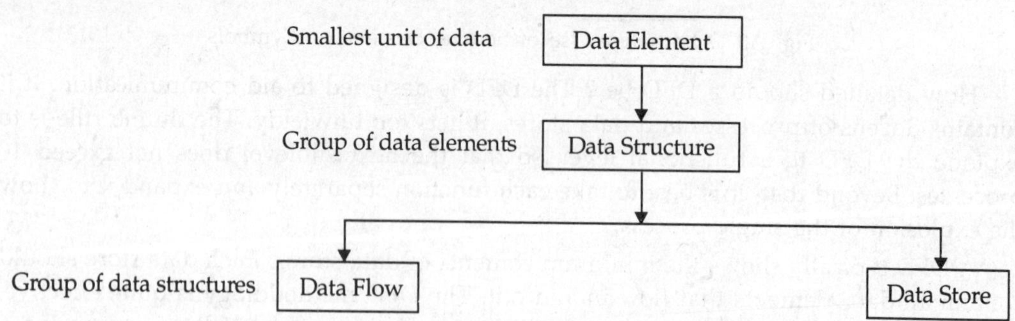

Fig. A4 Logical Data Description Hierarchy

In constructing a data dictionary, the systems analyst should consider the following points :

1. Each unique data flow in the DFD must have one data dictionary entry. There is also a data dictionary entry for each data store and process.
2. Definitions must be readily accessible by name.

3. There should be no redundancy or unnecessary definitions in the data definition. It must be simple to make updates.
4. The procedure for writing definitions should be straightforward but specific.

In essence, a data dictionary is an integral component of the structured specification. Without a data dictionary, the DFD lacks rigor, and without the DFD, the data dictionary is of no use.

Entity-relationship Diagram

An entity is something where one stores data. In a system, there may be several entity types such as customer, orders, products, employees, etc. The relationship between entity types is expressed in E-R diagrams. This diagram shows the relationship and certain properties of the relationship, especially the number of instances of one entity associated with an instance of the other entity. Relationships between entities are qualified by their cardinality. For example, seating arrangement in an examination hall there can be only one student per seat and only one seat per student. Also, there may be many students and the student entities are related by a one-to-many relationship. Relationships can be one-to-one, one-to-many, many-to-many, etc. The set of symbols used in E-R diagrams is shown in Fig. A5. A sample E-R diagram is shown in Fig. A6.

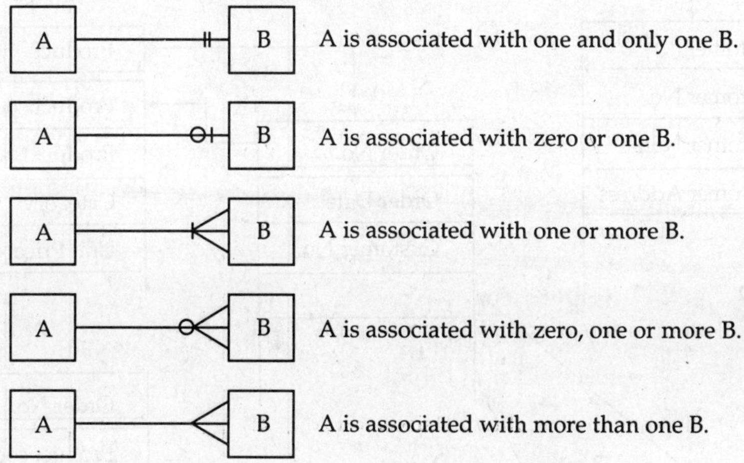

Fig. A5 Symbols Used in E-R Diagrams

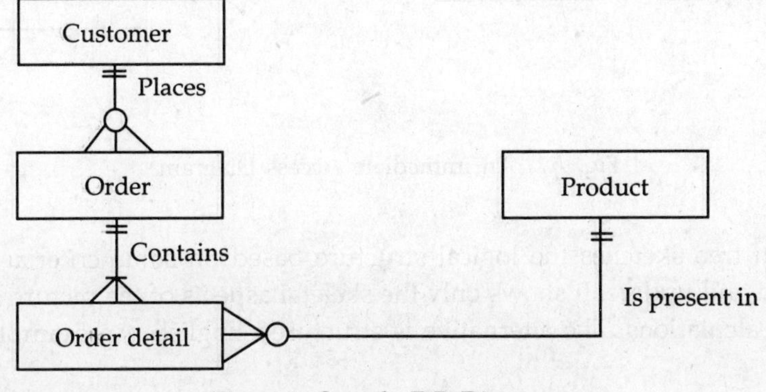

Fig. A6 Sample E-R Diagram

Entity relationship diagrams are used to understand the entities and design files. They illustrate the basic nature of data and are independent of current procedures, systems, department structures, etc. Sometimes they are also referred to as data structure charts.

Immediate Access Diagram

When data to be held in a system are shown by documenting data elements, data structures, data flows and data stores, systems analysts also need to understand the ways in which data may need to be accessed for queries in a system. For this purpose, immediate access diagram (also called Data Immediate-Access Diagram or DIAD) is used. This diagram is used only to understand all the accesses required, and is thereafter used to decide which accesses shall be provided for by the system, depending on the cost to fulfil the requirement. An example is shown in Fig. A7 using the entities CUSTOMER, ORDER, ORDER-DETAIL and PRODUCT. Systems personnel may use this diagram to discuss with the management what accesses are to be provided and their cost. With the approved accesses, the file and data design can be evolved.

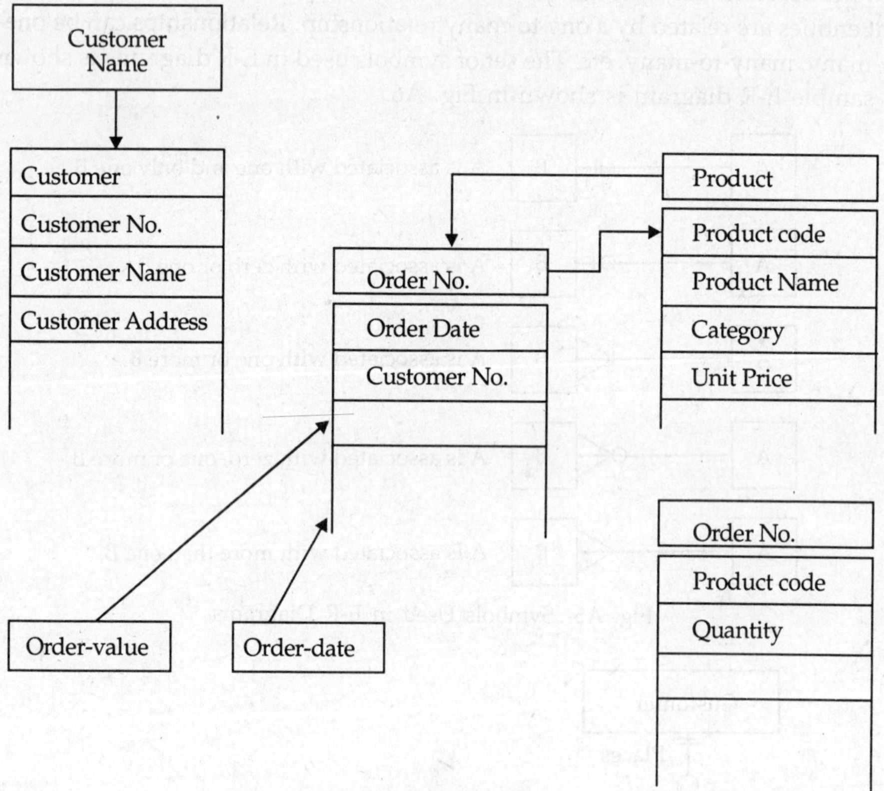

Fig. A7 An Immediate Access Diagram

Decision Tree

A decision tree sketches the logical structure based on some criteria. It is easy to construct, read and update. It shows only the skeletal aspects of the picture and does not lend itself to calculations. The alternative is structured English. An example is given in Fig. A8.

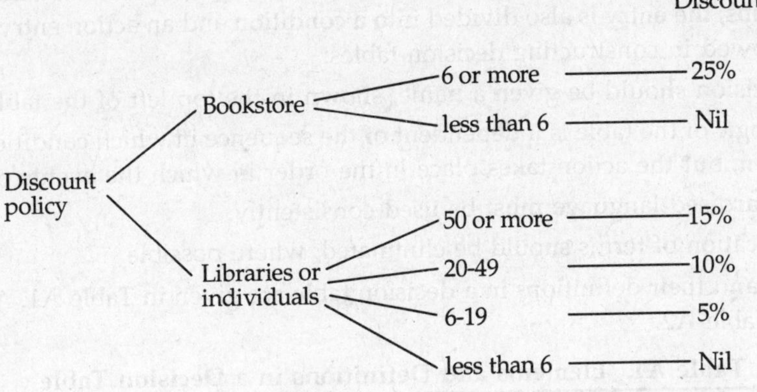

Fig. A8 Decision Tree

Structured English

Structured English uses logical constructs and imperative sentences designed to carry out instructions for action. Decisions are made through IF, THEN, ELSE, and SO statements. Processing logic is expressed using a combination of sequence, selection and iteration. *Sequence* is used when a set of processing instructions is to be executed in the order in which it appears. *Selection* is used when a choice is to be made between alternate courses of action. *Iteration* is used when a block of instructions has to be executed repeatedly till some particular condition is satisfied. Additional conventions such as *indenting, capitalising* or *underlining* certain words are followed for more clarity. An example is given in Fig. A9. The tool is highly correlated with the decision-tree.

```
     COMPUTE-DISCOUNT
  Add up the number of copies per book title
IF order is from bookstore
    AND-IF      order is for 6 copies or more per book title
        THEN : Discount is 25%
    ELSE        (order is for fewer than 6 copies per book title)
            SO : no discount is allowed
    ELSE (order is from libraries or individual customers)
    SO-IF       order is for 50 copies of more per book title, discount is 15%
        ELSE IF order is for 20 to 49 copies per book title, discount is 10%
        ELSE IF order is for 6 to 19 copies per book title, discount is 5%
        ELSE    (order is for less than 6 copies per book order)
            SO : no discount is allowed.
```

Fig. A9 Structured English

Decision Table

A decision table is a table of contingencies for defining a problem and the actions required to be taken. It is a single representation of the relationships between conditions and actions. The parts of the table are the stub and entry. The stub is divided into condition and action stubs; the entry is also divided into a condition and an action entry. Following rules are followed in constructing decision tables:

1. A decision should be given a name, shown in the top left of the table.
2. The logic of the table is independent of the sequence in which condition rules are written, but the action takes place in the order in which the events occur.
3. Standardised language must be used consistently.
4. Duplication of terms should be eliminated, where possible.

Elements and their definitions in a decision table are given in Table A1. An example is shown in Table A2.

Table A1. Elements and Definitions in a Decision Table

Elements	*Location*	*Definition*
Condition stub	Upper left quadrant	Sets forth in question form the condition that may exist
Action stub	Lower left quadrant	Outlines in narrative form the action to be taken to meet each condition
Condition entry	Upper right quadrant	Provides answers to questions asked in the condition stub quadrant
Action entry	Lower right quadrant	Indicates the appropriate action resulting from the answers to the conditions in the condition entry quadrant

In Table A2, answers are represented by a Y to signify yes, an N to signify no, or a blank to show that the condition involved has not been tested. In the action entry quadrant, an X (for a check mark will do) indicates the response to the answer(s) entered in the condition entry quadrant. Furthermore, each column represents a decision or a rule.

Table A2. Decision Table — Discount Policy

	Condition Stub	*Condition Entry*					
		1	2	3	4	5	6
	Customer is bookstore	Y	Y	N	N	N	N
	Order-size 6 copies or more ?	Y	N	N	N	N	N
IF	Customer librarian or individual ?			Y	Y	Y	Y
(condition)	Order-size 50 copies or more ?			Y	N	N	N
	Order-size 20-49 copies ?				Y	N	N
	Order-size 6-19 copies ?					Y	N
	Allow 25% discount	X					
THEN	Allow 15% discount			X			
(action)	Allow 10% discount				X		
	Allow 5% discount					X	
	No discount allowed		X				X
	Action Stub	Action Entry					

Flowcharts

Flowchart is used for expressing a solution to a given problem or representing a process. It is of two types : (*a*) Systems flowchart; and (*b*) Programming flowchart. A *systems flowchart* represents the flow of data within the entire data processing system, giving emphasis on inputs and outputs. It is a diagramming of the steps in a system. Figure A10 shows the symbols normally used in flowcharts. An example of a systems flowchart showing systems analysis and design itself is shown in Fig. A11.

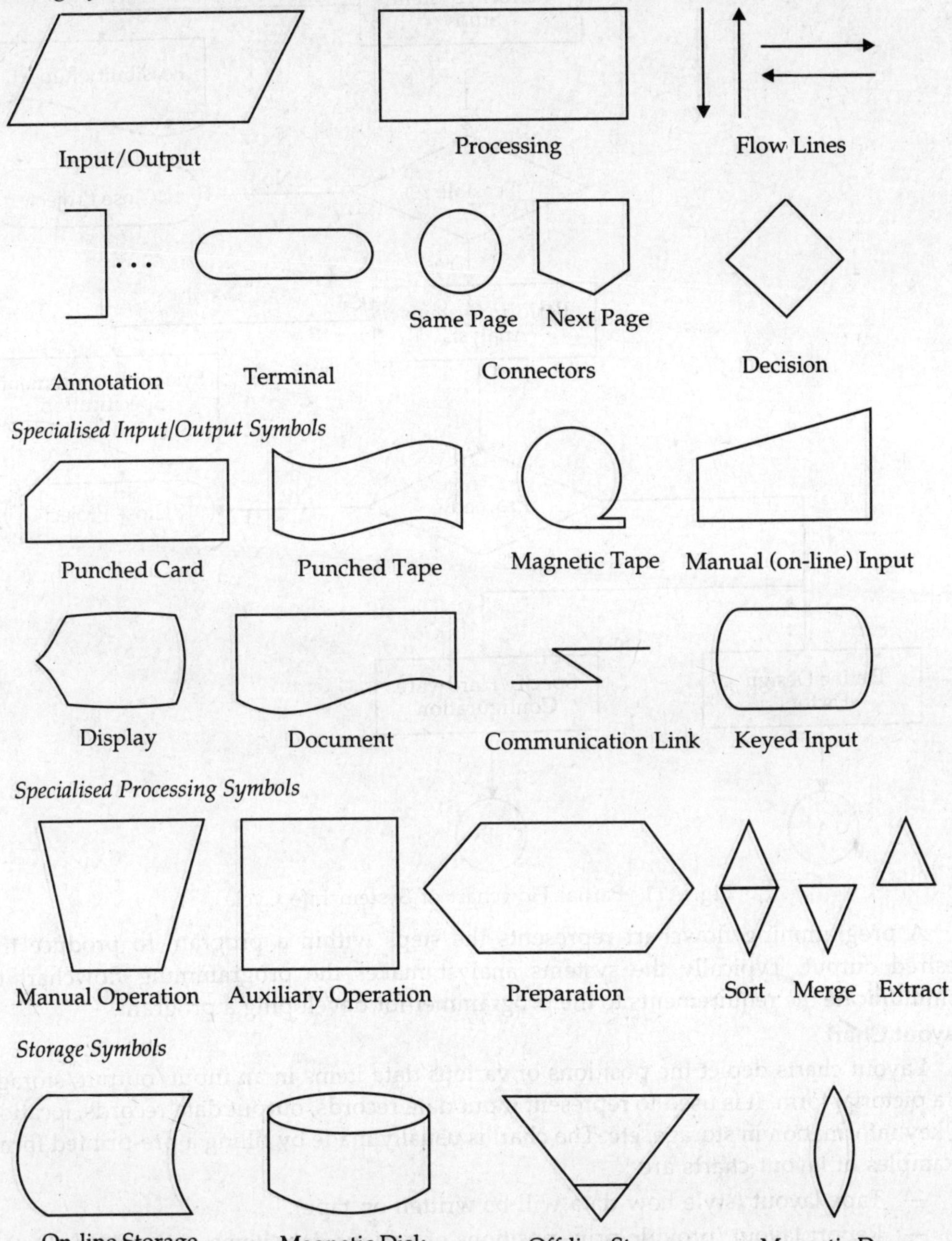

Fig. A10 Flowchart Symbols

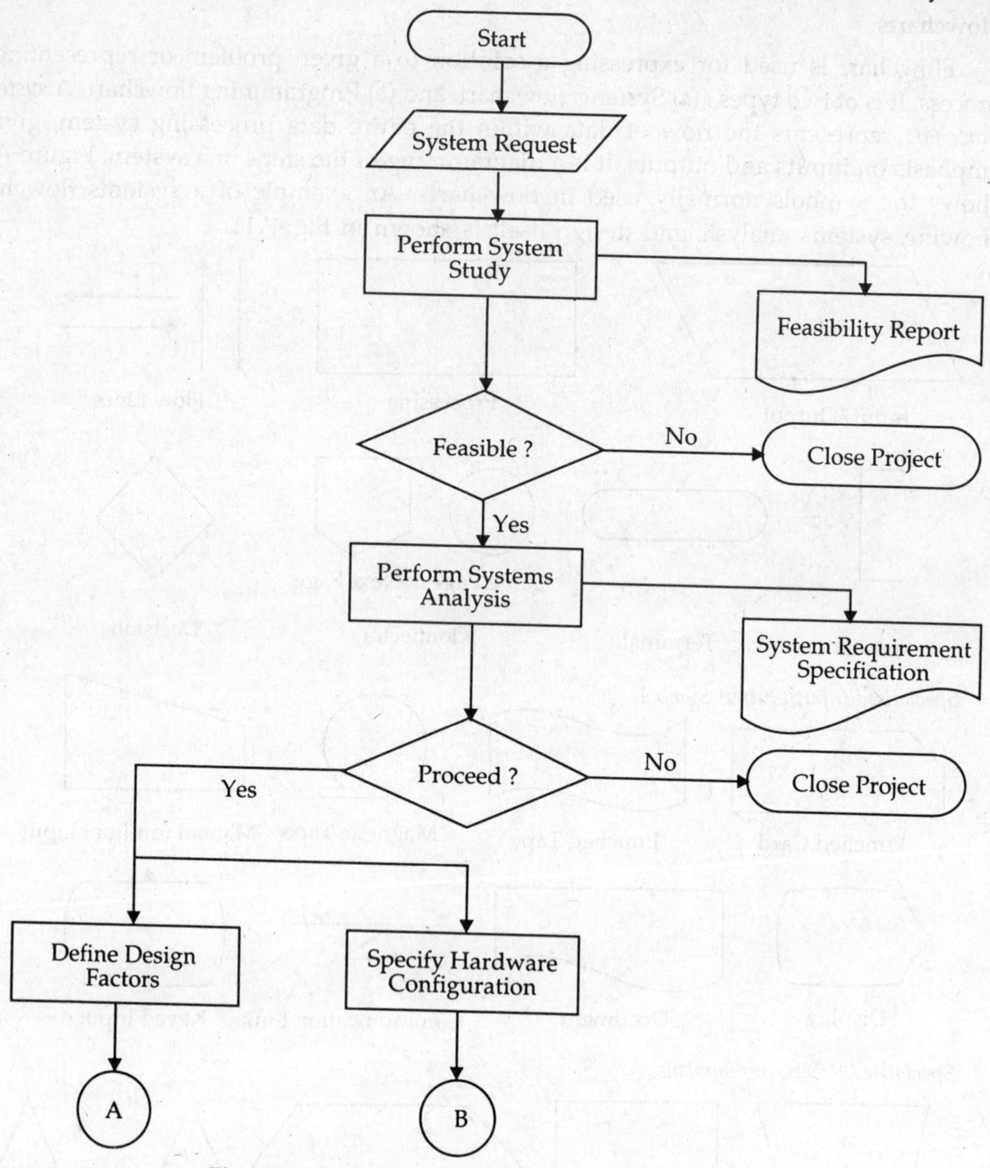

Fig. A11 Partial Flowchart of System Life Cycle

A programming flowchart represents the steps within a program to produce the desired output. Typically the systems analyst makes the programming flowchart to communicate the requirements to the programmer for developing a program.

Layout Chart

Layout charts depict the positions of various data items in an input/output/storage in a pictorial form. It is used to represent input data records, output data records, location of key information in storage, etc. The chart is usually made by filling a pre-printed form. Examples of layout charts are :

— Tape layout (style how data will be written on tape).
— Report layout (provide print positions of various data items on a print report).
— Card layout (show location of various data on a punched card).
— Screen layout (specifies positions of a screen with the data marked on it).

Appendix B

Design of Commercial Applications of Computers in MIS

Introduction

Computer applications to business and commerce started in the mid-50s when economic expansion and rapid technological development started throughout the industrial world. Today, most large and medium-size companies are almost totally dependent on their computers for numerous functions.

Overview of Functional Areas of Business

Every business consists of several well-defined functions. Often these functions are organised into areas/departments. These areas are known as the *functional areas* of business; in each functional area, a well-defined business function is performed. For example, the area within a business organisation responsible for pricing, coordinating consumer advertising efforts, and distributing the firm's products/services is known as the marketing function. The marketing function is usually performed by the marketing department. Similarly, the area within a firm responsible for making the product — if a product is indeed made — is the manufacturing department.

Three functional areas believed to be the most critical in business: finance, marketing, and manufacturing. Overviews of other functional areas — research and development, engineering, and personnel — are also included.

Table B1. Computerised Tasks in Various Functional Areas of Business

Functional Area	*Examples of Computerised Tasks*
Finance/accounting	Accounts payable
	Accounts receivable
	Budgeting
	Financial statement compilation
	Fixed assets control
	Payroll
	Portfolio analysis
Marketing	Market analysis
	Order entry
	Sales tracking
Production	Computer-aided manufacturing (CAM)
	Inventory control
	Manufacturing scheduling
	Material resource planning (MRP)

Research and development	Computer-aided design (CAD) Patent searches Specialised engineering functions
Personnel/human resources management	Employee evaluation Employee tracking Government report generation Recruiting

The backbone of an organisation's information system is its functional information systems, since these process transactions and make possible various housekeeping and administrative activities; they also provide most of the information useful for planning.

Overview of Accounting Information System

Accounting information system collects, maintain and report the financial information of a business organisation. One out of every five application programs in use today is an accounting program.

Accounting products and financial statements are prepared for two separate user groups, each with different interests, needs, and points of view. One group is external to the corporate body in an operational sense and is concerned principally with the financial strength and performance of the business. The other group, internal management, focuses primarily on (*a*) organisational planning through the use of budgets, and (*b*) data refined for use in control and decision making. Accounting information systems are concerned with *financial transactions,* that is, events (transactions) that are measured in terms of money. The accounting information system uses a highly structured framework that includes several sub-systems and usually utilises 'double entry accounting'. Because each financial transaction exchanges something of monetary value of something else of monetary value, it has a basic duality — something is given and something is received. Each half of this transaction — what is given and what is received — is recorded separately and is processed in different ways within the accounting information system.

The system can be divided into four separate areas :

1. The general ledger systems, which include the general ledger, budgeting and profitability reporting.
2. The cash receipts/disbursement systems which include the accounts payable, accounts receivable, payroll.
3. The production management systems which include material inventory control, manufacturing scheduling, and cost estimation.
4. The marketing management system includes finished goods inventory control, order processing, market analysis, and sales tracking.

Generally, outputs from accounting information systems take the following forms:

1. Audit trails in the form of activity lists and backup files.
2. Expected products that the systems were designed to yield, such as accounting statements, inventory balances, payroll checks and withholding statements, vendor checks and remittance advices, and production cost and status reports.
3. Updated master files of open (active) records, which constitute an input into subsequent processing cycles.

4. Data conditioned for input into other related sub-systems.
5. Processing exceptions designed to elicit external responses affecting future systems processing.

Some of the sub-systems are discussed here :

Accounts payable. Amount payable is a liability that is created as soon as goods (services) are received from vendors. The invoices and statements are validated against the actual receipt of goods found in the file and, if all information is in order, the payable is created on the books. The accounts payable system is the transaction processing sub-system that handles payments to suppliers. It keeps track of invoices from suppliers, determines the optimum time to pay invoices, produces checks to pay invoices and performs cash management activities (ensuring that cash is always available when bills must be paid).

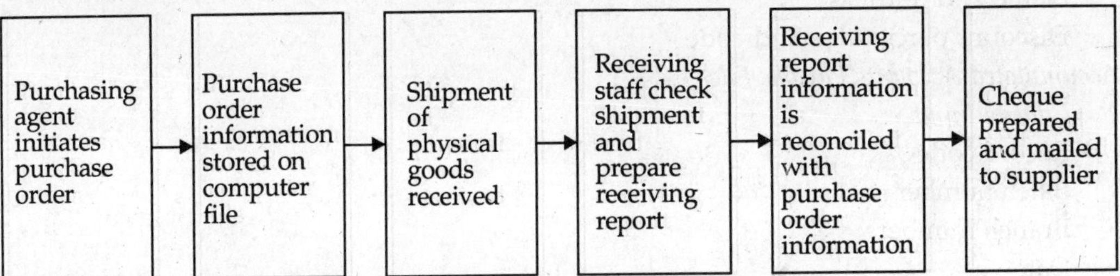

Fig. B1 Various Steps in the Accounts Payable Cycle

Initial input. When the material is purchased, a number of documents accompany the purchase of material from a vendor. The accounts payable system depends principally on three independently prepared documents : the transaction authorisation; purchase order; the supplier's request for payment after performance (the invoice) and the proof or acknowledgement of satisfactory performance (receiving report). When the terms of the contract specify that the buyer will absorb the freight charges, another source document, the freight bill, may be required to support the latter two documents.

A matter of particular importance in the accounts payable system is the official registration of each vendor document submitted for payment. It is common practice for vendors to provide duplicate copies of their invoices, particularly in cases where payment may be delayed pending the settlement of one or more of the discrepancies previously discussed. Such superfluous documentation should be identified and prevented from entering the normal system processing. In addition to the material identification, price, and quantity information normally expected on business transaction paper, documents entering the accounts payable system from outsiders must reflect sufficient information to permit matching with other related internal documents. The most important numbers in this interrelationship process are the purchase order serial number and the carrier's freight bill number. Upon receipt, a document control clerk will note the purchase order number on the vendor's invoice and make a cursory check to determine whether a previous billing has been recorded and paid or is still pending payment. If it is still pending, the clerk destroys the duplicate invoice. If not, the invoice is formally registered and entered into the system. By following this simple procedure, possible duplicate payment and distribution are avoided, along with the attendant reversal and corrective measures necessitated by erroneous data entering other systems such as inventory control, cash, and general ledger.

It can be seen that an invoice presented for payment, assigned a unique registration number, related to a specific purchase contract, and matched to a receiving report bearing the carrier's proof of delivery can be paid with confidence (and paid only once) — assuming, of course, there are no irreconcilable differences between the terms of agreement and actual performance. Subsequent to payment, which terminates the transaction cycle, the completed document sets are physically removed from the active files and stored in vendor name sequence in central files.

The contents of the vendor master file and accumulated accounts payable file are given below :

Vendor Master File

Record code
Vendor number
Name and address
Discount percentage and code

Accumulated Accounts Payable File

Control Input

Record code
Batch number
Branch number
Date
Control total

Keyed Input

Record code
Batch number
Vendor number
General ledger number
Invoice number
Invoice date
Invoice due date
Invoice amount
Invoice discount

The inputs, processes and outputs of accounts payable system are as follows :

Systems	*Inputs*	*Processes*	*Outputs*
Accounts Payable	Batches of invoices Purchase order Packing slip Invoices stating amount Other related records like receiving report	Verify and edit invoices Prepare disbursement vouchers Assemble disbursement vouchers Obtain batch totals Prepare control total slip Prepare disbursement voucher record Sort out disbursement voucher records Prepare transaction file Edit and print runs	Printed error list Printed batch total Edit list Vendor-wise disbursement voucher Account payable update

Payroll Accounting System

Every organisation pays to the people for the services they render. The basic purpose of the payroll system is to produce pay slips/pay checks for the employees every month. Organisations use standard methods for calculating salaries and wages. There is a basic component and additional allowances (house rent, city allowance, conveyance, etc.) which are linked with basic pay. Deductions are made from salary for provident fund, insurance premium, income-tax, etc. Consideration must also be given in such a system for special cases such as advanced payment of salaries for employees going on trips/vacations. Calculation of payroll is a tedious process and chances of making mistakes in any manual system are fairly high. Payroll, therefore, is seen as an area where most organisations would like to changeover to a computerised system. From the computerised payroll system, the employees get pay check/pay slip on pre-printed stationery.

Payroll master file. The master file used in payroll processing contains permanent as well as current data. Each record of this file holds such details as :

(*a*) *Employee information*
- Name
- Identification number
- Address
- Phone no.
- Designation
- Department
- Sex
- Date of birth
- Scale of pay
- Date of next increment
- Date of joining

(*b*) *Earnings*
- Basic pay
- Dearness allowance
- House rent allowance
- City allowance
- Conveyance allowance
- Other miscellaneous allowances

(*c*) *Deductions*
- Provident fund
- Voluntary provident fund
- Income-tax
- House rent
- Electricity

(*d*) Recovery of loans and advances

(*i*) Loans	—	Provident fund
		Conveyance
		House-building
(*ii*) Advances	—	Festival

(*e*) *Leave data*

Accumulated earned leave

Accumulated sick leave

Earned leave used current year

Sick leave availed current year.

The permanent portion of the file must be updated before current transactions are entered into the system. Prior to the actual processing of a payroll, the payroll office obtains data on new employees and on recent changes to existing employees. All changes to the employee master file are logged to an audit file.

Records of new employees are labelled 'added'. Similarly, when records are to be deleted from the file, these are labelled 'deleted'. However, when an employee is terminated, the year-to-date and other master file information for the employee is usually left on the file at least until the end of the fiscal year, since periodic reports require the appearance of terminated employee records to reflect the entire year-to-date payroll balance. Therefore, there is usually some provision for a termination date to indicate that an employee is no longer active. When employee records are adjusted in any way, these are labelled 'changed' on the audit report.

Input to the payroll system. After changes to the master file, the actual payroll run begins. Time sheets are submitted for data entry. This data entry procedure allows for waged and salaried employees to be selected for payment. The pay can be produced weekly, fortnightly, or monthly, as required, plus each employee can be paid by cash, cheque, or bank deposit. For waged employee, separate hours can be entered for each type of entry. For salaried employees, who are paid a regular salary, no timesheet or other document is submitted for determination of hours worked.

All income-tax amounts are calculated from a tax table which automatically accommodates for problems usually associated with annual leave, casual workers and partial pays. At data entry it is possible to select a number of allowances and/or deduction from the Allowances and Deductions file.

The inputs, processes and outputs of the payroll system are given below :

Systems	*Inputs*	*Processes*	*Outputs*
Payroll Accounting System	Personnel data like Record Code Employee no. Employee name Address Phone no. Department Salary Details Overtime Leave Particulars Payment Data	Execute payroll edit programme Payroll transactions file sorting Sorting transaction file Current period pay Old labour distribution Print journal report Complete master payroll file	Payment details employee-wise with all particulars Department-wise totals Whole Company Employees salary total Other required printouts

Financial Accounting

All organisations keep accounts. Accounts involves recording, classifying and summarising transactions and events that are of financial nature. The results are analysed. The financial accounting function is responsible for planning and controlling all financial procedures and the preparation of balance-sheets, trading and profit and loss accounts and ensuring that all business transactions are recorded in proper books of account. The function is also responsible, as custodian, for safeguarding the fixed and liquid assets of the business and implementing internal check procedures. Responsibilities also include the control of receipts and payments in accordance with various business transactions undertaken and the maintenance of statutory records relating to payroll applications and purchase and sales transactions.

Every transaction in a financial accounting system has a credit side and a debit side. The total debit amount in a transaction matches the total credit. One account head may be credited and another will be debited with the same amount. A transaction could involve multiple accounts being credited and debited while maintaining the credit amount total equal to the total debit amount.

The financial accounting system should have the following features :

Financial ratios. This is a concise report for the top management compiled through the shifting of data on hand. Some key accounting ratios or business measurements like current assets to capital, current assets to current liabilities, fixed assets to capital liquidity ratio, profit to sales, profit to capital, sales to inventory, sales to capital, acid test, etc. are presented.

Profit & loss statement. Besides giving year-to-date positions, this statement provides the current month's performance under each head of expense and income. To permit evaluation through comparisons, following additional information is given against each line item of income and expenses :

(*a*) Percentage of each item to sales;

(*b*) Year-to-date last year position — an average developed from the given last year's total base; and

(*c*) Year-to-date budget picture — an average compiled from the given total of this year budget.

Balance-sheet. Business status as of date along with status as of last month and year-end last year are presented side-by-side in the balance-sheet, making it a comprehensive business trend report for management. Flexibility in presentation as in case of profit & loss statement is also available to balance-sheet.

Day books. These basic registers required to be maintained for record and audit are provided by the system. There can be as many as 100 day-books and various format options are available to the user like double entry, single entry or columnar types.

With the columnar option, normal requirements of purchase/sales-tax registers can be met. In addition, special presentation needs of selected day-books like daily totals or progressive to-date totals are provided for.

Ledgers. All transactions entered in various day books are posted automatically in sub-ledgers or directly into the general ledger. A highly flexible chart of accounts can be developed by the user, taking into account future analytical needs, with the help of the six digit code structure available in a typical package. Within each such account, further subledger classification is normally possible to the extent of three digits. All, except the first high order position of the total nine digit code, is user controlled.

Following transactions are typical in most financial accounting system :

Systems	Inputs	Processes	Outputs
Financial Accounting	Sales invoices Purchase bills Payment voucher Receipt voucher Journal voucher Debit notes Credit notes	Validating the transactions (valid account number, debit equal to credit, etc.) Posting the transactions Summarising the accounts and transactions Printing details of accounts payable Printing the day books and ledgers Facilitating reconciliation of accounting entries	Cash book Bank book Sales day book Purchase day book General ledger Trial balance Profit & loss statement Balance-sheet Accounts receivable details Customer statement of account Annual profit & loss statement Annual balance-sheet

Inventory Control System

Inventory refers to a stock of materials/goods. The terms 'inventory' and 'stock' are usually seen as being synonymous and are used to describe materials which can be identified at various stages of the transformation process in organisations. The inventory for a manufacturing industry includes (*i*) raw material, (*ii*) semi-finished product, and (*iii*) finished product. Trading and retail organisations hold a stock of purchased goods which are to be sold.

The main purpose of the inventory control is the monitoring of the stock levels and this is achieved by recording stock movements on stock records. The system maintains files with item details and their stock levels. Transactions issue are entered when issues are made and the stock levels reduced by the issue quantity. When orders are placed, the quantity-on-order is incremented.

It must be appreciated that inventory forms a buffer to facilitate variations in supply and demand. As it often consumes a high proportion of working capital, it must be controlled in the most effective manner to achieve the following :

Avoidance of excessive stocks
Avoidance of excessive stocks shortages
Optimising cost of ordering supplies
Optimising cost of carrying inventory.

General Design of Inventory Systems

Inventory systems generally require the use of several data files. One file, usually referred to as the master file, keeps track of the quantity of each item presently available in stock. In addition, it may also keep track of the location of each item in the warehouse, the cost of the item, the reorder point, the quantity currently on order, and the name and address of the vendor from whom the item is purchased.

Most businesses also like to keep track of each individual transaction that occurs within the business. Information on these individual transactions is usually maintained in separate data files called *transaction files.* One such file might keep track of individual sales transactions : to whom items were sold, when, for how much, and the invoice or receipt number. A second transaction file might maintain an on-going record of all new stock received.

The transaction files maintain a history of all individual transactions involving the sale and receipt of goods, while the master file maintains the current status of goods in stock at any given moment by using information supplied directly from the two transaction files.

The sample file layouts for various files are given below :

Master file. The structure of master file, with a brief description of each field's contents, is shown.

Table B2. Structure for the Master Data File

Field name	*Width*	*Contents*
1. Part No.	5	Part number (key field)
2. Title	20	Item description
3. Quantity	4	Quantity in stock
4. Cost	9	Purchase price
5. Reorder	4	Reorder point
6. Order quantity	4	Quantity on order
7. Location	5	Location in warehouse
8. Vendor	25	Vendor's name
9. Vendor-add	25	Vendor's address
10. Vendors-CSP	25	Vendor's city, state, PIN code
11. Date	8	Date of last update
12. Order-date	8	Date of last order
13. New-order	4	Quantity to order

Sales file. A data file will be created to keep track of individual sales transactions:

Table B3. Structure for the Sales Data File

Field name	*Width*	*Contents*
1. Part number	5	Part number (key field)
2. Invoice No.	6	Invoice number
3. Sales Prs.	12	Salesperson's name (or code)
4. Customer	12	Customer's name
5. Quantity	4	Quantity sold
6. Price	9	Selling price
7 Date	8	Date sold

New stock file. The third file in the system will be used to keep track of goods received to replenish stock.

Table B4. Structure for the New Stock Data File

Field name	Width	Contents
1. Part number	5	Part number (key field)
2. Quantity	4	Quantity received
3. Cost	9	Purchase price
4. Date	8	Date received
5. Vendor	25	Vendor's name

The inputs, processes and outputs of inventory control system are as given.

Systems	Inputs	Processes	Outputs
Inventory Control System	Inventory master file Cash items Location of each item Cost of the item Re-order level Quantity currently on order Name and address of vendor Historical data	Compilation of files Structure of issue file Structure of new stock file Updation of inventory data and related particulars Value of items on hand and consumption	Inventory transactions Inventory ledger Customers' report Back order file Excess order file Excess stock Under stock Slow moving ABC class items Items to be ordered file

Sales Order Processing

The system described is suitable for a distributing company, where supplies to stock are purchased from several manufacturers and orders for stock are from many customers.

The typical order processing serves four primary functions :

1. It provides order-filling information used by warehouse storemen to collect the stock from inventory to be delivered to customers.
2. It updates computer inventory records based on incoming stock to inventory and the completed orders despatched to customers.
3. It retains records of orders completed so that invoices can be produced once the goods have been delivered.
4. It retains summary data for accounting and sales analysis purposes as well as for predicting future inventory requirements.

Input to the system. There are several types of input, other than adjustments to the stock-on-hand figure. The most familiar of these is the customer order which performs two functions. It provides information for filling the order *plus* information for updating the customer master file. Orders can be received in several ways. The bulk of the orders usually arrive by post, but a certain percentage may arrive by telephone or fax. When an order is telephoned or faxed, a standard order form may be used within the sales office to facilitate data entry. During order entry, an 'order number' is assigned to each order as it is entered. The customer number is verified and the customer name displayed. The responsible salesman and the delivery address may automatically be obtained from the customer file, or manually entered. Any special delivery instructions can also be entered at this stage. Each item on the order may be assigned a different discount percentage if necessary; and fully interactive outstanding order control is provided. Outstanding orders are orders that cannot be filled because of insufficient stock. New stock must arrive before outstanding orders can be filled. Hence, any unsatisfied balance of a customer order is placed on a special file called the *outstanding orders file.* After new stock has been received from the suppliers, the inventory record is updated. Thus, receipts of stock constitute another input to the system. Inventory receivings automatically update the average unit cost, selling price (if any price change), and quantity-on-hand in the inventory file.

Another input to an order processing is the credit memo, which is issued when goods are returned. It performs a dual function. So long as the goods can be resold, it is used to adjust the quantity-on-hand on the inventory file. Second, it is also used to adjust the customer details. If the customer has not been invoiced for the goods, then it is a simple matter of adjusting the details of the original customer order which will still be on file. If, however, the customer has been invoiced, then the credit memo will need to act as an input to the 'Sales Ledger' system, since invoice details are automatically interfaced with the Sales Ledger system. Thus, the customer, in effect, gets a refund for the goods returned.

System files. The main files in the order processing system are:

Inventory Master File;

Order Details File;

Outstanding Orders Files; and

Customer Master File.

The *Inventory Master File* contains (per stock item) such details as: item number, description, product category, quantity-on-hand, outstanding order quantity, reorder level, unit of issue, unit selling price, average unit cost price, month-to-date and year- to-date sales and cost of sales figures, taxable status, quantity discount rate and discount quantity. There are two different types of discounts normally offered in an order processing system. Quantity discounts apply when a customer orders more than a given amount of a particular item. Customer discounts apply to particular customers, and the details are kept on the customer master file.

The *Order Details File* contains information about the order itself (order header), as well as information about each item on the order (item details). The order header (one per order) would typically contain : order number, order date, customer number, customer's purchase order number, delivery instructions, delivery address, etc. The item details (one per item) would contain such data as order number, item number, bin location in warehouse, quantity ordered, quantity delivered, unit of issue, unit selling price, quantity discount rate (zero if no discount applicable).

The *Outstanding Orders File* also has one order header per order and as many details as there are items outstanding. The order header would contain: order number, customer number, order date, customer's purchase order number, delivery instructions, etc. The item details would contain : order number, item number, quantity outstanding, quantity discount rate (only applicable if the original quantity ordered exceeded the discount quantity).

A *Customer Master File* is also maintained containing customer number, customer name, invoice address, delivery address, customer code, salesman code, sales, customer type code and cost-of-sales, month-to-date (MTD) and year-to-date (YTD), taxable status, credit limit, and discount rate.

Order processing system. Order header information is entered followed by each order item. These are validated by reference to the Inventory File. Stock is allocated on the stock record, whether it is available or not, thus ensuring that stock committed to outstanding orders is not available for subsequent orders. If stock is available, then the order item details are merged with any available outstanding orders from the Outstanding File for the same customer. If stock is not available, then the order details are written to the Daily Outstanding Orders File. Those available item of the order *plus* any available outstanding items are then sorted and a copy of the order is then printed to act as a picking list for the storemen. The order details are then written to the Order Details File.

Once the goods have been picked, any amendments to the picking list are noted so that the quantities can be revised. These changes are used to update automatically the Order Details File, Inventory Master File, and the Daily Outstanding Orders File. The revised order is then used to print out a despatch note.

The Inventory Master File is updated with the goods inward data and an 'Inventory Receivings Report' is printed. A 'Purchasing Advice Report' is printed on request showing all items which fall below reorder level or went out of stock since the last printing of this report. Daily outstanding orders are merged with the Outstanding Orders File, the Stock File consulted, and picking lists printed for those outstanding orders which have been available for some days. The reason for waiting a number of days is to see whether another order from that customer comes in during this waiting period, and if so, those available outstanding items can be added to the new order rather than print a picking list for only one or two items. In the event that this does not happen, then the above procedure is followed and picking list printed.

Once the goods have been delivered, selected orders can be invoiced as and when required. Partial invoicing of an order is allowed, and adjustments to quantities delivered and quantities outstanding are still allowed. Miscellaneous charges, freight and any salesman commission amout or percentage due may also be entered at this time. The invoice names and addresses and customer discounts are received from the customer file and a multipart invoice set produced.

Other miscellaneous management reports are also produced such as the 'Outstanding Report by Item' which shows all the items outstanding for various orders, the 'Outstanding Order Report by Customer' which shows outstanding orders for each customer, the 'Sales Analysis by Product Category' as and when required. The sales analysis report shows sales, cost of sales, percentage of sales, profit and percentage of profit for each item within each category, both month-to-date and year-to-date, with a summary by category at the end.

The inputs, processes and outputs of sales order processing system are as given.

Systems	*Inputs*	*Processes*	*Outputs*
Sales Order Processing System	Receipt of customers Purchase order Sales order Authorisation to ship Quantity shipped	Assemble/compile record count, financial total of the values of items, last totals Assemble daily batch of remittance Additions of new records Credits for sale returns Verify and sort out sale records	Customer A/c no. Customer name and address Credit rating Balance due Transaction file Update A/c Delinquent A/c Invoices

Work-in-Progress Control System

The work-in-progress control system assigns materials, labour and overhead costs to production jobs or products. The objectives of the system are to cost jobs through the manufacturing process and provide management with information to assist in controlling cost, material utilisation and measuring the performance of departments. The system needs information about (*a*) materials requisitioned for each job, (*b*) labour employed on each job, (*c*) overhead costs allocated to each job, and (*d*) production status of each job.

The system interacts with the payroll, general ledger, finished goods inventory control, production scheduling and materials inventory control. Once manufacturing is complete, jobs are transferred from work-in-progress control to finished goods inventory control.

The inputs, processes and outputs of work-in-progress control systems are as given.

Systems	*Inputs*	*Processes*	*Outputs*
Work-in-Progress Control System	Job files Job identification no. Customer identification Promised completion date Estimated shipping date Estimated completion date Total estimated material cost Material cost to date Total labour cost Total standard overhead cost Overhead cost applied todate	Opening stock, stock on hand and despatches Scrap and re-work Pending for decisions Machinewise & cost centrewise analysis Working/worked hours Materials received, used and balance	Job cost Job status Dept. performance report Material utilisation Labour time Machine time Forecasted/predicted date for all pending orders

Production Control System

The purpose for production control system is to effectively utilise limited resources in the production of goods so as to satisfy customer demands and create a profit for investors. This involves forecasting and planning, routing, scheduling, despatching and expediting, and coordinating. These activities ensure the orderly supply and movement of materials, the performance applications of labour, and the use of machinery and equipment. As production control interrelates with functions outside itself, so do the components within production control have a complex flow of interactions. A simplistic view of these interactions might be as shown in Fig. B2. It should be apparent that decisions in one component — say, scheduling — have a distinct effect on other components. For example, one way to ensure that production is never slowed by lack of materials is to inventory an excess of those materials.

This might simplify the scheduling activity, but it does so at the expense of higher inventory expenses. For another example, one can ensure that production never misses a due date by increasing the delivery times, thus pushing customer demands off into the future. This makes the scheduling problem easier, but at the expense of customer satisfaction. The production control activity is a system, and it must be viewed in its totality. It may not always be wise to require that production resources never be idle or that inventory costs be minimized or that all due dates be met. The objective of the production control system should be the objective of the total organisation. Decisions that complement sales, production, and inventory are preferable to those that optimise only one function.

The system is shown (Fig. B2) as a cyclic activity starting with the customer and moving counterclockwise through the figure. At this point, one is concerned only with the activities located inside the larger box labelled "The Production Control System". Demand forecasting is the starting point for production control activity. For each class of product or service the future must be predicted. It is not unusual to have a lead time of many months between the time an order is placed to purchase raw materials and the time those materials are transformed and shipped out as finished goods, in which case the forecast must be for months into the future. This is called the forecasting horizon. In some cases, it is easy to predict sales for one to two years into the future. The delivery time between firm-order entries and deliveries may be a large fraction of the needed forecasting horizon. In other cases, accuracy beyond actual order entries may be difficult to attain. Without accurate forecasts it is impossible to accomplish the long-range capacity planning activity.

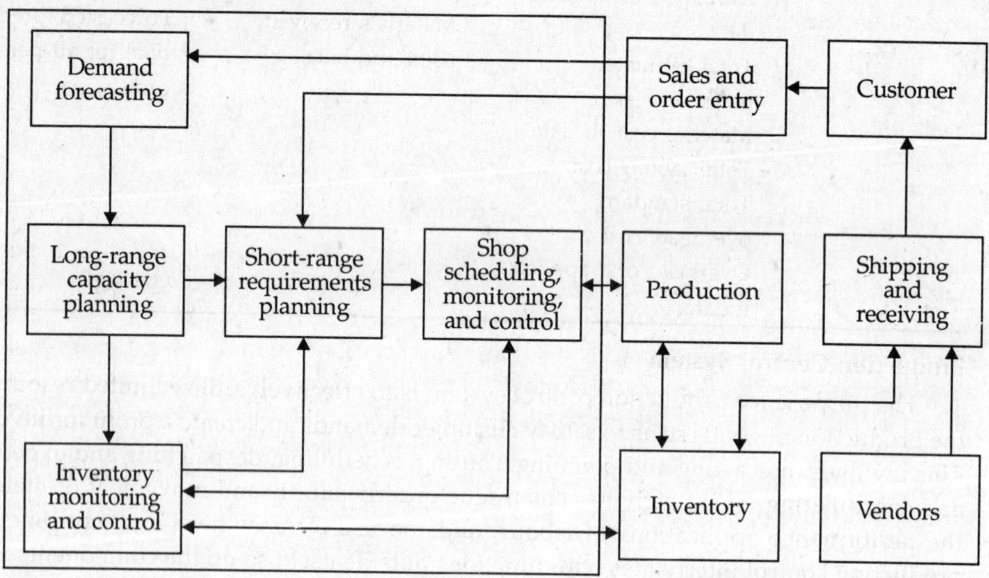

Fig. B2 Representative Production Control Information System

Capacity planning is the second step in the production control chain of events. The need is to know how many people to employ, how much overtime to schedule, and how much inventory to hold so that actual demand is economically met. If insufficient capacity or inventory is available, demand cannot be met and customers may be lost. If too much capacity and inventory exist, the company will be in a serious cash-flow bind. If the wrong products are in the pipeline, the company will be hurt at both ends, with unsatisfied customers and unsalable products. Without a reasonably accurate forecast of future demand, long-range capacity planning is not possible.

One concerns of capacity planning is the amount of inventory to be held. An often-used plan in the face of cyclic demand is to build more than is needed during slow periods, thereby increasing inventory. Then, when demand is high, it can be met, in part from inventoried items. Therefore, inventory levels will vary from period-to-period. With these variations in inventory, the quantities made on each production order will also vary. The control of inventory is the act of comparing what is actually on hand with the desired quantity. Inventory control thus is affected by the decision made in capacity planning.

A second activity that feeds off of the capacity planning output is short-range requirements planning. This activity also responds to the decisions of inventory control. In the near term, the need for production from rough machining to final assembly must be determined. In effect, the activity is one of looking at near-term production capacity and goals, existing inventory levels, and discrepancies between those levels and desired inventory, then creating a master schedule of what to do in each production department during the next week or month. To some extent, inaccuracies in the forecasted demand and changes in the capacity plan can be overcome at this stage. Items that need faster or greater production can be 'red-tagged' as urgent. Those items whose production levels can be reduced are easily handled with relatively minor impact on inventories. The amount of overtime and/or undercapacity can be adjusted. Thus, there is a degree of flexibility within the broader limits of the capacity plan. The resulting output is the short-range requirements plan, or master schedule.

The master schedule is made without reference to the dynamic changes in the shop situation. If people fail to arrive for work or if a machine breaks down, the schedule must be changed. If scrap parts are found or tooling is temporarily not available, the schedule must be adjusted. The master schedule then identifies the weekly production goals for each department but does not determine how those goals are to be met. This is the role of the shop scheduling activity. At the beginning of each shift, the shop foreman must review where he is in relation to the master schedule and what resources are available to him. He must then decide what to do during the shift, in what sequence the shop orders should be accomplished, and what resources to devote to those tasks. These production control decisions are then passed on to the production employee. Thus, the production control activity as a chain of interrelated events that function as a system. The decisions are made for different horizons in time and with different degree of accuracy. Yet they must all occur if the ultimate objective is to be met.

The benefits from computerised production control system can be summarised as:

1. Reduced work-in-progress and buffer stocks.
2. More accurate information updated as and when required.
3. Better communication.
4. Helps to plan ahead.
5. Reduced paperwork in use at any one time.
6. Over and under loads on facilities shown.
7. Long-term effects of management decisions shown.

Shop-floor input. Production control requires that information about the production operation be made available to decision makers in a timely fashion. This means that data have to be collected from all segments of the production operation : receiving, shipping, warehousing, manufacturing, maintenance, etc. These data must be stored, processed and subsequently presented in a format that is beneficial to the planner.

The primary inputs needed from the shop-floor are as follows :

1. Resource status (people, machines, tools, inspection equipment, and materials handling equipment) :
   (*a*) What resources exist.
   (*b*) Their operating status.
   (*c*) Their limitations/capabilities.
2. Job status
   (*a*) Work orders active in the schedule.
   (*b*) Operations that correspond to those orders.
   (*c*) The completion status of each order.
3. Material status
   (*a*) Which parts are in the plant.
   (*b*) Number of parts in inventory.
   (*c*) Number of parts allocated to active work orders.
   (*d*) Number of parts on order, and when delivery is expected.
4. Schedule status (for each scheduled resource)
   (*a*) Operations scheduled.
   (*b*) Expected processing time of each operation.
   (*c*) Total scheduled processing time.
   (*d*) Present sequence of operations.
   (*e*) Expected completion time of each operation.
5. Materials move status
   (*a*) Move tickets presently active.
   (*b*) Any tickets for urgent items.
6. Recent performance status
   (*a*) Percentage of resources used.
   (*b*) Average time in system for jobs.
   (*c*) Present value of existing inventory.
   (*d*) Average ratio of operation run time over standard run times for operations.
   (*e*) Percentage of items scrapped at inspection; number of inspection variations authorised.
   (*f*) Average time to complete a material move.
   (*g*) For all the preceding items, any resources, jobs, parts, and so on that performed out of acceptable limits.

All of these data items have to be collected in real time. Because the basic role of manufacturing is to perform jobs using various resources, monitoring jobs and resources is the key to data collection.

Reports. A wide variety of information output is used for manufacturing. They indicate the available capacity and scheduled future utilisation of labour and machinery. A sample of production control system is shown here.

Requirements planning reports

Product demand forecasts
Workforce and production plan
Finished product assembly plan, and master schedule
Parts production requirements plan
Projected work centre load report
Vendor parts delivery plan
Shipping dock plan
Bill of materials

Inventory control reports

Stock status
Items on order
Critical items exception

Operations scheduling reports

Work schedule
Work orders authorisation
Work orders location and status
Tooling delivery schedule
Production process routings
Rework orders
Maintenance work order

Materials handling reports

Work move ticket
Stock location
Parts receiving
Product shipping

Quality control reports

Inspection work order
Scrap reports
Quality control trend analysis

Assembly reports

Assembly schedule

Assembly procedure routings

Stock location

Shop floor control reports

Labour efficiency

Missing stock

Machine utilisation

Absenteeism analysis.

A typical production control database contains the following records :

1. Sales order records.
2. Sales order status records.
3. Shipping order status records.
4. Forecasted demand records.
5. Sales history records.
6. Part number master file.
7. Bill of materials records.
8. Assembly process records.
9. Production routing records.
10. Time standards records.
11. Manufacturing cost records.
12. Inventory cost and control records.
13. Raw materials inventory records.
14. In-process inventory records.
15. Finished goods inventory records.
16. Vendor-purchasing records.
17. Purchasing order status records.
18. Receiving order status records.
19. Shop loading-master schedule records.
20. Machine utilisation history records.
21. Shop order status records.

Share Accounting System

Share is an investment option used by many persons. Shares can be purchased either from the company (at the time of public or a rights issue) or from the share market. A share accounting system needs to maintain an updated list of shareholders. For each shareholder, the main information held is the name and address, names of joint holder (if any), the number of shares held and the identification of the certificates through which these shares are held. When a person purchases shares from a share holder, or share transfer form along with the certificates is sent by the buyer to the company for incorporating the transfer. The system records a change in ownership for the shares from the seller to the buyer. Periodically the company declares a dividend. Dividend warrants (cheques) need to be mailed on a particular day to various shareholders. Calculation of income-tax to be deducted at source is also done before the printing and mailing dividend warrants.

Other facilities usually provided in a share accounting system are :

1. Bank mandate facility, where the shareholders dividend warrant is sent to bank account at the shareholder's request.
2. Splitting of share certificates, where a single certificate having a large number of shares is splitted in a number of certificates containing a smaller number of shares.
3. Consolidation of shares, where many certificates belonging to a single shareholder are combined into one share certificate.
4. Mailing annual reports and invitation to various meetings.

The typical inputs, processes and outputs of share accounting system are given as follows :

Systems	*Inputs*	*Processes*	*Outputs*
Share Accounting System	Share holding date of a fresh issue Share transfer request Split request Consolidation request Request for duplicate certificate Request for duplicate dividend warrant Tax exemption forms Request for bank mandate	Recording the transfer of shares Handling (*a*) Splitting (*b*) Consolidation (*c*) Duplicate request Printing new certificates Calculation of dividend Calculation of income-tax to be deducted Printing annual reports	Transferred share certificates New certificates of splitting, consolidation and duplication Dividend warrants and counterfoils Statement of tax deduction Annual report

Appendix C

Controls in Information Systems/Organisations

INTRODUCTION

Robert Anthony suggested that controls in information systems for management planning are essential. Some aspects of control have been discussed in the previous chapter. In this chapter, the types of control one is looking at are:

- General controls—administrative controls and development controls
- Operational controls
- Controls in organisations
- Administrative controls are controls over data and the security thereof accomplished by means of administrative measures. Operational controls are measures incorporated into systems operations to ensure that processed information is accurate, complete, authorised and valid.

TYPES OF CONTROLS

Types of controls are : Input controls, processing controls, output controls, and master file controls.

Input Controls

Input controls in information systems are:

- Pre-numbered documents
- Sequence checks
- batch routines
- one-for-one verification.

Processing Controls

Processing controls in information systems are:

- Batch total agreement
- Check digits
- Master file matching
- Sequence number
- Range check
- Format check.

Output Controls

Output controls in information systems are:

- Batch total agreement
- End of report marker
- Distribution lists
- Exception reports.

Master File Controls

Master file controls in information systems are:

- Authorisation to update

- File balancing
- Master file matching
- Periodic verification.

THE PROBLEM WITH LOCAL AREA NETWORKS

The complexity of local area networks allows for many more breaches of security than a single computer and each breach can, of course, affect several computers. The main areas of concern are:

- Tapping into the cables
- Passwords and unauthorised log in
- Computer viruses
- Encryption
- File copying.

PASSWORDS

A password is a sequence of characters that must be presented to a computer system before it will allow access to the system or parts of that system. There are several inherent problems with passwords:

- authorised users may divulge their password to a colleague
- many passwords may have associations with the user
- passwords are often written down close to the computer.

The following measures help to counter the problems identified above:

- users should be required to change their passwords regularly
- passwords should be case-sensitive
- passwords should be a combination of numbers and letters
- users should be encouraged never to write down their passwords
- automatic passwords may be generated by the system
- an alternative to passwords is for the user to have a card or a badge.

LOGICAL ACCESS SYSTEM

Physical access involves restricting unauthorised access to the hardware of a system. *Logical access* controls the access of those who do have access to a computer/terminal.

A logical access system should be capable of the following:

- establishing the user's identity by means of an ID code
- verifying the user, usually by means of a password
- confirming that the user has authorised access to the requested data.

HACKING

Hacking is the deliberate accessing of on-line systems by unauthorised persons. Once the hacker has gained to the system, there are several damaging options available to him:

- gain access to the file which holds all ID codes, passwords, and authorisations
- discover the method used for generating/authorisation passwords
- develop a program to appropriate users IDs/passwords
- discover maintenance codes, which would render the system easily accessible
- interfere with the access control system, to provide the hacker with open access to the system

- generate information which is of potential use to a competitor organisation
- provide the basis for fraudulent activity
- cause data corruption by the introduction of unauthorised computer programs and processing onto the system (computer viruses)
- alter or delete files

Controls can be designed that will help prevent such activity occurring:

- physical security
- passwords
- data encryption
- system logs
- audit trails
- segregation of duties
- random checks.

COMPUTER VIRUSES

A computer virus is a small program which, having been introduced into the system, proliferates; its purpose is to spread extensively impairing both data and software. Viruses can be categorised as:

- **Trojans.** Whilst carrying on one program, secretly carries on another.
- **Worms.** Replicate within the systems.
- **Trap doors.** Undocumented entry points to systems allowing normal controls to be bypassed.
- **Logic bombs.** Triggered on the occurrence of a certain event.
- **Time bombs.** Triggered on a certain date.

Preventative steps may include:

- Control on the use of external software (e.g. checked for viruses before use).
- Use of only tested, marked discs within the organisation
- restricted access to floppy discs on all PCs/workstations.

ENCRYPTION

Encryption provides a defence to enhance physical security measures. It is the technique of disguising information to preserve the confidentiality; this should occur during transmission and when stored.

The response to a potential disaster, such as the loss of part of the computer system, can be effected by preparing a *contingency plan*. This is possible by creating multiple data processing facilities on separate sites.

CONTROLS IN ORGANISATIONS

The classical management theory was developed in the post-war period, often by practising management consultants, in an attempt to develop universal management theories. There are three major approaches:

- Scientific management
- Administrative theory
- Industrial psychology

All of these approaches have the common feature of assuming a *correct* solution—the only problem that is perceived is to identify the correct solution. The systems approach studies the organisation in the wider context of the environment in which it operates and recognises that the work situation involves both social and technical factors, which interact with each other, from this developed *contingency* theories of management. It sees the organisation as existing within a given environment, affected by both internal and external forces.

Analysing Organisational Structure

Organisational structure has been defined by Kast and Rosenzweig as the established pattern of relationships among the components/parts of the organisation. Lawrence and Lorsch claim that the process of structuring consists of two basic processes—*differentiation* and *integration.*

Differentiation consists of:

- vertical differentiation—establishing a hierarchy; and
- horizontal differentiation—setting up various departments.

Integration consists of both:

- Coordination, and
- Control.

Vertical differentiation. A typical organisation hierarchy could be:

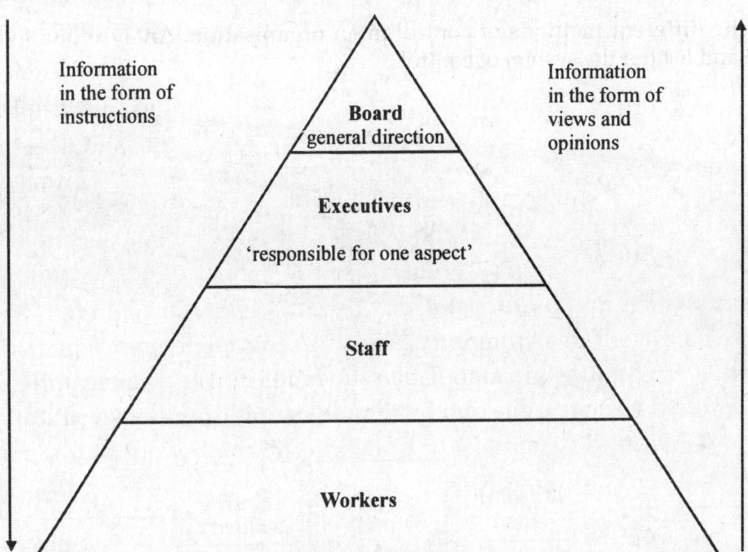

The basic argument concerning the vertical division of labour is whether an organisation should be **tall or flat**. *Span of control* is defined as the number of subordinates which can be supervised effectively by one manager. Hierarchies tend to produce an aristocratic, highly-stratified society based on status. An effective control on the quality of interpersonal relationships in crosswise communications is the requirement that subordinates keep their superior informed about their dealings with other departments.

HORIZONTAL DIFFERENTIATION. The total work of an enterprise must be divided into definite areas of activity in such a manner as to result in cooperation and integration for the attainment of the global objective. *Departmentalisation* will often occur in more than one form within the same organisation.

Organisations and Control

There is no single adequate definition of control, but two important related concepts are *dominance* and *regulation*. Dominance implies the ability to issue directions and rules, in that much of control consists of rules and regulations.

Review Questions

1. Define administrative controls and operational controls, with details of types of controls. Explain with examples.
2. Explain the problems with local area networks in controlling information systems.
3. What is a password? Explain the inherent problems with passwords and the measures to counter them in an effective manner.
4. Explain the logical access system.
5. What is hacking? List out the disadvantages of hacking. How controls can be designed to prevent such activities?
6. What do you understand by computer virus? Explain different types of viruses and the steps to prevent from such viruses.
7. What is encryption? Explain the methods for the same.
8. Explain the different methods of control in an organisation. Analyse one live organisation structure and list out the system of control.

Appendix D

Data Warehousing and Data Mining

INTRODUCTION

A *data warehouse* is a repository of subjectively selected and adapted operational data, which can easily answer any complex, statistical or analytical queries. It is situated at the centre of a decision support system (DSS) of an organisation and contains integrated historical data both summarised and detailed information—common to the entire organisation (Hammergren, 1997). Data warehousing enables easy organisation and maintenance of large data, in addition to fast retrieval and analysis, in a manner and depth required from time to time.

Data can be classified into three categories: Reference and transaction data, derived data, and denormalised data. *Reference and transaction data* originates from operational (source) systems and is normally kept in a conventional database system. At a predetermined periodicity, it will be loaded for refreshing the data warehouse. Once put in data warehouse, it cannot be modified. *Derived data* is only derived from the reference and transaction data, based on certain rules or computations. It can always be derived again on fresh or modified basis of derivation. *Denormalised data*, which is the basis for online analytical processing (OLAP) tools, is prepared periodically but is directly based on detailed reference (transaction) data.

Data mining is the process of extracting previously unknown, valid and actionable information from large data and then using the information so derived to make crucial business and strategic decisions. Data mining hierarchy in business decision support system can be represented as follows:

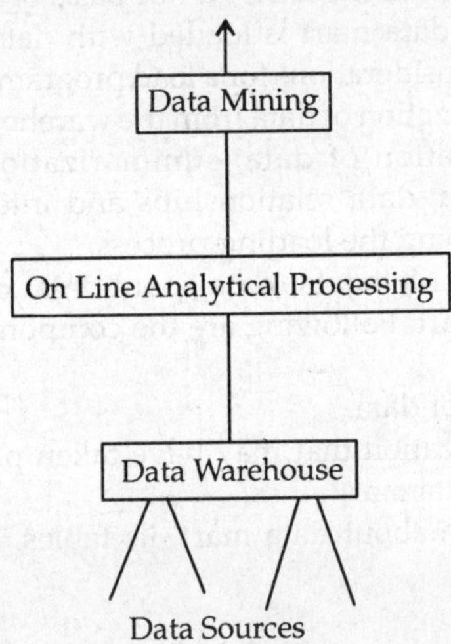

DATA WAREHOUSING

Data warehouses, along, with OLAP tools, are being increasingly developed to analyse historical or time series data to identify past patterns/trends which may be useful in forecasting the future. Data warehousing technology is becoming essential for effective business intelligence, business strategy formulation and implementation in a globally competitive environment, wherein longer and larger amount of data are required to be processed faster and faster for comprehension of its real meaning and impact.

Data Marts

A data mart is a body of DSS data for a department that has an architectural foundation of a data warehouse. In other words, from a data warehouse, data flows to various departments for their customised DSS usage. These individual departmental components are called *data marts*. Data mart in an organisation is much more popular than data warehouse, because every department of an organisation prefers to have a data mart instead of becoming part of the data warehouse. In such an event, the department can easily customize the data, without any necessity to meet the requirements of another department. The processing load is also limited in this case. Similarly, in the case of historical data, a department can choose to limit the historical data to its own department. The source of data that flows into the data mart is of current level detail. The detailed data is customized, sorted or summarised as it is placed in the data mart. In addition, the data mart can be fed by data from external sources.

It is important to note that issues related to data mart are equally relevant to a data warehouse, as data warehouse is only a collection of data marts.

Types of Data Marts. Data marts are of two types—multidimensional on line analytical processing (MOLAP) and relational on line analytical processing (ROLAP). In MOLAP, data mart, the numeric data, can be sliced or diced in a free fashion. In MOLAP, the data can be so viewed as to fully harness the natural multidimensionality. Queries can be asked based on this multidimensionality of data. Thus, query processing and analysis is much more powerful than what could be achieved in a conventional RDBMS environment. Similarly, ROLAP data marts may contain both text and numeric data, and are supported by RDBMS. These data marts are used for general purpose DSS analysis with many indices. ROLAP data marts can be analysed either on ad hoc basis or on preconceived queries.

Loading a data mart. The data mart is loaded with data from a data warehouse by means of a *load program*. Main considerations for a load program are : frequency and schedule; total or partial addition; customization of data from the warehouse (selection); re-sequencing and merging of data; aggregation of data; summarization; efficiency (loading time optimization); integrity of data; data relationships and integrity of data domains; and producing metadata for describing the loading process.

Metadata for a Data Mart. Metadata (data about data) describes about the data in a data warehouse or in a data mart. Following are the components of metadata for a given data warehouse/data mart :

1. Description of sources of data.
2. Description of customization that may have taken place as the data passes from data warehouse into data mart.
3. Descriptive information about data mart, its tables, attributes and relationships, etc.
4. Definitions of all types.

The linkages and relationships between metadata of a data warehouse and metadata of data mart have to be well established by the manager/analyst using the metadata. Further, the DSS analyst also requires to understand how calculations are made and how data is selected for the data mart environment. The metadata pertaining to the individual data mart should also be available to the end-user for effective usage.

Maintenance of a data mart. Periodic maintenance of a data mart means loading, refreshing and purging the data in it. Refreshing the data is performed in regular cycles as per the nature of frequency of data update. Refreshing may be daily, weekly, monthly, quarterly, yearly or decennially depending on the nature and frequency of the data availability. For purging of data in a data mart, the data mart is read periodically and some (old) data is selected for purging/removing. The criteria for purging depends on data, time and periodicity, based on any criterion decided by the application requirements.

Software components for a data mart. The software that can be found with a data mart includes DBMS, access and analysis software, software for automatic creation of data mart, purging and archival software, and metadata management software. The *access and analysis software*, which is the unique for a data warehousing application, allows the end-user to search through the data mart to find and compute or derive the data required by the user. This software also performs impressive presentation of the data so derived to the user.

Tables in the data mart. A data mart may include : summary tables, detailed tables, reference tables, historical tables, analytical (spreadsheet) tables, etc. The data are kept in the tables in the form of star joins normal tables.

Monitoring requirements for a data mart. Periodic monitoring is required on data mart behaviour. Monitoring mainly relates data usage to data content tracking. Data usage tracking has queries on the data mart such as:

What data are being accessed?
Which users are active?
What is the quantity of data accessed?
What are the usage timings?
The data content tracking includes the following queries:
What are the actual contents of the data mart?
What is the best way of accessing?
Is there any bad data in the data mart?
How and how much of the data mart is growing?

Monitoring of data mart will become essential and important only when the size of the data in the data mart grows significantly.

ONLINE ANALYTICAL PROCESSING

Online analytical processing (OLAP) systems are capable of analysing online a large number of past transactions or large number of data records and summarise them. The type of data is usually multidimensional in nature. This multidimensionality is the key driver for OLAP technology, which happens to control to data warehousing. On the contrary, regular, conventional online transaction processing (OLTP) systems consume large computing resources in terms of disk space, memory, and CPU time. In addition to response time and other resources, OLAP is a continuous iterative process and preferable interactive one.

OLTP and OLAP systems. Table shows a comparison between OLTP and OLAP systems.

Table Comparison between OLTP and OLAP systems

OLTP	OLAP
1. Only current data available (old data is replaced by current data by updating)	Both current and historic data available (current is appended to historic data)
2. Short transactions (single granularity or more)	Long database transactions

3.	Online update/insert/delete transactions	Batch update/insert/delete transactions
4.	High volume of transactions in a given period	Low volume transactions, periodic refreshing
5.	Concurrency control and transaction recovery	No concurrent transactions and therefore no recovery upon failures required
6.	Largely online ad hoc queries, requiring low level of indexing	Largely pre-determined queries requiring high level of indexing

Data modelling. In the data warehousing environment, the requirements of data modelling are quite different, as the users' expectations from the integrated data warehouse have to be considered. Since the data warehouse comprises of a central repository of data collected from divergent sources, the integrated user's view of the data warehouse will form the basis for any data modelling of the data warehouse. In other words, the data collected from different source systems and integrated together in the data warehouse cannot be used, unless it is modelled and organized based on the end-users' perspective of the data. The better the understanding of the user's perspective, the more will be effectiveness of the data warehousing application. Therefore, the outcome of the understanding of the users' requirements and perspectives should be thoroughly captured in the data model for the data warehouse.

Star schema. The star schema provides a multidimensional view. Business data analysis of any application will require analysis in multiple dimensions. From the data organisation angle, a star schema is a relational schema. Star schema is organised around a central table, called *fact in* table, which contains raw numeric items that represent relevant business facts.These facts are additive and are accessible via dimensions. The performance of star schema, either in a conventional RDBMS environment or in other environments, will not be efficient. For object oriented data models, the star schema definition may be required to be made a fresh, which is an open area of research.

Multifact star schema/snow flake schema. As a data warehouse grows in complexity, the diversity of subjects covered grows which adds more perspectives to access the data. In such situations, a better technique, called *multifact* or *snow flake* schema can be utilised. It provides aggregation at different levels of hierarchies in a given dimension.

OLAP tools. OLAP tools can be broadly classified into two categories: MOLAP tools and ROLAP tools. *MOLAP* based products organise, navigate and analyse data typically in an integrated form. Applications requiring iterative and comprehensive time series analysis of trends are well suited for MOLAP technology (e.g. financial analysis and budgeting). Examples include Arbor Software's Essbase, Oracle's Express Server, Pilot Software's Lightship Server, Sinper's TM/1, Planning Science's Gentium and Kenan Technology's Multiway.

Some of the problems faced by users are related to maintaining support to multiple subject areas in an RDBMS. These problems can be solved by some vendors by maintaining access from MOLAP tools to detailed data in an RDBMS, as shown in Fig.

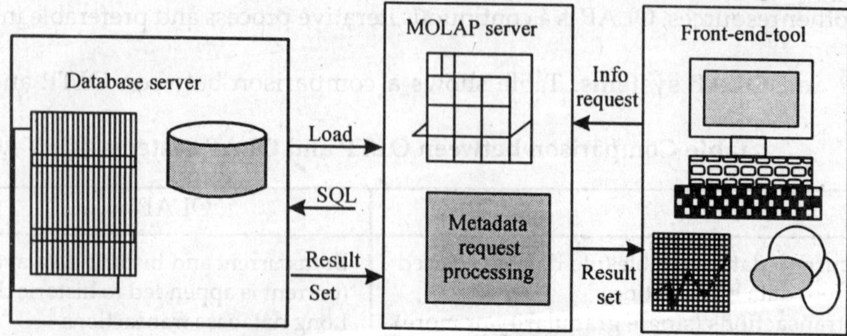

Fig. An architecture for MOLAP

ROLAP. *Relational OLAP* (*ROLAP*) is the latest OLAP technology segment in the market. By supporting a dictionary layer of metadata, the RDBMS products have bypassed any requirement for creating a static, multidimensional data structure as shown in Fig.

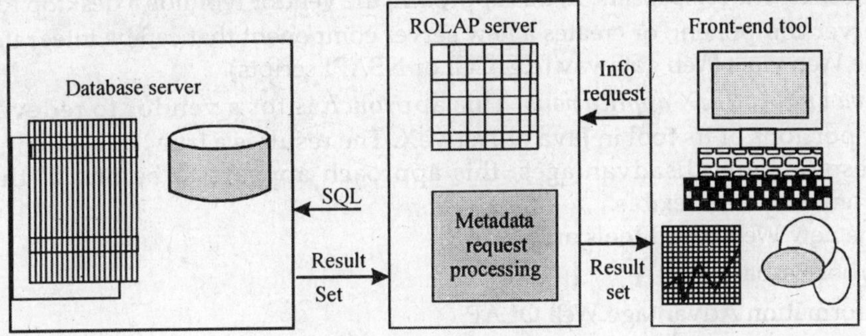

Fig. ROLAP architecture

Important vendors of such products are Microstrategy (DSS Agent/DSS Server), Platinum/Prodea Software (Beacon), Information Advantage (AxSys), Informix/Stanford Technology Group (Metacube) (now acquired by IBM) and SyBASE (High Gate Project).

OLAP tools and the Internet. The Web technologies are the natural choice for adaptation for data warehousing. The internet is virtually a free resource which provides a universal connectivity within and between organisations and also individuals. Some of the Web facilities are as under:

- The Web eases complex administrative tasks of managing distributed environments.
- The Web allows companies to store and manage both data and applications on servers that can be centrally managed and updated, thus eliminating problems with software and data accuracy.
- The emerging third generation Web sites replace HTML gateways with Web-based application servers. These servers can download Java applets or ActiveX applications that execute on clients, or interact with corresponding applets running on servers-servlets. The third-generation Web servers provide users with all the capabilities of existing decision-support applications without requiring them to load any client software except a Web browser.

Vendors of decision support applications, especially query, reporting and OLAP tools, are rapidly converting their tools to work on the Web vendor approaches for deploying tools on the Web include the following:

- *HTML publishing*. This approach involves transforming an output of a query into the HTML page that can be downloaded into browser. This approach does not support interactive access to data or reports.
- *Helper applications*. In this approach, a tool is configured as a helper application that resides within a browser. This is the case of a 'fat' client, in which, once the data is downloaded, users can take advantage of all capabilities of the tool to analyse data. However, maintaining these helper applications becomes another tasks for system administrators.
- *Plug-ins*. A variation on the previous approach, plug-ins are helper applications that are downloaded from the server prior to their initial use. Since the plug-ins are downloaded from the server, their normal administration and installation tasks are significantly reduced. However, typically, plug-ins are browser-specific and

may not run on all platforms or with all browsers. Also, as browsers get updated, these plug-ins may have to be upgraded as well, creating additional administration workload.

- *Server-centric components*. In this approach, the vendor rebuilds a desktop tools as a server component, or creates a new server component that can be integrated with the Web via a Web gateway (e.g. CGI or NSAPI scripts).
- *Java and ActiveX applications*. This approach is for a vendor to redevelop all or portions of its tool in Java or ActiveX. The result is a true `thin' client model. Despite some disadvantages, this approach appears to be one of the most promising and flexible.

Some of the new Web-based tools are:

- Arbor Essbase Web
- Information Advantage Web OLAP
- Microstrategy DSS Web
- Brio Technology.

Data Warehouse Implementation

Following are the steps of the data warehouse implementation:

1. Collect and analyse business requirements.
2. Create a data model and physical design for the data warehouse after deciding the appropriate hardware platform.
3. Define data sources.
4. Choose the DBMS and software platform for data warehouse.
5. Extract the data from operational data sources, transfer it, clean-up and load into the data warehouse model or data mart.
6. Choose database access and reporting tools.
7. Choose database connectivity software.
8. Choose the data analysis (OLAP) and presentation (client GUI) software.
9. Keep refreshing the data warehouse periodically.

DATA MINING

Data mining process is a natural and logical continuation to data warehousing. An organisation that may have already invested in a data warehouse would naturally like to reap the benefits of a data warehouse by adopting data mining process. It is, however, possible that an organisation can take up data mining even without having built a data warehouse by using either direct transactional data records or a single database of transactions of data on which mining is required to be done. Therefore, a data warehouse will always be the right foundation for taking up data mining process.

Process of Data Mining

The stepwise data mining process is as follows:

1. Deciding business objectives for data mining.
2. Data preparation

- Data selection (identification and extraction of data).
- Data pre-processing (data sampling and quality assurance).
- Data transformation (data conversion into an analytical model).

Data mining and analysis of results go hand in hand, interactively and iteratively. The analysis of results is the most important step in the entire cycle of data mining. Using visualisation aids and tools, analysis of data can be done by a highly skilled data analyst with the help of a business analyst.

Finally, the business analyst identifies the stages for implementation of assimilating business knowledge (gained by mining process) into actual real-life business processes for availing the benefits of data mining exercise performed. The ultimate benefit will be a recognition or a new focus on importance of data as an asset of the organisation. Its value is better understood and focused by data mining operations, thus resulting in a data-oriented culture in the organisation which enhances interest and motivation for related activities such as development of data warehousing activities.

Data Mining Tools

The tools for data mining are so trendy that many vendors at other software (as for decision-support functions) are attempting to add data mining capabilities. The emerging generic title for these tools is 'siftware', mainly because they 'sift' through a large amount of data. The tools for data mining can be classified into three categories:

- Commercial tools
- Public domain tools
- Research prototypes.

Commercial tools can be identified as follows:

1. 'Intelligent Miner' from IBM.
2. 'SAS' System from SAS Institute.
3. 'Thought' from Right Information Systems.
4. 'Data Mining Suite' from Information Discovery Inc.
5. MineSet from Silicon Graphics Inc.
6. 'Data Mining Marksman' from HNC Software.
7. 'Data Crusher' from DataMind Corp.
8. 'Cross/z' from Cross/z International.
9. 'Clementine' from Integral Solution Ltd.

Public domain tools include largely freeware with just registration fee: 'Brute' from University of Washington and 'MCL++' from Stanford University, California.

Some of the research prototypes may find their way into commercial market.

Review Questions

1. Define data warehouse and explain the purpose of creating a data warehouse in an organisation.
2. Explain different types of data and their originating source.
3. What are data marts? Explain the differences between the data warehouse and data marts. Name the two types of data marts.
4. What do you understand by metadata? Explain the components of metadata for a given data warehouse/data mart.
5. Explain in detail the system of maintenance of a data mart, its software components, and different types of tables available for use.
6. What is online analytical processing? How is it different from online transaction processing?
7. Explain the uses of different types of data modelling.
8. Outline the significant uses of MOLAP and ROLAP tools of OLAP. Explain the same with diagrammatic representation.
9. List out the steps for data warehouse implementation.
10. How is Web technology useful for adaptation of data warehousing? Explain the role of Internet for this purpose.
11. What do you understand by data mining? Explain the data mining process in detail.
12. What are the available data mining tools? Identify the different commercial tools available.

Glossary

Acceptance testing. Developers and users test the system under actual or simulated operated conditions to ensure that it is acceptable to users.

Agile manufacturing. The activities of manufacturing environments that are dynamic and flexible to produce instantaneously customised goods and services in different quantities and switchover from one product to another without any problem.

Application control. Application control in the areas of input, processing, output and storage of data, information, and programs.

Application software. Software designed to perform people-related tasks such as word processing, graphics and so on.

Application-dedicated software. Specialised or customised applications designed to meet the particular needs of an organisation.

Archie. An information search tool for the internet that identifies and indexes all files on anonymous ftp servers; user must know the file name, or at least part of it.

Arithmetic-logic unit (ALU). The portion of the CPU used for arithmetic and logical operations.

Artificial intelligence. The study and use of computers to replicate or improve upon such intelligent human thought processes as reasoning or learning.

Assembler. A program used to translate assembly language into machine language.

Assembly language. A machine-dependent, second-generation language. Each instruction typically consists of a name or label field, an operation code, an operand, and a comment field.

Attribute. Each column in a relational table represents a field, also referred to as an attribute.

Audit trail. The path of data recordings, transcriptions, and processing that a data item takes as it flows through a business information system.

Automatic teller machine (ATM). Machine at banks that process inputs and outputs using magnetic strips affixed to cards.

Backlog. Information systems which are waiting to be developed because of lack of resources.

Backup files. Copies of files that are pressed into operation when the originals are damaged/destroyed.

Backup procedures. Procedures for copying data and programs on to spare magnetic tapes/disks to provide security.

Bandwidth. The data-carrying capacity of a data-cummunications channel.

BASIC. A high-level programming language that is easy to learn, yet possesses great power in writing formulae expressing input/output instructions.

Baseband. Transmits digital signals directly over the network; can transmit only one signal at a time. It is most commonly used in LANs.

Batch processing. Data are accumulated over a period of time before they are processed periodically when the use of a computer is likely to be cost-effective.

Binary digit (bit). A binary digit conventionally represented by '0'and '1'. It is a fundamental unit of storage in all digital computers.

Bits per second (bps). A measurement describes the speed at which a communication device sends and receives data.

Broadband. Transmits multiple streams of analog signals over the network using frequency division multiplexing. Useful for transmitting large amounts of data over long distance.

Bus topology. A local area network in which computer devices are connected to a common cable.

Business information system. A set of manual and/or computerised components for collecting, storing, and processing business data and converting such data into useful, decision-oriented information.

Business intelligence. Internal and external data helping a firm assess and analyse the business environment and identify any possible opportunity and threat.

Byte. An 8-bit group used to represent a single letter, number, or special symbol in a computer.

Cache memory. A primary memory designed to increase the efficiency of the CPU. It is made up of memory cells that are used to store data and instructions temporarily.

CASE. It is also known as computer aided software engineering. It automates several phases of information system development. It graphically represents system requirements and automatically converts system requirements into program code.

CD-ROM. Compact Disk-Read Only Memory — a special kind of optical disk that has excellent storage capabilities and stores different kinds of data, such as text, picture, audio, and video.

Cell (in a spreadsheet). A memory location in a spreadsheet identified by its row and column coordinates and used to store labels, numbers, formulae, or instructions.

Cellular phones. It contains a base station with a radio transmitter, a receiver, an antenna, and a computer. The user's calls are handled using radio waves with a unique set of frequencies that are assigned to each cell.

Central processing unit (CPU). A device that performs the actual data processing tasks of a computer system.

Centralised environment. All computer facilities, systems and resources are in one central location and other parts of the organisation are linked to the central facility through telecommunication networks.

Channel. A data communications path through a medium that can take to accomplish a communications task.

Client. A smaller computer, usually a PC or a workstation, on a network shares some of its tasks and computing power with the server; both the client and the server share tasks and processes.

Client-server system. A distributed system in which a server, such as a mainframe, stores commonly used data and programs. The client asks the server for data and programs.

Closed system. A system that neither transmits nor receives any information from the outside world.

Coaxial cable. A copper or aluminium wire wrapped in one or more layers of insulating metallic and/or fibrous sheathing, and that protects the data-carrying wire from external electrical static and noise.

COBOL. A high-level programming language that uses instructions resembling English statements and imposes an overall framework for a program.

Coding. The process of writing instructions for a computer program in a specific language.

Common carrier. A firm that furnishes voice and data communication services both to businesses and to the general public.

Communication satellite systems. Commercial satellites launched into geosynchronous orbit at an altitude of about 22,300 miles above the equator. These are powered by solar panels and carry different types of signals.

Compiler. A program that translates high-level programming language instructions into machine code.

Computer. An electronic device with ability to (*a*) accept user-supplied data, (*b*) input, store, and execute programmed instructions, (*c*) perform mathematical and logical operations, and (*d*) output results according to user specifications.

Computer aided design. A computerised application used primarily for research and design of new products.

Computer aided manufacturing. A computerised application used by industrial manufacturers to produce products.

Computer graphics. The graphical display of computerised information.

Computer hardware. Computer equipment such as a CPU, disk drive, CRT, or printer.

Computer software. Programs that instruct a computer how to process data and documentation that explains how these programs should be used.

Computer vision. A field of study that endows computers with the ability to recognise objects.

Configuration. The customisation of a PC to meet the information needs of a particular user.

Context diagram. It provides a broad, abstract, top-down view of an entire system by identifying its major inputs, outputs, and processes.

Control unit. A part of the CPU that accesses data and instructions stored in the computer memory and transfers them to the ALU.

Creeping requirements. New requirements that keep emerging throughout the development of life-cycle. These can seriously jeopardize system development.

Data. The raw material from which information is generated. Data appear in the form of text, numbers, figures, or any combination of these.

Database. A set of one or more computer files used by one or more application programs and that minimises data redundancy.

Database administrator. An individual who is in-charge of an organisation's databases.

Database management system (DBMS). Special computer programs that enable users and application programs to create, maintain, manipulate, and retrieve file data and create useful reports to management.

Data communication carriers. Telephone and telecommunication firms that provide telecommunication services to move data.

Data definition language. A programming language that enables a database user to identify the data fields of a new file and to enter data for individual file records.

Data dictionary. A computer file that contains descriptive information about data items in other files.

Data encryption. The process of translating communicated data into secret codes in order to safeguard the data.

Data field. The set of characters comprising a data item in a file record (*e.g.*, name, address, employee number).

Data flow diagram (DFD). It is derived from a context diagram. It graphically portrays the inputs, outputs, data stores, and processes associated with each subsystem of the overall system. It breaks down the single process shown in the context diagram.

Data hierarchy chain. The data stored in a database is organised in a hierarchy: databases, files, records, fields, bytes, and bits.

Data independence. A system allowing the user to access data simply based on the contents of data, without knowing the physical location of the data.

Data manipulation language (DML). A programming language that enables the user to access, update, replace, delete, sort, index, or protect data base records.

Data mart. Individual departmental DSS data.

Data mining. Process of extracting previously unknown, valid or actionable information from large data and using the information to make business and strategic decisions.

Data redundancy. It occurs when data are duplicated in different files.

Data transcription. The process of converting source documents into machine-readable format for computer processing.

Data transmission. The process of sending data from one location to another within a computer or between computers and/or other equipment.

Data warehouse. Repository of subjectively selected and adapted operational data, which can easily answer any complex, statistical or analytical queries.

Decentralised environment. Each individual site designs, develops, acquires and maintains systems that meet its local needs.

Decision support system (DSS). A set of computer programs capable of handling unstructured or semi-structured problems through the use of one or more corporate databases, user databases, model databases, and a special dialogue or planning language.

Decision table. A graphical tool that outlines system logic. The table shows the conditions and the actions to be taken if the conditions are met.

Decision tree. A graphical representation of the logic in a decision-making process and the sequence of decision points that constitutes the decision.

Desktop publishing. The production of office documents such as memos, newsletters, price lists, technical manuals, etc.

Difference engine. A prototype computer device developed by Charles Babbage in 17th century that would calculate the roots of polynomial equations.

Digital computer. A device whose fundamental unit of storage is the binary digit or bit.

Digital signatures. Verify the authenticity and integrity of the message and the claimed identity of the sender.

Direct access. A type of secondary storage in which any record can be directly accessed.

Direct cutover. During system implementation, the old system is removed and the new system is installed.

Direct distance dialing. Network that transmits voice and data.

Direct file organisation. Organisation of files based on a unique key for each file, which is accessed directly through the memory address of the key.

Disaster recovery plan. It specifies how a firm will maintain its information systems and services if a disaster strikes.

Distributed database. Databases distributed over single- or multi-vendor hardware located in different geographic areas.

Distributed management. Policies and procedures designed to manage the distributed systems in an organisation.

Distributed systems. Multi-vendor systems that reside on PCs and mainframes, that are linked by networks.

Document management systems. Computer-based tools that allow users to access text and graphics, irrespective of their location and form.

Dot-matrix printer. A serial, impact printer that creates characters out of a 'grid' or a matrix of tiny dots.

Drill-down. A feature that allows the user to get information at any desired level of detail from an EIS.

DSS generator. It consists of programs such as data management tools, electronic spreadsheets, report generators, and statistical packages to facilitate system development.

DSS shell. A computer program used to build a customised DSS. It has a skeletal version of a database, a model base, and an interface.

E-commerce. Based on virtual corporation paradigm through the combination of intranets and extranets.

E-Governance. Delivery of govt. services and information to the public using electronic means, and allows citizens to participate in govt. decision-making process.

E-mail. The use of a computer for personal or business communications, in which users leave short, written message in each other's computer 'mail boxes'.

Electronic cash. Executes cash payments using computers connected over networks.

Electronic data interchange. A direct computer-to-computer exchange of data over a telecommunications network.

Encryption. Provides a defence to enhance physical security system.

End-user. Usually non-technical individuals who use computer resources to accomplish daily tasks.

End-user computing. The design, development, and maintenance of information systems by system users, rather than by the IS department.

Enterprise modelling. An important prerequisite before selection/implementation of an ERP system.

Enterprise resource planning. Software architecture facilitating the flow of information among different functions of an organisation.

Entity. A person, place, thing, or idea about which data are collected.

Entity relationship diagram. A graphical tool that models the entities in a system and the relationships among them.

Exception report. A report that identifies data that appear to be exceptional, where an exception is the difference between actual performance and expected performance.

Executive information system. A program that allows top managers to quickly retrieve, analyse, and disseminate data and information.

Expert systems. A software designed to capture the experience, decision rules, and thought processes of one or more experts in a given area. It consists of three main components : a knowledge base, an inference engine, and a user interface.

External strategic systems. Systems that are used by a firm's customers, clients, suppliers, or other external entities.

Extranet. An extension of an intranet which makes the latter accessible to outside companies/individuals with or without an intranet.

Fax. A technology that uses telephones, modems, and scanners to transmit text and graphics to an individual/organisation anywhere in the world.

Field. A meaningful group of characters. A record consists of fields; a field is made up of bytes.

File. A collection of records of the same type grouped together.

Flat file. A collection of similar computer records in which each record on the file is the same as every other record in terms of importance or use.

Flexibility. The ease with which system designers can adapt an existing computer system to changing circumstances.

Floppy disk. This is a 5.25-inch or 3.5-inch storage diskette made of polyester film with a magnetic coating, used mostly on microcomputers. It has fairly large memory capacity (between 720 KB and 2.88 KB).

FORTRAN. A high-level programming language developed by IBM in 1957 for expressing formulae, writing equations, and performing reiterative calculations.

Fourth-generation programming languages (4GLs). These high-level languages include the data manipulation languages of electronic spreadsheets, wordprocessors, and DBMS.

ftp. File transfer protocol allows users to send or receive files from a remote computer.

Full duplex. A data exchange device in which both parties can send and receive information at the same time.

Functional requirements. System specifications identified by asking who, what, where, when, and how; who are the users ? What are their needs ? Where, when, and how do they want the information ?

Fuzzy logic. A set of mathematical and logical principles that make it possible to use incomplete, inconsistent, and imprecise knowledge in an expert system.

General-purpose software. A software that is mass-produced for a broad range of common business applications, such as word processing.

GIGO (garbage-in, garbage-out). An acronym that means if inaccurate data is input into a computer system, useful information cannot be output from the system.

Goal seeking. The process of determining the input values required to achieve a certain goal. This process can be viewed as the reverse of 'what-if' analysis.

Gopher. A menu-based interface that provides access to information residing on Gopher sites.

Group decision support systems. Information systems that facilitate the free flow and exchange of ideas and information among group members while maintaining their anonymity.

Groupware. Communication tools, such as E-mail, voice mail, fax, and video conferencing that foster electronic communication and collaboration with groups.

Hacking. Deliberate accessing of online systems of unauthorised persons.

Half-duplex. A data exchange device in which two parties alternate sending data. In this system, one device 'talks' while the other can only listen. Commonly used to communicate with peripherals.

Hand-held computer. A smaller than a notebook computer used primarily to collect field data.

Hard-copy output. Computer output that is printed on paper.

Hard disk. A type of secondary storage medium that actually consists of several disks, a read/write head mechanism, and an electronic drive interface.

Hardware. The physical devices of a computer system, *e.g.*, keyboard, monitor, disk drive, or printer.

Hashing. A method where the record key of a file record is transformed directly to a disk address and no dictionary is used.

Hash total. An otherwise meaningless control total used as a check against a computer-generated version of the same number.

Hierarchical database. A database that uses parent-child relationships to organise file records. It is also called a tree-structure.

Hierarchical model. A model in which the logical relationships among data elements are represented as a hierarchy using 1-M relationships.

High-level programming languages. Computer languages that improve on assembly language and machine language because they are English-like and require fewer instructions.

Home page. An electronic description of an individual, institution, or organisation. Home pages can be accessed through the Internet.

Host computer. A large computer, often a mainframe, serves as the central receiving and switching computer in local, regional, or national computer networks.

Icon. A tiny picture typically displayed on a computer screen to identify processing choices.

Imaging software. Programs that scan data and information and convert them into digital images.

Imaging systems. A document management system that converts paper, microfilm, microfiche, and electronic data into digitised images that can be printed, faxed, or viewed on a computer screen.

Indexed-sequential file. A file in which data are stored in a sequence and an index is created showing the memory address of each piece of data.

Inference engine. It is a component of an expert system. It is the control mechanism that applies reasoning to the knowledge in the knowledge base and decides what knowledge to apply and when and where to apply it.

Informal systems. Systems created by ad hoc, informal work groups to support information needs that cannot be met by formal systems.

Information. Facts, figures, or statistics that have meaning, typically because they are useful in reaching a decision.

Information resource management. The process of managing all components of an information system that collect, store, process, retrieve, and disseminate information. The resources include hardware, software, networks, systems, and personnel.

Information superhighway. A network of networks full scalable, with no central controlling entity, and cannot determine the user's profile.

Information system. A system that creates, processes, stores and retrieves information.

Information technology. Tools and techniques supporting the design and development of information systems.

Input controls. It ensures that input data are authorised, accurate, and timely by preventing users from entering incomplete, erroneous, or inappropriate data.

Integrated Services Digital Network. Digital network which uses commercial telephone systems allowing users to transmit voice and data.

Intelligent support systems. Systems designed to assist intuitive decision making, *e.g.*, DSS, EIS, and ES.

Internal strategic systems. Systems used by employees within an organisation and designed to enhance productivity.

Internet. Network of networks linking computer users all over the world. It serves as a repository of information on a variety of subjects.

Interorganisational systems. Computerised information systems shared by more than one organisation.

Interpreter. A software that translates and executes one statement at a time.

Interrecord gap. A space on a secondary storage device that is used to separate physical file records from one another.

Intranet. Business transactions across its internal departments and subsidiaries, which can span the entire globe in case of multinationals. Intranets respond to this challenge.

Joystick. An input device commonly used with microcomputers and often designed in the shape of handles.

Key. It identifies each record in a database.

Key field. A field that serves as a unique identifier of instances of that record in the file.

Keyboard. A common and popular method of inputting data into a computer.

Knowledge acquisition. The process of acquiring knowledge from different sources.

Knowledge base. The understanding required by individuals before they can use a system intelligently.

Knowledge representation. The conversion of the knowledge and judgement of the expert into a form the system can use.

Laptop microcomputer. A microcomputer about the size of a briefcase that is compact, light weight, and designed for portability.

Laser printer. A page-at-a-time printer, capable of printing 600 dpi or more.

Leased lines. Telephone lines are leased to organisations for its exclusive use in setting up WANs.

Line printer. A printer that assembles an entire line of output at one time.

Local area network. A geographically confined configuration of computer equipment that has been connected together for communication purposes.

Logical access. Controls the access of those who do not have access to a computer/ terminal.

Logical file. A conceptual file that satisfies the data requirements of an application program.

Logical record. One record in a file containing information about one file entity.

Logical view. The logical relationships among data elements in a database.

Logic field. A field used to store a 'true' or 'false' condition.

Looping. The process of executing the same instructions over and over.

M-commerce. Means to pay for merchandise services or information through a mobile phone using wireless application protocol.

Machine-dependent programming language. A computer language that can only run on the machine(s) for which it was designed.

Machine language. A first-generation computer language that is expressed in a binary code and can therefore be stored and executed directly by a computer.

Magnetic disk. Storage medium which provides direct access to data from both large and small computers.

Magnetic Ink Character Recognition. A type of data input that uses machine-readable ink containing magnetic particles.

Magnetic tape. A secondary storage medium. One side of the tape has a magnetic oxide coating used to record data while the other side is used as backing.

Mainframe computer. A fully configured computer intended for substantial, high volume data processing. It contains large primary memory, substantial processing capabilities, the ability to attach numerous peripheral devices, and data communication capabilities.

Management information systems. 1. Any type of information systems designed primarily for management use. 2. A specific type of computer information system developed after EDP systems that focuses on outputting useful, decision-oriented information useful to managers as opposed to operational workers.

Manufacturing information systems. A system that supports manufacturing functions of purchasing, receiving, quality control, inventory management, material requirements planning, capacity planning, production scheduling, and plant design. It applies to both manufacturing and service environments.

Many-to-many (M-M). A relationship in which a record can have multiple parents and multiple children.

Marketing information system. An information system that collects, maintains, and reports data related to sale of goods, customer support following sales, sales forecasts, sales performance, marketing research, and advertising for a firm.

Master file. A permanent record of all transactions that have occurred in a firm.

Meta data. Describes about the data in a data ware house or in a data mart.

Metropolitan area networks. High bandwidth WANs that link electronic devices distributed over a metropolitan area and are used for LAN-to-LAN connections, high-speed data transmission, backup network facilities, full-motion video, and image transmission.

Microcomputer. The smallest and least-expensive computer. Often called a lap-top microcomputer, personal computer, or portable microcomputer.

Microfiche. Small film sheets that store information in miniaturised form.

Microprocessor. A chip in a microcomputer that contains the arithmetic/logic and control functions. The speed of a microcomputer is measured in MHz.

Minicomputer. A small, powerful multiuser system with high memory capabilities and processing speed. It is less powerful than a mainframe but more powerful than a PC.

Mixed chaining. The use of both forward and backward chaining to solve problems. Most expert systems are equipped to use both.

Model management system. A component of a DSS that stores and accesses models that managers use to make decisions.

Modem. A data communication device standing for 'modulator-demodulator' and which translates digital signals into analog ones and *vice-versa.*

Modules. When a large program is divided into smaller ones, more manageable units, these units are termed as modules.

Mouse. A hand-held 'point-and-click' input device that can be moved over a smooth surface to control the position of the cursor on the screen.

Multimedia. An interactive system that combines several types of media, such as text, graphics, animation, audio, and video. Most multimedia applications require a sound card, a video card, and a CD-ROM drive.

Multiplexer. A data communication device that allows several users to share communication channels.

Multiprocessing. The use of two or more processing units that are linked together to accomplish data processing tasks.

Multiprogramming. A computer system in which a number of users can run multiple programs on a single CPU at the same time.

Multi-user operating system. An operating system that enables several users to access a computer and run different programs at the same time.

Natural-language interface. A technology that enables computers to recognise and respond to the languages in which human beings communicate with one another.

Network. A system that transmits data to and from a number of locations that are geographically dispersed.

Network architecture. A set of standards, or protocols, for telecommunication hardware and software.

Neural networks. Programs that model the capabilities of the human brain. They have good pattern-recognition capabilities and can also learn new information and behaviour.

Non-procedural language. Language that focuses on *what* needs to be done, without specifying exactly *how* it should be done.

Object-oriented programming. A powerful programming language that enhances the productivity of programmers and reduces software development time. Another use is code reusability.

Office automation system. Computer-based information systems whose primary aim is to facilitate oral and written communication between individual and groups, e.g., desktop publishing, voice mail, E-mail, work processing, and multimedia systems.

One-to-many (1-M). A relationship in which each node can have only one parent, but can have multiple children.

One-to-one (1-1). A relationship between two entities.

Online analytical processing. Capable of analysing online a large number of data records and summarise them.

Online transaction processing (OLTP). Data are processed as they are created; since there is no time lag between data creation and data processing, the information is always current.

Open system. A system with a feedback mechanism that promotes the free exchange of information between the system and external entities.

Operating system. A set of programs that controls the operations of the CPU and enables users to communicate with a computer system.

Optical character recognition (OCR). A method of reading printed, typed, or hand-written data directly from source documents by interpreting the pattern.

Organisation-wide system. System that provides comprehensive overall long-term information about the entire organisation. These systems integrate information from multiple sources to present a complete view of the organisation.

Organisational structure. It identifies the level of responsibility, authority, management, and scope of control of employees in the organisation. There are two types of organisational structure : pyramid and task-based.

Output controls. Controls designed to ensure accurate outputs from a computer and to restrict the distribution of outputs to authorised recipients.

Outsourcing. Hiring professional services from outside to meet the in-house needs of an organisation. Using external agencies to create, process, manage, and maintain information systems and provide information-related services.

Parallel conversion. A method of system implementation in which data processing is performed on both the old system and the new system for a trial period to assure the workability of the new system.

Parallel processing. The ability of a computer to execute several instructions concurrently instead of sequentially.

Password. Sequence of characters presented to a computer system before it will allows access to the system.

Peer-to-peer relationship. An arrangement whereby all devices on a network have equal status and privileges, in which a central computer controls and coordinates all other devices on the network.

Pen-based computing. Portable computer that use an electronic writing pad and a light-sensitive pen to input data into a computer. The writing is converted into digital input and stored in a file in the computer.

Personal computer. A device that contains greater capabilities than either home or portable microcomputers. A PC typically can add options through expansion slots. The term 'Personal Computer' is misleading, since many are used for business purposes and/ or are networked.

Personal information systems. Systems that support the information needs of individual decision makers for solving structured, semi-structured, and unstructured problems, *e.g.*, PCs.

Phased conversion. The new system is slowly phased into its operational environment by replacing parts of the old system with parts of the new system.

Physical access. Restrict unauthorised access to the hardware of a system.

Pilot study. Uses one department or unit to test a system before installing it throughout the organisation.

Pointers. Data stored by a computer to establish links between records.

Primary storage. The computer's main memory is called primary storage and is part of the central processor. It is made up of memory cells that are used to store data and instructions temporarily. Four types of memory are : RAM, ROM, cache, and registers.

Private branch exchange (PBX). An electronic switching device that provides connections between the organisation's telephone lines and those of the outside lines.

Procedural language. A general-purpose programming language, with its own syntax and grammar, that is used to write software.

Process controls. Controls concerned with the manipulation of data inside a central processing unit.

Production systems. It relates to production of goods and services. Specifically addresses information needs relating to raw materials, equipment, manpower, and other issues.

Program. Stored instructions that tell a computer how to process data.

Program flowchart. Illustrates the flow of logic in a computer program. It is built around the three software constructs of sequence, selection and iteration.

Programmable read only memory (PROM). A type of read only memory that can be programmed by a special device called a 'ROM programmer'.

Programming language. A special type of computer language, with its own syntax and grammar, that is used to write software.

Protocols. Rules and formats that ensure efficient and error-free electronic communication.

Prototyping. A system development methodology in which the system is iteratively developed using prototypes. Also, referred to as rapid application development (RAD).

Pyramid structure. It is an organisational hierarchy with the chief executive at the top and non-managerial employees at the bottom. Middle managers are somewhere between the two.

Quality information system. Stand-alone or embedded systems that help an organisation to achieve its quality goals. The quality plan is derived from the strategic information plan.

Query language. A problem-oriented programming language that enables a user to retrieve selected information from a database file.

Random access file. A direct-access file, typically stored on disk, in which file records can be accessed in random order.

Random access memory. Primary memory used to store data or instructions that can be altered by the user.

Re-engineering. Re-evaluating and radically redesigning the way in which a firm does business; driven by the question, 'why do we do what we do ?'

Read only memory (ROM). Primary memory used to store data and instructions that cannot be changed by the user. It is a non-volatile memory.

Record. A group of interrelated fields in a database. A collection of records is a file.

Register. A special storage location in arithmetic/logic portion of a computer where arithmetic and logic computations take place.

Relational model. Two-dimensional tables made up of columns and rows. Each column represents a field and each row a record.

Report writers. Software packages that allow users to generate static questions.

Resolution. The sharpness of an image. It is determined by the number of pixels on the screen.

Ring topology. An arrangement whereby networked computers are arranged in a ring. The ring network transmits a message to all the nodes between the sending node and the receiving node.

Risk analysis. A function of DSS and EIS that allows managers to assess the risks associated with various alternatives.

Robots. Machines that are capable of human-like tactile perception and motor activities. It can perform routine tasks and more challenging ones. Robotics is the study of AI.

Runaway projects. Projects that are behind schedule and over budget.

Satellite communications. Satellites, which organisations lease or purchase, used to transmit data.

Schema. Information that describes the relationships between data in a database.

Secondary storage. It is a non-volatile memory that resides outside the CPU on devices as magnetic disks and tapes. Two types of secondary storage are sequential storage and direct-access storage.

Semi-structured decisions. The decisions fall between structured decisions, which are routine and repetitive, and unstructured decisions, which are unique and non-repetitive.

Sequential file. A file that has been organised in ascending or descending record-key sequence.

Sequential storage. Data that can be accessed and retrieved only in the order in which it was entered.

Server. A large central computer that serves as a repository of data and programs commonly accessed by a number of users.

Shell. A set of tools and techniques that allows developers to build the prototype of a system.

Single computer system. The simplest type of GDSS, designed primarily for single users, uses a video display system through which each group member can communicate with the others.

Source document. The document that is generated at the source where the transaction occurs, *e.g.*, sales receipt.

Speech recognition. Computer recognition of the human voice. It allows users to communicate with machines just as they do with other human beings.

Star schema. Provides a multidimensional view.

Star topology. An arrangement whereby a central host computer receives messages from computers on the network and passes them to others on the same network, *e.g.*, PBX.

Strategic business plan. A plan that identifies a firm's goals to achieve the organisa-tion's mission. It includes SWOT analysis.

Strategic information system. A system that delivers information products and services that play a direct and prominent role in helping the firm achieve its strategic goals.

Structure chart. A graphical tool that shows the hierarchy of software modules and the relationships among modules.

Structured decisions. Decisions that are routine and straightforward.

Structured english. It describes the logic in a program using simple, easy-to-understand English phrases.

Structured programming. Program development that takes a top-down view of the system and also breaks down the system into modules.

Structured query language. A database language that allows users to query a database and receive ad hoc reports or planned reports.

Structured tools. Tools and techniques that support the various phases of traditional development methodologies such as SDLC.

Subschema. A subset of database information that is made available to specific end-users or application programs.

Subsystem. A unit within a system that shares some or all of the characteristics of that system.

Sustainable competitive advantage. The ability of an organisation to introduce a product, service, or technique that provides an ongoing benefit of competitive significance.

System. A set of components that work together to accomplish one or more common goals.

System analysis. A detailed problem analysis undertaken in order to understand the nature, scope, requirements, and feasibility of the new system.

System design. A plan that shows system developers how to convert system requirements into system features.

System development software. Software packages and programs that assist programmers and system analysts in designing and developing information systems.

System flowchart. A diagram documenting the computer files and other inputs, outputs, and computer programs involved in an entire computer system.

System implementation. The process of installing a new computer system, including such tasks as site selection and preparation, training, testing, file conversion, and changeover.

System maintenance. The last, longest, and most expensive part of the life-cycle of a computer system, in which computer programs are updated and changed as management needs dictate.

System software. Software that performs the basic functions necessary to start and operate a computer.

System testing. Tests that examine the ability of several programs to interact and process data accurately in a job stream.

Task-based structure. A structure in which a group of people, required to execute a given activity, are brought together based on their skills rather than on their places in the organisational hierarchy.

Telecommunication media. The means by which data are transmitted. Two types of media exist : bounded and unbounded.

Telnet. A command that connects the user to a remote machine located anywhere on the internet. This allows the user to type commands to the remote machine, such as activating a program.

Terminal. A device consisting of a display screen on printer and a keyboard that is capable of sending data to a computer and receiving data from one.

Throwaway prototype. A prototype that is discarded after several iterations.

Time-sharing environment. A method of permitting different users to use the CPU at the same time.

Top-down approach. A structured-design method for creating computer programs/ systems of starting with the overall system objectives and developing finer input/ processing/output details in successively lower levels.

Topology. The physical configuration of devices on a network. There exists *three* network topologies : bus, ring and star.

Touch screen. A CRT screen that allows a user to merely touch the screen to make a choice from a menu.

Transaction file. Temporary tape or disk files whose records are used to update master files.

Transaction processing system (TPS). Information systems that record internal and external transactions. The output of the TPS becomes the input to an MIS.

Transmission direction. Three directions in which data can be transmitted : simplex, half-duplex, and full duplex.

Transmission mode. Two modes of data transmission over a network exists : synchronous and asynchronous. Synchronous transmission moves several characters at a time; asynchronous transmission, one character at a time.

Tuple. Each row in a relational database represents a record, also called a tuple.

Unstructured decisions. Decisions that are unique and non-repetitive.

Unstructured task. A task that relies heavily on intuition, judgement and experience.

User interface. Software that helps a user to interact with the computer.

Utility programs. Programs that perform routine, repetitive tasks. These programs make it easier to use the computer.

Value-added networks (VANs). Public data networks that add value to basic communication services provided by common carriers by providing additional services, *e.g.*, e-mail, correction of transmission errors, and videoconferencing.

Very high-level languages. Also called 4GLs, these are efficient, user-friendly, and English-like languages.

Videoconferencing. A type of electronic meeting system that uses telephone, video, computer, and communication links to enable geographically separated decision makers to hear and see each other.

Virus. A small program which, having been introduced into the system, proliferates.

Virtual corporation. A firm whose employers and employees are not limited by a physical work environment, but instead use communication technology to work from elsewhere and at any time.

Voice mail. The transmission, storage, and retrieval of spoken messages using computers. Eliminates many problems associated with telephones.

Voice recognition. An input device that responds to the human voice to execute computer commands.

Volatile memory. Primary or secondary computer memory that is lost when there is no electrical power to the computer.

'What-if' analysis. The process of a powerful managerial planning for deciding among several potential strategies.

Wide area networks (WANs). A computer network spanning a regional, national, or global area.

Word processing. A computerised method to create, edit, and manage text.

Work-group information system. A system designed to support group decision making. Such systems promote the free flow of information among group members.

Working memory. A component of an expert system. It is a temporary storage area where the initial data, the intermediate results, and the problem-solving steps are stored.

Workstation. A combination of input/output device or set of devices that typically include a keyboard and a video screen, and is typically used by data entry clerks.

World Wide Web (WWW). A hyper-text based Internet tool that allows users to display documents stored on any server on the Internet.

Write-Once, Read-Many (WORM). A special kind of CD-ROM : Write-Once, Read-Many. An optical disk that can be written to once, but read many times.

Selected References

Alter, S and M. Ginzberg. 'Managing Uncertainty in MIS Implementation.' *Sloan Management Review*, vol. 20, Fall 1978.

Alter, S.L. 'Decision Support Systems : Current Practice of Continuing Challenges.' *Addison-Wesley*, Reading, MA 1980.

Aronoff, S. 'Geographic Information Systems.' *WDL Publications*, Ottawa, 1994, p. 39.

Bacon, C.J. 'The Uses of Decision Criteria in Selecting Information Systems/Technology Investments.' *Management Information Systems Quarterly*, vol. 16, no. 3, September 1992, pp. 335-352.

Barrett, S.S. 'Strategic Alternatives and Interorganisational System Implementations: An Overview.' *Journal of Management Information Systems*, Winter 1986-87.

Boynton, A.C. *et al*. 'The Influence of Information Technology Management Practice on Information Technology Use in Large Organisations.' *Management Information Systems Quarterly*, September 1994, pp. 299-319.

Brien, B.O. 'Information Management Decisions.' *Pitman Publishing*, London, 1995.

Broderick, R. and J.W. Boudreau. 'Human Resource Management, Information Technology, and the Competitive Edge.' *Academy of Management Executive*, vol.6, no. 2, 1992, pp. 7-17.

Byrd, T.A. 'Implementation and Use of Expert Systems in Organisations : Perception of Knowledge Engineers.' *Journal of Management Information Systems*, vol. 8, no. 4, Spring 1992.

Cerveny, R.P., *et al*. 'The Application of Prototyping to System Development: A Rationale and Model.' *Journal of Management Information Systems*, no. 3, Fall 1986.

Cox, J.F. and S.J. Clark. 'Problems in Implementing and Operating a Manufacturing Resource Planning Information System.' *Journal of Management Information Systems*, no. 1, Summer 1984, pp. 81-101.

Curtis, Graham. 'Business Information Systems — Analysis, Design and Practice.' *Addison-Wesley Longman Publishing Company*, New York, 1998.

Date, C.J. 'An Introduction to Database Systems.' *Addison-Wesley*, Reading, MA, fifth edition, 1990.

Davenport, T.H. 'Process Innovation : Re-engineering Work through Information Technology.' *Harvard Business School Press*, 1993.

Davis, G.B. 'Strategies for Information Requirements Determination.' *IBM Systems Journal*, no. 1, 1982.

Davis, G.B. and M.H. Olson, 'Management Information System.' *McGraw-Hill International edition*, second edition, 1984.

Deiotel, H.M. 'An Introduction to Operating Systems.' *Addison-Wesley Publishing Company*, Reading, MA, revised first edition, p. 11.

DeJong, J. 'RAD to the Rescue.' *Information Week*, February 6, 1995, pp. 54-55.

DeSanctis, G. and R.B. Gallupe. 'A Foundation of the Study of Group Decision Support Systems.' *Management Science*, vol. 33, no. 5, May 1987.

Dickson, G.W. and J.C. Wetherbe. 'The Management of Information Systems.' *McGraw-Hill Book Company*, Singapore, 1985.

Dos Santos, B. 'Justifying Investments in New Information Technologies.' *Journal of Management Information Systems*, vol. 7, no. 4, Spring 1991.

Dosick, R.W. 'The Business Bible.' *Harper Collins Publishers*, 1995.

Duchessi, P.S. *et al.* 'Implementing a Manufacturing Planning and Control Information System.' *California Management Review*, vol. 31, Spring 1989, pp. 75-90.

Eliot, L. 'Moving into Client/Server Technology.' *Decision Line*, vol. 24, March 1993, pp. 5-6.

Finlay, Paul. 'Introducing Decision Support Systems.' *NCC Blackwell Ltd.*, Manchester, UK, 1994.

Gerritsen, R. and E.G. Brand. 'State-of-the Art Client/Server.' *DBMS*, February 1993, pp. 54-60.

Giuliano, V.E. 'The Mechanisation of Office Work.' *Scientific American*, vol. 247, September 1982, pp. 148-164.

Grover, Varun and James Teng. 'How Effective is Data Resource Management.' *Journal of Information Systems Management*, Summer 1991.

Grudnitski, G. 'Eliciting Decision Makers' Information Requirements.' *Journal of Management Information Systems*, Summer 1984.

Gupta, A.K. 'Management of Systems.' *Macmillan India Ltd.*, New Delhi, 1997.

Gupta, A.K. and S.K. Sarkar. 'Systems Analysis, Data Processing and Quantitative Techniques.' *Galgotia Publications (P) Ltd.*, New Delhi, 1997.

Gupta, U.G. and A. Gupta. 'Outsourcing the Information System Function.' *Journal of Information System Management*, vol. 9, no. 3, Summer 1992, pp. 44-50.

Hall, W.A. and R.E. McCauley. 'Planning and Managing a Corporate Network Utility.' *Management Information Systems Quarterly*, December 1987.

Hansen, W.C. The Integrated Enterprise. *In : Foundations of World Class* Manufacturing Systems : Symposium Papers, Washington DC, 1991.

Hammer, M. and G. Mangurian. 'The Changing Value of Communications Technology.' *Sloan Management Review*, Winter 1987.

Hammer, M. and J.A. Champy, 'What is Re-engineering ?' *Information Week*, May 5, 1992, 10 ff.

Hoffman, K. Management of Enterprise-wide Integration Programs. *System Integration*, Vol. 10, pages 4-13, 1992.

Johnston, H.R. and S.R. Carrico. 'Developing Capabilities to Use Information Strategically.' *Management Information Systems Quarterly*, vol. 12, no. 1, March 1988.

Joseph, C. and K. Muralidhar. 'Integrated Network Management in an Enterprise Environment.' *IEEE Network Magazine*, vol. 4, July 1990, pp. 7-13.

Keen, Peter G.W. 'Competing in Time.' *Ballinger Publishing Company*, Cambridge, MA, 1986.

Keen, Peter G.W. 'Shaping the Future: Business Design through Information Technology.' *Harvard Business School Press*, Cambridge, MA, 1991.

King, W.R. 'Alternative Designs in Information System Developments.' *Management Information Systems Quarterly*, December 1982.

Konsynski, B.R. 'Advances in Information System Design.' *Journal of Management Information Systems*, no. 1, Winter 1984-85.

Kumar, Vijay. 'Current Trends in Transaction Processing Systems.' *Journal of Systems Management*, vol. 41, January 1990, pp. 33-37.

Lang, Larry. 'Management Information Systems.' *Prentice-Hall International edition*, 1992.

Laudon, K.C. and J.P. Laudon. 'Management Information Systems : Organisation and Technology.' *Macmillan*, third edition.

Lee, S. 'The Impact of Office Information Systems on Potential Power and Influence.' *Journal of Management Information Systems*, vol. 8, Fall 1991, pp. 135-151.

Leifer, R. 'Matching Computer-based Information System with Organisational Structures.' *Management Information Systems Quarterly*, vol. 12, no. 1, March 1988, pp. 63-73.

Leonard, B. 'The Myth of the Integrated Human Resource Information System.' *Personnel Journal*, vol. 70, September 1991, pp. 113-115.

Leonard-Barton, Dorothy and J.J. Sviokla. 'Putting Expert Systems to Work.' *Harvard Business Review*, March-April 1988.

Lewis, Paul. 'Information Systems Development.' *Pitman Publishing*, London. 1994.

Lucey, T. 'Management Information System.' *ELBS Low-Priced Edition*, 1993.

Mcleod, Raymond Jr., *et al.* 'Management Information Systems.' *Prentice-Hall*, Englewood Cliffs, New Jersey 07632.

Michaelson, R. and D. Michie. 'Expert Systems in Business.' *Datamation*, November 1983.

Milliman, Z. and J. Hartwick. 'The Impact of Automated Office Systems on Middle Managers and Their Work.' *Management Information Systems Quarterly*, vol. 11, no. 4, December 1987.

Montgomery, D.B. and G.L. Urban. 'Marketing Decision Information Systems: An Emerging View.' *Journal of Marketing Research*, vol. 7, May 1970, pp. 226-234.

Myers, W. 'Introduction to Expert Systems.' *IEEE Expert*, no. 1, Spring 1986.

Navathe, S.B. 'Evolution of Data Modeling for Databases.' *Communication of the ACM*, vol. 35, September 1992, pp. 112-113.

Orlikowski, W.J. 'CASE Tools as Organisational Change : Investigating Incremental and Radical Changes in System Development.' *Management Information Systems Quarterly*, September 1993, pp. 309-340.

Payne, A.C. *et al.* 'Management for Engineers.' *John Wiley & Sons*, UK, 1996.

Ricciuti, M. 'The Best in Client/Server Computing.' *Datamation*, March 1, 1994, pp. 26-35.

Robson, W. 'Strategic Management and Information Systems : An Integrated Approach.' *Pitman Publishing*, London, 1994.

Sarkar, S.K. and A.K. Gupta. 'Elements of Computer Science.' *S. Chand & Co. Ltd.*, New Delhi, 1998.

Schoderbek, P.P. et al. 'Management Systems: Conceptual Considerations.' *BPI/Irwin*, fourth edition, Homewood II, 1990.

Senn, J.A. 'Information Systems in Management.' *Wadsworth Inc.*, 1990, pp. 173-174.

Sinha, Alok. 'Client-Server Computing.' *Communications of the ACM*, vol. 35, July 1992, pp. 77-97.

Sproull, L. and S. Kiesler. 'Connections: New Ways of Working in the Networked Organisation.' *MIT Press*, Cambridge, MA, 1992.

Turban, E. 'Decision Support and Expert Systems.' *Macmillan Publishing Company*, second edition, New York, 1993.

Turban, E. and P.R. Watkins. 'Integrating Expert Systems and Decision Support Systems.' *Management Information Systems Quarterly*, June 1986.

Vitale, M.R. 'The Growing Risks of Information Systems Success.' *Management Information Systems Quarterly*, December 1986.

Ward, J. and Pat Griffiths. 'Strategic Planning for Information Systems.' *John Wiley & Sons Ltd.*, second edition, England, 1997.

Wasson, R.E. 'Organising for Future Technologies.' *Datamation*, vol. 36, April 1, 1990, pp. 93-95.

Watson, H.J. and M.M. Frolick. 'Determining Information Requirements for an EIS.' *Management Information Systems Quarterly*, September 1993, pp. 255-269.

Willis, T.H. and D.B. Tesch. 'An Assessment of Systems Development Methodologies.' *Journal of Information Technology Management*, vol. 2, no. 2, 1991, pp. 39-45.

Yadav, S.B. 'Classifying an Organisation to Identify Its Information Requirements: A Comprehensive Framework.' *Journal of Management Information Systems*, no. 2, Summer 1985, pp. 39-60.

Yoon, Y. and L. Peterson. 'Artificial Neural Networks : An Emerging New Technique.' *DATABASE*, vol. 23, Winter 1992, pp. 55-57.

Yoon, Y. and T. Guimaraes. 'Developing Knowledge-based Systems: An Object-oriented Organisational Approach.' *Information Resources Management Journal*, vol. 5, Summer 1992, pp. 15-32.

Index

NOTES

NOTES

NOTES

NOTES

NOTES

NOTES